# Future of Business and Finan

The Future of Business and Finance book series features professional works aimed at defining, describing and charting the future trends in these fields. The focus is mainly on strategic directions, technological advances, challenges and solutions which may affect the way we do business tomorrow, including the future of sustainability and governance practices. Mainly written by practitioners, consultants and academic thinkers, the books are intended to spark and inform further discussions and developments.

Francisco J. Martínez-López • Yangchun Li •
Susan M. Young

# Social Media Monetization

Platforms, Strategic Models and Critical
Success Factors

🐎 Springer

Francisco J. Martínez-López
Department of Business
Administration 1
University of Granada
Granada, Spain

Yangchun Li
School of Management
Zhejiang University of Technology
Hangzhou, China

Susan M. Young
Gabelli School of Business
Fordham University
New York, NY, USA

ISSN 2662-2467      ISSN 2662-2475    (electronic)
Future of Business and Finance
ISBN 978-3-031-14577-3      ISBN 978-3-031-14575-9    (eBook)
https://doi.org/10.1007/978-3-031-14575-9

This Springer imprint is published by the registered company Springer Nature Switzerland AG
The registered company address is: Gewerbestrasse 11, 6330 Cham, Switzerland

# Preface

Social media has become a dominant presence in our everyday lives. We use Facebook to make friends and observe posts shared by others. YouTube is an online platform we use to watch interesting videos and listen to music. TikTok, a social video app, has gained momentum among Gen Z users. LinkedIn is a professional social networking site we use to build professional networks. Social media platforms essentially penetrate every aspect of our society from presidential elections to philanthropic social campaigns. People can use social media platforms for shopping, discovering interesting products or services and they are an ideal place for tourists to find destinations for their next trip. The platforms have also helped establish a large number of digital celebrities and influencers. Their opinions and views considerably influence how we interpret world events. Facebook, Instagram, Twitter, TikTok, and many other social media platforms are offered free of charge, so how do they earn profits and survive? The companies behind these social media platforms are not non-profit organizations. With this question in mind, we delve into the history of social media, observe the business practices of social media companies, and attempt to uncover the dynamics of social media monetization. We study social features and economic models of social media platforms and present a holistic view of social media monetization.

In many cases, social media monetization is not straightforward or explicit. Many social media platforms impose restrictions on the creation and sharing of commercial content or social media advertisements. The commercialization of a social circle can be disturbing and annoying for users. People do not enjoy unwanted commercials when socially interacting with friends. Therefore, social media platforms need to be deliberate when monetizing their users. Powered by frontier technologies such as machine learning, data mining and analytics, and cloud computing, social media platforms have demonstrated how these technologies can be used in advertising and social commerce, and, most importantly, how to earn profits with these technologies. When we swipe left or right on a social media platform, the monetization system of the platform is automatically recording and processing our actions. The algorithmic system memorizes our actions, analyzes our preferences, and monetizes users by pushing social media content, explicitly or implicitly, that contain advertisements or commercial features. How a social media platform monetizes its users is novel and offers a glimpse of future advertising and Internet commerce. Social media has been touted as the most effective channel for advertisers to reach target customers. Social media platforms even offer advertisers automatic and efficient budget spending options and bidding strategies in advertisement auctions. Advertisers' bids, advertisements' relevancy, and viewers' estimated action rates are all considered when deciding what content to be displayed for which viewers. This algorithm-based content recommendation mechanism is then beneficial to both advertisers and viewers. The social media platform earns profits on the basis of this reciprocal relationships.

This monetization model is exciting from a business viewpoint, because it concurrently considers the heterogeneity of social media users and the interests of advertisers. It offers personalized content recommendations for social media users. In contrast, traditional mass media such as television and newspapers rely on feeding audiences the same programs or media content. Another encouraging aspect of social media monetization is that social media platforms can create a gig economy based on the media platforms. YouTubers create and share videos on YouTube to obtain a share of YouTube's advertising revenue. Premium social media content can cause users to become addicted to the media platform, which makes the platform more attractive for advertisers. Social media platforms have become a user-driven content production and exchange platform and many content producers are able to earn a living from the platforms. Social media features have been largely diversified in recent years: social ecommerce, live streaming, subscribed content, etc. These new features enable ordinary people to participate and reach monetization through their talents.

However, social media monetization presents a set of problems which may suggest that there are trade-offs along with the benefits. We question whether monetization should be the underlying algorithmic logic, or the sole metric, in deciding which piece of social media content is displayed for which users. In other words, is it ethical for a social media company to merely see users as monetizable resources? This monetized interpretation of user attention is problematic and raises serious ethical issues, which may eventually jeopardize a social media company's long-term success. This book critically reviews social media platforms' existing problems, analyzes these problems in depth, and offers strategies for potential resolutions and theoretical contributions for social media research.

Social media monetization is based on algorithmic content recommendations. Driven by the needs for monetization, the algorithm may inevitably be biased and unfair. The algorithmic system prioritizes those social media posts with greater monetization potential. In this case, social media pushes social media content which may seem more attractive, more relevant, and more addictive for users. The experiences of social media users are therefore determined by backend algorithms. The algorithms know each users' interests and preferences, and consistently feed users desirable content. This preference-based monetization model may not be satisfactory for users but instead create forms of addiction. Apart from creating more social media addicts, monetization is achieved by leveraging users' private data. Many social media platforms offer an application programming interface (API) to third parties which provides access to user data and allows third parties to collect insights about social media users. The data accessibility benefits third parties, and at the same time leaves opportunities for a significant breach of privacy. Moreover, this algorithmic monetization system will demonetize particular videos or video channels following specific content moderation policies and guidelines. Social media demonetization like YouTube's Adpocalypse also creates considerable impact on the gig economy and the social media platform. A demonetization policy allows a social media platform to determine which content follows their policy, which jeopardizes free speech on social media, and thus may lead to a polished, sanitized, and "family-friendly" content ecosystem.

This book is comprised of four parts. Part I (Chap. 1) introduces the social media monetization issue and discusses the importance of examining this issue. Part II (Chaps. 2–5) offers an overview of social media monetization and introduces potential monetization strategies for various parties. Part III (Chaps. 6–9) focuses on how firms such as brands and retailers use social media to earn profits and build markets. Part IV (Chaps. 10–14) shifts attention to the social media platforms, delves into how social media platforms reach monetization, and discusses the side effects of social media monetization. We conclude with Chap. 15, which adopts a futuristic approach and identifies potential monetization strategies and issues in the era of frontier technologies such as big data, artificial intelligence, and smart devices. This academic monograph has received financial support from Research Start-Up Fund of Zhejiang University of Technology (Grant number: 2021132007929).

Granada, Spain                                       Francisco J. Martínez-López
Hangzhou, China                                                    Yangchun Li
New York, NY                                                     Susan M. Young

# Contents

**Francisco J. Martínez-López**, MSc in Marketing, and European PhD in Business Administration (2005), with Extraordinary Doctoral Prize, from the University of Granada (Spain), is a Professor of Business Administration at the University of Granada and at the Open University of Catalonia (Barcelona, Spain). He has been a visiting researcher at the Zicklin School of Business (CUNY, USA), Rutgers Business School (Rutgers University, USA), Aston Business School (Aston University, UK), the University of Chicago Booth School of Business (USA), the Michael Smurfit School of Business (University College Dublin, Ireland), LUISS Business School (Rome, Italy), and the Complutense University Business School (Madrid, Spain).

**Yangchun Li** is a lecturer at Zhejiang University of Technology (China). He obtained his doctorate from the University of Granada (Spain). His research interests include social media monetization and e-commerce return management. His work has been publishedin Journal of Business Research, Electronic Commerce Research and Applications, Journal of Retailing and Consumer Services, Journalof Organizational and End User Computing, Journal of Global Information Management, etc.

**Susan M. Young**, who holds a PhD from the University of Southern California, is an associate professor at the Gabelli School of Business, Fordham University. She studies financial decision-making, investor use of financial information, and capital-market responses. Her work has been published in *Human Resource Management Journal of Management Accounting Research, the Accounting Review*, the *Journal of Business, Finance and Accounting, Review of Behavioral Finance*; and Accounting Horizons. Professor Young has previously held positions at Emory University, Baruch College of the City University of New York and is an adjunct faculty member at Columbia University.

# Part I

# An Introduction to Social Media Monetization

## 1.1    The Business Value of Social Media

Social media is gaining momentum in generating commercial value. According to recent social media statistics, social media ad revenue for the year 2017 reached a staggering $41 billion (see Singh, 2018). These statistics also found that 87% of shoppers reveal that social media plays a role in helping decide what to purchase, and 90% of brand followers try to contact brands via social media (see Singh, 2018). According to Facebook's financial report from the fiscal year 2018 (Facebook, 2019), Facebook's total revenue is $16,914 million, which is predominately driven by its advertising business ($16,640 million). Social media is not solely a platform to increase brand awareness, but is also used to sell products such as smartwatches, facial masks, phone cases, speakers, and VR products (see Singh, 2018). The ROI produced by social media is surpassing emails which were deemed the most profitable marketing channel previously (Boyle, 2018). There are several real-world examples that have shown that brands can garner monetary value by launching social media campaigns; Nike sold out their new products—Air Jordan III "Tinker" shoes—in a record 23 min via Snapchat (Dickey, 2018). Another example is Umbro, an English athletic brand that ran ads on Facebook and stated that ad viewers' purchase intentions increased by 6% (Keath, 2012). Finally, State Bicycle promoted cycling-related events to Facebook users and achieved $500,000 sales from this campaign (Keath, 2012).

The commercial value that social media can offer can be encapsulated in "6C": content, community, commerce, connection, collaboration, and conversation (Singh, 2018). First, social media empowers advertisers to generate and spread content. Social media content has commercial features by which users can click to download/view/purchase and complete commercial activities. In addition, social media analytic tools and methods can be employed to analyze users' behavioral pattern and preferences (Ketonen-Oksi et al., 2016). Second, social media organizes users into interrelated communities. Communities can offer financial and nonfinancial values for companies (Iskoujina et al., 2017), including product sales, product awareness,

F. J. Martínez-López et al., *Social Media Monetization*, Future of Business and
Finance, https://doi.org/10.1007/978-3-031-14575-9_1

corporate reputation, and brand loyalty. Companies can use communities to find their targeted customers because members of a community share similar interests or goals. Third, social media enables companies and brands to sell products and establish marketplaces for e-commerce activities. Most social media companies allow retailers to use hypertext links to lead shoppers to external commercial websites and complete purchases. For example, Instagram has recently allowed buyers to buy things directly through their platform (Frier, 2019). Fourth, social media offers more capacity to reach potential customers by taking advantage of numerous connections. Without social media, most brands can only directly contact a handful of followers. With social media, brands can reach many more followers through such followers' connections with others (Martínez-López et al., 2015). Fourth, social media is an online collaboration platform by which an extensive number of users can jointly create value for brands or companies. Social media enables collaborative marketing tactics by which social media users can generate e-word-of-mouth (eWOM) for brands or report pain points in companies' business processes (Garcia, 2017). Last, social media enables peer-to-peer conversations. One of the pain points in traditional e-commerce is that traditional e-commerce cannot offer a social shopping experience. Even though traditional e-commerce can offer a cheap and broad selection of products and brands, shoppers may still not feel satisfied because they do not want a solitary shopping experience (Parker, 2017). Shoppers sometimes want to share product photographs and reviews with fellow users, and many brands try to satisfy shoppers' social needs. Social media can also offer other noteworthy commercial values when fused with inspiring technical and commercial features such as mobile payment, quick response code readers, artificial intelligence, cloud computing, and Big Data analytics. Given these opportunities, consumers can use social media apps to conduct commercial activities in more common situations, such as paying a check directly to a restaurant. The "6C" represents the core commercial values that social media offers.

In summary, social media possesses enormous commercial value. It will play a more and more crucial role in the future business world. Companies can realize monetization by embracing the effective use of social media.

## 1.2   Challenges and Problems that Firms Need to Consider in Social Media Monetization

Though social media can bring about many benefits for business, this book advises business leaders to not launch into their social media monetization plans without considering its drawbacks. In other words, companies need to consider how to overcome pitfalls before and after launching their social media monetization strategies and learn to adjust or abandon such strategies if those strategies fail or do not reach the company's expectation.

Companies need to understand that the success of a social media monetization strategy relies on user-generated content. However, social media enables all online users to co-create value as well as co-destroy value. One example of this destruction involved negative online product reviews shared by social media trolls. In particular, social media users can complain about a company's products or services by sharing bad consumption experiences or posting to a company's social media account. If the company cannot quickly and effectively respond to social media complaints, negative online reviews can undermine the company's online image. This example implies that user-generated content is not beneficial to companies in all cases.

From a user's perspective, people do not want the overcommercialization of their online social circle. Imagine people are in a social gathering and a merchant suddenly appears selling a product to them; these people would likely feel uncomfortable (Clemons, 2009). On Instagram, users can find plenty of photographs of things such as luxury cars and houses shared by their friends. These photographs present the property owners' decadent lifestyle and may make many viewers feel like they are in a worse life than most other users (Galer, 2018). Though social media companies get consent from users, users would still be wary of anyone misusing their social media data and content. For example, Facebook ran into several crises related to how they cope with the misuse of Facebook users' data and content. Up to 87 million Facebook users' data were improperly shared with Cambridge Analytica (Badshah, 2018). This scandal shows that Facebook "deceived consumers by telling them they could keep their information on Facebook private, and then repeatedly allowing it to be shared and made public" (Brodkin, 2019). Every Internet platforms involves similar privacy risks, but social media data become more vulnerable as people spend more and more digital time on social media (Galer, 2018) and social media data can reflect many aspects of an individual such as location information, preferences, and behavioral patterns.

Free riding is another drawback of social media. Users who discover products or services on social media may eventually complete purchases at other places. In the case of Instagram, US Internet users who found brands on Instagram eventually complete purchases on the brand's website (40%), Amazon (29%), the brand's physical store (20%), other e-retailers (17%), or other bricks-and-mortar stores (14%); only 19% of purchases are directly completed via Instagram (Garcia, 2018). Companies or brands need to consider this free riding behavior before monetizing social media. Their marketing dollars may be spent for the benefit of others. In addition, conversion rates are of paramount importance for the performance of Internet business. Touted as the future of digital advertising, social media does not always lead to a satisfactory conversion rate. Social media platforms' conversion rates such as Facebook, Twitter, Snapchat, and YouTube all are lower than Google and Bing (Priceonomics, 2018).

Research reveals that it appears difficult to make a profit from social media. In a survey of Fortune 500 companies, over 80% of CMOs revealed that they did not find that the use of social media brought about new customers (see John et al., 2017). Twitter, the well-known social media platform reported its first-ever profitable quarter after having been public for 4 years (see Flynn, 2019). This company finally reported $91 million in profits for the fourth quarter of 2017 (see Flynn, 2019). From a brand's perspective, it seems that opening a social media account, accumulating likes and followers, or running social ads is not necessarily associated with more sales. John et al. (2017) conducted 16 studies and found no evidence that following a brand on social media alters consumers' buying behaviors. These researchers also found that liking a brand's Facebook page does not change consumers' purchasing behavior (John et al., 2017).

In summary, business leaders need to consider the drawbacks of social media when devising their social media monetization strategy. Even social media giants such as Facebook and Twitter did not cope well with drawbacks in their pathway toward monetization.

## 1.3    The Importance and Necessity of Studying Social Media Monetization

This book examines how economic agents (brands, firms, and social media platforms) make money using social media platforms. Though a handful of researchers and practitioners have studied several aspects related to social media monetization, their contributions are largely limited by their strategic focus on a particular economic agent or a certain research context. We provide a brief summary of the prior literature below.

Clemons (2009) examined the complexity of monetizing online social networks. The author explored why advertising-based business models are dying and revealed approaches that companies can use for online social networks to earn a profit (Clemons, 2009). We note that as this article was written a decade ago, advances in technology have brought about fundamental changes for social media platforms. For example, the emergence of social media payment technologies has transformed how users use social media. Social media wallets make money transfer among users easier and faster. Our book formulates how economic agents use social media to make profits considering such technological changes. Also, while Clemons presents several approaches or business models that social media companies can use to monetize, social media monetization is not only an issue of selecting a proper monetization approach or business model, but also an entire process of how companies identify monetization opportunities and harvest monetary value from them. This process encompasses opportunity identification, approach to business modeling, planning, specifying strategies and tactics, and implementing the monetization plan. Our book will remedy this gap in the literature by providing a holistic solution for social media monetization.

Sokhatska and Oleksyn (2012) constructed a roadmap toward monetization for companies or brands using social media. In contrast to their work, our book extends the analysis to additional economic agents such as social media companies. This extension is not solely a matter of considering more economic agents who can earn money from social media. Social media companies or platform providers should also consider how to improve in-platform brands' monetization performance. If brands can garner more sales and traffic from running ads on social media, they should be more willing to pay a higher ad fee to the platform, which in turn improves the platform's monetization performance. Our book will consider all major forms of social media monetization and view social media as an entire business ecosystem. We will offer helpful insights for improving all economic agents' monetization activities from a holistic perspective. Specifically, after a critical analysis of approaches to improving monetization performance for brands, this book will offer solutions for social media companies to cultivate a value co-creation ecosystem in which each party can benefit from collaborating with others.

Dohrmann et al. (2015) argued that social media companies need to balance social welfare and monetary income and they revealed how business model changes affect monetization performance. However, as previously noted, business models are not the sole determinant in influencing monetization performance. If monetization opportunities of a business were not real money-making opportunities and misidentified as opportunities by entrepreneurs, any business model would not remedy this strategic mistake and successfully earn money. In fact, strategy is a crucial component of the successful monetization of social media. Our book considers the interdependent relationship between strategy and business models and offers a pathway toward monetization that encompasses both.

Zajc (2015) explained why social media users willingly provide "free labor" by continually generating monetizable content. Most social media companies do not pay users for their content creations. Instead, social media platforms use user-generated content to attract advertisers and earn increased ad revenue. Zajc (2015) argued that the exploitation of such free labor on social media unveils a unique economic process in which users tolerate this exploitation and social media companies profit from user-generated content. However, this article focuses on more conceptual and theoretical discussions of this economic process and delivers less practical implications for social media companies or brands to improve monetization performance. In contrast, our book will connect more closely to the practical aspects of social media and point out roadmaps for monetizing social media. Diverse business cases will be discussed in this book. Furthermore, as we will take into account different forms of economic agents' characteristics and will approach the newest social media practices, original contributions regarding previous research will be made.

Several monetization-related articles (e.g., Lambrecht et al., 2014; Voigt, 2016) have studied how companies make money in general Internet business contexts such as World Wide Web. However, the social media context can alter companies' money-making practices. Social media monetization can entail conventional monetization approaches used by general Internet business such as advertising, e-commerce, commissions, donations, and premium service. However, the unique characteristics of social media could alter some of the conclusions got by previous Internet business research. For example, social media includes novel interactive elements among users such as online video streaming. There are companies that have employed the interactive feature to monetize social content by encouraging users to buy e-gifts for streamers. In general, it is to specify yet how a firm incorporates social media's social and interactive components into their business model and strategy. Therefore, it is interesting to specifically study the monetization issue in social media contexts.

Studying social media monetization is important and necessary in a practical sense as well. The number one mistake that entrepreneurs make is that they focus too much on technology, storytelling, leadership, and organizational growth instead of monetization (Rettig, 2018). Entrepreneurs need to consider monetization before they launch their business (Vijayashanker, 2014). Companies can identify customer needs and to what extent customers are willing to pay for their value proposition. Before offering a developed product, firms can present crucial benefits for early customers and anticipate the performance of their monetization strategy. This book will provide a holistic solution for how brands, firms, and social media companies use social media to make money. The insights presented should prove helpful in improving monetization performance and increase the likelihood of monetization success.

In conclusion, it is as important as it is necessary to study social media monetization because this topic can lead to both interesting theoretical and practical implications.

## References

Badshah, N. (2018). *Facebook to contact 87 million users affected by data breach.* Retrieved August 29, 2019, from https://www.theguardian.com/technology/2018/apr/08/facebook-to-contact-the-87-million-users-affected-by-data-breach#img-1

Boyle, P. (2018). *Recart guide to Facebook messenger for shopify stores.* Retrieved February 12, 2019, from https://blog.recart.com/2018/06/20/recart-guide-to-facebook-messenger-for-shopify-stores/

Brodkin, J. (2019). *Facebook may face multi-billion dollar fine for Cambridge Analytica scandal.* Retrieved February 15, 2019, from https://arstechnica.com/tech-policy/2019/02/facebook-may-face-multi-billion-dollar-fine-for-cambridge-analytica-scandal/

Clemons, E. K. (2009). The complex problem of monetizing virtual electronic social networks. *Decision Support Systems, 48*(1), 46–56.

Dickey, M. R. (2018). *Nike teamed up with Snap and Darkstore to pre-release Air Jordan III 'Tinker' shoes on Snapchat.* Retrieved February 12, 2019, from https://techcrunch.com/2018/02/19/nike-teamed-up-with-snap-and-darkstore-to-pre-release-air-jordan-iii-tinker-shoes-on-snapchat/

Dohrmann, S., Raith, M., & Siebold, N. (2015). Monetizing social value creation—A business model approach. *Entrepreneurship Research Journal, 5*(2), 127–154.

Facebook. (2019). *Annual Report 2018.* Retrieved August 22, 2022, from https://www.annualreports.com/HostedData/AnnualReportArchive/f/NASDAQ_FB_2018.pdf

Flynn, K. (2019). *Twitter is \*finally\* profitable for the first time ever.* Retrieved February 15, 2019, from https://mashable.com/2018/02/08/twitter-profitable-earnings-2017-first-time/?europe=true#Lz13p_acPaqS

Frier, S. (2019). *Instagram will now let you buy things directly through the app.* Retrieved August 29, 2019, from https://www.bloomberg.com/news/articles/2019-03-19/instagram-gets-into-the-e-commerce-business-with-checkout-tool

Galer, S. S. (2018). *How much is 'too much time' on social media?* Retrieved February 15, 2019, from http://www.bbc.com/future/story/20180118-how-much-is-too-much-time-on-social-media

Garcia, A. (2017). *How co-creation is fueling the future of marketing.* Retrieved February 12, 2019, from https://www.socialmediatoday.com/marketing/how-co-creation-fueling-future-marketing

Garcia, K. (2018). *Instagram is giving the buy button a makeover*. Retrieved February 15, 2019, from https://retail.emarketer.com/article/instagram-giving-buy-button-makeover/5aec9eadebd40003a0c24684

Iskoujina, Z., Ciesielska, M., Roberts, J., & Li, F. (2017). Grasping the business value of online communities. *Journal of Organizational Change Management, 30*(3), 396–416.

John, L., Mochon, D., Emrich, O., & Schwartz, J. (2017). What's the value of a like. *Harvard Business Review, 95*, 108–115.

Keath, J. (2012). *105 Facebook advertising case studies*. Retrieved August 29, 2019, from https://www.socialfresh.com/facebook-advertising-examples/

Ketonen-Oksi, S., Jussila, J. J., & Kärkkäinen, H. (2016). Social media based value creation and business models. *Industrial Management and Data Systems, 116*(8), 1820–1838.

Lambrecht, A., Goldfarb, A., Bonatti, A., Ghose, A., Goldstein, D. G., Lewis, R., et al. (2014). How do firms make money selling digital goods online? *Marketing Letters, 25*(3), 331–341.

Martínez-López, F. J., Anaya, R., Aguilar, R., & Molinillo, S. (2015). *Online brand communities: Using the social web for branding and marketing*. Springer.

Parker, S. (2017). *What is social commerce and why should your brand care?* Retrieved February 12, 2019, from https://blog.hootsuite.com/social-commerce/

Priceonomics. (2018). *The advertising conversion rates for every major tech platform*. Retrieved February 15, 2019, from https://www.forbes.com/sites/priceonomics/2018/03/09/the-advertising-conversion-rates-for-every-major-tech-platform/#7d9dc75f5957

Rettig, T. (2018). *The no. 1 mistake young, aspiring entrepreneurs make*. Retrieved February 18, 2019, from https://medium.com/swlh/the-no-1-mistake-young-aspiring-entrepreneurs-make-e8f7c01ede36

Singh, S. (2018). *Social networks e-commerce gateways in 2018* [infographic]. Retrieved February 12, 2019, from https://socialnomics.net/2018/06/05/social-commerce-in-2018/

Sokhatska, O., & Oleksyn, T. (2012). Social media monetization in global informational environment. *Journal of European Economy, 11*(1), 99–108.

Vijayashanker, P. (2014). *Monetize before you launch: One entrepreneur's lessons learned*. Retrieve February 18, 2019, from https://www.entrepreneur.com/article/241061

Voigt, S. (2016). *Monetization strategies for internet companies*. Doctoral dissertation, Technische Universität Darmstadt.

Zajc, M. (2015). The social media dispositive and monetization of user-generated content. *Information Society, 31*(1), 61–67.

# Part II

# A Strategic Framework for Social Media Monetization

# How Companies Can Exploit the Commercial Value of Social Media Through Advertising

**2**

## 2.1 Social Media Advertising: What It Is and Why It Is Important

Social media advertising is becoming a winning strategy for firms, brands, and retailers (He & Shao, 2018). Statistics demonstrated the staggering growth of the global social media advertising market: Marketers' spend on social media advertising had grown to over $89 billion in 2019; it was estimated that this ad spend would produce a yearly growth rate of over 8% and likely reach over $100 billion in 2020 (Zote, 2020). In contrast to traditional media's limited reach capability, promotional messages on social media can connect and reach over one billion customers (Shareef et al., 2019; Schulze et al., 2014). Social media also outperforms traditional print media because it incorporates more social, informative, and interactive elements in firm–customer communication (Alalwan, 2018; Barreda et al., 2016; Lee & Hong, 2016; Mangold & Faulds, 2009; Swani et al., 2017; Wu, 2016). Although social media ads cannot be directly converted into sales, the promotion of such ads can be a facilitator in building customers' awareness toward brand or product, spread brand and product-related knowledge to customers influencing customers' brand or product perceptions, and eventually nudging customers to make purchases (Alalwan et al., 2017; Duffett, 2015; Kapoor et al., 2018).

Surprisingly, many marketers and researchers understand social media advertising as a form of online advertising focusing on social networking services, which lacks a more precise definition that reveals the essence of social media advertising. For instance, marketing professionals understand social media advertising as "social advertising is any advertising in which you're paying the social media company to display your content" (Sherman, 2019a, 2019b). In fact, if social media only was deemed as an advertising platform equivalent to platforms such as TV, radio, and newspapers, crucial commercial value behind social media advertising could be overlooked by marketers and firms. For example, some informal user-generated organic ads could lead to more superior business outcomes than formal social media ads (Shareef et al., 2019). Traditionally, print media like newspapers and billboards is a unidirectional communication platform, in which marketers develop ad content (Shareef et al., 2019) and users can only passively receive commercial information. In contrast, social media is a bidirectional communication platform whose social elements enable social media users to add value (e.g., shares, likes, and comments) to marketer-generated social ads. Social media advertising also differs from traditional advertising due to more advanced targeting capabilities (Deshpande, 2019). Traditional advertising employs a carpet-bombing approach, wherein ads are delivered to an audience regardless of their demographic and contextual background; social media enables marketers to target ideal customers based on their geographic, demographic, and behavioral attributes (Deshpande, 2019).

There is a handful of literature that sheds light on this conceptual issue of social media advertising and incorporates social and information elements in illuminating its concept and characteristics. Social media advertising can be understood as a form of advertising based on social information in developing, targeting, and forming firm–customer communication (He & Shao, 2018). This special advertising follows a value co-creation logic. By using comments, sharing, and other functions embedded in social media platforms, users can engage in the social media advertising processes (Azeem & Haq, 2012; He & Shao, 2018). In 2009, the Interactive Advertising Bureau referred to social media advertising as running "an online ad that incorporates user interactions that the consumer has agreed to display and be shared. The resulting ad displays these interactions along with the user's persona (picture and/or name) within the ad content" (see Chu, 2011, p. 32). It is plausible that this definition incorporates social elements such as user interactions and user persona in defining social media advertising. However, user interactions and user persona are not always included with social media ads. For example, YouTube's in-stream ads do not involve user interactions now. In this case, social media ads are akin to traditional TV ads. Therefore, based on the above discussion, social media advertising refers to commercial or noncommercial content which incorporates social or informative elements that can be displayed or shared on social media for fulfilling commercial purposes and building public awareness. Social elements refer to social or interactive features such as sharing, commenting, and liking. Informative elements encompass content (e.g., product and brand information) displayed on social media and content formats (e.g., texts, pictures, and videos) supported by social media. In practice, different social media ads show different orientations. Facebook ads such as sponsored posts include social elements and informative elements. Facebook users can share, comment, and like sponsored posts as well as access product or brand information by viewing ad content. YouTube ads such as in-stream ads focus on offering informative content toward viewers. YouTube viewers cannot socially add value to such ads now.

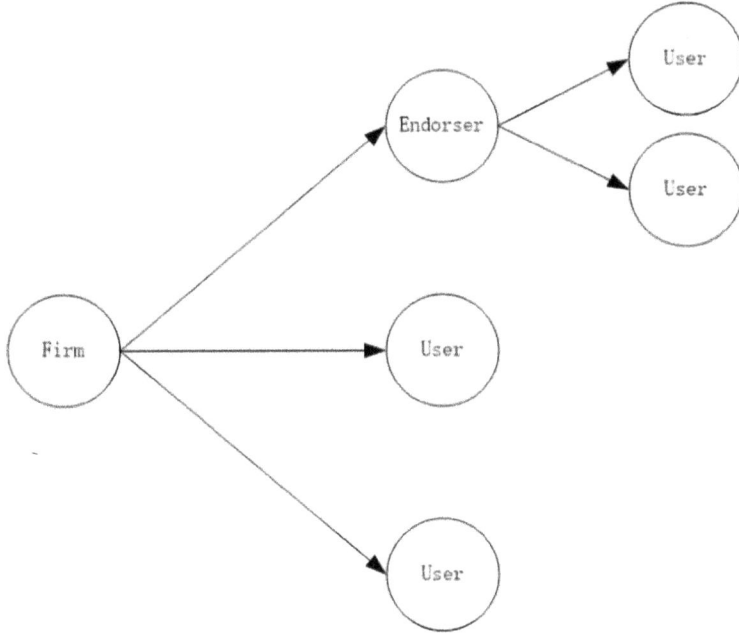

**Fig. 2.1**  Push-based social advertising

## 2.2    Push-Based Social Advertising

Push-based social advertising refers to proactively pushing commercial messages to recipients via social media (Higgs, 2008). In push-based social advertising, social ads are adaptions of traditional mass media ads such as TV ads and newspaper ads into social media contexts. Push-based social advertising entails explicit commercial messages delivered through social media (Taylor et al., 2011). Push advertising is a traditional advertising strategy, which employs a direct, straightforward structure (see Fig. 2.1). The major goal of push-based social advertising lies in the direct promotion of products and services to consumers (John et al., 2017). There are a variety of push ads in social media. Firms and brands use such ads to market their products and services.

Banner ads are a form of push ads widely seen in social media websites and platforms. Banner ads are clickable banners in-between content viewed by website visitors or app users. In order to increase the public awareness of banner ads, content that viewers want to access could be overlaid with banner ads. It is expected that such banner ads could hardly achieve marketing purposes because such ads' appearance is usually annoying for viewers who desire to access contents behind banners. In particular, marketers should be aware that the rise of ad blockers could be used to block their banner ads shown in viewers' devices. Ad blockers are widely available in many browsers such as Chrome, Firefox, Opera, Safari, and Internet Explorer

Web browsers (Shewan, 2019). Therefore, marketers can seek other ad forms which are less likely to be blocked by ad blockers. For example, native ads, which look and read like other regular contents, can be out of reach for ad blockingtechnology (Shewan, 2019).

Albeit Facebook's advertising business model has been controversial due to its infringement of user data privacy, technological innovations made by Facebook have described what social ads should look like in practice. Many other social media platforms offer similar advertising features used by Facebook. Over 65 million firms run their business on Facebook and 4 million of them are running social ads (Quick, 2018). Regarding ad spend on Facebook, the average cost per click in the United States was only 26 cents, which is considerably low, and an affordable option for small businesses with limited budgets (Quick, 2018). Sponsored posts and Facebook ads are two means by which brands and retailers can push product and service information directly to consumers. Sponsored posts refer to posts that a firm pays for influencing a larger audience (Main, 2018). We conclude these posts can be a form of push-based social advertising if their aim is to increase public awareness of products or services. Sponsored posts can be created through a Facebook business profile and run for 7 days at most (Main, 2018). A sponsor can frame an ad as a friend's story sharing the person's real experience with a product, which can be integrated into the news feed and mixed with other organic contents (Cox, 2011; Lin & Kim, 2016; Villiard & Moreno, 2012). This enables viewers to be involved in an immersive brand experience and gives viewers access to the information (e.g., likes and shares) added by fellow users (Dyrud, 2011; Lin & Kim, 2016).

In the eyes of Facebook, sponsored posts are not designed for social advertising. These posts are simply purchased to get more visibility. The goal of sponsoring a post can be commercial or noncommercial. In contrast, "Facebook ads" are advertising features Facebook offers for advertisers. Before running a Facebook ad, firms will be asked about the goals of their ad campaign (Sherman, 2019a, 2019b). For example, specific marketing or advertising goals need to be set before launching Facebook ads. Facebook will run such ads to reach a specific audience based on established marketing goals. In other words, Facebook ads offer more sophisticated targeting and customization that help brands and retailers zero in on their target customers (Sherman, 2019a, 2019b).

Facebook's advertising model has also caused considerable controversy. Facebook can offer more precise advertising because its ad appearance is based on users' profile information and use pattern, therefore more reliable for advertisers in contrast to banner ads (Barreto, 2013; Lin & Kim, 2016). Vast amounts of personal information were shared on user profile pages (Van Reijmersdal et al., 2017). Information such as age, gender, and hobbies is publicly accessible for advertisers (Van Reijmersdal et al., 2017). Advertisers use such information for commercial purposes, reaching target customers (Köster et al., 2015; Van Reijmersdal et al., 2017; Villiard & Moreno, 2012). But research also revealed that Facebook users' concerns about privacy negatively influence users' attitude toward Facebook advertising (Lin & Kim, 2016; Taylor et al., 2011). The unexpected appearance of sponsored ads in users' news feed could also provoke their perceived intrusiveness of Facebook advertising (Lin & Kim, 2016). The privacy infringement and ad intrusiveness inevitably jeopardize the effectiveness of Facebook advertising. On the one hand, advertising generates revenue on which social media platforms rely to survive; on the other hand, excessive commercialization by running social ads can damage the appeal of Facebook (Taylor et al., 2011). As Stone wrote in The New York Times: "when it doesn't work, it's not only creepy but offputting" (Stone, 2010). Research indicated that around 8% of consumers had abandoned a social media platform due to excessive advertising, and approximately 13% of consumers had abandoned a social media platform due to their privacy concerns (see Taylor et al., 2011).

To combat weaknesses of social ads using user profile information and social media use pattern, brands and retailers have started to seek alternatives. Celebrity endorsement is widely used in advertising because marketers presume that celebrities can increase consumers' attention in product ads and celebrities' attractive personal traits can be transferred to endorsed products or services (Chung & Cho, 2017). A celebrity endorser refers to "anyone who enjoys public recognition and who uses this recognition on behalf of a consumer good by appearing with it in an advertisement" (McCracken, 1989, p. 310). A survey among in-house marketers in the United Kingdom demonstrated that 77% of marketers said celebrities were highly effective in social media promotion, which was deemed more effective than TV advertising (40%) and radio advertising (28%) (Statista Research Department, 2019). Social media is a useful platform for advertisers to run celebrity-endorsed ads. Many celebrities use a vast array of social media platforms such as Facebook, Twitter, and Instagram to interact with fans and sustain online visibility. Several celebrities such as Lady Gaga, Katy Perry, and Justin Beiber had over 60 million followers on Twitter or Facebook (Chung & Cho, 2017). The large number of followers and considerable influence a celebrity could have on followers determine that celebrity endorsement can be an effective advertising strategy for advertisers. For example, Steph Curry is considered one of the best shooters in NBA history. Curry partnered with a water filter brand, Brita, to create a hilarious video skit (for this case story, see Mediakix, n.d.). In the video, he promotes a Brita filter to achieve a healthier lifestyle. He also posted a sponsored Instagram video containing an excerpt from the video, and as a result, a staggering engagement rate of 10.8% was achieved. His post received over one million likes and 15,000 comments.

Social media is a content sharing platform by which creators can build their influence among followers by sharing premium contents. These influential creators are called "influencers" which refer to "someone who has built a loyal following through their online content creation" (Bailis, n.d.). In contrast to celebrities, influencers can win over more consumer trust and add more value in endorsement ads (Schouten et al., 2020). Research also showed that 92% of consumers trust an influencer more than an advertiser (Mau, 2017). According to a survey in 2019, 89% of marketers stated that ROI from influencer marketing is comparable to or better than other marketing channels (Bailis, n.d.). In contrast to formal corporations, influencers deemed as peer consumers are more trusted by viewers; viewers also tend to evaluate products or services based on information offered by such peer consumers (Lee & Koo, 2012). Among all forms of influencer endorsement, experience-based product information shared by influencers acts a crucial role in shaping viewers' evaluation of product or service attributes before purchasing (Lu et al., 2014). Product reviews are crucial social proof letting viewers know that other people have bought the product (Santora, 2019). Marketers have leveraged product reviews to increase brand awareness and social proof. Thus sponsored, product recommendation posts should be included as a form of social advertising because such posts are injecting regular social messages with specific, product promotion purposes other than regular consumer experience sharing or product assessment (Lu et al., 2014; Zhu & Tan, 2007). For instance, regular consumer experience sharing or product assessment could be against marketers' interests; consumers could reveal weaknesses associated with product use and recommend others not to buy it. Moreover, influencers or product reviewers are usually offered compensation in exchange for posting positive comments, reviews, or blogs parallel to marketers' advertising goals (Forrest & Cao, 2010; Lu et al., 2014; Zhu & Tan, 2007).

Apart from the above social ad forms, video ads are common push ads shown on social video sharing platforms such as YouTube. First, there are the pre-roll ads, which are usually skippable after they have played for over 5 s. Second, there are the in-stream ads, which could suddenly start to play commercial ads when viewers are viewing a video. The maximum length of in-stream ads is 15 s; non-skippable in-stream ads can be 30 s long and cannot be used in some product categories (Yang et al., 2014).

## 2.3  Pull-Based Social Advertising

Pull-based social advertising is an alternative approach used to increase public awareness of particular social contents which can fulfill a firm's commercial purposes. Many firms hold a mistaken opinion that sales will naturally occur if they establish a social media page and push social ads occasionally (Duffett, 2015). Previously, firms would spread commercial messages on mass media, hoping consumers would develop a preference for their products. But the reality is that 44% of consumers never click on Facebook ads and 31% rarely clicked (Duffett, 2015; Greenlight, 2012). Regarding our research focus on social media monetization, a key question that every social media marketer should ask: Firms spend billions of dollars each year on social advertising campaigns, but do these campaigns really increase revenue?[1] Marketers who push social ads to a large audience who follow their social media account may see sales growth from push-based social ads. But it could be because those customers already show a positive attitude toward a brand and are therefore more likely to follow it in the first place and consequently buy more (John et al., 2017). In this case, social advertising is a means of converting

---

[1] See John et al. (2017) for more details about social marketers' current dilemma.

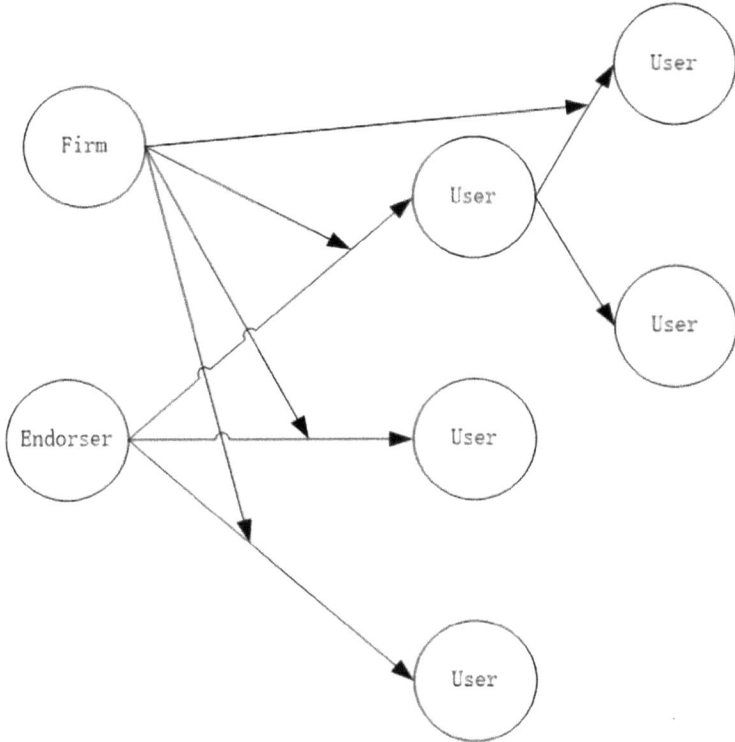

**Fig. 2.2**  Pull-based social advertising

existing loyal customers into purchasers, not acquiring valuable, unsought customers. Since social media has fundamentally revamped the delivery of information, seller-centric, push-based marketing messages or posts are no longer as effective (Lu et al., 2014). Pull-based social advertising, therefore, merits social marketers' specific advertising efforts.

It is reasonable to assume that push-based social advertising is less effective in influencing social media users. Social media is designed for a purpose of social interactions, i.e., messaging, connecting, commenting, and sharing content. In essence, social media is not an online advertising platform. Even nowadays, it is questionable whether Facebook should switch to a new business model (e.g., subscription or membership for an ad-free version) instead of precise advertising based on user personal information and private hobbies. WeChat, China's answer to Facebook, strictly controls the number of ads displayed in users' news feed.

Pull-based social advertising is a consumer-centric approach. As shown in Fig. 2.2, in pull-based social advertising, the publicity of content, which fall into a firm's interests, is achieved by viral sharing and pass along among social media users. This influential mechanism is different from push-based social advertising which relies more on direct firm–consumer communication. This unique mechanism can help us rethink the concept of advertising. Advertising has been deemed as a firm action and a unidirectional information flow from a firm or advertising agents to recipients. Social media, however, enables users to actively pass along content, which eventually can also cause advertising effects or the publicity of brands, products, or services. In this pull-based advertising mode, marketer-generated formal ads or commercials can be absent. In other words, it is a novel means of advertising with or without formal ads or commercials which are orchestrated and launched by firms or advertising agents. Advertising effects (e.g., acquisition of prospects, publicity, reputation, and credibility) can be achieved with or without a nominal "advertisement." In a situation where a social ad is absent, this pull-based social advertising refers to the noncommercial product or service promotion among social media users for commercial purposes (Hayes & King, 2014; Shareef et al., 2018).

The popularity of pull-based social advertising does not mean that firm actions are trivial in the era of social media. Measures need to be taken to boost social electronic word of mouth (eWOM) which can benefit a firm and lead social media users to form positive perceptions toward advertised products, services, or events. Companies such as Dell conduct social listening programs and gather customers' comments and opinions. Companies also advertise key customers' positive eWOM or product comments within social networks to increase brand awareness. Brands also adopted a practice of "seeding social endorsements" by paying influencers to try products or services and send such social endorsements to more social media users (John et al., 2017). The Red Robin restaurant chain hired customers as "brand ambassadors," nudging them to send recommendations to their friends (for this case story, see Taylor et al., 2011). Approximately 1500 customers with an average of 150 friends participated in this social advertising campaign, which eventually spawned around 225,000 positive responses. A China-based fashion retail company, LY, requires all employees in physical stores to share in-store customers' try-on pictures on WeChat. As an exchange, LY offers those customers store credits or discounts. In some cases, firms also needed to conduct actions which were not directly related to their advertising initiatives. For example, Lego uses social media channels to collect customers' opinions related to new product development. The Dutch airline KLM uses Twitter as a key channel for customer feedback and service (see John et al., 2017). All these efforts, no matter whether they are directly or indirectly related to advertising efforts, are a crucial proxy of achieving a positive, well-known social media presence. These measures can pull customers to a brand's product line and convert customers or followers into a great asset: Customers actively engage in value co-creation activities and offer constructive comments for a brand's product line; customers also recommend products or services to peers. Based on the above discussion, we can see that pull-based social advertising is fundamentally different from push-based social advertising in terms of marketing practices.

Existing literature has explained why pull-based social advertising can be effective and tailored to social media contexts. Social media users do not exhibit much resistance toward persuasive contents shared by informal sources or peers (Shareef et al., 2019). Social media users can garner hedonic or other benefits from viewing and passing along content and responding to that content (Shareef et al., 2019). In contrast to marketer-generated advertising content, social media users place more reliance on information shared by fellow users in a social network because content generated by fellow users can more easily elicit their sense of belonging (Choi et al., 2017).

Viral advertising is an example of a successful case of pull-based social advertising. A successful viral advertising case can reach millions of social media users from all over the world. This novel advertising approach is defined as peer-to-peer, self-organized, and viral spreading of content that reflects a firm's interests (Hayes & King, 2014; Porter & Golan, 2006). The Ice Bucket Challenge, a worldwide, popular viral advertising case, can be used to further clarify the essence and characteristics of viral advertising. The Ice Bucket Challenge was a viral, social event introduced by the ALS association (the disease amyotrophic lateral sclerosis) in the United States to raise funds or donations for ALS-related activities and to increase public awareness of this disease. The vision of this viral event was to create a world without ALS (Robinson, 2015). If a person was challenged by another person on social media, she had to pour a bucket of ice water over her head or donate money to the organization. This viral social event involved dozens of celebrities such as Chris Pratt, Oprah, LeBron James, and Bill Gates. The involvement of celebrities further heightened the virality of the Ice Bucket Challenge. As to the awareness of the disease and the advertised association, many people did not know about this disease or the organization before the campaign. This social media campaign allowed many people to become educated about ALS and this resulted in a large number of donations to the organization. As a consequence, this viral event led to over three million donors and the ALS association received over one million donations in the summer of 2014 (The ALS Association, 2014). Based on a story from the New York Times, over 1.2 million videos were shared between June 1 and August 13, 2014, and the event was mentioned over 2.2 million times on Twitter between July 29 and August 17, 2014 (Steel, 2014).

The success of the Ice Bucket Challenge has many implications for social marketers, albeit this event is not for pure commercial purposes such as advertising or branding a given product or service. First, as we mentioned, firm actions were determinant in spawning a viral event. An inspirational vision needs to be created in order for the vision to be shared by massive amounts of social media peers. In this case, the vision, a world without ALS, was so inspiring that many citizens voluntarily participated in this event and added value by co-producing viral content for the vision. Second, endorsers, a regular advertising approach in push-based strategy, are needed to fuel the bandwagon effect of the advertised opinion or content. Research shows that marketers should facilitate peer-to-peer communication by connecting social endorsements with discounts, giveaways, and other sale promotions (Wan & Ren, 2017). In particular, the involvement of celebrity endorsers or influencers is a key facilitator of viral advertising. Third, in viral advertising, a firm's commercial purpose (e.g., fundraising) does not need to be explicitly pronounced, but this purpose needs to be clearly integrated into shared contents. In this example, a person challenged by another has to accept the Ice Bucket Challenge or make a donation to the ALS association.

## 2.4 A Combined Use of Push- and Pull-Based Social Advertising

Considering the weaker advertising effects (e.g., purchase consideration levels) of push-based advertising compared to pull-based advertising (Barreto, 2013; Duffett, 2015), it has not been uncommon to see marketers' commenting about the end of push-based advertising and the rise of pull-based advertising (John et al., 2017). However, research also shows that advertising strategy could be suboptimal if only a pull-based strategy is used; an optimal strategy could be a combined use of push- and pull-based advertising strategies (Hyder, 2019).

A combined use of push- and pull-based advertising strategies can mitigate weaknesses of a sole advertising strategy. It is common to see that push-based advertising could lead to a trust crisis because advertisers' commercial, persuasive intention can be explicitly perceived by customers. This perception can lead to customer distrust in the respective advertised product or service. However, when pull-based advertising strategy is adopted, the advertising effect can be improved if a social ad is shared or delivered through more trusted ties among large numbers of social media users. In push-based advertising, as ads are pushed toward viewers without considering viewers' personal needs, the advertising effectiveness could be lower. In pull-based advertising, as social media users would like to present a favorable social presence and keep nice relationships with their social contacts, viewers' specific needs can be considered when users share advertised content. For example, an ad related to the promotion of the brand new iPhone X could be pushed to a large audience. The ad can be persuasive for most ad viewers, but many individuals who just bought a new phone or feel it unnecessary to replace their current phone are mistakenly targeted by advertisers and saturated by iPhone ads. The situation is different in pull-based advertising in which peer-to-peer communication is based on everyday interactions. The advertised iPhone message can be more precisely delivered to a person who wants to buy a new phone because the message sender is a friend of the person and knows the person's specific need in buying a phone. Also, a commercial message shared by the sender is more effective than regular online ads in terms of advertising effects because this peer-to-peer information sharing is based on more trusted ties (Hayes & King, 2014).

Push-based ads are needed for social media marketers. Massive amounts of content are generated every day in social media. With the variety of content mix in social media, it is unlikely that firms can only rely on pull-based strategies to influence target customers. By targeting specific profiles with ads, firms can find relevant customers. Therefore, push-based social advertising is suitable for newly born firms or brands to get clicks and website visitors (Hyder, 2019). Many social media platforms also offer advertising analytics for paid ads, which is helpful for companies to access constructive feedback for advertising outcomes. Push-based strategies can also be effective for short-term organizational goals such as increasing clicks, leads, and sales (Wan & Ren, 2017), while pull-based strategy, requiring customer participation in social media activities (Rishika et al., 2013), can bring about long-term outcomes such as fans, connections, and communities. In a word, a combined use of push- and pull-based advertising strategies is recommended for social media marketers. We note that this chapter mainly illuminates the concept, variety, and characteristics of social advertising. More specifics will be discussed in later chapters which offer more thorough business solutions for firms and social media marketers.

At the end, we use a case to clarify the combined use of push- and pull-based social advertising. Castrol Moto is the motorcycle division of Castrol [the case study is adapted from Hyder (2019)]. The company conducted a 1-year social advertising initiative. The goal was to increase customer engagement with the brand in the region of North American. During the first 6 months, the company focused on using organic contents to engage customers in Facebook. Five thousand fans and over 25,000 social interactions were garnered in these 6 months. These outcomes were quite satisfactory considering the company's Facebook page had just been created. But a major problem was that, in a pull-based strategy scenario, 80% of the 5000 fans were less relevant for the company's interests which focus on customers in North America. This was because the company could not place restrictions on the target region of social ads unless they used Facebook's profile-targeting feature. During the second 6 months, Castrol used a combination of pull- and push-based social advertising strategy. Paid ads were posted by targeting customers in the specific region. The results were astonishing. The company garnered over 30,000 new fans; 50% of these new fans were in the target region. The results have shown that the combination of pull- and push-based social advertising strategy can be successful.

# References

Alalwan, A. A. (2018). Investigating the impact of social media advertising features on customer purchase intention. *International Journal of Information Management, 42*, 65–77.

Alalwan, A. A., Rana, N. P., Dwivedi, Y. K., & Algharabat, R. (2017). Social media in marketing: A review and analysis of the existing literature. *Telematics and Informatics, 34*(7), 1177–1190.

Azeem, A., & Haq, Z. (2012). Perception towards internet advertising: A study with reference to three different demographic groups. *Global Business and Management Research: An International Journal, 4*(1), 28–45.

Bailis, R. (n.d.). *The state of influencer marketing: 10 influencer marketing statistics to inform where you invest*. Retrieved from https://www.bigcommerce.com/blog/influencer-marketing-statistics/#conclusion

Barreda, A. A., Bilgihan, A., Nusair, K., & Okumus, F. (2016). Online branding: Development of hotel branding through interactivity theory. *Tourism Management, 57*, 180–192.

Barreto, A. M. (2013). Do users look at banner ads on Facebook? *Journal of Research in Interactive Marketing, 7*(2), 119–139.

Choi, Y. K., Seo, Y., & Yoon, S. (2017). E-WOM messaging on social media. *Internet Research, 27*(3), 495–505.

Chu, S. C. (2011). Viral advertising in social media: Participation in Facebook groups and responses among college-aged users. *Journal of Interactive Advertising, 12*(1), 30–43.

Chung, S., & Cho, H. (2017). Fostering parasocial relationships with celebrities on social media: Implications for celebrity endorsement. *Psychology and Marketing, 34*, 481–495.

Cox, C. (2011). *Facebook to show sponsored ads in news feed in 2012.* Retrieved from http://abcnews.go.com/Technology/facebook-put-sponsored-ads-timeline-newsfeed-january-2012/story?id=15205346#.UzPiAv7KEVE.email

Deshpande, I. (2019). *What is social media advertising? Definition, costs, best practices, benefits, and examples.* Retrieved from https://www.martechadvisor.com/articles/social-media-marketing-2/what-is-social-media-advertising/#

Duffett, R. G. (2015). Facebook advertising's influence on intention-to-purchase and purchase amongst Millennials. *Internet Research, 25*(4), 498–526.

Dyrud, M. A. (2011). Social networking and business communication pedagogy: Plugging into the Facebook generation. *Business Communication Quarterly, 74*(4), 475–478.

Forrest, E., & Cao, Y. (2010). Opinions, recommendations and endorsements: The new regulatory framework for social media. *Journal of Business and Policy Research, 5*(2), 88–99.

Greenlight. (2012). *Facebook sponsored advertisements—44% of people say they would 'never' click on them.* Retrieved from www.bizcommunity.com/Article/196/12/75429.html

Hayes, J. L., & King, K. W. (2014). The social exchange of viral ads: Referral and coreferral of ads among college students. *Journal of Interactive Advertising, 14*(2), 98–109.

He, J., & Shao, B. (2018). Examining the dynamic effects of social network advertising: A semiotic perspective. *Telematics and Informatics, 35*(2), 504–516.

Higgs, B. (2008). On location. *Marketing Magazine*, pp. 82–84.

Hyder, S. (2019). *Paid or organic social media marketing? Do you know which to use . . . and why?* Retrieved from https://zenmedia.com/blog/paid-organic-social-media-marketing-know-use/

John, L. K., Mochon, D., Emrich, O., & Schwartz, J. (2017). *What's the value of a like.* Retrieved from https://hbr.org/2017/03/whats-the-value-of-a-like

Kapoor, K. K., Tamilmani, K., Rana, N. P., Patil, P., Dwivedi, Y. K., & Nerur, S. (2018). Advances in social media research: Past, present and future. *Information Systems Frontiers, 20*(3), 531–558.

Köster, M., Rüth, M., Hamborg, K. C., & Kaspar, K. (2015). Effects of personalized banner ads on visual attention and recognition memory. *Applied Cognitive Psychology, 29*(2), 181–192.

Lee, J., & Hong, I. B. (2016). Predicting positive user responses to social media advertising: The roles of emotional appeal, informativeness, and creativity. *International Journal of Information Management, 36*(3), 360–373.

Lee, K. T., & Koo, D. M. (2012). Effects of attribute and valence of e-WOM on message adoption: Moderating roles of subjective knowledge and regulatory focus. *Computers in Human Behavior, 28*(5), 1974–1984.

Lin, C. A., & Kim, T. (2016). Predicting user response to sponsored advertising on social media via the technology acceptance model. *Computers in Human Behavior, 64*, 710–718. https://doi.org/10.1016/j.chb.2016.07.027

Lu, L. C., Chang, W. P., & Chang, H. H. (2014). Consumer attitudes toward blogger's sponsored recommendations and purchase intention: The effect of sponsorship type, product type, and brand awareness. *Computers in Human Behavior, 34*, 258–266.

Main, K. (2018). *Facebook sponsored posts: What they are & how they work.* Retrieved from https://fitsmallbusiness.com/facebook-sponsored-posts/

Mangold, W. G., & Faulds, D. J. (2009). Social media: The new hybrid element of the promotion mix. *Business Horizons, 52*(4), 357–365.

Mau, D. (2017). *Alexa Chung's app Villoid pivots to become online influencer marketplace.* Retrieved from https://fashionista.com/2017/12/alexa-chung-villoid-influencer-app

McCracken, G. (1989). Who is the celebrity endorser? Cultural foundations of the endorsement process. *Journal of Consumer Research, 16*, 310–321.

Mediakix. (n.d.). *Celebrity influencer marketing: How brands win with the world's biggest stars.* Retrieved from https://mediakix.com/blog/celebrity-influencer-marketing-instagram-examples/

Porter, L., & Golan, G. (2006). From subservient chickens to brawny men: A comparison of viral advertising to television advertising. *Journal of Interactive Advertising, 6*(2), 4–33.

Quick, T. (2018). *Why Facebook sponsored ads need to be part of your advertising strategy.* Retrieved from https://instapage.com/blog/facebook-sponsored-ads

Rishika, R., Kumar, A., Janakiraman, R., & Bezawada, R. (2013). The effect of customers' social media participation on customer visit frequency and profitability: An empirical investigation. *Information Systems Research, 24*(1), 108–127.

Robinson, R. (2015). *Buckets of ice heat up ALS research.* Retrieved from http://web.alsa.org/site/DocServer/Vision_Winter_2015.pdf?docID=122341&_ga=2.43202924.855738741.1567482896-1424647728.1558037434

Santora, J. (2019). *9 ways to get more product reviews and increase social proof.* Retrieved from https://optinmonster.com/get-more-product-reviews/

Schouten, A. P., Janssen, L., & Verspaget, M. (2020). Celebrity vs. influencer endorsements in advertising: The role of identification, credibility, and product-endorser fit. *International Journal of Advertising, 39*(2), 258–281.

Schulze, C., Schöler, L., & Skiera, B. (2014). Not all fun and games: Viral marketing for utilitarian products. *Journal of Marketing, 78*(1), 1–19.

Shareef, M. A., Mukerji, B., Alryalat, M. A. A., Wright, A., & Dwivedi, Y. K. (2018). Ads on Facebook: Identifying the persuasive elements in the development of positive attitudes in consumers. *Journal of Retailing and Consumer Services, 43*, 258–268.

Shareef, M. A., Mukerji, B., Dwivedi, Y. K., Rana, N. P., & Islam, R. (2019). Social media marketing: Comparative effect of ad sources. *Journal of Retailing and Consumer Services, 46*, 58–69.

Sherman. (2019a). *Facebook sponsored posts vs. Facebook ads: Which is best for your business?* Retrieved from https://www.lyfemarketing.com/blog/facebook-sponsored-posts/

Sherman. (2019b). *FAQ: What is social advertising & how does it impact my sales?* Retrieved from https://www.lyfemarketing.com/blog/what-is-social-advertising/

Shewan, D. (2019). *The rise of ad blockers: Should advertisers be panicking?(!!).* Retrieved from https://www.wordstream.com/blog/ws/2015/10/02/ad-blockers

Statista Research Department. (2019). *How effective are celebrities as part of the following marketing strategies?* Retrieved from https://www.statista.com/statistics/711291/celebrity-marketing-effectiveness-in-the-uk/

Steel, E. (2014). *'Ice bucket challenge' has raised millions for ALS association.* Retrieved from https://www.nytimes.com/2014/08/18/business/ice-bucket-challenge-has-raised-millions-for-als-association.html?_r=1

Stone, B. (2010). Ads posted on Facebook strike some as off-key. *New York Times.*

Swani, K., Milne, G. R., Brown, B. P., Assaf, A. G., & Donthu, N. (2017). What messages to post? Evaluating the popularity of social media communications in business versus consumer markets. *Industrial Marketing Management, 62*, 77–87.

Taylor, D. G., Lewin, J. E., & Strutton, D. (2011). Friends, fans, and followers: Do ads work on social networks? How gender and age shape receptivity. *Journal of Advertising Research, 51*(1), 258–275.

The ALS Association. (2014). *The ALS association expresses sincere gratitude to over three million donors.* Retrieved from http://www.alsa.org/news/media/press-releases/ice-bucket-challenge-082914.html

Van Reijmersdal, E. A., Rozendaal, E., Smink, N., Van Noort, G., & Buijzen, M. (2017). Processes and effects of targeted online advertising among children. *International Journal of Advertising, 36*(3), 396–414.

Villiard, H., & Moreno, M. A. (2012). Fitness on Facebook: Advertisements generated in response to profile content. *Cyberpsychology, Behavior, and Social Networking, 15*(10), 564–568.

Wan, F., & Ren, F. (2017). The effect of firm marketing content on product sales: Evidence from a mobile social media platform. *Journal of Electronic Commerce Research, 18*(4), 288–302.

Wu, C. W. (2016). The performance impact of social media in the chain store industry. *Journal of Business Research, 69*(11), 5310–5316.

Yang, K. C., Yang, C., Huang, C. H., Shih, P. H., & Yang, S. Y. (2014). *Consumer attitudes toward online video advertising: An empirical study on YouTube as platform*. In 2014 IEEE International Conference on Industrial Engineering and Engineering Management, pp. 1131–1135.

Zhu, J., & Tan, B. (2007). Effectiveness of blog advertising: Impact of communicator expertise, advertising intent, and product involvement. *ICIS 2007 Proceedings*.

Zote, J. (2020). *55 critical social media statistics to fuel your 2020 strategy*. Retrieved from https://sproutsocial.com/insights/social-media-statistics/

# How Companies Can Use Social Media for Social Selling

**3**

## 3.1 Social Selling: What It Is and Why It Is Important

A staggering number of stores, around 9000, failed from Jan 2019 to Oct 2019, significantly higher than the 5844 stores that failed in the entire 2018 (Coresight Research, 2019). Businesses know that sales are crucial for a firm's survival in the current volatile, competitive business environment. With steady sales of products or services, a firm can monetize its resources, maintain its business operation, and be able to conduct risky, high-return activities such as market expansions, new product development, and digital innovations.

However, increasing sales can be difficult for most firms. A survey on companies' top sales priority showed that over 30% of the surveyed companies stated that closing more deals is their first priority, followed by increasing sales efficiency and shortening the length of the sales cycle (Brudner, 2019). The average sales conversion rate across all industries is considerably low, 2.46–3.36% (Statista, cited in Gerencer, 2020). Traditional selling approaches are becoming more difficult. Brian Carroll, CEO of InTouch Inc., and author of the book, Lead Generation for the Complex Sale, once said "[t]here's the old adage that 90 percent of people hate cold-calling and the other 10 percent are lying" (InsideView, 2011). For every 330 cold calls, only approximately one appointment was set (Lampertz, 2012). Customers are less captured by salespeople's traditional selling initiatives (Ancillai et al., 2019; Fidelman, 2012; Giamanco & Gregoire, 2012; Minsky & Quesenberry, 2016). Research found that over 75% of all B2B buyers had very limited interactions with salespeople (Andersen et al., 2017). This phenomenon does not only happen with traditional simple offerings (e.g., household appliances) but also with complicated, value-based offerings (e.g., digital business solutions) in which salespeople must interact with customers in order to identify customer needs (Adamson et al., 2012; Ancillai et al., 2019; Terho et al., 2017). These changes put considerable pressure on salespeople and organizations which rely on traditional sales initiatives (Ancillai et al., 2019).

F. J. Martínez-López et al., *Social Media Monetization*, Future of Business and Finance, https://doi.org/10.1007/978-3-031-14575-9_3

In contrast, social selling normally generates more positive outcomes. Buyers have become accustomed to using social media in their buying process or purchase journey (Ancillai et al., 2019; Fidelman, 2012; Giamanco & Gregoire, 2012; Wiese, 2017). 82% of the business-to-business (B2B) buyers stated that the winning seller's social content can significantly influence their purchase decision (Minsky & Quesenberry, 2016). Skilled social sellers are six times more likely to exceed sales quota over sellers with limited or no social selling skills (Biro, 2015). Around 84% of the companies used social media in their sales function and around 90% monitored and collected social data (Kiron et al., 2013).

Social selling is understood by some researchers as a process whereby "salespeople use social media platforms to research, prospect, and network by sharing educational content and answering questions" (Minsky & Quesenberry, 2016, p. 3). Social selling can encompass the entire buying process from awareness to the moment when a consumer decides to buy (MacDonald, 2020). Existing literature also reveals that social media is a channel to garner intelligence and knowledge about consumers; thus, social selling should also involve using intelligence and knowledge about customers in the sales cycle (Trainor, 2012). By integrating current studies, Ancillai et al. (2019) offered a conclusive definition on social selling: "a selling approach which leverages social and digital channels for (1) understanding, (2) connecting with, and (3) engaging influencers, prospects and existing customers at relevant customer purchasing journey touchpoints for building valuable business relationships" (p. 294). We prefer this definition to the one offered by Minsky and Quesenberry, because it considers the value co-creation characteristic of social media. Content of interest about social sellers does not necessarily have to be produced by sellers. Consumers can also generate influential content and bring about prospects and sales. This definition reflects a value co-creation view of selling (Hartmann et al., 2018). This concept reveals three key elements of social selling: (1) collecting consumer knowledge and intelligence; (2) connecting various factors such as endorsers, consumers, and sharers via social channels and digital touchpoints; and (3) engaging consumers via firm-generated or user-generated content to facilitate social sales (Ancillai et al., 2019).

In addition to customer satisfaction, social reach, brand reputation, and other metrics, sales is a major metric in assessing social media initiative success (Kiron et al., 2013). In the eyes of top management (i.e., CEO, CFO, CIO, and CMO), increasing sales is a key goal of using social media (Kiron et al., 2013). Social media is frequently used by sales representatives to discover and meet customer needs (Warren, 2016). There is significant evidence that the use of social media does create sales. For example, the University of Michigan ran a social selling campaign to sell individual football tickets in 1 day that generated $86,000 in sales (Smith, 2012). In another example, after adopting social selling initiatives and LinkedIn's Sales Navigator, marketing software company Eloqua reduced its average sales cycle time by 20 days and increased the rate of leads converting to opportunities by 25% (Sexton, n.d.).

Despite these examples, firms' adoption of social selling does not necessarily lead to success. First, on social media, while customers can "like" and "friend" a sales rep, customers can also "hide" and "unfollow" a sales rep, with just one click (DSN Staff, 2011). Second, social media is not designed for commercial activities. It is centered on social interaction. Therefore, consumers have a natural ad aversion on social media (Crowl, 2019). Third, as social media does not have a professional product webpage like e-commerce websites do, social content is not as effective as e-commerce websites in displaying product attributes. This characteristic could affect a product's online social presence and a brand's social authenticity, which could turn customers away at the point of sales (Crowl, 2019). Last, for many sales managers, they have been used to "dialing for dollars" because they feel sales reps should be "on the phones" (Warren, 2016) and erroneously think that social selling is just using social media channels to sell. This reflects that many sales reps and managers lack an accurate understanding of social selling and its characteristics. In order to overcome these barriers in social selling success, key success factors and key activities on social selling need to be identified.

Many managers do not notice the differences between social media marketing and social selling. Social selling focuses more on building one-to-one relationships than reaching an extensive number of social media users (Stevanovic, 2019). In contrast, social media marketing aims to increase brand awareness by generating viral content that users can share and pass along within social networks (Minsky & Quesenberry, 2016). In the traditional selling model, marketers first create public awareness of products and services and generate a list of prospects' emails and phone numbers. Then, sales reps contact such prospects and try to convert prospects into buyers. In the social selling model, marketers and sales reps are closely aligned. The interactive and social element of social media can help sales reps be involved earlier in the sales cycle (Minsky & Quesenberry, 2016). Sales reps can use marketer-generated content to find and connect prospects and actively find sales opportunities, rather than waiting for customers to become aware of their products or services. In addition, another characteristic of social selling is that social interactions with a prospect do not necessarily lead to a direct sale in a week or a few months, but could lead to a big sale within a year (Minsky & Quesenberry, 2016). Social selling is not another channel that sales reps use to "cold call" prospects (Rowley, 2017). Social selling is about nurturing and maintaining relationships over time (Rowley, 2017). Sales should come naturally if interpersonal trust is built and sales reps offer products or solutions based on customers' pain points and problems.

To summarize, social selling is a novel selling approach. The core components of social selling are finding, understanding, and engaging customers via social media channels (Ancillai et al., 2019). The implementation of social selling is reliant on a social media-based selling mindset by which firms can transform their selling models. Social selling is not about replacing traditional firm–customer communication methods such as ads, commercials, online meetings, and face-to-face interactions (Rowley, 2017), but these can be used to integrate a firm's social selling system.

## 3.2   Critical Success Factors of Social Selling

Although social selling is a unique selling approach, many firms fail to produce satisfactory outcomes through its use. Therefore, it is necessary to identify key success factors of social selling so that firms can improve social selling performance by placing more priority on such factors. From an academic viewpoint, current research on critical success factors of social selling is scarce. A majority of the research focuses on the use of social media in team collaboration (see Zeiller & Schauer, 2011), marketing (see Mohammadian & Mohammadreza, 2012), advertising, staying updated, and sharing relevant company information (see Campbell et al., 2013). This chapter aims to close this research gap, by specifically identifying the critical success factors of social selling. The chapter is built on reviews of existing literature, case studies, and the industrial experience in a China-based digital business solution supplier.

1. *Organizational Adoption of Social Media in Selling*. Social media should not be solely used by sales reps. Sales managers and top executives in sales and marketing should prioritize social media in selling in both a strategic level and a tactical level. Otherwise, top-performing salespersons who are good at social selling could be misunderstood by their managers and leadership, resulting in an organization that does not offer a conducive atmosphere for growing its social selling capability.

2. *Building Meaningful Relationships with Customers*. Social media is used for building and maintaining relationships with others. In today's volatile, competitive business environment with the wide application of Internet platforms, prospects can contact several companies at the same time. Therefore, sales reps should not overlook the role of customer relationship management because it is becoming harder to identify a prospect and win a deal among several competitors. Therefore, a key facet of successful social selling is building meaningful relationships with customers and prospects (Selledge, 2020).

3. *Collecting and Analyzing Customer Information*. In any selling approach, customer information is crucial for winning a deal. Sales reps collect customer information and discern customers' needs and pain points. With social media, sales reps can visit customers' profile page and communicate with customers easily and smoothly. By collecting and analyzing customer information, sales reps can identify "right" prospects whose needs can be met by particular products or services and thereby convert prospects into buyers.

4. *Developing Content Oriented toward Customers' Pain Points and Problems*. Sharing content of quality is a key to customer engagement on social media. Social content shared on social media encompasses product or service information, brand information, corporation information, etc. In social selling, successful customer engagement is reliant on the relevance and value of the content developed by sales reps or marketers (Ancillai et al., 2019). In particular, the relevance and value of the content can be curated and designed by focusing on customers' problems and pain points. This can empower customers to envision potential

benefits they could have if they bought the product or service in question (see Agnihotri et al., 2012; Ancillai et al., 2019; Bocconcelli et al., 2017).

5. *Selecting Appropriate Metrics for Social Selling.* Measuring what matters is crucial for social selling success (Agnihotri et al., 2012; Kiron et al., 2013). However, it is difficult to apply unified, specific metrics for various social selling initiatives at different stages of the sales cycle (DSN Staff, 2011). The essence of social selling is dynamic, complex, and variant across market segments and selling situations. Some social selling professionals argue that activity-focused metrics should be applied for assessing salespeople's performance (Ancillai et al., 2019). Moreover, metrics should not only focus on the quantity, but also stress the quality of the activities in order to achieve optimal outcomes (Ancillai et al., 2019). For instance, at an early stage of social selling, leads generation is a major goal for salespeople. Therefore, sales managers at this early stage should roll out metrics relevant to this goal such as the number of leads, the number of customers who visited the firm's website, but left without being taken care of, and the number of customers who followed the firm's social account or made a subscription for more updating information. At this stage, managers should place less weight on actual sales that a salesperson generates when assessing this person's performance. For example, SAP avoided using specific measures in defining all social media initiatives; instead, they set different goals and metrics for each initiative (Agnihotri et al., 2012). Activity-focused metrics do not imply that sales performance cannot be strictly assessed and managed. The popularity of social selling does not mean that cold calls or traditional selling approaches are no longer of use. Social media use should be advocated by firms, but it does not mean that every firm should fundamentally transform their business model. Having a result-oriented view in mind, sales managers can assess and measure each salesperson's performance by setting uniform metrics, such as sales quotas and ROI at the mid-year or at year-end.

6. *Aligning Marketing and Sales in Social Media Initiatives.* It is found that when sales and marketing are well aligned, organizations can obtain higher ROI, revenue, and employee satisfaction (Granath, 2019). Research also demonstrates that when an organization's marketing and sales work in silos, the win rates of deals are usually smaller than their counterparts in which marketing and sales are aligned and cohesive (Schenk, 2019). As a consequence, sales and marketing alignment is stressed by many organizations (Bailey, 2015). The alignment of sales and marketing can be created through frequent and direct communication between the two departments (Bailey, 2015). What is more, sales and marketing alignment can be achieved by building a shared language and a shared body of knowledge of social selling, thereby increasing the visibility of each department for the other and helping to define a shared customer journey (Granath, 2019). The boundary between sales and marketing should be removed in social selling initiatives. Social professionals have even introduced a new concept, *smarketing*, which would encourage social-oriented organizations to merge sales and marketing into one entity (Bailey, 2015). However, many executives do not have such a boundary-spanning mindset. In particular, many marketers and executives often

misunderstand social selling. They erroneously understand social selling as using social media channels to boost the awareness of brands, products, or services. One successful case of marketing and sales alignment is used to illustrate how companies can align marketing and sales. A China-based digital business solutions supplier stresses the role of marketing and sales alignment in social selling. The supplier's executive first developed a shared language and a shared body of knowledge on social selling. Then, as deals are closed via a project organization (this organization is assembled for fulfilling a specific task and dismissed after the task has been completed), marketers and salespersons work together to close a deal cohesively. Next, driven by a selling-orientation approach, a sales manager is appointed as the project leader in order to avoid disagreements and conflicts between salespersons and marketers. Finally, the company's sales and marketing teams are united in winning and closing deals.

7. *Taking Security and Privacy Measures*. Security and privacy are customers' basic needs in using social media. Customers do not want their personal information misused by sales reps and other third-party organizations for commercial purposes. However, customers' social media profiles are used by social media companies to offer profile-targeting advertising as well as to help social media marketers identify ideal targets. Therefore, because customer information collection and analyses are inevitable, security and privacy measures should be taken by social sellers. Social sellers can provide security and privacy notices in their posts in an attempt to demonstrate their integrity in protecting customers' information security and privacy and guaranteeing transaction safety.

8. *Leadership Support*. This factor is commonplace in determining strategy success. Also, leadership support is a necessity for social selling success (Kiron et al., 2013). For example, Michael Dell's leadership has contributed to Dell's social media strategy growing from the early stage to the mature stage (Kiron et al., 2013). Pitney Bowes, a global technology company, started using LinkedIn to build the credibility of salespeople, and this initiative quickly saw considerably positive outcomes: a significant increase in selling opportunities (Walsh, 2017). The critical success factor for Pitney Bowes was having leadership support, which made it easier for salespeople to participate and succeed in social selling (Walsh, 2017). From a managerial viewpoint, selling strategy, regardless of whether it is social selling or traditional selling, should be strictly managed and supported by top executives. Shared strategic visions, language, and key metrics (e.g., sales growth rates) should be centrally managed by leadership. Because social selling is a completely different selling approach (in contrast to traditional cold calling), salespeople should be able to successfully work between-function boundaries and be equipped with a certain degree of freedom to interact with internal (e.g., marketers) and external (e.g., clients) actors within social networks. Therefore, leaders should support selling activities, as well as empower front-line salespeople to win deals via social media or other tools.

## 3.3 Key Activities in Social Selling: How to Convert "Social" into "Sales"

### 3.3.1 Social Media Lead Generation

Social media lead generation refers to the process of identifying and cultivating prospects for a firm's product or service via social media channels. Traditional examples of lead generation strategies are cold calling, running paid ads, giving away freebies, and roadshows. In social media contexts, leads can be generated through more natural and organic approaches, such as viral social content, product recommendations, and brand communities. Current social media lead generation practice involves several problems:

1. *A Mistaken Mindset.* As mentioned previously, social selling is becoming more popular and profitable in contrast to traditional selling strategies. Traditional push strategies can generate leads through spreading product or service information among a large audience. The problem is that often managers may employ an obsolete mindset, requiring salespeople to make cold calls and wait for customers to become aware of their products or services. Alternatively, salespeople can generate leads using social media channels and technologies. For example, salespeople can create viral social content without explicit commercial information to spawn social media leads which can then be converted into prospects. Particularly in the context of social media communication, organic lead generation content is more preferable than their sales-oriented counterpart because organic content can be useful as well as unobtrusive to viewers (Das et al., 2015). Therefore, organizations should be more flexible with lead generation approaches and allow marketers and salespeople to use social media channels and technologies to attract prospects.

2. *Erroneously Assume That Social Traffic Will Develop.* An erroneous assumption is simply to build a social media page, pay to run ads, and then wait for social traffic to develop. A social media page should not just display an online corporate image. It should be a key platform for interacting with users and building relationships with them. Social media lead generation needs companies to spend time and resources on the process. Paid social ads are crucial for startups and new brands which lack enough public awareness to generate primary leads or "social seeds." But paid social ads do not necessarily lead to successful lead generation in the long term. Organic, native content can also be incorporated in a firm's social media page. It is reasonable to expect that social posts with a "sponsored" label will more easily make viewers perceive posters' commercial intention. Social traffic will develop when firms proactively curate social content and nurture relationships with customers in a timely manner. It is unlikely that social traffic will come out of just a social presence without many marketing and selling efforts involved.

3. *Leading Viewers to a Generic Landing Page.* When a few digital touchpoints are used simultaneously for generating leads, a mistake is leading all viewers or

visitors to generic landing pages. The problem associated with this approach is that visitors could perceive standard content and e-commerce websites as less relevant to their individual needs. Albeit making a sale is a firm's ultimate goal for all social selling initiatives, this does not mean that social media users will buy from a firm's commercial posts which are disguised as regular social posts. The shortest path from discovery to purchase may not be straightforward and linear. It is plausible that firms delve into why users are interested in their social posts, designing specific landing pages tailored to users' interests and needs.

4. *Not Moving Social Media Users Forward in the Social Selling Process.* It is not enough to lead social media users to a specific landing page that meets their interests and needs. In the service of the ultimate goal of achieving sales, firms should take steps to move visitors forward in the social selling process. This does not mean that a click-to-buy button or other notices need to be displayed in the landing page. Social salespeople can befriend those visitors and kindly contact them for sales opportunities later on. Sales managers can keep an eye on the progress that sales reps make. A sales manager can require sales reps to report leads they get and their sales planning in detail. In particular, a manager can assess a sales rep's job performance by examining whether a sale rep regularly contacts each lead and makes efforts in cultivating sales opportunities. On the other hand, if sales can be achieved directly, for instance, products are low priced, it is likely that consumers will buy impulsively. In these circumstances, pain points in a customer's path to purchase should be removed. A click-to-buy button can be used to seamlessly connect a social platform with an e-commerce platform. For example, customers clicking a buy button in social ads will be directly led to the respective product webpage without wasteful efforts such as website registration and login-in. As e-commerce involves the physical separation between sellers and buyers, e-commerce could be naturally risky and uncertain for online consumers. Steps should be taken by sellers to remove consumers' security and privacy concerns and move them forward in the social selling process.

### 3.3.2  Managing Customer-Related Social Media Data and Information

As mentioned previously, social media data collection is a critical success factor of social selling success. Regarding the management of customer-related social media data and information, social sellers need to overcome several challenges and know how to effectively use such data and information.

1. *Social Listening.* Social media can generate a large amount of data, encompassing user-generated content, likes, shares, and comments, etc. Social selling companies can exploit this data and find insightful and valuable digital assets to guide new product development and strategic innovations, ultimately improving social selling performance. However, the large volume and wide variety of social media data can make data and information management difficult (Stieglitz et al.,

2018). Even big companies such as Dell need to plan for years to perform social listening activities. Since 2006, Michael Dell, the founder and CEO of Dell Technologies, has discussed the possibility of social listening with his employees. Many social digital platforms for social listening have been developed. These include Dell Techcenter (launched in 2006, this online community connects IT experts to customers, employees, and other stakeholders), IdeaStorm (launched in 2007, this website allows customers to submit ideas to Dell), Social Media Listening Command Center (launched in 2010, this center for managing social listening activities), Social Net Advocacy (launched in 2013, this tool measures social sentiment) (see Kiron et al., 2013). The case of Dell demonstrates that social listening requires a long-term plan for arranging relevant activities and launching digital platforms for social listening.

2. *Collecting and Processing Data and Information across Various Silos.* Data or information silos refer to non-integration or incompatibility between various information systems and different sectors, functions, data providers, and channels (Ma et al., 2018). Customer-related data and information could be stored across many sources. First, marketing and sales departments could have access to diverse customer data and information. From a marketing viewpoint, marketers could be more informed about what social content nudges viewers to follow a brand. From a selling viewpoint, salespeople could be more knowledgeable about a particular prospect's social activities and preferences. Second, social media platforms such as Facebook, LinkedIn, Instagram, and Twitter can be deemed as information systems by which firms access and manage information associated with customers. While some social media platforms have started to offer connections with third-party companies' websites and systems (e.g., Weibo offers data connections with Alibaba; WeChat is connected to Pinduoduo; and Facebook introduced the Facebook Application Programming Interface (API) to build the connectivity and interactivity between Facebook and other apps), most social media platforms focus on their social business. Therefore, as social media platforms are not used for commercial activities, it is not uncommon to find data and information silos between social media platforms and a company's CRM systems or e-commerce systems. Finally, social selling does not imply that sales activities have to rely on social media channels. The role of social media can simply lead customers to brick-and-mortar stores or e-commerce websites. Customers' cross-channel behaviors can also result in data or information silos between online channels and offline channels.

   Breaking down data and information silos could involve a holistic solution encompassing strategy, culture, organizational redesign, information systems integration, and business process re-engineering. For instance, decentralized organizational design can mitigate data and information silos between functions. In social selling settings, we would focus on strategies that can break down data or information silos related to organizational functions, information systems, and channels. First, regarding data and information silos between marketing and sales, firms can consider increasing data and information sharing between these two functions. As previously mentioned, marketing and sales alignment is a critical success factor for social selling. Second, with regard to data or information silos between different systems, data and information connections or interfaces can be introduced to connect different information systems. Social media data such as views, likes, comments, and shares can be transferred to social selling companies' business systems such as CRM systems and selling platforms. Finally, data or information silos across various channels should be minimized by examining the big picture of online and offline channels. It is plausible that companies can build a holistic and systematic view of omni-channels (Verhoef et al., 2015). Based on this view, even in social selling settings, social media channels are merely a channel among others for winning deals and achieving sales. The ultimate goal of social selling is closing more deals or achieving sales. Hence, data or information silos between channels can be decreased when an integral omni-channel management view is established. Specifically, how data or information flows from one channel to another should be dependent on whether a firm can extract maximum value from both channels. For example, Semir, a China-based fashion retail group, has an online channel and an offline channel. Semir's offline channel generates the most sales and acts a strategic role in the firm. Social media data and information processing should act as a secondary role in the entire business and offer insights for selling activities in brick-and-mortar stores. In this case, as the role of social media channels and physical retailing channels are clearly defined, the data and information silos between the two channels can be avoided.

3. *From Social Media Analytics to Social Media Intelligence.* After discovering, collecting, managing, and processing social media data and information, firms should then place their focus on analyzing data and information in order to deliver practical and managerial implications. Social media analytics refers to the analysis of data gathered from social media channels (Gandomi & Haider, 2015). In practice, social media analytics can impose technical barriers for many firms, particularly small businesses which have very limited resources. In other words, it is extremely difficult for small firms to create a competitive advantage over firms which have professional social media analysts and specialists in data science. Advanced technologies such as artificial intelligence (automatic analytics and prediction), big data technology (analysis of a huge amount of data), decision support systems connecting social media analytics to strategic decision making, and content analysis techniques can be applied to social media analytics. But this barrier does not mean that small firms should just drop their social selling initiatives. Small firms can garner benefits from social media analytics by using third-party analytics applications for social media initiatives. First, it is necessary to clarify why social media analytics are so crucial for the success of social selling and other social media initiatives. The role of social media analytics is *explaining* why a social selling initiative is effective or ineffective and *predicting* future key social selling strategies. Social media analytics can help firms evaluate the influence of social selling initiatives and create optimal strategic decisions (Expert System Team, 2016). Second, social media analytics include analyses of three aspects: social content analysis, social influence analysis, and social links

and networks analysis (Gandomi & Haider, 2015). By analyzing social content, firms become informed about how consumers react to their marketing communication and social presence. Specifically, built on social listening, social content analyses entail analyses of customer emotion, preferences, and behavioral patterns. By analyzing the social influence of their marketing communication, firms will know what content leads to sales. A typical social influence analysis of a social selling campaign is comparing the sales before and after the campaign and also calculating how many likes, comments, and followers are obtained in the campaign. By analyzing social links and networks, firms can discern what customer is most influential with their social network. This analysis can help firms select brand endorsers or social media influencers which have been proven to be influential with social networks. By continually gathering insightful information or intelligence from social media analytics, companies can build a route from social media analytics to social media strategy making. Ultimately, companies could form a valuable corporate asset: social media intelligence. This intelligence refers to the capability of handling social media data and information and then generating smarter, more precise, and more effective decision making for social selling initiatives. It is expected that, if a company is equipped with a high level of social media intelligence, this company could face changes in business models and corporate strategy. Such strategy and business models need to consider information and intelligence produced by social media analytics. Concerning social selling, companies should design socially focused business models and selling strategies. Socially focused business models or strategies add social and interactive elements to the firm–customer interface, such as social eWOM, online product reviews, and brand communities. Having in mind that this chapter only aims to introduce social selling and key aspects of it, more details about social media analytics and social media intelligence will be specifically discussed in a later chapter.

Two examples are introduced to clarify how social media analytics and intelligence are used in practice. Lispy London, a female fashion-related company, employed social media analytics to analyze and predict social media users' linguistic pattern and online behaviors, in an attempt to engage the right customers at the right time in their purchase journey (Petersen, 2015). Social media analytics was used to redesign paid and organic content marketing and other relevant marketing campaigns (Petersen, 2015). This process produced a 350% increase in sales and brought thousands of prospects to the company (Petersen, 2015). In another example, H&M, a multinational fashion retail company, found its endorsement ads saw different outcomes in different markets (Petersen, 2016). In order to explain and find out what caused the differences, the company monitored the volume of conversations following its social media campaigns (Petersen, 2016). H&M found that different cultures and customs can influence the effectiveness of the company's marketing campaigns (Petersen, 2016). H&M can extract value from social media analytics by reshaping and redesigning its marketing strategy according to a target market's culture and custom characteristics.

### 3.3.3  "Friending" and Networking Customers

Social selling is a process of finding, nurturing, and monetizing relationships with social media users. Relationship building therefore is a core component of social selling success. Previous literature provides evidence on relevant academic topics such as social capital (Brass, 2001; Envick, 2005), guanxi (Farh et al., 1998), strong or weak ties (Granovetter, 1973; Ren et al., 2016; Ruef, 2002), and networking (Yang et al., 2018; Zhang & Zhang, 2006). We find that there is limited research that addresses issues related to building and nurturing customer relations. In social selling contexts, existing knowledge is fragmented and should be refined. Current research on social capital and guanxi offers a fundamental understanding on why it is needed to build and nurture relationships. Having a large number of followers and building intimate relationships with them can be social capital that continually generates profit for organizations or individuals (Brass, 2001). Guanxi, a particular form of informal interpersonal relationships involving exchanges of favors (Zhang & Zhang, 2006), can also be found in social media networking: Guanxi can be established and maintained using social networking services. Guanxi is an informal exchange mechanism by which an individual with guanxi can garner a comparative advantage in contrast to one without guanxi, particularly in a business environment in which mature institutions and administrative policies are absent. The concept's use of "strong ties and weak ties" is also meaningful in online social networking contexts (Schroeder, 2013). A strong tie refers to a close, strong relationship on which each individual spends a lot of resources (Dong & Wang, 2018; Krämer et al., 2014; Williams, 2006). In online social networking contexts, a person's strong relationships with family members, acquaintances, and colleagues can be deemed as strong because this person has been spending a lot of time, efforts, and money on sustaining and nurturing such relationships. A weak tie refers to a loose relationship in which a person starts to get to know another in an attempt to gain new and useful information or resources (Dong & Wang, 2018; Krämer et al., 2014; Shen et al., 2016). A person's relationships with another who he is unfamiliar with can be deemed as weak because he could spend no resources or efforts in establishing this relationship and would intentionally contact another in order to get new information or resources.

Strong ties and weak ties play different roles in social selling. Strategic partnerships with clients that are strong ties can produce steady cash flow for companies. For example, social selling is a selling approach widely adopted by digital business solution companies. A digital business solution company's strategic clients are able to generate a large amount of revenue for the company because such clients have bought specific software and digital business solutions. Factors such as IT asset specificity and IS familiarity drive clients to a continual use of the IT and IS solutions offered by the company. As a consequence, this kind of clients is willing to pay for software renewal or innovative services. Newly established relationships with prospects are also beneficial for companies. Prospects perhaps are inspired by professionals' blogs or product demos shared on social media and thus contact sales reps to gather more information and explore possible cooperative opportunities. By delving into weak ties, new business opportunities can be sought, developed, and converted into sales. For example, sales reps, apart from maintaining relationships with paying customers, also share knowledge and insights for future business directions and opportunities on social media. These professional social media posts perhaps attract additional prospects to whom sales reps can sell. While current literature can offer primary insights for social selling, strategies and know-how related to relationship building and maintenance in social selling are still quite limited. This section aims to introduce key points relevant to this issue.

1. *Quality Relationships Matter.* In social selling, customers are divided into two types: buyers who make a single purchase and never return and repeat buyers who make purchases many times. The relationship quality of the latter is higher than that of the former. Repeat buyers can contribute more value to sellers in the long term than ones who make a single purchase and leave (WebFX, n.d.). Research has suggested that quality is more important than quantity in relationship building (WebFX, n.d.). Specifically, in nonpositive macroeconomic scenarios, previous quantity-oriented relationship building is becoming less effective. Companies need to make the most of existing limited business opportunities. Therefore, quality-oriented relationship building is advantageous in a volatile, competitive business environment. Also, in the eyes of salespeople, given that a person can maintain 150 relationships maximum simultaneously (Dunbar, 1992; Schroeder, 2013), quality-oriented relationship building is more appropriate for a salesperson's limited cognitive ability. Loyal customers who have a good inter-personal relationship with salespeople are willing to recommend given products or services to their social friends. These quality relationships can help salespeople access new resources or find new prospects within social networks.

2. *Quality Relationships Deriving from Responsive Customer Service.* Research states that 67% of customers have engaged a brand's social media for social customer service needs (J.D. Power and Associates, 2013). 42% of the surveyed customers expected a response from a company within 1 h (Baer, n.d.). If a company failed to resolve customers' concerns quickly enough, customers' anger could spread across social media (Carter, n.d.). Hence, relationships that were built with significant resources could be in vain. Responsive customer service does more than maintain quality relationships; it is also able to improve social selling performance. For example, according to a study of airlines' use of Twitter, the average time for the observed airlines to provide a first response to a customer inquiry is around 22 min (some even respond in 3 s) (Huang, 2015). It has been found that if an airline responds to a customer inquiry in less than 6 min, the customer is willing to spend, on average, $20 more on the company in the future (Huang, 2015). In a word, fast, appropriate responses are a key guarantee for maintaining quality relationships with customers and also generate more profits for companies.

3. *Building Quality Relationships with Personalized Messages and Content.* A standard message can be applied in all social selling situations. However, social media enables one-to-one communication in which a personalized conversation

serves the goal of building quality relationships (Carter, n.d.). Building a relationship with a customer requires salespeople to treat the customer as a friend.
Therefore, apart from an ability of professionally revealing product advantages
and attributes, social salespeople also need to develop an ability of building
informal, intimate relationships with customers. This spotlights customers as
the center of social selling activities rather than the products or services. We
think that products and services are a means of satisfying customers' needs in
social selling. Therefore, personalized messages and content closely relevant to
customers' pain points, problems, and needs are essential to building and
maintaining relationships with social media users.

4. *Building a Brand Personality on Social Media.* Brand personality is a key
   concept in marketing research (Aaker, 1997; Grohmann, 2009; Malär et al.,
   2012; Wentzel, 2009) and management practice (see Aufreiter et al., 2003).
   Brand personality refers to a set of characteristics that relate to the human side
   of a brand (Aaker, 1997). Social selling is not a new channel for cold calling.
   With the proliferation of social media, social media marketers are able to refine
   current weaknesses in remote relationship maintenance. Social media features
   (contents, networks, communities, and conversations) enable firms to build a
   particular type of brand personality and show their human side. This approach fits
   the online social networking context in which people make online social
   interactions. In a social media context, if a firm suddenly appears and spreads
   commercial posts on a social network, this can be deemed intrusive and annoying.
   In contrast, a brand's social media can display a particular personality and post
   specifically designed content reflecting this personality. As a consequence, these
   efforts give the brand "a heart" (Carter, n.d.). For example, many well-known
   brands' social media are not always pushing commercials or ads; in many cases,
   they share posts less relevant to products or services to help build a unique
   personality tailored to the brand's value perspectives.

### 3.3.4  Achieving Sales

Lead generation, customer data management, and customer relationship management all serve the ultimate goal of achieving sales. We do not concur with comments
such as "social selling is not about selling" (Digital Sales Institute, 2016; Fields,
2015; Rowley, 2017). Social selling in essence is a selling approach and not just
about building and nurturing relationships with customers. This selling approach is
not an excuse for low sales performance. Management is a strict, administrative
mechanism for ensuring the fulfillment of organizational goals and optimizing the
deployment of organizational resources. Its *maintenance* nature drives most management tools and measures to be *retributive* and *restrictive* rather than *laissez-faire*.
Sales management requires all sales agents and resources to move forward in a given
track and achieve or outperform a planned sales quota. The completion of sales goals
determines a firm's ability to thrive or decline. The introduction of social selling may
require a company to change tack and look for new approaches to achieve sales. But

the ultimate goal of all selling approaches remains unchanged: achieving sales. If adopting social selling is deemed as a critical change to organizations, this change should generate better outcomes, achieving higher sales in particular, as compared to previous selling models. Without this, the change would be meaningless.

In summary, these key activities help achieve sales. Lead generation produces prospects for salespeople to take follow-up actions. Customer relationship management spawns quality relationships with customers, which is a solid base for future social selling success. Customer data and information management can offer marketing and sales insights for improving sales activities and ultimately heighten social sales performance.

## References

Aaker, J. L. (1997). Dimensions of brand personality. *Journal of Marketing Research, 34*(3), 347–356.

Adamson, B., Dixon, M., & Toman, N. (2012). The end of solution sales. *Harvard Business Review, 90*(7), 61–68.

Agnihotri, R., Kothandaraman, P., Kashyap, R., & Singh, R. (2012). Bringing "social" into sales: The impact of salespeople's social media use on service behaviors and value creation. *Journal of Personal Selling and Sales Management, 32*(3), 333–348.

Ancillai, C., Terho, H., Cardinali, S., & Pascucci, F. (2019). Advancing social media driven sales research: Establishing conceptual foundations for B-to-B social selling. *Industrial Marketing Management, 82*, 293–308.

Andersen, P., Archacki, R., De Bellefonds, N., & Ratajczak, D. (2017). *How digital leaders are transforming B2B marketing*. Retrieved from https://www.bcg.com/publications/2017/marketing-sales-how-digital-leaders-transforming-b2b.aspx

Aufreiter, N. A., Elzinga, D., & Gordon, J. W. (2003). Better branding. *McKinsey Quarterly, 4*, 28–39.

Baer, J. (n.d.). *42 percent of consumers complaining in social media expect 60 minute response time*. Retrieved from https://www.convinceandconvert.com/social-media-research/42-percent-of-consumers-complaining-in-social-media-expect-60-minute-response-time/

Bailey, C. (2015). *Smarketing: A sales & marketing love story*. Retrieved from https://www.socialmediatoday.com/marketing/christinebailey99/2015-10-22/smarketing-sales-marketing-love-story

Bocconcelli, R., Cioppi, M., & Pagano, A. (2017). Social media as a resource in SMEs' sales process. *Journal of Business and Industrial Marketing, 32*(5), 693–709.

Biro, M. M. (2015). *Study: Skilled social media users are six times more likely to exceed quota*. Retrieved from https://www.forbes.com/sites/meghanbiro/2015/05/22/study-skilled-social-media-users-are-6x-more-likely-to-exceed-quota/#5d2aef812847

Brass, D. J. (2001). Social capital and organizational leadership. In *The nature of organizational leadership: Understanding the performance imperatives confronting today's leaders* (pp. 132–152). Jossey-Bass.

Brudner, E. (2019). *Is social selling all hype?* [Data]. Retrieved from https://blog.hubspot.com/sales/sales-professionals-guide-to-social-selling

Campbell, S. R., Anitsal, I., & Anitsal, M. M. (2013). Social media's key success factors: An analysis of customer reactions. *Business Studies Journal, 5*(1), 43–56.

Carter, R. (n.d.). *8 tips to build customer relationships with social media*. Retrieved from https://sproutsocial.com/insights/build-customer-relationships/

Coresight Research. (2019). *Weekly US and UK store openings and closures tracker 2019, week 43: Destination maternity files for chapter 11 bankruptcy protection.* Retrieved from https://coresight.com/research/weekly-us-and-uk-store-openings-and-closures-tracker-2019-week-43/

Crowl, J. (2019). *The new e-commerce social media strategy: Why direct selling is the future of retail.* Retrieved from https://www.skyword.com/contentstandard/the-new-e-commerce-social-media-strategy-why-direct-selling-is-the-future-of-retail/

Das, S., Soni, A., Venkatesan, A., & Donato, D. (2015). *Organic vs. sponsored content: From ads to native ads.* In 2015 IEEE/WIC/ACM International Conference on Web Intelligence and Intelligent Agent Technology.

Digital Sales Institute. (2016). *5 benefits of social selling.* Retrieved from https://medium.com/social-media-selling-and-marketing/5-benefits-of-social-selling-fbcd7ce1931d

Dong, X., & Wang, T. (2018). Social tie formation in Chinese online social commerce: The role of IT affordances. *International Journal of Information Management, 42,* 49–64.

DSN Staff. (2011). *Top 10 mistakes direct selling companies make in social media.* Retrieved from https://www.directsellingnews.com/top-10-mistakes-direct-selling-companies-make-in-social-media/

Dunbar, R. I. M. (1992). Neocortex size as a constraint on group size in primates. *Journal of Human Evolution, 20,* 469–493.

Envick, B. R. (2005). Beyond human and social capital: The importance of positive psychological capital for entrepreneurial success. *The Entrepreneurial Executive, 10,* 41–52.

Expert System Team. (2016). *Social Media Analytics helps companies meet business goals.* Retrieved from https://expertsystem.com/social-media-analytics-helps-organizations-meet-business-goal/

Farh, J. L., Tsui, A. S., Xin, K., & Cheng, B. S. (1998). The influence of relational demography and guanxi: The Chinese case. *Organization Science, 9*(4), 437–534.

Fidelman, M. (2012). *The rise of social salespeople.* Retrieved from https://www.forbes.com/sites/markfidelman/2012/11/05/the-rise-of-social-salespeople/

Fields, J. (2015). *Why social selling is not about selling.* Retrieved from https://www.forbes.com/sites/sap/2015/06/01/why-social-selling-is-not-about-selling/#4dd0f2d70a74

Gandomi, A., & Haider, M. (2015). Beyond the hype: Big data concepts, methods, and analytics. *International Journal of Information Management, 35*(2), 137–144.

Gerencer, T. (2020). *200+ sales statistics [cold calling, follow-up, closing rates].* Retrieved from https://zety.com/blog/sales-statistics

Giamanco, B., & Gregoire, K. (2012). Tweet me, friend me, make me buy. *Harvard Business Review, 90*(7), 89–93.

Granath, E. (2019). *Smarketing: The powerful result of sales and marketing alignment.* Retrieved from https://www.vainu.com/blog/smarketing-sales-and-marketing-alignment/

Granovetter, M. S. (1973). The strength of weak ties. *American Journal of Sociology, 78,* 1360–1380.

Grohmann, B. (2009). Gender dimensions of brand personality. *Journal of Marketing Research, 46*(1), 105–119.

Hartmann, N. N., Wieland, H., & Vargo, S. L. (2018). Converging on a new theoretical foundation for selling. *Journal of Marketing, 82*(2), 1–18.

Huang, W. (2015). *Consumers spend after positive customer service interaction on Twitter.* Retrieved from https://blog.twitter.com/en_us/topics/insights/2015/Consumers-spend-after-positive-customer-service-interaction-on-Twitter.html

InsideView. (2011). *The death of cold calling—Ending the debate.* Retrieved from https://blog.insideview.com/2011/03/18/the-death-of-cold-calling-ending-the-debate/

J.D. Power and Associates. (2013). *Poor social media practices can negatively impact a businesses' bottom line and brand image.* Retrieved from https://www.jdpower.com/business/press-releases/2013-social-media-benchmark-study

Kiron, D., Palmer, D., Phillips, A. N., & Berkman, R. (2013). Social business: Shifting out of first gear. *MIT Sloan Management Review, 55*(1), 7–11.

Krämer, N. C., Rösner, L., Eimler, S. C., Winter, S., & Neubaum, G. (2014). Let the weakest link go! Empirical explorations on the relative importance of weak and strong ties on social networking sites. *Societies, 4*(4), 785–809.

Lampertz, D. (2012). *Has cold calling gone cold?* Retrieved from https://www.baylor.edu/content/services/document.php/183060.pdf

Ma, R., Lam, P. T., & Leung, C. K. (2018). Potential pitfalls of smart city development: A study on parking mobile applications (apps) in Hong Kong. *Telematics and Informatics, 35*(6), 1580–1592.

MacDonald, S. (2020). *Social selling: A sales reps guide to social media success.* Retrieved from https://www.skyword.com/contentstandard/the-new-e-commerce-social-media-strategy-why-direct-selling-is-the-future-of-retail/

Malär, L., Nyffenegger, B., Krohmer, H., & Hoyer, W. D. (2012). Implementing an intended brand personality: A dyadic perspective. *Journal of the Academy of Marketing Science, 40*, 728–744.

Minsky, L., & Quesenberry, K. A. (2016). How B2B sales can benefit from social selling. *Harvard Business Review, 8*, 2–5.

Mohammadian, M., & Mohammadreza, M. (2012). Identify the success factors of social media (marketing perspective). *International Business and Management, 4*(2), 58–66.

Petersen, R. (2015). *7 case studies show social media analytics pay off.* Retrieved from https://barnraisersllc.com/2015/11/23/7-case-studies-show-social-media-analytics-pay-off/

Petersen, R. (2016). *12 inspiring social media monitoring case studies.* Retrieved from https://biznology.com/2016/08/12-inspiring-social-media-monitoring-case-studies/

Ren, S., Shu, R., Bao, Y., & Chen, X. (2016). Linking network ties to entrepreneurial opportunity discovery and exploitation: The role of affective and cognitive trust. *International Entrepreneurship and Management Journal, 12*(2), 465–485.

Rowley, J. (2017). *What social selling isn't.* Retrieved from https://blog.hubspot.com/marketing/what-social-selling-isnt

Ruef, M. (2002). Strong ties, weak ties and islands: Structural and cultural predictors of organizational innovation. *Industrial and Corporate Change, 11*(3), 427–449.

Schenk, T. (2019). *For social selling, aligning sales and marketing is key.* Retrieved from https://www.csoinsights.com/blog/for-social-selling-aligning-sales-and-marketing-is-key/

Schroeder, H. (2013). *The art of business relationships through social media.* Retrieved from https://iveybusinessjournal.com/publication/the-art-of-business-relationships-through-social-media/

Selledge. (2020). *The ultimate guide to social selling in 2020.* Retrieved from https://leadgenerationinstitute.com/the-ultimate-guide-to-social-selling-in-2020/

Sexton, K. (n.d.). *7 ways sales professionals drive revenue with social selling.* Retrieved from https://business.linkedin.com/content/dam/business/sales-solutions/global/en_US/site/pdf/ti/linkedin_7_ways_playbook_us_en_130606.pdf

Shen, G. C. C., Chiou, J. S., Hsiao, C. H., Wang, C. H., & Li, H. N. (2016). Effective marketing communication via social networking site: The moderating role of the social tie. *Journal of Business Research, 69*(6), 2265–2270.

Smith, M. (2012). *Survey: More schools beefing up ticket efforts.* Retrieved from https://www.sportsbusinessdaily.com/Journal/Issues/2012/06/04/Colleges/College-tickets.aspx?hl=%22Using+social+media+to+sell+tickets%22+michigan&sc=0

Stevanovic, I. (2019). *23 social selling statistics you need to know in 2020.* Retrieved from https://www.smallbizgenius.net/by-the-numbers/social-selling-statistics/#gref

Stieglitz, S., Mirbabaie, M., Ross, B., & Neuberger, C. (2018). Social media analytics—Challenges in topic discovery, data collection, and data preparation. *International Journal of Information Management, 39*, 156–168.

Terho, H., Eggert, A., Ulaga, W., Haas, A., & Böhm, E. (2017). Selling value in business markets: Individual and organizational factors for turning the idea into action. *Industrial Marketing Management, 66*, 42–55.

Trainor, K. J. (2012). Relating social media technologies to performance: A capabilities-based perspective. *Journal of Personal Selling and Sales Management, 32*(3), 317–331.

Verhoef, P. C., Kannan, P. K., & Inman, J. J. (2015). From multi-channel retailing to omni-channel retailing: Introduction to the special issue on multi-channel retailing. *Journal of Retailing, 91*(2), 174–181.

Walsh, S. (2017). *6 case studies of social selling success*. Retrieved from https://blog.anderspink. com/2017/05/6-case-studies-of-social-selling-success/

Warren, C. (2016). Social media and outbound ticket sales: Examining social media strategies among top-performing salespeople. *Journal of Applied Sport Management, 8*(4), 49–62.

WebFX. (n.d.). *Why your company should use social media to build customer relationships*. Retrieved from https://www.webfx.com/blog/general/why-your-company-should-use-social-media-to-build-customer-relationships/

Wentzel, D. (2009). The effect of employee behavior on brand personality impressions and brand attitudes. *Journal of the Academy of Marketing Science, 37*(3), 359–374.

Wiese, M. (2017). *Death of a salesman: The rise of social selling*. Retrieved from https://www. forbes.com/sites/forbesagencycouncil/2017/06/29/death-of-a-salesman-the-rise-of-social-selling/

Williams, D. (2006). On and off the'Net: Scales for social capital in an online era. *Journal of computer-mediated communication, 11*(2), 593–628.

Yang, Z., Huang, Z., Wang, F., & Feng, C. (2018). The double-edged sword of networking: Complementary and substitutive effects of networking capability in China. *Industrial Marketing Management, 68*, 145–155.

Zeiller, M., & Schauer, B. (2011). Adoption, motivation and success factors of social media for team collaboration in SMEs. In *Proceedings of the 11th international conference on Knowledge Management and Knowledge Technologies*.

Zhang, Y., & Zhang, Z. (2006). Guanxi and organizational dynamics in China: A link between individual and organizational levels. *Journal of Business Ethics, 67*(4), 375–392.

# How Social Media Profits from Advertising and Social Commerce

4

## 4.1 Advertising as a Major Revenue Source for Social Media

Social media advertising comprises a major revenue source for many large social media platforms. The Interactive Advertising Bureau defines social media advertising as "an online ad that incorporates user interactions that the consumer has agreed to display and be shared. The resulting ad displays these interactions along with the user's persona (picture and/or name) within the ad content (see Chu, 2011, p. 32)." Social media advertising is quite different from traditional mass media advertising. Social media advertising incorporates more social elements in the advertising process. Social media ads can be interactive, immersive, and influential when social media users are browsing social media content. Social media users can comment, distribute, and like social ads. Social media ads can also be presented in an organic form which looks similar to regular social content displayed in users' online social circles. The more shares or impressions a social ad creates, the more influential it will become. For example, Snapchat, an American social media platform, is largely favored by younger users. Snapchat nicely represents what a social media platform should look like in the future (Martin, 2017). As reported in Snap's earning report,[1] Snap has the following advertising products (the following illustrations are adapted from this earning report):

- *Single Image or Video Ads*: Skippable ads can contain an attachment for Snapchatters to take a specified action or to swipe up.
- *Story Ads*: Branded ads that can be in either a video format or an image format and are displayed in the Discover section of the Stories tab.
- *Collection Ads*: Tappable ads that can present several items at the same time, offering users a frictionless way to browse and buy.

---

[1] Snap Earnings 2020-12-31. Retrieved 19 April 2021 from https://q10k.com/SNAP#CONSOLIDATED_BALANCE_SHEETS

F. J. Martínez-López et al., *Social Media Monetization*, Future of Business and Finance, https://doi.org/10.1007/978-3-031-14575-9_4

45

**Table 4.1**  Major social media revenue in 2019 and 2020

| Social media platform/ company | Fiscal 2020 revenue | Fiscal 2019 revenue (in millions USD) |
|---|---|---|
| Facebook | 84,169 (Facebook Earnings 2020-12-31. Retrieved 19 April 2021 from https://q10k.com/FB) | 69,655 (Facebook Earnings 2020-12-31. Retrieved 19 April 2021 from https://q10k.com/FB) |
| YouTube | 19,772 (Alphabet Google Earnings 2020-12-31. Retrieved 19 April 2021 from https://q10k.com/GOOG) | 15,149 (Alphabet Google Earnings 2020-12-31. Retrieved 19 April 2021 from https://q10k.com/GOOG) |
| Twitter | 3207 (Twitter Earnings 2020-12-31. Retrieved 19 April 2021 from https://q10k.com/TWTR) | 2993 (Twitter Earnings 2020-12-31. Retrieved 19 April 2021 from https://q10k.com/TWTR) |
| Snapchat | 2507 (Snap Earnings 2020-12-31. Retrieved 19 April 2021 from https://q10k.com/SNAP#CONSOLIDATED_BALANCE_SHEETS) | 1716 (Snap Earnings 2020-12-31. Retrieved 19 April 2021 from https://q10k.com/SNAP#CONSOLIDATED_BALANCE_SHEETS) |
| Kuaishou | 3357 (Annual Financial Report as of 31 December 2020. Retrieved 19 April 2021 from https://ir.kuaishou.com/system/files-encrypted/nasdaq_kms/assets/2021/03/23/6-46-25/%E6%88%AA%E8%87%B32020%E5%B9%B412%E6%9C%8831%E6%97%A5%E6%AD%A2%E5%B9%B4%E5%BA%A6%E6%A5%AD%E7%B8%BE%E5%85%AC%E5%91%8A.pdf) | 1139 (Annual Financial Report as of 31 December 2020. Retrieved 19 April 2021 from https://ir.kuaishou.com/system/files-encrypted/nasdaq_kms/assets/2021/03/23/6-46-25/%E6%88%AA%E8%87%B32020%E5%B9%B412%E6%9C%8831%E6%97%A5%E6%AD%A2%E5%B9%B4%E5%BA%A6%E6%A5%AD%E7%B8%BE%E5%85%AC%E5%91%8A.pdf) |
| Weibo | 1486 (Weibo released its fourth-quarter and full-year financial results for 2020. Retrieved 21 April 2021 from https://finance.sina.com.cn/stock/usstock/c/2021-03-18/doc-ikkntiam4887520.shtml) | 1530 (Weibo released its fourth-quarter and full-year financial results for 2019. Retrieved 21 April 2021 from https://tech.sina.com.cn/i/2020-02-26/doc-iimxyqvz6003265.shtml) |

Source: Self-elaborated from different data sources

- *Dynamic Ads*: Social media ads that are powered by Snapchat's machine learning algorithm and can match an ad to the right Snapchat user at the right time.
- *Commercials*: Ads that are non-skippable for 6 s and can run for 3 min maximum.

Snapchat has also created augmented reality (AR) ads. The AR ads are a lens which users can add to their videos (Sloane, 2018). The AR ads can lead users to a shopping page, an app install page, a video, or a website without leaving Snapchat (Sloane, 2018). As shown in Table 4.1, advertising made up a considerable amount of revenue for social media companies. The revenues reported in Table 4.1 are based on financial reports, and therefore, they may not represent the exact advertising revenue. For example, as indicated in Snapchat's fiscal 2020 report, "we generate substantially all of our revenues by offering various advertising products". It does

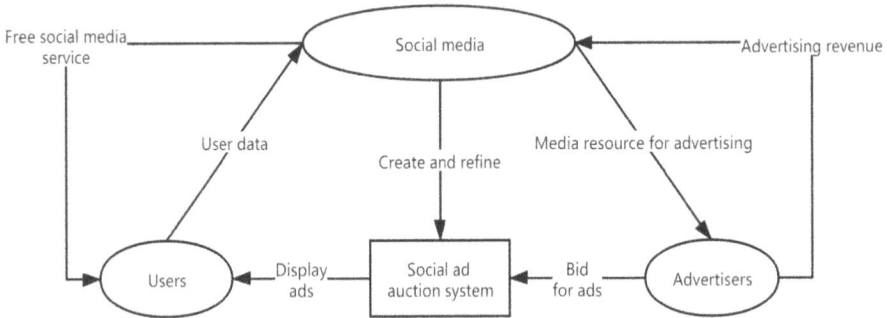

**Fig. 4.1** Advertising business model of social media

not mean that Snapchat's revenues as indicated in Table 4.1 only include advertising revenue. In most circumstances, advertising generates substantially all revenue for social media companies. This reflects that current social media companies, including Facebook, did not find a reliable alternative monetization approach.

From a critical viewpoint, social media's advertising business model is inherently problematic (see Fig. 4.1), particularly in cases where social media offers self-service advertising business. With self-service advertising business, anyone can leverage the power of social media to find a target audience. Facebook has been lambasted for distributing objectionable media content, fake news, and Russia-backed ads that influenced the 2016 U.S. presidential campaign (Angwin, 2018; Schaefer, 2018). First, social media is collecting user data through free social media service. Then, the collected data are used for increasing the advertising precision of advertisers who are a major revenue source for social media companies. Second, in order to obtain media resource for promoting their products or services, advertisers need to bid for ads in the social media's social ad auction system. The bid winners are able to display ads to users. Finally, the most problematic part of the advertising business model is that the ad auction system or ad display mechanism is created and refined on the basis of user data. Advanced advertising technologies, such as artificial intelligence and machine learning, need significant amounts of user data to train and improve the system so that a target audience can be more precisely identified and the precision of social media advertising is further elevated.

On the basis of value analysis, social media's advertising business model is creating and capturing social value. Social value refers to the necessary products or services offered by organizations with social purposes such as creating a connected world, removing information asymmetry and digital divide, and advocating for more inclusive and fairer policies (Felício et al., 2013). The value proposition of social media bases on creating and offering social value for people. It mainly offers two-way access to the collective stream of information, enabling people to collaborate and connect with others. For example, Facebook describes itself as "a social utility that helps people communicate more efficiently with their friends, family and coworkers... Anyone can sign up for Facebook and interact with

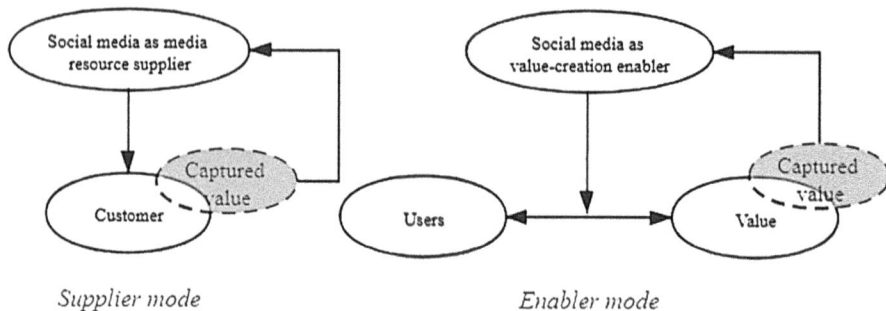

**Fig. 4.2**   Social media's supplier mode and enabler mode

the people they know in a trusted environment." (Facebook, cited in Chaffey, 2013) This value proposition explicitly indicates Facebook is *a social utility*. This value proposition is inspiring for the social welfare of the entire society, but it also reveals the inherent defect of social media's advertising model. Supposedly, social media companies could be deemed unethical in that they finance their free social media service by monetizing the social value it creates. Users' free access to social media service does not imply that social media's commercial use of user data (e.g., created content, viewed content, and user locations) is ethical. Existing literature has suggested measures to refine social media's advertising business, such as imposing fines for data breaches, policing political ads, creating ethics review boards, and building accountability systems (Angwin, 2018). Apart from relying solely on leveraging user data and advertising revenue, social media can profit from alternate methods. Despite the fact that there is not a standard solution for a social media company to ethically profit from their social business, it is plausible that social value can be monetized by switching revenues *from* the social mission to revenues *with* the social mission (Dohrmann et al., 2015). This implies that social media can also be monetized when the platform finds a way to switch from a *supplier* who profits from transacting with customers to an *enabler* who empowers users to create more value and also to receive monetary returns (see Fig. 4.2). A possible path to becoming an enabler is to create an online marketplace for commercial activities that users have with others via social media.

## 4.2   Social Commerce and the Online Marketplace

There are two forms of social commerce: e-commerce sites integrated with social media features for encouraging online shopping and interactions with consumers (Meilatinova, 2021) and social media platforms integrated with e-commerce features (Han & Kim, 2016). Previous research had focused on the former and has not paid enough attention to the latter. This could mostly be because current social media platforms have not found a mature way to monetize via e-commerce. Most social media platforms still heavily rely on advertising to earn profits. The immaturity of social commerce led previous researchers and pundits to question this business model. Previous research even argued that it could be very difficult for social media platforms to monetize through online commerce between users (Clemons, 2009; Halzack, 2016).

As shown in Table 4.2, major social media platforms have attempted to incorporate e-commerce features into their own platforms. For example, social media buy buttons are a navigation element leading social media users to make purchases through the platform. The incorporation of a buy button in social media content or posts can make viewers easily perceive sellers' selling intention. This perception is not in line with the original purpose of introducing social media: connecting and interacting with others. Prior literature has indicated that social media users could be annoyed due to merchandising content when they are interacting with others in an online social gathering (Clemons, 2009). Social media research has found that 45% of U.S. adults stated that they were not interested in using buy buttons (see Business Insider Intelligence, 2016). Even though Facebook and Twitter have offered their buy button since around 2014, over 30% of the people surveyed argued that they had never bought an item directly through a social media platform (Statista, 2017). Twitter, one of the most popular social media platforms in the world stopped its e-commerce operation and removed its buy button (Del Rey, 2017). Nevertheless, social media companies are actively exploring social commerce and trying to find a reliable approach to monetize via e-commerce.

To date, American companies have merely dabbled in social commerce; it constitutes only 3% of U.S. e-commerce (Wei and Banjo, cited in Liu, 2019). In contrast, according to a forecast offered by the Internet Society of China, social commerce comprised over 30% of China's entire online retail business in 2020 (Yu, cited in Liu, 2019). Social commerce has taken over China (Shen, 2021). The market scale of social commerce in the USA, around 22 billion Chinese Yuan in 2018, was merely one-tenth of the size of the market scale in China (Liu, 2019). China's vibrant social commerce can be attributed to two aspects. On the one hand, due to the Internet censorship policy in China, major western social media platforms such as Facebook, YouTube, and Twitter are not available in China. China's own social media platforms, such as WeChat, Weibo, and Kuaishou, have fewer competitors and are able to focus on the China market which has substantial users to monetize. In 2019, the number of China's social media users reached 882 million (Thomala, 2020). The large population of China's social media users offers a solid base for social media companies to conduct social commerce businesses. In particular, novel marketing strategies, such as influencer marketing, have been adopted for promoting commercial activities on social media. For example, Becky Li was a top WeChat influencer (Chernavina, 2020). Her WeChat Official Account "Becky's Whimsical World" was followed by approximately ten million women, with each of her post creating more than 100,000 views (Chernavina, 2020). In 2017, Becky collaborated with MINI to endorse the "MINI YOURS Caribbean Blue Limited Edition" and sold out 100 custom cars within a mere 4 min (Chernavina, 2020). Western brands have seized the opportunity to market their products in China. Lululemon is a popular athletic apparel brand and focuses on experiential marketing and increasing

**Table 4.2** Social media with e-commerce features

| Social media | E-commerce feature | How it is used |
|---|---|---|
| Facebook | Facebook buy button<br>Facebook ads<br>Facebook Marketplace<br>Facebook Pay | The buy button lets Facebook users complete the entire purchase process within Facebook (Constine, J. (2014). Facebook Tests Buy Button To Let You Purchase Stuff Without Leaving Facebook. Retrieved 23 April 2021 from https://techcrunch.com/2014/07/17/facebook-buy-button/)<br>An advertiser can customize their Facebook ads by leading ad viewers from Facebook to a shopping app the advertiser chooses (Help: Choose the Right Ad Objective. Retrieved 2 December 2020 from https://www.facebook.com/business/help/1438417719786914)<br>Facebook Marketplace is an online marketplace by which a user can find photographs of items that people near him/her have posted for sale (Tillman, M. (2020). What is Facebook Marketplace and how can you use it to buy and sell? Retrieved 23 April 2021 from https://www.pocket-lint.com/apps/news/facebook/139045-what-is-facebook-marketplace-and-how-can-you-use-it-to-buy-and-sell)<br>Facebook Pay enables Facebook users to pay others or to buy items online (Kishore, A. (2019). What Is Facebook Pay and How to Use It: Plus the key differences between PayPal. Retrieved 23 April 2021 from https://www.online-tech-tips.com/software-reviews/what-is-facebook-pay-and-how-to-use-it/#:~:text=How%20To%20Use%20Facebook%20Pay%201%20Open%20a,you're%20using%20the%20desktop%20version%20of%20the%20site.) |
| Instagram | Shop<br>Instagram Shop<br>Live Shopping<br>Shoppable Sticker<br>Instagram Checkout | Shop is a storefront on a business profile page letting users shop directly on the page (What is Instagram Shopping?\|Instagram for Business. Retrieved 2 December 2021 from https://business.instagram.com/shopping)<br>Instagram Shop is an in-app shopping destination where Instagram users find products and brands they love (What is Instagram Shopping?\|Instagram for Business. Retrieved 2 December 2021 from https://business.instagram.com/shopping)<br>Live Shopping enables broadcasters to sell items through Instagram Live (What is Instagram Shopping?\|Instagram for Business. Retrieved 2 December 2021 from https://business.instagram.com/shopping)<br>A Shoppable Sticker can be added into Instagram Stories It lets brands tag products from their inventory or e-commerce site in the story. When users tap on the sticker, they can find the product name, price, and description (Warren, J. (2020). Instagram Checkout: Everything You Need to Know. Retrieved 23 April 2021 from https://later.com/blog/instagram-checkout/#:~:text=Instagram%20Checkout%20is%20now%20available%20to%20all%20eligible,process%20to%20converting%20Instagram%20followers%20into%20loyal%20customers) |

(continued)

**Table 4.2**  (continued)

| Social media | E-commerce feature | How it is used |
| --- | --- | --- |
|  |  | The checkout feature lets users purchase an item without leaving Instagram, creating a smooth process for Instagram shopping (Warren, J. (2020). Instagram Checkout: Everything You Need to Know. Retrieved 23 April 2021 from https://later.com/blog/instagram-checkout/#:~: text=Instagram%20Checkout%20is%20now%20available %20to%20all%20eligible,process%20to%20converting% 20Instagram%20followers%20into%20loyal%20 customers) |
| Twitter | Twitter Buy Button | The buy button allows users to make a purchase directly from Twitter's interface (What is Twitter's buy button? Retrieved 23 April 2021 from https://www.bigcommerce. com/ecommerce-answers/what-twitters-buy-button/) |
| YouTube | Click-to-shop | The click-to-shop allows users connect to brand websites to make purchases they see in pre-roll ads simply by clicking a buy button that is shown on a card during the pre-roll ad (YouTube offering advertisers "click-to-shop" buy buttons on videos. Retrieved 23 April 2021 from https://www.b2bnn.com/2015/05/youtube-offering-advertisers-click-to-shop-buy-buttons-on-videos/) |
| Snapchat | Snap Ads<br>AR Ads<br>Camera Search | Snap Ads and AR ads enable users to make a purchase through Snap (Snap Earnings 2020-12-31. Retrieved 19 April 2021 from https://q10k.com/ SNAP#CONSOLIDATED_BALANCE_SHEETS)<br>Snap also teams up with Amazon to roll out the Camera Search feature. The feature lets users use Snap camera to identify a product and then find purchase information at Amazon (WeChat's digital solution for retail companies is entirely adapted from https://work.weixin.qq.com/nl/ index/industry?category=retail) |
| WeChat | WeChat Mini Programs<br>Official Account<br>WeChat Pay | Mini Programs are mobile applications running within WeChat. E-commerce platforms such as JD and Weipinhui have developed their shopping Mini Programs for WeChat users to shop without exiting WeChat (Can the US Replicate China's $63B Livestream Shopping Industry? Retrieved 25 April 2021 from https://www. wearerockwater.com/blog/livestream-selling-china-us)<br>Official Account is a WeChat account specifically for business purposes. Official Account users can embed an e-commerce system on their WeChat information pages<br>WeChat Pay enables consumers to transact and interact with merchants in the WeChat ecosystem. WeChat Pay can be used for Mini Program payment and Official Account Payment (paying for products inside a merchant's Official Account) (The example is entirely adopted from HUYA 2019 Annual Report. Retrieved 25 April 2021 from: http:// ir.huya.com/index.php?s=120) |
| Weibo | Weibo Pay |  |

(continued)

**Table 4.2**  (continued)

| Social media | E-commerce feature | How it is used |
|---|---|---|
| | | Weibo Pay is a mobile payment solution that Weibo offers to provide online shopping. It is built on Alipay (a digital payment application offered by Alibaba) and Weibo's social networks (Facebook Earnings 2020-12-31. Retrieved 19 April 2021 from https://q10k.com/FB). It aims to create a more profound marketing solution for Weibo merchants and streamline the marketing and service process. It is a socially focused payment solution by which merchants find, establish, and reach Weibo users. This payment solution can report explicit social interaction behaviors (shares, comments, likes, followers, and subscriptions) and implicit relations data for merchants to optimize their social commerce |
| Kuaishou | Kuaishou Store Current Promoted Product Shopping Cart | Kuaishou Store is an in-app e-commerce destination where users can find broadcasters who are promoting products A Current Promoted Product is a shoppable button appearing in a broadcaster's live chat room. It enables viewers to purchase a product that is being promoted by the broadcaster A Shopping Cart is a shoppable icon appearing in a broadcaster's live chat room. Viewers can tap on this icon and find products that have been promoted by the broadcaster |
| Pinterest | Shop the Look Pins | A shoppable Pin that brands are able to use to add product tags. It enables users to hit the pin to shop on Pinterest |

Source: Self-elaborated from different sources

consumer loyalty (Liu, 2019). Considering the fact that the Chinese market is comprised of young and wellness-conscious people, Lululemon hired influencers as brand ambassadors to reach its targeted customers (Liu, 2019). The Canadian brand also regularly posts quality content for its followers on WeChat and converts likes into sales by using the Mini Program feature (Liu, 2019). As Lululemon owns a number of physical stores in China, its store network covers over 30 Chinese cities.[2] Store visitors and workshop attendees actively use social media to share their shopping experience (Liu, 2019).

There are several ways to monetize via social commerce. First, on the basis of paid advertising, social commerce features can be free to use for merchants, but if they want greater exposure to audiences, they need to pay for increasing the publicity of their ad. Facebook, Instagram, and Weibo use this approach to monetize via social commerce. Second, taking a cut or commission from each sale is another way to earn money from social commerce. For content creators on Facebook, Facebook takes a cut of up to 30% cut from their proceeds (Ha, 2019). Finally, in some cases where a

---

[2]The store information of Lululemon was taken from Baidu Map.

social media platform does not charge an adverting fee or take a cut from proceeds, a technical service fee is charged for allowing merchants to use e-commerce features developed by the platform. For example, WeChat charges bloggers a technical service fee (Tong & Jia, 2020), so that they can embed a buy button in their article.

## 4.3    Digital Business Solutions

Social media can offer business solutions for enterprises. This type of social media platform is referred to as enterprise social media. It refers to the organizational use of social media platforms such as Yammer, Chatter, and WeChat that prompt internal communication, collaboration, and knowledge sharing (Razmerita et al., 2016). As this chapter focuses on social commerce, we introduce how such digital business solutions can help firms to conduct social commerce activities.

Social commerce is more than just creating an e-commerce site within social media. It also entails other activities in social commerce. In social commerce, consumers would be unlikely to make an immediate purchase without further deliberation upon viewing a commercial. Social purchasing is built on social interactions, which in turn foster consumer trust in a firm or a brand and eventually facilitate consumer purchase and repurchase. Social media can be used for instant messaging between consumers and firms. It can also be used by a firm or a brand to collaborate simultaneously with its upstream or downstream partners.

WeChat has rolled out a digital solution for retail companies.[3] WeChat injects social media features into a retail company's operation, helping them effectively manage and retain consumers. The solution also entails business features such as internal work groups. It is an enterprise version of WeChat. First, store associates can friend consumers via this version and create loyalty programs for them. Once connected, store associates can simultaneously contact consumers and send them the latest promotion or coupon information, resulting in more consumer repurchases. Second, store associates can create a group of loyal consumers in WeChat in the service of group buying, fans management, and contract renewal, among others. The retail firm can manage multiple consumer groups at the same time and collaborate with upstream suppliers and downstream distributors by directly leveraging information from consumer groups. A consumer group can contain 500 persons maximum. Third, store associates can share store promotions, expertise, and promoted items on WeChat's Moment, similar to Facebook's News Feed, so that branded content naturally appears in consumers' online social circles. Store associates can use the enterprise version of WeChat to interact with consumers. Finally, the retail company can use this version to create store groups, store manager groups, and supervisor groups. This enterprise version of WeChat is easier for communicating with organizational members and helps to respond to front-line problems in a timely

---

[3]WeChat's digital solution for retail companies is entirely adapted from https://work.weixin.qq.com/nl/index/industry?category=retail

manner. This version of WeChat is better than its conventional version counterpart because communication and social networks are centrally managed and supervised by the retail company. It facilitates the information and knowledge sharing between organizational members and creates an organizational structure which is more connected and oriented to organization collaboration and partnership. In summary, social media platforms can leverage their social computing capability and social media service to roll out digital business solutions, ultimately profiting from this business.

## 4.4    Livestreaming

Livestreaming e-commerce incorporates e-commerce elements and functionality into livestreaming. It is another variety of social commerce. Livestreaming e-commerce is a way for livestreaming platforms to monetize users via e-commerce activities. Livestreaming merits e-commerce practitioners' attention. Projected to generate $129 billion in 2020, livestreaming e-commerce was significant in defining consumption experiences for China's online consumers.[4] Taobao Live, merely one of many livestreaming platforms, was estimated to sell to over 500 million consumers in 2020 and engender over 500 billion transactions during 2021–2023. The livestreaming e-commerce strategy has also been adopted by U.-S. companies. This was particularly important during the period of COVID-19, as people were minimizing social contact and avoiding shopping in physical stores. Livestreaming e-commerce is prevalent because people can purchase items remotely and interact with merchants virtually. Instagram has rolled out a livestreaming e-commerce feature. Broadcasters on Instagram can include a shoppable icon, Add to Bag, in their live chat room. Viewers in the chat room can purchase items by tapping on the icon and make payments using Checkout on Instagram. For example, Nikita Dragun, a beauty influencer, launched livestreaming on Instagram and has attracted 43,000 followers (Flora, 2020).

Apart from taking a cut from e-commerce sales, livestreaming e-commerce offers other ways for social media companies to monetize. Livestreaming e-commerce relies heavily on a broadcaster's personal talent and performance. Successful broadcasters go beyond merchandising items. They build viewers' emotional attachment (Wan et al., 2017) or affective commitment to them (Hu & Chaudhry, 2020). In many cases, broadcasters are not oriented to merchandising items. They present their talent and perform shows (e.g., gaming, singing, dancing, and playing an instrument) to social media fans. Therefore, purchasing items from a beloved broadcaster is merely a form of fans' support for the broadcaster. Rewarding the broadcaster (e.g., purchasing and giving virtual gifts) directly is also commonplace in livestreaming. In

---

[4]Can the US Replicate China's $63B Livestream Shopping Industry? Retrieved 25 April 2021 from https://www.wearerockwater.com/blog/livestream-selling-china-us

practice, social media companies take a percentage from broadcasters' livestreaming proceeds.

In Huya's 2019 annual report, the company notes that livestreaming has been deemed a major monetization approach for the company.[5] Huya rolled out a number of virtual gifts for users to purchase, such as thumbs-up, planes, or treasure boxes. Purchasing and giving these gifts to broadcasters are key way for users to participate in the livestreaming. Most users choose to watch live shows free of charge; however, broadcasters are more likely to interact with paid users. Huya also asserted that they share livestreaming revenue with broadcasters and talent agencies. This simple monetization model has led Huya to become one of the most popular livestreaming platforms in China. In 2018, Huya completed its initial public offering (IPO) in New York. Huya's focus on livestreaming avoids high content acquisition cost without losing much user engagement (General Expert, 2018). Because Huya inherited this monetization model from its parent company JOYY Inc. (listed on NASDAQ), its monetization potential is more predictable (General Expert, 2018).

Advertising and social commerce are the most commonplace monetization approaches in social media. This chapter introduces monetization approaches that have been adopted by firms in practice. However, monetization is more than just selecting an appropriate monetization approach. Monetization also requires that social media firms address more relevant issues, e.g., how a monetization approach can be integrated into a firm's existing business operation and business model. In a later chapter, we will discuss more deeply and holistically how the monetization process can cohesively integrate advertising and social commerce.

## References

Angwin, J. (2018). *Four ways to fix Facebook*. Retrieved April 22, 2021, from https://business-ethics.com/2018/04/08/four-ways-to-fix-facebook/

Business Insider Intelligence. (2016). *Buy buttons fail to show return on investment*. Retrieved November 10, 2020, from https://www.businessinsider.com/buy-buttons-fail-to-show-return-on-investment-2016-12?IR=T

Chaffey, D. (2013). *Facebook case study*. Retrieved April 22, 2021, from https://www.smartinsights.com/social-media-marketing/facebook-marketing/facebook-case-study/#:~:text=Facebook%27s%20value%20proposition%20In%202013%2C%20the%20Facebook%20mission,more%20efficiently%20with%20their%20friends%2C%20family%20and%20coworkers

Chernavina, K. (2020). *Chinese Influencers that sell out products in minutes!* Retrieved from https://www.hicom-asia.com/chinese-influencers-that-sell-out-products-in-minutes/

Chu, S. C. (2011). Viral advertising in social media: Participation in Facebook groups and responses among college-aged users. *Journal of Interactive Advertising, 12*(1), 30–43.

Clemons, E. K. (2009). The complex problem of monetizing virtual electronic social networks. *Decision Support Systems, 48*(1), 46–56.

---

[5]The example is entirely adopted from HUYA 2019 Annual Report. Retrieved 25 April 2021 from: http://ir.huya.com/index.php?s=120

Del Rey, J. (2017). *Twitter's 'Buy' button is officially dead*. Retrieved November 10, 2020, from https://www.vox.com/2017/1/18/14311230/twitter-buy-button-dead-killed-shuts-down

Dohrmann, S., Raith, M., & Siebold, N. (2015). Monetizing social value creation–a business model approach. *Entrepreneurship Research Journal, 5*(2), 127–154.

Felício, J. A., Gonçalves, H. M., & da Conceição Gonçalves, V. (2013). Social value and organizational performance in non-profit social organizations: Social entrepreneurship, leadership, and socioeconomic context effects. *Journal of Business Research, 66*(10), 2139–2146.

Flora, L. (2020). *Instagram's livestream shopping sees early beauty adopters*. Retrieved from https://www.glossy.co/beauty/instagrams-livestream-shopping-sees-early-beauty-adopters/

General Expert. (2018). *Why Huya is the best Chinese streaming IPO*. Retrieved April 27, 2021, from https://seekingalpha.com/article/4186158-why-huya-is-best-chinese-streaming-ipo

Ha, A. (2019). *Facebook will start taking a cut of fan subscriptions in 2020*. Retrieved April 10, 2021, from https://techcrunch.com/2019/07/09/facebook-subscription-revenue-share/

Halzack, S. (2016). *Why the social media 'buy button' is still there, even though most never use.* Retrieved November 10, 2020, from https://www.washingtonpost.com/news/business/wp/2016/01/14/why-the-social-media-buy-button-is-still-there-even-though-most-never-use-it/?utm_term=.974a7f94c3f8

Han, M. C., & Kim, Y. (2016). Can social networking sites be e-commerce platforms? *Pan-Pacific Journal of Business Research, 7*(1), 24–39.

Hu, M., & Chaudhry, S. S. (2020). Enhancing consumer engagement in e-commerce live streaming via relational bonds. *Internet Research, 30*(3), 1019–1041.

Liu, X. (2019). *The rising tide of social commerce—And why China is leading it*. Retrieved April 24, 2021, from https://www.asiapacific.ca/research-report/rising-tide-social-commerce-and-why-china-leading-it

Martin, J. (2017). *13 times Facebook cloned snapchat*. Retrieved April 21, 2021, from https://www.quertime.com/article/13-times-facebook-cloned-snapchat/

Meilatinova, N. (2021). Social commerce: Factors affecting customer repurchase and word-of-mouth intentions. *International Journal of Information Management, 57*, 102300.

Razmerita, L., Kirchner, K., & Nielsen, P. (2016). What factors influence knowledge sharing in organizations? A social dilemma perspective of social media communication. *Journal of Knowledge Management, 20*(6), 1225–1246.

Schaefer, M. (2018). *Facebook's biggest problem isn't ethics, hate or fake news. It's Facebook*. Retrieved April 15, 2021, from https://businessesgrow.com/2018/01/08/facebooks-biggest-problem/

Shen L. (2021). *Social commerce has taken over China. Can it do the same overseas?* Retrieved April 24, 2021, from https://www.protocol.com/manuals/transforming-2021/chinese-social-commerce

Sloane, G. (2018). *Selfie commerce: Snapchat adds shopping to its augmented reality ads*. Retrieved April 21, 2021, https://adage.com/article/digital/snapchat-puts-shopping-option-augmented-reality-ads/313192

Statista. (2017). *Social media platform on which social media users in the United States last made a purchase directly from a social media post as of October 2017*. Retrieved November 10, 2020, from https://www.statista.com/statistics/250909/brand-engagement-of-us-online-shoppers-on-pinterest-and-facebook/

Thomala, L. L. (2020). *Number of social media users in China 2017–2025*. Retrieved April 24, 2021, from https://www.statista.com/statistics/277586/number-of-social-network-users-in-china/

Tong, Q., & Jia, D. (2020). *WeChat tests pay-to-read feature for public blogging accounts*. Retrieved March 30, 2021, from https://www.caixinglobal.com/2020-01-16/wechat-tests-pay-toread-feature-for-public-blogging-accounts-101504591.html

Wan, J., Lu, Y., Wang, B., & Zhao, L. (2017). How attachment influences users' willingness to donate to content creators in social media: A socio-technical systems perspective. *Information and Management, 54*(7), 837–850.

# How Social Media Can Monetize by Offering Premium Service or Content

**5**

## 5.1 Premium Service

Social media is mainly offered free of charge. Facebook, Twitter, YouTube, LinkedIn, and many other applications are free to users. Hence, it is interesting to study how free-to-use social media achieves monetization. Previously, we have discussed the possibility of monetizing via social advertising. We will not reiterate this here but focus on an alternative approach to monetization of social media users: premium service or content.

Premium service or content is service or content of which the quality is higher than basic, free-of-charge service. For example, YouTube, a social video sharing platform, enables users who have paid for premium service to enjoy more privileges such as ad-free viewing (view everything on YouTube without ads), YouTube originals (access to original video content), background playing (smartphone users can play the sound of the video even if the smartphone display is shut down), video downloads (download videos or playlists on given devices), and YouTube Music Premium (access to YouTube music services) (Vicente, 2020). For YouTube, premium services are these additional features or services designed for creating better user experiences and privileges. However, there are other forms of premium features. A major feature of social media is creating substantial and extensive social networks in which content creators can attract fans or followers by producing creative, informative, or entertaining content. Recently, social media companies have noticed this wave and rolled out premium content and other fan-related premium services. Facebook rolled out a premium content feature by which an original content creator can charge a fee to viewers. Basically, viewers need to pay a fee to access exclusive content created by the creator. This premium content feature benefits original content creators because they can earn money from their creations. They are motivated by monetary incentives to produce original content for viewers. At the same time, social media platforms can take a share of viewers' payments. For example, Facebook takes a cut of up to 30% from users' payments for exclusive content and a fan badge (Ha, 2019).

F. J. Martínez-López et al., *Social Media Monetization*, Future of Business and Finance, https://doi.org/10.1007/978-3-031-14575-9_5

Users can access basic service for free, while they need to pay for premium service. The integration of free basic service and premium service is defined as "freemium" (Liu et al., 2014). It has been an increasingly dominant business model for today's digital services (Hamari et al., 2017). In a freemium business model, a basic product or service is offered for free, though app users wanting additional services or a better consumption or use experience can buy a premium subscription or make in-app purchases (Mäntymäki & Islam, 2015). For example, YouTube offers premium service at around $10 per month (Mann, 2020). Currently, there are 20 million premium subscribers (Mann, 2020), generating approximately $2.4 billion per year. Regarding the relationship between social advertising and premium subscriptions, Twitter's CEO Jack Dorsey once said premium subscriptions are complementary to advertising, and asserted that Twitter could offer premium service soon.

> We want to make sure any new line of revenue is complementary to our advertising business. We do think there is a world where subscription is complementary, where commerce is complementary, where helping people manage paywalls... We think is complementary. (cited in Lee, 2020)

## 5.2    Ad-Free as a Premium Feature

Despite the fact that many firms have monetized from freemium business models, the model seems more difficult to integrate into social media platforms' dominant advertising models. There is little reason for social media users to pay for additional premium service, considering the fact that major social media features (friending, messaging, networking, etc.) are offered at no charge. WPS Office is an office suite for Microsoft Windows, iOS, and Android operating systems. Unlike Microsoft Office, WPS Office's Word, Excel, PowerPoint, and other applications are offered at no charge, but users must pay if they need to use premium features such as a larger cloud storage, more templates, easier processing of pictures, and others. These features are easy to use and can meet a users' particular needs. However, it is harder for social media to "force" free users to upgrade to paid users.

As mentioned in previous chapters, advertising is a main revenue source for social media platforms. Advertising can cover the costs for free, basic social media functions such as friending, messaging, and networking. Accordingly, ad-free is a premium service that creates a seamless browsing experience for social media users and is considered to be a major reason why social media users would agree to pay. For example, Facebook was in a debate about whether it should introduce a premium, ad-free service for paid users. Facebook's advertising business model has been criticized for its data collection strategy. It collects user data in order to increase advertising precision, which threatens Facebook users' data privacy. Annoying commercials unexpectedly appearing in users' News Feed negatively influence users' Facebook use experiences. Hence, paying for ad-free premium would remove all ads in paid users' Facebook, and at the same time, such users' data would not be collected. But Mark Zuckerberg is not on the same page:

> I personally don't believe that very many people would like to pay to not have ads... It may still end up being the right thing to offer that as a choice down the line, but all the data that I've seen suggests that the vast, vast, vast majority of people want a free service, and that the ads, in a lot of places, are not even that different from the organic content in terms of the quality of what people are being able to see. (cited in Wagner, 2019)

Zuckerberg's argument is that it would not be fair to stop gathering data about particular paid users (Wagner, 2019). Indeed, the creation of ad-free premium does not de facto refine its current advertising business model. As to those free users, their private data are still collected for commercial purposes. Furthermore, this user discrimination strategy could engender an unfair setting between free users and premium users.

## 5.3   Premium Social Media Content

Social media is a platform created for the dissemination of content through online social interactions (Botha & Mills, 2012). Furthermore, the dissemination of social media content is a major feature of social media platforms. Charging a fee for premium social media content shows respect for content creators' intellectual property (Zhao et al., 2018). Some social media platforms introduced a paywall for premium social media content so that users must pay to access particular content; as a consequence, it is unlikely for users to know whether the premium content merits purchase beforehand. Previous research has indicated that if value producers cannot capture enough value, their motivation to consistently generate value will be depleted (Lepak et al., 2007). The premium social media content can motivate content creators with payments from their followers or fans. Previous research has revealed that content sharing in an online platform is mostly fueled by monetary incentives (Lee et al., 2013). It is harder for social factors to motivate users to share content in the platform (Lee et al., 2013). This finding implies that social factors (social interactions, social connections, and community activities) which social media platforms bring about may not be enough to motivate social media users to continually generate meaningful content. Apart from Facebook, there are other social media platforms that have noticed the business value behind premium social media content. WeChat introduced a paywall that allows content creators to monetize posts they create (Zhang, 2020). The creators can charge followers up to $30 per article (Tong & Jia, 2020). WeChat, in turn, charges the creators a fee to earn money from this premium feature (Tong & Jia, 2020). It was reported that Weibo, China's Twitter, earned 26.8 billion Chinese yuan (around $3.83 billion) for content creators by launching the premium content business (Sina Tech, 2018).

## 5.4    Premium Digital Items or User Privileges

Premium digital items include fan badges, virtual gifts, virtual decorations, and other digital items available for user purchase on a social platform; these items are offered by most social platforms. Premium digital items have been studied in previous research related to online social platforms (e.g., Animesh et al., 2011; Guo & Barnes, 2011; Kim et al., 2011, 2012; Shang et al., 2012; Mäntymäki & Salo, 2013, 2015).[1] Online streaming platforms have incorporated similar premium features such as digital fan badges and special user privileges. Huya is a Chinese live streaming platform. In Huya, followers of a streamer pay 1 Chinese yuan to obtain an exclusive fan badge. The fan badge will be shown in their favorite streamer's streaming room, so that these paid followers are distinguishable from free followers. Furthermore, paid followers must maintain or upgrade their fan badges to keep watching the streamer's streaming videos or give virtual gifts to the streamer; otherwise, the exclusive fan badge will disappear. Huya also offers users premium privileges. There are seven levels for privileges. Each privilege provides users with premium features such as a virtual mount or a virtual VIP seat. The higher the privilege level, the better the premium features available to the users. The lowest level charges users around 10 Chinese yuan per month (50 Chinese yuan for the first month), while the highest level can cost users more than 1.5 million Chinese yuan. Live streaming contributed around 7.98 billion Chinese yuan in revenue for Huya in 2019, which is approximately ten times the amount (0.79 billion Chinese yuan) reported in 2016 (Huya Inc., 2020). Unlike Facebook, advertising only represented a small portion (less than 5%) of Huya's total revenue (see Huya Inc., 2020). In summary, we see that Huya has presented a path to monetization via premium digital items and user privileges versus relying on advertising.

## 5.5    Managing Multiple Monetization Models

Most social media platforms build their monetization models on advertising. Premium service is an alternative monetization model to monetize social media users. These two monetization models could, however, negatively influence each other. Previous research has indicated that a cannibalization effect occurs when free service reduces the number of paid users because they have access to the free service (Bawa & Shoemaker, 2004). For example, when a social media platform offers an ad-free premium service or version, with the increase in paid users, advertisers become unwilling to spend money on the social media platform. Paid users who subscribe to an ad-free premium indicate their preference for the ad-free, uninterrupted

---

[1] It is worth mentioning that many of these studies focused on decorative, virtual items (e.g., digital accessories, furniture, and clothes for digital avatars), and social virtual communities such as Cyworld (Kim et al., 2011), Second Life (Animesh et al., 2011; Guo & Barnes, 2011), Habbo (Kim et al., 2012; Mäntymäki & Salo, 2013, 2015), and iPart (Shang et al., 2012), which are not commonplace social media platforms, e.g., Facebook, YouTube, Twitter, and WeChat.

experience. These users, formerly the target customers of the product or service ads, will no longer see the ads nor will they be present in these users' social circles. On the other hand, with the increase in free users, advertisers are more willing to spend money on the social media platform. In particular, when a social media platform attracts significant users by free services, it is easier for advertisers to find their target customers on the platform and thus willing to run paid ads. Previous research has revealed that free users add value by creating a network effect and producing digital content (Wagner et al., 2014). In social media contexts, social media content generated by free users attracts more new users who adopt the social media and participate in creating and sharing more content. Platforms must finance free users for the platform to sustain the extensive social network, which the revenue from paid users alone usually does not cover (Wagner et al., 2014). The above discussion reveals an inherent conflict between multiple monetization models. It is harder for a firm to manage multiple monetization models, particularly when there exist intertwined influencing relationships. For example, Tinder, a dating app, was at risk when it introduced its subscription-based premium service (Cook, 2015). Tinder became popular by creating a casual experience for finding potential dating partners. However, when Tinder offered premium services for paid users and imposed limitations on free users, its app rating dropped considerably (Cook, 2015).

Research has indicated that it is not always optimal for a provider to adopt advertising and premium services simultaneously as a hybrid business model (Xu & Duan, 2018). This research found, particularly when users are unlikely affected by advertising, social media platforms should focus on a subscription-based model (Xu & Duan, 2018) and remove ads to create better user experiences.

On the other hand, if advertising does create revenue for social media platforms, social media platforms that have launched premium service or content features need to create coherence between these two monetization models. The coherence of multiple monetization models refers to an optimal state in which multiple monetization models work hand in hand and capture maximum value from users. Research has shown that companies with higher coherence scores produce more returns for stakeholders than their counterparts with lower scores (Yadavalli et al., n.d.). In fact, in recent years, more social media platforms, (e.g., Facebook, YouTube, and Weibo) that previously monetized via advertising, now place their attention on premium service or content. In the following chapter, these social platforms' premium service and content business are introduced.

## 5.6   Social Media Platforms Monetizing via Premium Service or Content

There are several ways to monetize premium service or content. With premium service or content offered by social media platforms, the user can be charged a monthly or annual subscription fee or a single fee. With premium content offered by content creators in a social media platform, the user can also be charged by a monthly or annual subscription fee or a single fee. In most cases, users can cancel these subscriptions at any time. In this section, we will introduce different social media platforms' premium service or content.

(1) *YouTube*. We have introduced YouTube Premium previously. To summarize, YouTube offers premium services including ad-free viewing, access to original video content, background playing, video downloads, and premium music services (Vicente, 2020). The subscription cost is $11.99 per month in the USA. The subscription costs vary by country (Dutta, 2020). Inspired by Patreon's business model, YouTube also allows creators to offer special perks including merchandise, product/service offers, and discounts to channel subscribers who pay $4.99 per month for membership (Dutta, 2020). At the same time, YouTube keeps 30% of the membership fee paid by these subscribers (Dutta, 2020).

(2) *Facebook*. Facebook is continually exploring new monetization options. Facebook tested a monthly subscription feature that allowed users to pay their favorite creators directly (Constine, 2018). The monthly subscription costs $4.99 per month (Constine, 2018). Facebook refrained from taking a portion of these fees during the testing period (Constine, 2018). Recently, the Director of Media Monetization, Kate Orseth, asserted that Facebook is committed to allowing content creators to keep 70% of their earned income (minus taxes and fees) (Ha, 2019). When compared to other mobile platforms' policies which gather their 30% fee on first-year subscriptions, this implies that Facebook will not take any commission (Ha, 2019).

(3) *Weibo*. Weibo may be most mature in terms of premium content. Weibo has been launching paid content features since around 2014 (Incitez China, 2014). Weibo has launched V+ membership and paid Q&A services allowing content creators to make a living from their creative content (Chan & Segal, 2019). For example, Weibo blogger Hong Huang has over 14 million followers. She opened the paid subscription feature V+ membership. Paid subscribers who pay 51 Chinese yuan per year can access all her new content and Weibo answers. Particularly, subscribers can access professional articles shared by her and participate in fan activities offline. Ms. Huang also offers paid consulting service via the social media platform. Each question is priced at 10 Chinese yuan. It is noteworthy that Weibo introduced an interesting share allocation mechanism. If a paid questioner submits an interesting question, other users ("bystanders") can pay 1 Chinese yuan for access to the answer. The paid questioner will then take a 50% share of the bystanders' payments. This policy encourages more Weibo users to use the paid Q&A feature.

(4) *LinkedIn*. LinkedIn is a social networking site specifically built for developing professional relationships. It was acquired by Microsoft in 2016. LinkedIn connects professionals across the world to help them obtain more social capital and has revamped the way firms hire, market, sell, and interact with other firms (Microsoft, 2020). LinkedIn offers basic services such as creating and displaying a personal profile, friending other professionals, and job seeking. It also offers premium services: Talent Solutions, Learning Solutions, Marketing Solutions,

Sales Solutions, and Premium Subscriptions (Microsoft, 2020). Paid LinkedIn users can access these additional premium services. For example, users who have paid for premium subscriptions can enable experts to refine their identity, expand their social network, and reach more talented users via premium services like premium search (Microsoft, 2020). LinkedIn Premium offers four levels which range in price from $29.99 to $59.99 per month for job seekers, $79.99 per month for sales representatives, and $119.95 per month for human resource managers; purchasing the service for a whole year results in slight discounts (Florentine & Kapko, 2019).

(5) *Tinder.* Tinder is an online dating app. It recommends singles in a users' current geographic area. It will prioritize matches that have common friends, common interests, and relationships with the user on Facebook. A Tinder user can use the Swipe Right feature to like someone, and if someone likes him or her back, it is considered a match. The people who liked the other can have a meeting and get connected. Tinder offers premium features such as Message before matching, Prioritized Likes, and See Who Likes You. For example, Message before matching is an approach to show a user's interest in a potential match by attaching a message to his/her Super Like.[2] When a message is left for a potential match, viewers will see it on the user's profile before they Like or Nope. Tinder currently offers three tiers of premium service: Tinder Plus, Tinder Gold, and Tinder Platinum. Tinder Gold has all the features from Tinder Plus. Tinder Platinum is the highest tier and contains all features from lower tiers. The highest tier is around $12 per month (a 6-month subscription) (SwipeHelper, 2020).

In conclusion, this chapter has introduced the concept of premium service or content and has discussed major premium services or contents that have been adopted by social media platforms. Furthermore, this chapter has highlighted the potential problem related to introducing premium service or content business. We close with several cases which show how major social media platforms like YouTube and LinkedIn monetize with premium services or content. This chapter presents major monetization approaches via premium service/content, but it is not enough for social media firms to just select a monetization approach. The journey to monetization requires firms to create specific monetization strategy and perfect their existing monetization models. As premium service or content is a novel feature recently adopted by major socially focused media platforms, monetizing via premium service/content could positively or negatively influence their existing revenue source: advertising. A holistic view is needed for social media firms to obtain maximum revenue from all businesses. This chapter has aimed to briefly introduce monetization approaches; how social media firms create specific strategies, business policies, monetization models, and manage the relationship between the premium service/content and advertising business will be addressed in a later chapter.

---

[2]This feature can be seen at Tinder's official site: https://www.help.tinder.com/hc/en-us/articles/3 60046358932-Message-Before-Match-

# References

Animesh, A., Pinsonneault, A., Yang, S. B., & Oh, W. (2011). An odyssey into virtual worlds: Exploring the impacts of technological and spatial environments on intention to purchase virtual products. *MIS Quarterly, 35*(3), 789–810.

Bawa, K., & Shoemaker, R. (2004). The effects of free sample promotions on incremental brand sales. *Marketing Science, 23*(3), 345–363.

Botha, E., & Mills, A. J. (2012). Managing the new media: Tools for brand management in social media. In A. Close (Ed.), *Online consumer behavior: Theory and research in social media, advertising and E-tail* (pp. 83–100). Taylor and Francis.

Chan, C., & Segal, A. (2019). *Making a living off 'likes': The new influencer paradigm.* Retrieved from https://a16z.com/2019/12/19/making-a-living-off-likes/

Constine, J. (2018). *Facebook builds Patreon, Niche clones to lure creators with cash.* Retrieved from https://techcrunch.com/2018/03/19/facebook-creator-monetization/

Cook, J. (2015). *Tinder's paid subscription service could ruin everything that made it great.* Retrieved from https://venturebeat.com/2015/02/08/tinders-paid-subscription-service-could-ruin-everything-that-made-it-great/

Dutta, A. (2020). *YouTube business model\How does YouTube make money?* Retrieved from https://www.feedough.com/youtube-business-model-how-does-youtube-make-money/

Florentine, S., & Kapko, M. (2019). *Why LinkedIn Premium is worth the money.* Retrieved from https://www.cio.com/article/2877153/why-linkedin-premium-is-worth-the-money.html

Guo, Y., & Barnes, S. (2011). Purchase behavior in virtual worlds: An empirical investigation in Second Life. *Information and Management, 48*(7), 303–312.

Ha, A. (2019). *Facebook will start taking a cut of fan subscriptions in 2020.* Retrieved from https://techcrunch.com/2019/07/09/facebook-subscription-revenue-share/

Hamari, J., Hanner, N., & Koivisto, J. (2017). Service quality explains why people use freemium services but not if they go premium. *International Journal of Information Management, 37*(1), 1449–1459.

Huya Inc. (2020). *2019 annual report.* Retrieved from https://www.file:///C:/Users/K/Desktop/HUYA%202019%20Annual%20Report.pdf

Incitez China. (2014). *Weibo launched paid content and buy-me-a-coffee features for premium publishers.* Retrieved from https://www.chinainternetwatch.com/8090/weibo-launched-paid-content-buy-me-a-coffee-features-for-premium-publishers/

Kim, H. W., Chan, H. C., & Kankanhalli, A. (2012). What motivates people to purchase digital items on virtual community websites? The desire for online self-presentation. *Information Systems Research, 23*(4), 1232–1245.

Kim, H. W., Gupta, S., & Koh, J. (2011). Investigating the intention to purchase digital items in social networking communities: A customer value perspective. *Information and Management, 48*(6), 228–234.

Lee, T. (2020). *Twitter could be considering adopting a subscription model.* Retrieved from https://www.ubergizmo.com/2020/07/twitter-could-adopt-subscriptions/

Lee, U., Kim, J., Yi, E., Sung, J., & Gerla, M. (2013). Analyzing crowd workers in mobile pay-for-answer Q&A. In *Proceedings of the SIGCHI Conference on Human Factors in Computing Systems,* pp. 533–542.

Lepak, D. P., Smith, K. G., & Taylor, M. S. (2007). Value creation and value capture: A multilevel perspective. *Academy of Management Review, 32*(1), 180–194.

Liu, C. Z., Au, Y. A., & Choi, H. S. (2014). Effects of freemium strategy in the mobile app market: An empirical study of google play. *Journal of Management Information Systems, 31*(3), 326–354.

Mann, H. (2020). *How much is YouTube worth? $170bn in 2020.* Retrieved from https://mannhowie.com/youtube-valuation

Mäntymäki, M., & Islam, N. (2015). Gratifications from using freemium music streaming services: Differences between basic and premium users. In *Proceedings of the ICIS.*

Mäntymäki, M., & Salo, J. (2013). Purchasing behavior in social virtual worlds: An examination of Habbo Hotel. *International Journal of Information Management, 33*(2), 282–290.

Mäntymäki, M., & Salo, J. (2015). Why do teens spend real money in virtual worlds? A consumption values and developmental psychology perspective on virtual consumption. *International Journal of Information Management, 35*(1), 124–134.

Microsoft. (2020). *Annual report 2020.* Retrieved from https://www.microsoft.com/investor/reports/ar20/index.html

Shang, R. A., Chen, Y. C., & Huang, S. C. (2012). A private versus a public space: Anonymity and buying decorative symbolic goods for avatars in a virtual world. *Computers in Human Behavior, 28*(6), 2227–2235.

Sina Tech. (2018). *Weibo empowered content writers to earn 26.8 billion yuan the content ecosystem is more active.* Retrieved from https://tech.sina.com.cn/i/2018-12-21/doc-ihmutuee1410472.shtml

SwipeHelper. (2020). *Tinder platinum—The new subscription tier above tinder gold. Release date, price, and features as they unveil.* Retrieved from https://www.swipehelper.com/2020/07/17/tinder-platinum-new-subscription-tier-above-tinder-gold-rumored-release-date-price-features/

Tong, Q., & Jia, D. (2020). *WeChat tests Pay-to-read feature for public blogging accounts.* Retrieved from https://www.caixinglobal.com/2020-01-16/wechat-tests-pay-to-read-feature-for-public-blogging-accounts-101504591.html

Vicente, V. (2020). *What is YouTube premium, and is it worth it?* Retrieved from https://www.howtogeek.com/659597/what-is-youtube-premium-and-is-it-worth-it/

Wagner, K. (2019). *Mark Zuckerberg explains why an ad-free Facebook isn't as simple as it sounds.* Retrieved from https://www.vox.com/2019/2/20/18233640/mark-zuckerberg-explains-ad-free-facebook

Wagner, T. M., Benlian, A., & Hess, T. (2014). Converting freemium customers from free to premium—The role of the perceived premium fit in the case of music as a service. *Electronic Markets, 24*(4), 259–268.

Xu, J., & Duan, Y. (2018). Subscription price and advertising space decisions for online content firms with reference effect. *Electronic Commerce Research and Applications, 30*, 8–24. https://doi.org/10.1016/j.elerap.2018.05.007

Yadavalli, S., Kapoor, P., Bruun-Jensen, J., & Freilich, R. (n.d.). *Business model coherence.* Retrieved from https://www2.deloitte.com/content/dam/Deloitte/us/Documents/consumer-business/us-cb-m-and-a-match-making-consumer-products.pdf

Zhang, W. (2020). *WeChat is letting bloggers add paywalls. Will the experiment work?* Retrieved from https://www.sixthtone.com/news/1005086/wechat-is-letting-bloggers-add-paywalls.-will-the-experiment-work%3F

Zhao, Y., Zhao, Y., Yuan, X., & Zhou, R. (2018). How knowledge contributor characteristics and reputation affect user payment decision in paid Q&A? An empirical analysis from the perspective of trust theory. *Electronic Commerce Research and Applications, 31*, 1–11.

# Part III

# Know-how for Companies to Monetize Social Media

# Monetization Process for Companies

# 6

A monetization process encompasses six activities: market research, social media strategy formulation, social media listening and social media intelligence, influencer marketing, performance assessment and reporting, and community management and customer care. All activities serve the ultimate goal of increasing corporate profit via social media. The six activities are not arranged in a causal sequence. For example, social media listening could be performed earlier than market research. These activities can constitute the entire monetization process, but not all activities are necessary in different forms of social media monetization. This chapter offers an overview of the monetization process. The key activities will be discussed in further detail in later chapters.

## 6.1    Market Research

Market research refers to the systematic collection of market information for the formulation of a marketing strategy (Kao, 1986). Market information includes buyer personas, products, competitors, market distribution, and trends. Market research can enhance entrepreneurial performance, marketing, or advertising effectiveness and increase the likelihood for success of a new product launch. Social media has become a pivotal marketing channel in many firms' marketing strategy. It has been reported that social media marketing budgets can comprise as much as 75% of a firm's total marketing budget (see Mirreh, 2019). Hence, it is necessary to perform sophisticated market research and planning to effectively monetize social media.

Social media encompasses a wide variety of users. Users' intention to employ a social media platform is quite diverse, from building and sustaining social networks to browsing social media content in a particular field (e.g., health, beauty, and sports). A firm needs to know *who their customers are*. In other words, firms need to identify their buyer persona. This includes demographics, preferences, behavioral patterns, needs, and purchase motivations. For social media marketing to succeed, it is necessary to collect information about target customers' social media preferences, browsing habits, needs, etc. For example, a fashion brand producing youth clothes can focus on Instagram which is preferred by young people versus other social media sites.

In addition to customer insights, competitor information is another aspect of market research for social media marketing. For example, when a competitor is creating viral content on social media, a firm can accordingly imitate similar, but more attractive content to attract competitors' social traffic. Competitor information also helps the firm assess its social media campaign effectiveness. Benchmarking competitors' social media advertising performance is a useful reference point for the firm to see how successful the firm has performed vis-à-vis competitors.

Furthermore, on the basis of market research, an actionable marketing plan can be created. Project management techniques, such as work breakdown structure (WBS), RACI (responsible, accountable, consulted, informed) matrix, and critical path method (CPM), are available for firms to curate a plan. In particular, firms need a plan to allocate their marketing budget. For example, Estée Lauder spent around $900 million on influencer marketing solely in the USA and recruited influencers to considerably boost sales and brand awareness (Mirreh, 2019). Another key aspect of a firm's marketing plan is to create engaging social media content. Social media pioneers, such as Nike, Adidas, and Coca-Cola, all stress the role of social media content quality in ensuring the success of a social media campaign. Research has revealed that the information quality of social media content is closely related to customers' involvement in a firm's social media page (McClure & Seock, 2020) and the level of influence of the content (Francalanci & Hussain, 2014). In order to keep customers engaged, firms need to consistently create captivating content that is congruent with a firm's brand identity (Tanha, 2018).

## 6.2   Social Media Strategy Formulation

Despite the fact that the concept of social media strategy has been widely used in practice, we believe this concept is narrowly understood as a social media publishing strategy or a social media marketing strategy. More business values (e.g., new competitive advantage and business model innovation) are attainable if this concept can be more broadly defined. Essentially, strategy is about choosing what to do and what not to do and makes a firm stand out from its competitors. Social media strategy refers to the choice of social media as a strategic enabler to create a unique and valuable competitive position. Based on this definition, not all firms are suited to adopt a social media strategy because this strategy requires firms to use social media to strengthen their competitive position and potentially innovate their business models. A firm should not assert that they have a social media strategy because a social media marketing department has been created or Facebook ads are running. Social media strategy needs to inject a "social gene" into a firm. Human resources, business processes, corporate culture, and business models can be fundamentally transformed by leveraging the power of social media. For example, Dell's social media strategy is "to create a level of involvement that means the Web can inform

| Market research | | | Influencer marketing |
| Social media listening | Social media strategy | | Performance assessment and reporting |
| Social media intelligence | | | Community management and customer care |

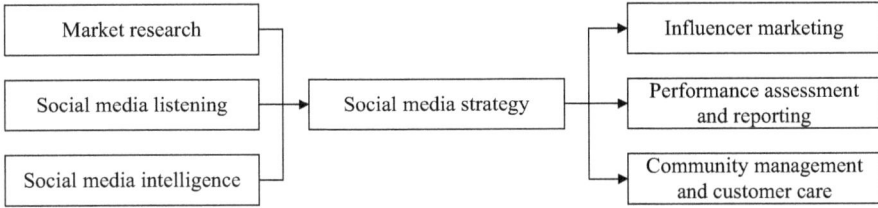

**Fig. 6.1** Key role of social media strategy in social media monetization process

every part of the business (Shaughnessy, 2011)." Dell created internal and external social media listening programs for co-creating unique and valuable products with internal employees and external customers. This social media strategy brought fundamental changes to Dell's production management and customer relationship management. In doing so, Dell places social media as a key element in shaping its production strategy and customer relationship management. Another example, Pinduoduo, an e-commerce firm, uses social media to launch team purchases; social media acts as a platform to assemble buyers who may then purchase goods in a team. The business model based on team purchases is relatively novel in contrast to the conventional e-commerce model which creates a solitary shopping experience for customers. This team purchase social media strategy enabled Pinduoduo to become the second largest e-commerce player in China. Research has shown that social media features can influence firms' business models, relationship with customers, and value proposition (Wikström & Ellonen, 2012). Social media strategy formulation and implementation entail social media channel selection, social media content creation, social organization design, and social media measurements among others. Social media strategy is a key nexus in the social media monetization process (see Fig. 6.1). Because this chapter is simply an introduction on monetization processes, we will discuss how to specifically formulate and implement social media strategy in a later chapter.

## 6.3    Social Media Listening and Social Media Intelligence

Social media listening is a process of monitoring websites or social media channels to see what is being said about a firm's brand, product, service, and businesses (Andzulis et al., 2012; Chumwatana & Chuaychoo, 2017). Social media listening platforms have features including automated sentiment analysis, volume metrics, geographic breakdowns, and limited content analysis (Moe & Schweidel, 2017). Firms engage in social media listening for the purpose of monitoring brand health, monitoring the success of social media campaigns, and gleaning deeper insights about customers (Moe & Schweidel, 2017; Ngo & Pilecki, 2016). Social media listening has been widely applied across sectors including beauty, airlines, consumer electronics, and fashion. By combining the reporting capabilities of social media listening with social media analytics, firms can better leverage the data offered by social media users (Moe & Schweidel, 2017) and ultimately generate social media intelligence.

Social media intelligence is the capability of handling social media data and information, thereby generating smarter, more precise, and more effective decision making for social selling initiatives. Social media intelligence is an advanced application that can automatically generate actionable insights for a firm's marketing campaigns. Not all firms ultimately develop social media intelligence which is largely reliant on sufficient organizational resources and capabilities. For example, artificial intelligence (AI) was widely used for social media listening and cultivating social media intelligence. Despite the fact that there are several social media listening platforms such as Brandwatch, Crimson Hexagon, and Salesforce (Moe & Schweidel, 2017), research has shown that companies cannot blindly rely on conclusions drawn from AI-powered social media listening platforms (Hayes et al., 2021). Because results generated by AI can be biased, more elaborate algorithm documentation and training data sets are necessary for a firm to make more complex decisions based on social media listening (Hayes et al., 2021).

## 6.4    Influencer Marketing

Influencer marketing has become an effective approach for firms to connect with consumers via social media influencers (Tafesse & Wood, 2021). Influencer marketing refers to a marketing mode in which marketers leverage social media influencers' social influence to promote their brands or products. Social media influencers can be divided into macro-influencers and micro-influencers. According to Phlanx.com,[1] the number of an influencer's followers on Instagram is negatively associated with their average engagement rate. Macro-influencers, defined as having over one million followers, see the lowest average engagement rate at 1.97%. In contrast, micro-influencers, defined as having between 1000 and 5000 followers, witness the highest average engagement rate at 5.60%. Hence, it could be concluded that influencer marketers should not rely solely on macro-influencers.

Influencer marketing entails two crucial aspects: discovering influencers and avoiding influencer risks. When discovering influencers, three dimensions should be considered when vetting them: influencer content, influencer attributes, and audience attributes. Influencer content is social media content generated by the influencer. For example, if an influencer shares social media content related to cosmetics products and makeup techniques, she could be a useful influencer for beauty brands. Influencer attributes entail expertise, trustworthiness, attractiveness, gender, age, and past engagement rates, among others. According to Ohanian's source credibility model, product endorsement effectiveness depends on an endorser's expertise, trustworthiness, and attractiveness (Ohanian, 1990). The

---

[1] Data source: https://phlanx.com/engagement-calculator. The macro-influencers' and the micro-influencers' average engagement rates are taken from this website.

match-up hypothesis in advertising also requires that product endorsers be congruent with the product they endorse. Audience attributes include demographics (e.g., income, education, age, and gender), purchase preferences, and brand affinity among others. A digital and social media manager comment on how an advertising agency selects influencers: The agency first examines how the influencer aligns with the brand by examining the past and present social media endorsements given by the influencer to determine whether he or she properly fits their brand (see Childers et al., 2019). The agency also examines the influencers' previous social media content for up to 2 years and checks for content, sentiment, engagement, and legal issues of actual posts (see Childers et al., 2019).

An influencer is used to create a positive association between the influencer and the product or brand he or she endorses. However, negative associations could occur. For example, a celebrity influencer who is involved in a scandal is putting at risk brands that he or she is endorsing. Inappropriate content posted by an influencer ultimately also affects the brand image that the influencer endorses. In addition, the engagement rate is a key metric to monitor the endorsement effectiveness of an influencer; however, this metric is subject to influencer fraud. A survey has shown that as much as $255 million of the $1.4 billion spent on Instagram was lavished on accounts with fake followers (Monllos, 2020). Despite the fact that Instagram has taken several anti-fraud measures to avoid influencer fraud, from September to December 2019 the fake engagement rate for accounts with fake followers increased because some influencers were able to find ways to circumvent the social media platform's anti-fraud methods (Monllos, 2020). To summarize, monitoring an influencer should be based on several metrics, instead of the sole metric of engagement rate. Multiple metrics should also be considered when deciding whether an influencer fits well with the product or brand.

## 6.5  Performance Assessment and Reporting

Regardless of the social media strategies chosen, precise performance assessment is a key to examining whether the strategy met expectations. The success of a social media campaign should be predefined. In other words, key performance indicators (KPIs) or social media metrics should be set based on the purposes of a social media campaign. For example, Coca-Cola wanted to create personalized customer experiences, creating a "Share a Coke" campaign on multiple social media platforms. The major purpose of this social media campaign was to change customers' established image of Coca-Cola and to let them know that Coca-Cola bottles can be customized.

Performance assessment and reporting should indicate actionable insights for a firm. For example, using social media analytic tools can help reveal the ROI of each social media channel. Using this information, marketers can optimize their social media marketing spending and select the most effective social media channel to reach optimal monetization. A challenge for managers is the need to collect and manage data across various information systems including social media platforms, customer relationship management (CRM) systems, and retail systems. Currently, some social media measurement tools, such as Sprout Social and Power My Analytics, are available to help resolve this issue.

## 6.6    Community Management and Customer Care

Community management is a key activity for the success of social media monetization. Previously, we have illustrated how social media is used for communicative purposes, such as using influencers to deliver brand value. Community management is quite different. It aims to create a branded community where members interact with each other and voluntarily promote brands or products. Community members are basically customers or users of the same product or brand, so social posts shared in the community are much more relevant for community members. This is a major difference of brand community from social media posts and profile pages. A brand community is more oriented to building and nurturing relationships. Research shows that the use of brand community helps increase brand loyalty and brand trust (Coelho et al., 2018).

Customer care means offering what is necessary for customers in need. In an active community, customers often ask questions related to products or services, particularly for complex products such as computers and software. Responsiveness to such questions helps elicit customers' favorable reactions to a product. Effective and timely responses show the brand community cares about their consumption or product use experiences. The provision of customer care in a brand community is also beneficial for increasing customers' attachment to the community and ultimately increasing customer loyalty. For example, Xiaomi, a leading smartphone manufacturer in China, created "Mi Community." In the Spanish community, a user shared a story that he used a mobile, Mi 10T Pro, to make a short film. In the post, the user said that, thanks to the 4K recording, even the smallest details were captured. This user-generated post helped with the promotion of Xiaomi's smartphone.

To summarize, social media monetization entails key activities from market research to community management. The most important of these activities is formulating a social media strategy. In fact, all other activities are in the service of successfully implementing a social media strategy.

## References

Andzulis, J. M., Panagopoulos, N. G., & Rapp, A. (2012). A review of social media and implications for the sales process. *Journal of Personal Selling and Sales Management, 32*(3), 305–316.

Childers, C. C., Lemon, L. L., & Hoy, M. G. (2019). #Sponsored# Ad: Agency perspective on influencer marketing campaigns. *Journal of Current Issues and Research in Advertising, 40*(3), 258–274.

Chumwatana, T., & Chuaychoo, I. (2017). *Using social media listening technique for monitoring people's mentions from social media: A case study of Thai airline industry*. In 2017 2nd International Conference on Knowledge Engineering and Applications (ICKEA), pp. 103–106.

Coelho, P. S., Rita, P., & Santos, Z. R. (2018). On the relationship between consumer-brand identification, brand community, and brand loyalty. *Journal of Retailing and Consumer Services, 43*, 101–110.

Francalanci, C., & Hussain, A. (2014). A visual approach to the empirical analysis of social influence. In *Proceedings of 3rd international conference on data management technologies and applications (DATA-2014)*, pp. 319–330.

Hayes, J. L., Britt, B. C., Evans, W., Rush, S. W., Towery, N. A., & Adamson, A. C. (2021). Can social media listening platforms' artificial intelligence be trusted? Examining the accuracy of Crimson Hexagon's (Now Brandwatch Consumer Research's) AI-Driven analyses. *Journal of Advertising, 50*(1), 81–91.

Kao, R. W. (1986). Market research and small new-venture start-up strategy. *Journal of Small Business and Entrepreneurship, 3*(4), 36–42.

McClure, C., & Seock, Y. K. (2020). The role of involvement: Investigating the effect of brand's social media pages on consumer purchase intention. *Journal of Retailing and Consumer Services, 53*, 101975.

Mirreh, M. (2019). *Estée Lauder commits 75% of its advertising budget to influencers*. Retrieved from https://talkinginfluence.com/2019/08/27/estee-lauders-commits-75-of-its-advertising-budget-to-influencers/

Moe, W. W., & Schweidel, D. A. (2017). Opportunities for innovation in social media analytics. *Journal of Product Innovation Management, 34*(5), 697–702.

Monllos, K. (2020). *'Definitely a concern': Influencer fraud is on the rise again on Instagram*. Retrieved from https://digiday.com/marketing/definitely-concern-influencer-fraud-rise-instagram/

Ngo, S., & Pilecki, M. (2016). *The Forrester wave: Enterprise social listening platforms, Q1 2016*. Retrieved from https://www.forrester.com/report/The1Forrester1Wave1Enterprise1Social1Listening1Platforms1Q112016/-/E-RES122523

Ohanian, R. (1990). Construction and validation of a scale to measure celebrity endorsers' perceived expertise, trustworthiness, and attractiveness. *Journal of Advertising, 19*(3), 39–52.

Shaughnessy, H. (2011). *Dell social business strategy—The secret sauce*. Retrieved from https://www.forbes.com/sites/haydnshaughnessy/2011/12/01/dell-social-business-strategy-the-secret-sauce/?sh=4c043b2b2bae

Tafesse, W., & Wood, B. P. (2021). Followers' engagement with Instagram influencers: The role of influencers' content and engagement strategy. *Journal of Retailing and Consumer Services, 58*, 102303.

Tanha, M. A. (2018). An introduction to brand building via social media. *International Journal of Management Research and Reviews, 8*(6), 1–12.

Wikström, P., & Ellonen, H. K. (2012). The impact of social media features on print media firms' online business models. *Journal of Media Business Studies, 9*(3), 63–80.

# Social Media Strategy Design

7

## 7.1 Strategy Design Overview

A social media strategy is comprised of six elements: why, who, where, what, when, and how (5Ws 1H). Before a social media strategy is decided upon, a firm needs to resolve these six issues:

1. Why should a social media strategy be formulated in a particular format?
2. Who should be responsible for each activity in the monetization process?
3. Where should social media content be distributed?
4. What social media content or campaigns should be created?
5. When should social media content be posted on particular social media channels?
6. How should a firm perform a successful social media campaign and how do firms measure the success of the strategy?

The questions above will be approached, not necessarily in order or separately, in this chapter.

## 7.2 Strategy Design for Social Media

### 7.2.1 Strategic Focus

The creation of strategic focus offers direction for a firm's advertising strategy. The strategic focus explains the "why" issue. A different strategic focus drives firms to perform different actions. In this section, we present major strategic focuses in social media strategy.

***Customer Engagement*** Gartner, a well-known global and research advisory firm, indicates that customer engagement can yield many positive outcomes: increased customer loyalty and trust, valuable customer feedback and insight, improved customer experiences, and accelerated sales velocity (Briglia, 2020). Customer engagement has been used as a major objective of many social media campaigns. The form of customer engagement is more than just likes, shares, or comments on social media posts. It also contains an inclusive business strategy that encourages customers to participate in the value creation process. For example, Starbucks has viewed Twitter as a key platform to boost customer engagement. Starbucks ran the @MyStarbucksIdeas campaign on its Twitter page where customers were encouraged to share their opinions about how to optimize existing products (e.g., coffee flavor), propose new product ideas, or discuss the coffee giant's local franchise (Naylor, 2018). The firm has adopted over 300 ideas directly from this campaign. The campaign not only engages consumers by allowing them to submit their opinions, but also makes them feel as if they were a part of the brand that aims to be inclusive (Naylor, 2018).

***Retargeting Effectiveness***  Retargeting ads are effective for nudging on-the-fence customers to buy (Lazar, 2018). Customers who find retargeted ads are 70% more likely to convert (Lazar, 2018). The average click-through rate (CTR) for retargeted ads is 10 times that of regular ads (Lazar, 2018). Most major social media platforms support retargeting ads. For example, Facebook created the Facebook Pixel feature by which firms can retarget customers who have abandoned a shopping cart, viewed product webpages, or subscribed to online campaigns (Lee, 2018). Kimberly-Clark, a major provider of sanitary paper products and surgical and medical instruments, also relies on retargeting ads to boost sales. The company has seen impressive results from applying a strategy focusing on retargeting ads including a 50–60% higher conversion rates among customers who visit their property and express interest (Abramovich, 2012).

***Physical Store Traffic***  Researching online, purchasing offline (ROPS) is a new norm for consumers (Skrovan, 2017). Sixty-seven percent of consumers said they at least occasionally research products via the Internet before shopping for them in physical stores (Skrovan, 2017). According to a study in 2016, 56 cents of every dollar spent in a physical store was affected by digital research (Simpson et al., 2016), demonstrating that social media is able to convert social traffic into store traffic. Facebook in particular offers several options to segment an audience. The potential audience near a physical store can be targeted by leveraging this social media feature. Facebook for Business (2014) reported an interesting case demonstrating how IKEA used Facebook ads to drive physical store traffic.[1] Customer data in a geo-fenced area around the IKEA Cardiff store were collected by running geo-targeted Facebook ads. In order to ensure the advertising precision, IKEA staff, people who lived in the area, and passers-by were removed from the scope of the geo-targeting advertising. This strategy created a 31% increase in young

---

[1]The text related to the case is adapted from Facebook for Business (2014). More information can be accessed at the website: https://www.facebook.com/business/news/IKEA-Footfall-Study

consumers visiting IKEA Cardiff. Furthermore, the geo-targeted ad campaign yielded a 6:1 return on investment against the media spending on Facebook and received 1.4 million impressions; an impressive resulte, considering that only a specific portion of people were targeted.

***Customer Relationship Quality*** Managing and retaining good relationships with customers are crucial objectives of using social media. Research shows that social media interactions with customers do indeed ease the upselling efforts and can offset the service cost related to more frequently interacting with customers (Maecker et al., 2016). For example, social media has been widely used by airline companies to increase customer relationship quality. Social media outperforms conventional phone-based customer service. Airline staff can use social media to check on a traveling child, seek a lost bag, cope with a venting customer, and upgrade a seat in just minutes (Wolfe, 2018). JetBlue, a North American airline, achieved a staggering 4 min 50 s response time to customer inquiries received through social media (Lekach, 2018). Considering the efficiency of "social care," many customers are increasingly skipping phone calls to the airline customer service and are instead taking their inquiries to Twitter and Facebook (Wolfe, 2018). Airlines are also expanding their social media staff and providing them with additional resources needed to help passengers (Wolfe, 2018).

***Conversion Rates*** Based on the specific goals of a social media campaign, a conversion rate refers to the number of customers who made a subscription, a purchase, or a reservation, signed a petition, or downloaded an app. Conversion rates are the most effective indicator of whether or not a firm's social media efforts are ultimately successful (Helmy, cited in Drell, 2013). Other metrics a firm can examine (e.g., page flows, bounce rates, and traffic sources) are mainly figures that offer helpful hints on where the firm is succeeding or not succeeding in boosting the conversion rate (Helmy, cited in Drell, 2013). RageOn, a Fashion brand, focused on creating a seamless shopping experience for Instagram users in order to increase conversion rates. The brand created a landing page tailored to mobile shoppers (Barnhart, 2019). The landing page is scrollable and includes large, bright buttons (Barnhart, 2019). It is noteworthy that many social media platforms have also taken several measures to boost conversion rates for brands. Instagram rolled out Checkout on Instagram, which largely streamlines the process from product discovery to checkout.

## 7.2.2   Social Media Channels

There are a variety of social media platforms that serve different customers or offer different social media content. In order to find targeted customers and offer them social media content that is a good fit for the firm, firms need to recognize and select proper social media channels, resolving the "where" issue. In a later chapter, we discuss the specific features of some major social media channels. In the present chapter, we mainly introduce what social media channels are prevalent and suitable for commercial use.

**Facebook**  Facebook is a social media channel that has the potential to access a significant customer base and therefore increase profits due to Facebook ad campaigns. In terms of Monthly Active Users (MAU), Facebook users outnumber the total number of users of Twitter, Instagram, Pinterest, and LinkedIn combined (Vrountas, 2019). Facebook is also a major source of product and purchase information. On average, Facebook users click one ad every 3 days (Newberry, 2019a). In particular, this Facebook statistic also implies that users pay attention to Facebook ads, rather than just tuning ads out (Newberry, 2019a). Furthermore, Facebook takes the lion's share (80.4%) of US social referral to e-commerce sites in comparison to other platforms, Instagram (10.7%), Pinterest (8.2%), Reddit (0.4%), and Twitter (0.3%) (eMarketer, 2019). In other words, Facebook can effectively convert social traffic into website traffic. The average cost per mile (CPM, cost per 1000 impressions) on Facebook is $7.19, but the cost per click (CPC) is quite low at $0.97 (Teng, 2019).

**Instagram**  One billion people use Instagram every month (Newberry, 2019b). Data shows that 75.3% of U.S. businesses will use Instagram in 2020 (Newberry, 2019b). With a set of sophisticated shopping features, when running into an interesting product, Instagram users usually try to purchase it right away. Instagram has a unique feature, Stories. It allows a user to share photographs and videos to their "Story." Most interestingly, these stories will disappear after being public for 24 h (Bernazzani, 2020): 500 million users use this feature every day (Functionalmedia, 2020). This feature also benefits firms that want to garner commercial value. One-third of the most viewed stories are from businesses (Functionalmedia, 2020). The CPM on Instagram is slightly more expensive than Facebook's at approximately $7.91, and the CPC is much higher at $3.56 (Teng, 2019).

**WeChat**  WeChat is a social media platform mainly used by Chinese users. Its MAU has surpassed 1.2 billion (Thomala, 2020). Different from other social media platforms, WeChat is "an app for everything," providing gaming, ridesharing, e-shopping, and e-government services (Sehl, 2019a). WeChat is quite different from Facebook. It does not rely as much on advertising to earn profits as Facebook does. WeChat limits the number of ads running on the platform and focuses more on offering several types of business accounts for companies: Subscription Account, Service Account, Mini Program, and WeChat Work. WeChat has been widely adopted as an instant messaging tool for firms to have real-time interactions with customers.

**Pinterest**  Pinterest is an image-focused social media platform designed for the discovery of inspiration and ideas (Gershgorn, 2019). According to a recent report, Pinterest had 335 million MAUs (Pinterest, 2020). Among these users, 73.7% are users outside the USA (Pinterest, 2020). Pinterest meets customers' needs for searching images and can be useful for a business. For example, approximately 84% of weekly active users (WAU) use Pinterest to help decide what to buy (Sehl, 2019b) and 83% of WAU have bought an item on Pinterest (Sehl, 2019b). However, the cost of Pinterest marketing is high, with a CPM of $30 and a CPC of $1.50 (Teng, 2019).

*Twitter* The average monetizable daily active user of Twitter reached 145 million in the third quarter of 2019, a 17% increase year over year (Twitter, 2019). Twitter users are younger, more likely to identify as Democrats, and have more education and higher incomes than the average US adult (Wojcik & Hughes, 2019). Twitter users are 15% more likely to inform friends and family about new products and spend 26% more time on ads than other major social media platforms (see @TwitterBusiness, 2019). Firms may consider using Twitter as a key social media channel because Twitter is used to share updates and industry news and engage with customers (Roy, 2019). As previously noted, US airlines are using Twitter for customer service. Airline customers are skipping phones and turning to Twitter to book a flight and upgrade their seat. Twitter is a relatively low-cost platform to invest in, with a CPM of $6.46 and a CPC of $0.38 (Teng, 2019).

*YouTube* YouTube is quite different from the previously mentioned social media platforms in that YouTube focuses on the social sharing of videos. YouTube has over two billion MAUs, and every day, YouTube users watch over a billion hours of video and produce billions of views.[2] It is also the second largest search engine, behind only Google (Tafesse, 2020). People are increasingly likely to watch videos online because videos can bring about an immersive experience in contrast to pictorial or textual content. It is estimated that by 2022, online videos will make up more than 82% of all online traffic—15 times greater than in 2017 (Cisco, cited in Norris, 2020). To leverage this engaging video content format, firms are investing in YouTube more broadly (Tafesse, 2020). The average CPM on YouTube is approximately $10 and the CPC is $3.21 (Teng, 2019).

*LinkedIn* Social media platforms can be used not only for social communication, but also for work-related communication. LinkedIn is a social media platform that is mainly used for the latter. It has been reported that LinkedIn has up to 722 million users worldwide (Hutchinson, 2020). Among these users, around 30 million are companies (Iqbal, 2020a, 2020b). Because so many companies are using LinkedIn for business, 94% of B2B marketers use LinkedIn for content marketing and 89% use it for lead generation (Cooper, 2020). LinkedIn has been used to build and nurture relationships with clients. Moreover, LinkedIn is also a fundamental part of a firm's fundraising and talent-recruitment. According to a recent study, the average number of followers that a firm's founders have on LinkedIn was positively associated with the amount of funds raised by the firm (Banerji & Reimer, 2019). In other words, founders with more social connections on LinkedIn can more easily

---

[2] Data source: https://blog.youtube/press/. Retrieved on December 14, 2020.

raise funds. LinkedIn's advertising costs are among the highest, with a CPM of $6.59 and a CPC of $5.26 (Teng, 2019).

***TikTok***   TikTok is a new favorite social media app targeted toward young people. Its MAUs are estimated at 800 million (Iqbal, 2020b). TikTok focuses on offering short social videos whose lengths vary from around 30 s to 3 min. The video content encompasses beauty, fashion, sports, news, finance, and music. Basically, users can scroll on their mobile devices to access videos one by one. Statistics show that 90% of all TikTok users use the app multiple times every day (Mohsin, 2020). Despite the fact that this social app was recently introduced into markets, there are businesses using the app for advertising. For example, Clean & Clear used the app to promote its new face wash product, My Swag, and received a 9% lift in purchase intention and a 100.9% lift in message association.[3]

The selection of social media channels is largely reliant on a firm's social media strategy. The strategy defines the business goals in social media campaigns. When specific business goals are set, each social media channel's unique attributions should be taken into consideration. The social media channels mentioned above are targeting different audiences. For example, Instagram is preferred by young consumers, while LinkedIn is preferred by companies. Furthermore, each popular social media platform has its own unique features or focuses on a specific format of digital content. For example, Pinterest focuses on images, while YouTube mainly offers video content. The content format could affect the marketing effectiveness. While video content seems more engaging and captivating, the creation and elaboration of video content take more time. Small businesses may not have the time, efforts, and resources to continually create video content. Also, advertising costs vary across different social media platforms. Firms need not be focused on a particular social media platform. They can consider using a social media platform that will reach their target audience and that also minimizes costs. In practice, many firms, such as Coca-Cola, employ multiple social media channels for their social media strategy. Based on our observations, Facebook currently remains the most popular social media platform for advertising and monetizing.

## 7.2.3   Content

### 7.2.3.1  How to Use User-Generated Content for Business

User-generated content (UGC) is the central element of most social media platforms. UGC refers to media content created by the general public rather than by paid professionals (Daugherty et al., 2008). A social media platform aims at disseminating UGC online. UGC is a major part of "what" social media content should be delivered to consumers. Research indicates that UGC exhibits a greater

---

[3]Information related to this case was adapted from https://www.tiktok.com/business/es/inspiration/1

influence than marketer-generated content on consumer purchase behavior (Goh et al., 2013). UGC has also been used in branding. Positive brand-related UGC can benefit brands because it elicits consumers' electronic word of mouth (eWOM) behavior, brand engagement, and purchase behaviors (Kim & Johnson, 2016).

UGC can be used for business, but first firms need to acquire captivating UGC. Many customers are unwilling to produce relevant, meaningful, and captivating social media content for companies. Posting social media content online makes a person's activity public and accessible to everyone. It could constitute a threat to customer privacy. Another issue is that customers may not be able to produce quality content. Most customers merely use their smartphone to produce simple pictures or videos, and their photographic techniques are not as good as professional content producers. In fact, low-quality UGC could be misleading and make viewers feel that the product presented in the UGC does not deserve to be purchased. In this section, we will discuss how firms can garner captivating UGC and how they can use such content for business.

***Leverage the Power of Hashtags***  A hashtag, written with a # symbol, is used to index keywords or topics.[4] Hashtags are used to categorize social media posts by keywords. The inclusion of hashtags in social media posts can help promote social media campaigns. Customers can engage in a social media campaign by including a specific hashtag into their social media posts; hence, such posts are more easily found by peers who are also interested in the campaign. This practice has been adopted by many firms. Warby-Parker, a retailer of prescription glasses and sunglasses, allowed customers to try on its glasses at home (Vrountas, 2020). Before they buy, the glasses company encourages trial wearers to post photographs of themselves to social media with the hashtag #warbyhometryon (Vrountas, 2020). As a consequence, 20,446 relevant UGC were eventually posted on Instagram (Vrountas, 2020). As another example, Red Bull launched a #PutACanOnIt campaign in which customers held a can of Red Bull in front of an object that is far away, making it look like the object is carrying the can (Sharma, 2017). In just a few months, almost 10,000 original user-generated photographs were uploaded and hashtagged with #PutACanOnIt across Instagram and Twitter (Sharma, 2017).

***Create Social Virality***  Going viral on social media is a common goal for users. In fact, the creation of millions of user-generated social media posts is driven by the social virality of a particular topic or theme. Social virality is determined by three key components. The first component is an inspirational idea or vision. The inspirational idea allows customers to create social media posts that add value. For example, the Ice Bucket Challenge was aimed at creating a world without a disease (amyotrophic lateral sclerosis or ALS). This was very inspirational and drove people

---

[4]The discussion of hashtags is adapted from Twitter's Help Center: https://help.twitter.com/en/using-twitter/how-to-use-hashtags. Twitter was one of the earliest social media platforms to adopt hashtags.

to promote the social media campaign related to raising funds for ALS research. The second component is to empower people to create social media posts. As mentioned previously, in Red Bull's #PutACanOnIt campaign, customers can put a can on an object that is far away, making the can interestingly interact with the object. The objects posted included cars, bikes, teenagers, and even pets. The social media campaign provoked customers' creativity in posting interesting pictures by putting the can on objects they have. The last component is key influencers. The virality of a social media campaign depends on its influence on significant numbers of social media users. It is difficult to reach a large number of users by relying solely on a firm or an individual. Influencers can help distribute the social media campaign by exerting their personal influence on their followers. Their followers, in turn, influence additional users' involvement in the campaign.

***Offer Rewards*** Rewarding customers who are willing to generate social media content is always an effective strategy. In practice, customers who share their purchase choice on social media are rewarded with discounts or coupons for their next orders. Firms also connect customers sharing content on social media to their loyalty programs. Customers posting social media content have privileges to purchase items at a lower price or access to more services. iSeeMe, a manufacturer of children books and personalized gift boxes, rewards customers sharing the story of their purchase on Facebook with an exclusive coupon for their next purchase (Mathew, 2020). Every time a customer makes a purchase on iSeeMe's website, a dialog window pops up for customers to leave a comment on the purchase and share it on Facebook (Mathew, 2020).

***Choose the Best Times to Reach Social Media Users*** The "when" issue in social media strategy formulation is a key element in defining the success of social media strategy. Research shows that it is more effective to post social media content during certain time periods in order to generate higher levels of UGC. For example, Facebook found that the most consistent user engagement occurred during the period of Tuesday through Thursday, 8 a.m.–3 p.m. (Arens, 2020). Social media professionals have also found evidence that the posting time for various types of content (e.g., consumer goods, education, healthcare, finance, and recreation) is different (Arens, 2020). It is recommended that firms study target social media users' usage behaviors and schedule a firm's social media content tailored to these behaviors. Scheduling the posting of social media content based on user behavior can help increase the visibility of the content.

From a business perspective, the creation of UGC is not directly related to the success of a social media campaign. The key is how firms use UGC to accomplish its social media strategy. Here, we will discuss several approaches to use UGC for commercial purposes.

***Incorporate UGC into Marketing Channels*** E-commerce websites are a place to achieve monetization. Displaying quality user-generated photographs or reviews on a firm's e-commerce websites or other marketing channels is an approach to leverage the power of UGC. Dune London, a fashion footwear and accessories brand, incorporated UGC into its e-commerce and email channels. The brand has introduced UGC (customer-generated photographs of customers wearing Dune shoes or accessories) to the product pages on its e-commerce website in order to inspire consumers when they are shopping on the website. Dune found this social proof feature did significantly increase sales (Rigby, 2017). The brand's email campaign featuring UGC related to its "Your Style" gallery saw 55% more click-throughs in contrast to emails not featuring UGC (Rigby, 2017). The gallery led to a sixfold increase in revenue (Rigby, 2017). UGC has an advantage over marketer-generated content: UGC exhibits how products are used or presented in real-life settings. Hence, UGC has a closer psychological distance with regular shoppers and is more convincing in merchandising.

***Use UGC in Advertising***  The inclusion of UGC in ads benefits advertisers: Marketers have seen higher return on ads including UGC versus ads that do not (Desai, 2020). When an influencer endorsement is featured in an ad and that influencer is more similar to regular consumers, the advertising effectiveness is higher. Product endorsement research has also indicated that the effect of product endorsement relies on the congruence between endorsers and consumers (Gaied & Rached, 2010; Xu & Pratt, 2018). Marketers choose the best UGC that is most relevant to their interest and post these as paid ads on Facebook or Instagram (of course, the permission to use such UGC has been granted by respective customers).

***View UGC as the Voice of the Customer (VOC)***  Viewing UGC as the VOC can benefit a firm in two ways. First, customers dissatisfied with a product or service can share their consumption experiences on social media. Particularly in service settings, social media has been widely used by travelers to complain about low or unstable service quality. It is not uncommon to see such negative UGC receive thousands of views. The online presence of such negative UGC may prevent other travelers from using the service. Research has indicated that negative UGC results in an overall negative brand perception and damages the brand equity (Wouters, 2016). Viewing negative UGC as the VOC can help firms fulfill dissatisfied customers' unmet needs and take action before the negative UGC further damages the firm. Second, valuing UGC can make consumers feel that they are a part of the firm's community and this sense of belonging can create loyal consumers (Organic Advertising, 2020). On Twitter, many firms' Twitter accounts retweeted customers' tweet to show that customers' voices are valuable for firms. The users who create content related to a brand or a product are normally the ones who are loyal to the brand or the product (Organic Advertising, 2020). In other words, actively responding to UGC can help build customer loyalty.

### 7.2.3.2  How to Design and Launch Social Media Campaigns for Business

During the process of social media strategy formulation, launching social media campaigns must respond to the "how" issue. Marketing effectiveness of social media campaigns largely determines the outcomes of a social media strategy. In this section, we will present some social media campaigns that have been used by firms and have proven suitability.

## A Combined Use of Celebrities, Social Ads, and Targeting Techniques

The combined use of celebrities, social ads, and targeting techniques aims to deliver relevant content to customers. The approach was reported in Tencent Advertising's successful cases.[5] Weltmeister, an electric car brand, arranged a music festival for customers on the opening day of its smart car factory. In order to strengthen its brand image and increase the effectiveness of branding communication, the car brand uses several measures to fully leverage the power of social media.

*Use Celebrities for Brand Endorsement to Catch Young Consumers' Attention* Weltmeister employed Jike Junyi, Ma Di, and other celebrities to produce marketing content for brand endorsement. Celebrity endorsers are specially highlighted in marketing content to amplify their influence.

*Use Social Ads to Reach Customers with Different Demographics* Weltmeister posted WeChat ads in various ad positions including Moment (similar to News Feed in Facebook) and Official Accounts (social media accounts for business purposes). Also, Weltmeister varied content to fit customers with different demographics. These measures guarantee the maximum reach of social ads.

*Recognize Targeting Customers to Reach Precision Marketing* It is cumbersome to recognize targeting customers. Therefore, Weltmeister's social advertising agent used targeting techniques to recognize the fans of celebrities, in-store customers, and prospects. The followers of celebrities likely are more interested in the brand endorsed by the celebrity. In-store customers and prospects are potential customers who may be interested in purchasing the car. Identifying targeted customers increased the marketing effectiveness of the social media campaign. Furthermore, Weltmeister's advertising agent created a creative landing page for social ads. The landing page was designed to be more interactive for social media users. Users could directly make a reservation on the landing page. As a consequence of the combined use of the above measures, Weltmeister's campaign received hundreds of millions of views. The overall marketing cost was much lower than the average cost in the car industry.

## Cultivate Social Value for More Repeat Purchases

Repeat purchasing usually generates more value for a firm because marketing costs for consumers who have previously bought are lower than for consumers who have not. Repeat purchasing is even more valuable for nondurable products such as

---

[5]The discussion related to the case was adapted from Tencent Advertising's cases "'Low Cost, High Sound Wave' Smart Factory Music Festival Received Hundreds of Millions of Exposures."

cosmetics, apparel, and shoes. Social media campaigns for increasing repeat purchases face two major hurdles: how to identify valuable customers who will make repeat purchases and what marketing efforts should be taken to encourage such customers to make repeat purchases.

Li-Ning, a sport brand, offered an interesting social media campaign paradigm. In summary, Li-Ning used a Mini Program and an Official Account in WeChat and partnered with Tencent's business analysis and data asset management platform to increase repeat purchases.[6] Li-Ning created a business model for acquiring consumers and cultivating consumer equity and achieved the hacked growth of Gross Merchandise Value (GMV).

Mini Programs are applications within the WeChat ecosystem. First, Li-Ning created an e--commerce Mini Program. Second, the brand partnered with Tencent to analyze buyer personas. Third, based on analysis results, a more precise advertising strategy was devised. Social media ads, i.e., WeChat ads, were targeted at customers as depicted in given buyer personas. Fourth, consumers tapping on such ads could directly buy in the e-commerce Mini Program. This social commerce feature is easy to use. Consumers could purchase Li-Ning's products directly via WeChat, using their WeChat account to login into the e-commerce system and make the payment. Paid consumers were asked to follow the brand's Official Account. This approach precisely recognized actual buyers. Finally, the brand produced social media activities for their followers and nurtures the relationships with the followers. This approach ultimately increased the repeat purchase rates.

Outcomes:

1. The commercials received over 97 million exposures and over one million clicks, seeing a 1.09% click-through rate.
2. The average return on investment was 2.41.
3. Total sales surpassed 3.61 million yuan, and the average order value amounted to 320 yuan, which was much higher than the average value in the fashion industry.
4. The repeat purchase rate is around 20–30%.

As reported in the case, Li-Ning created an online business model from acquiring consumers and encouraging them to make repeat purchases. Social media WeChat plays a key role in depicting buyer personas, acquiring consumers, and enabling consumers to make repeat purchases.

---

[6]The discussion related to the case was adapted from Tencent Advertising's cases "Create a new online business model with a one-day ROI of more than 6.6." It can be retrieved from https://e.qq. com/success/detail/?pid=3786

**Go Beyond Paid Advertising to Focus on Creating Relevant Social Media Content and Influencer Marketing**
Social media advertising is more than paying to boost an ad post. In order to achieve higher consumer engagement, firms should place their attention on creating sophisticated social media content.

Estée Lauder, a beauty brand, is skilled in brand building on social media. The brand's social media success is reliant on creating relevant, meaningful social media content. The brand underscores the quality of social media posts and professionally produces high-quality content. For example, in order to promote its new lip products, the brand hired several professional models and used professional filming techniques to create a sophisticated video on social media (Parisi, 2017).

Estée Lauder does not only create branded content itself, but also uses influencers to do so. The firm spent over $900 million in the USA alone on influencer marketing (Mirreh, 2019). The beauty company has a portfolio of brands including Mac, Mecca, Clinique, La Mer, Estée Lauder, Glossier, and Aesop. In order to promote these brands, 60 influencers were recruited to promote products in the brand portfolio (Stewart, 2018). Interestingly, influencers were offered the freedom to choose the products they want to endorse and create social media content in their fashion (Stewart, 2018). The autonomy in endorsement choice and content creation enables influencers to exert their creativity and create authentic and convincing social media posts (Thomas, 2018). As a result, Estée Lauder obtained 120 pieces of content created by the influencers, which reached over 3.3 million consumers and achieved an overall engagement rate of 3.8% (Stewart, 2018).

### 7.2.4  Organizational Design for Social Media Monetization

Building an organization oriented to social media monetization should guarantee the successful implementation of the social media strategy. An organization oriented for social media monetization should be made up of a social media manager, a social media content creator and editor, a community manager, a social media advertiser, a social media analyst, and a social media influencer manager, among others (Nitu, 2019). This organizational design responds to the "who" issue in strategy formulation.

***Social Media Manager***  Social media managers are responsible for the success of a social media strategy. They are the nexus between the CEO and other organizational members. Social media managers are accountable for all activities involved in the social media monetization process. Monetization is more than running an ad and achieving social sales. It involves marketing, sales, and additional supportive activities (e.g., IT infrastructure and e-commerce platforms). The social media manager's duty is also different from personnel from marketing, sales, and other supportive functions. If a monetization project cannot be completed in a timely and economic manner, a firm could lose its competitive advantage or gradually perish with its obsolete business model. Therefore, we argue that a social media manager's duty is as an innovator that allocates internal and external resources to bring about a profit or develop a new capability generating sustainable revenue by using social media. When a firm earns the sought profit or develops the sought capability, the social media manager should continue looking for other monetization opportunities and proposing new projects for the firm. A social media marketing professional's responsibilities for a social media managers includes designing and tracing social media strategy, planning campaigns, building brand and product awareness and an online reputation, creating leads and conversions for sales, and contacting internal and external stakeholders (Nitu, 2019).

***Social Media Content Creator and Editor***   As previously mentioned, social media content quality is of paramount importance for the success of a social media campaign. Estée Lauder, Nike, Adidas, and other name brands create curated social media content which is created by professional content production teams. Based on our observation, the quality of social media content has been increasing during recent years. The role of the social media content creator and editor is a key in a social media marketing team. A social media content creator and editor are responsible for creating and editing various forms of social media content, and this content should be entertaining, informative, useful, and attractive (Ahmed, 2019). The social media content can be textual and visual. Captivating content produced by social media content creators and editors is the key to attract traffic, increase engagement, and generate revenues (Ahmed, 2019).

***Community Manager***   A community manager focuses on developing the brand community and cultivating customer equity. The manager acts as a brand ambassador, developing the community by conducting community activities and interacting with community members. The community manager often seeks new ways to engage the brand community and increase community members' sense of belonging, ultimately bringing about loyal consumers. The social media community allows the community manager to interact with community members under the brand name and also create more intimate relationships with community members. Social interactions between community managers and community members can help link the managers to the brand (Chen, 2020), creating a positive association between brand managers and the brand. Furthermore, Nitu (2019) indicates that community managers are responsible for managing brand advocates and fans and building brand visibility.

***Social Media Advertiser***   Social media advertisers are specialists in advertising strategy who possess a strong sense for advertising budgets and a strong understanding of different social media platforms (Nitu, 2019). Previously, we have categorized social media advertising into push-based advertising and pull-based advertising. Push-based social media advertising requires advertisers to push commercial messages to consumers through social media (Higgs, 2008). In this mode, social media ads are adaptions of traditional mass media ads such as radio and TV commercials but within social media contexts. In pull-based social media advertising, the advertising effect is achieved by viral sharing and pass along among social media users, for example, Red Bull's #PutACanOnIt campaign. In this situation, an explicit ad is absent. The advertising effect is more implicit, but entails commercial purposes (Hayes & King, 2014; Shareef et al., 2018). In the case of Red Bull's #PutACanOnIt campaign, despite the fact that the beverage brand did not explicitly advertise a particular drink, the brand creates a favorable image by engaging young consumers in the campaign. Social media advertisers are responsible for devising and projecting how to use social media for advertising and create synergistic effects when social media and traditional mass media (e.g., television and radio) are all adopted for the firm's advertising strategy.

*Social Media Analyst*   An expert social media analyst not only knows the data to be analyzed and how to analyze such data, but also knows how to use data to offer actionable and valuable recommendations for current social media practices. A social media analyst normally uses significant social media data mining to find information about return on investment to optimize the firm's social media practice (Ramakrishnan, 2020). Specifically, social media analysts analyze whether social media campaigns reached their given objectives. For example, if a social media campaign aims at leading social traffic to an e-commerce website, the social media analyst should report the click-through rates of social ads. An effective social media analyst also actively conducts social media listening programs in order to recognize trends and future monetization opportunities.

*Social Media Influencer Manager*   Social media influencer managers are in charge of managing the relationships with social media influencers and ensuring the social media content that influencers produce falls into the firm's interests (Nitu, 2019). According to a recent survey, as much as $255 million of the $1.4 billion spent on influencers at Instagram was wasted due to influencers' fake followers (Monllos, 2020). Influencer vetting is the priority of an influencer manager's job responsibility. A great influencer manager can find appropriate influencers with authentic followers. Influencer managers also need to monitor the performance of influencers to see whether the influencers are posting social media content in a timely manner and that the content is appropriate, legal, and not misleading. Influencers involved in a scandal could put a brand's reputation at risk. Influencer managers act as a brand safeguard in the influencer marketing process.

To summarize, an organization oriented for social media monetization goes beyond hiring these talents: The existing departments (e.g., marketing, sales, IT, and human resources) should closely collaborate with these talents. Firms need to create a workflow based on their industrial and organizational peculiarities.

## 7.2.5   Metrics for Strategy Assessment

Establishing metrics for strategy assessment is a key component in strategy formulation. From a business perspective, economic metrics (e.g., return on investment) can be used to report the outcomes or performance of strategy implementation. These metrics resolve the "how" issue in the strategy formulation. Furthermore, firms are able to evaluate whether the dollars spent on social media campaigns merit what was achieved by the campaigns. Selection of metrics is closely related to a firm's strategic focus (e.g., customer engagement, conversion rates, retargeting effectiveness, and store traffic) or specific objectives (e.g., fulfillment of sales quota). In particular, it is noteworthy that different metrics can be used in the different stages of the monetization process. For example, at the stage of generating leads, suitable metrics are more related to prospects and product awareness. However, at the stage of closing deals, suitable metrics are more related to transactions and sales.

The metrics currently widely used by social media marketers, and companies are those offered by social media platforms. For example, Facebook offers a set of objectives for Facebook ads that offer three major[7] objectives or metrics: awareness, consideration, and conversions. However, we argue that firms cannot just directly employ these prepackaged metrics to monitor and report their social media strategy performance. On the one hand, metrics offered by social media platforms are derived from data that are accessible for social media platforms. There are valuable data to which social media platforms have no access, for example, in-store traffic. It is beneficial to add more metrics tailored to a firm's social media strategy. On the other hand, metrics offered by social media platforms are related to the advertising business on such platforms. In reality, firms can monetize social media platforms by other approaches such as selling tangible or intangible products on social media. In order to tackle these issues, major metrics that have been used in practice are discussed: consumer behavior, consumer engagement, and company profit (Petrova, 2017).

***Consumer Behavior***  This refers to actions that consumers take after viewing or interacting with social media content. Behaviors can be divided into online and offline consumer behaviors. Online consumer behaviors are related to actions consumers take on a firm's commercial platform, e.g., page views, average time on page, the number of visitors, page depth, pages per session, bounce rates, new and returning consumers, and traffic source (Petrova, 2017). Offline consumer behaviors are related to actions that consumers take at physical stores. They can be measured by store visits, store traffic pattern, average basket size, and customers who access loyalty programs (Ellsworth, 2019).

***Consumer Engagement***  This is a common metric for social media campaigns (Ashley & Tuten, 2015; Barger et al., 2016; Tafesse, 2016). Most social media platforms can directly offer indicators for this metric. Likes, impressions, shares, subscriptions, and comments are widely used to measure consumer engagement with

---

[7]Regarding Facebook-for-Business's given ad objectives, see: https://www.facebook.com/business/help/1438417719786914

a social post. On the firms' side, they can also include consumer inquiries, reservations, and orders to measure consumer engagement.

*Company Profit* The ultimate goal of monetization is achieving higher profits. Profit is comprised of two aspects: revenue and cost. Revenue can be further divided into revenue from existing consumers and revenue from new consumers. It can also be divided by the social media platform used, for example, revenue derived from Facebook, revenue derived from Instagram, and revenue derived from YouTube. Revenue can also be divided from a competitor perspective, like share of market and share of wallet. Regarding costs, cost per mile, cost per click, cost per action, cost per lead, and consumer acquisition cost have been used in current social media marketing practices. To reflect the overall profits of a firm, return on investment (ROI) and net profit (NP) are two key indicators. ROI measures the amount of ROI that firms spent on social media activities and campaigns. NP measures the profit that remains after deducting all costs involved in the social media campaigns.

To summarize, in this chapter, we have discussed the 5W1H issues in formulating a social media strategy. We have not delved into the specifics of a particular social media strategy because any particular strategy needs to consider a firm's external and internal environment, capabilities, and resources. In the following chapters, we will examine the specifics of a social media strategy, discuss major social media platforms, and offer pragmatic implications derived from firms' successful cases.

## References

@TwitterBusiness. (2019). *Agency playbook*. Retrieved from https://cdn.cms-twdigitalassets.com/content/dam/business-twitter/resources/agency-playbook-2019/Twitter_Agency_Playbook_2019.pdf

Abramovich, G. (2012). *Inside Kimberly-Clark's digital strategy*. Retrieved from https://digiday.com/marketing/inside-kimberly-clarks-digital-strategy/

Ahmed, E. (2019). *How to become a content creator on social media and earn revenues*. Retrieved from https://www.socialmediamagazine.org/content-creator-on-social-media/#:~:text=A%20Content%20Creator%20on%20Social%20Media%20is%20responsible,be%20of%20several%20types-%20blogs%2C%20videos%2C%20infographics%2C%20

Arens, E. (2020). *The best times to post on social media in 2020*. Retrieved from https://sproutsocial.com/insights/best-times-to-post-on-social-media/

Ashley, C., & Tuten, T. (2015). Creative strategies in social media marketing: An exploratory study of branded social content and consumer engagement. *Psychology and Marketing, 32*(1), 15–27.

Banerji, D., & Reimer, T. (2019). Startup founders and their LinkedIn connections: Are well-connected entrepreneurs more successful? *Computers in Human Behavior, 90*, 46–52.

Barger, V., Peltier, J. W., & Schultz, D. E. (2016). Social media and consumer engagement: A review and research agenda. *Journal of Research in Interactive Marketing, 10*(4), 268–287.

Barnhart, B. (2019). *8 ways to boost your social media conversion rate*. Retrieved from https://sproutsocial.com/insights/social-media-conversion/

Bernazzani, S. (2020). *Instagram stories: What they are and how to make one like a pro*. Retrieved from https://blog.hubspot.com/marketing/instagram-stories

Briglia, C. (2020). *Why customer engagement is important*. Retrieved from https://www.gartner.com/en/digital-markets/insights/why-customer-engagement-is-important#:~:text=Why%20is

%20customer%20engagement%20important,and%20collect%20valuable%20customer%20 information

Chen, J. (2020). *Social media manager vs. community manager: What's the difference?* Retrieved from https://sproutsocial.com/insights/social-media-vs-community-manager/

Cooper, P. (2020). *20 LinkedIn statistics that matter to marketers in 2020*. Retrieved from https://blog.hootsuite.com/linkedin-statistics-business/

Daugherty, T., Eastin, M. S., & Bright, L. (2008). Exploring consumer motivations for creating user-generated content. *Journal of Interactive Advertising, 8*(2), 16–25.

Desai, J. (2020). *How to use UGC marketing to grow your business*. Retrieved from https://www.jeffbullas.com/how-to-use-ugc-marketing/

Drell, L. (2013). *Marketing 101: The importance of conversion*. Retrieved from https://mashable.com/2013/11/21/conversions-metrics/?europe=true

Ellsworth, M. (2019). *How to measure consumer behavior: 3 metrics for brands and retailers*. Retrieved from https://blog.wiser.com/how-to-measure-consumer-behavior-3-metrics-for-brands-and-retailers/

eMarketer. (2019). *US social referral share to ecommerce sites, by platform, Q1 2019 (% of total)*. Retrieved from https://www.emarketer.com/chart/227803/us-social-referral-share-ecommerce-sites-by-platform-q1-2019-of-total

Facebook for Business. (2014). *IKEA footfall study*. Retrieved from https://www.facebook.com/business/news/IKEA-Footfall-Study

Functionalmedia. (2020). *The 8 types of Instagram stories you need to be using*. Retrieved from https://functional-media.com/the-8-types-of-ig-stories-you-need-to-be-using/

Gaied, A. M., & Rached, K. S. B. (2010). The persuasive effectiveness of famous and non famous endorsers in advertising. *IBIMA Business Review, 2010*, 474771.

Gershgorn, D. (2019). *Pinterest is distancing itself from social networks as it goes public*. Retrieved from https://qz.com/1579086/pinterest-is-distancing-itself-from-social-networks-as-it-goes-public/

Goh, K. Y., Heng, C. S., & Lin, Z. (2013). Social media brand community and consumer behavior: Quantifying the relative impact of user-and marketer-generated content. *Information Systems Research, 24*(1), 88–107.

Hayes, J. L., & King, K. W. (2014). The social exchange of viral ads: Referral and coreferral of ads among college students. *Journal of Interactive Advertising, 14*(2), 98–109.

Higgs, B. (2008). On location. *Marketing Magazine*, pp. 82–84.

Hutchinson, A. (2020). *LinkedIn up to 722 million members, Continues to see 'Record levels of engagement'*. Retrieved from https://www.socialmediatoday.com/news/linkedin-up-to-722-million-members-continues-to-see-record-levels-of-enga/587956/

Iqbal, M. (2020a). *LinkedIn usage and revenue statistics (2020)*. Retrieved from https://www.businessofapps.com/data/linkedin-statistics/

Iqbal, M. (2020b). *TikTok revenue and usage statistics (2020)*. Retrieved from https://www.businessofapps.com/data/tik-tok-statistics/

Kim, A. J., & Johnson, K. K. (2016). Power of consumers using social media: Examining the influences of brand-related user-generated content on Facebook. *Computers in Human Behavior, 58*, 98–108.

Lazar, M. J. (2018). *These 2018 retargeting statistics prove it works*. Retrieved from https://www.readycloud.com/info/these-2018-retargeting-statistics-prove-it-works

Lee, K. (2018). *How to master Facebook ad targeting & zero-in on your audience*. Retrieved from https://sproutsocial.com/insights/facebook-ad-targeting/

Lekach, S. (2018). *Airlines keep upping their social media game, but it's far from the perfect system*. Retrieved from https://mashable.com/2018/01/10/airlines-social-media-customer-service/?europe=true

Maecker, O., Barrot, C., & Becker, J. U. (2016). The effect of social media interactions on customer relationship management. *Business Research, 9*(1), 133–155.

Mathew, G. (2020). *4 ways to generate user-generated content (UGC) to market your business.* Retrieved from https://themanifest.com/digital-marketing/resources/4-ways-generate-ugc-marketing-your-business

Mirreh, M. (2019). *Estée Lauder commits 75% of its advertising budget to influencers.* Retrieved from https://talkinginfluence.com/2019/08/27/estee-lauders-commits-75-of-its-advertising-budget-to-influencers/

Mohsin, M. (2020). *10 TikTok statistics that you need to know in 2020 [infographic].* Retrieved from https://www.oberlo.com/blog/tiktok-statistics

Monllos, K. (2020). *'Definitely a concern': Influencer fraud is on the rise again on Instagram.* Retrieved August 23, 2021, from https://digiday.com/marketing/definitely-concern-influencer-fraud-rise-instagram/

Naylor, T. J. (2018). *How brands are using social media to boost customer engagement.* Retrieved from https://www.socialmediatoday.com/news/how-brands-are-using-social-media-to-boost-customer-engagement/514872/

Newberry, C. (2019a). *33 Facebook stats that matter to marketers in 2020.* Retrieved from https://blog.hootsuite.com/facebook-statistics/#advertising

Newberry, C. (2019b). *37 Instagram stats that matter to marketers in 2020.* Retrieved from https://blog.hootsuite.com/instagram-statistics/

Nitu, L. (2019). *How to build the perfect social media team—From roles to goals & tools.* Retrieved from https://planable.io/blog/social-media-team/

Norris, A. (2020). *Over 82% of internet traffic will be online videos by 2022: How publishers can scale their content production.* Retrieved from https://whatsnewinpublishing.com/over-82-of-internet-traffic-will-be-online-videos-by-2022-how-publishers-can-scale-their-content-production/

Organic Advertising. (2020). *How to use UGC for your campaigns.* Retrieved from https://www.adquadrant.com/blog/how-to-use-ugc-for-your-campaigns

Parisi, D. (2017). *Estée Lauder's multipart #LipsToEnvy campaign shows Facebook video confidence.* Retrieved from https://www.luxurydaily.com/estee-lauders-multipart-lipstoenvy-campaign-shows-facebook-video-confidence/

Petrova, A. (2017). *23 essential metrics to measure your content performance.* Retrieved from https://www.semrush.com/blog/measure-your-digital-content-performance/

Pinterest. (2020). *Pinterest Q419 Earnings Report.* Retrieved August 23, 2021, from https://s23.q4cdn.com/958601754/files/doc_financials/2019/q4/2019-Q4-IR-Earnings-Presentation-12320.pdf

Ramakrishnan, V. (2020). *What does a social media analyst do?* Retrieved from https://www.falcon.io/insights-hub/topics/social-media-strategy/what-does-a-social-media-analyst-do/

Rigby, C. (2017). *User-generated content helps lift sales for Dune London.* Retrieved from https://internetretailing.net/themes/user-generated-content-helps-lift-sales-for-dune-london

Roy, A. (2019). *Why Twitter is still important for your business.* Retrieved from https://clutch.co/agencies/social-media-marketing/resources/why-twitter-still-important-your-business#:~:text=Businesses%20should%20invest%20in%20Twitter,platforms%20based%20on%20active%20users

Sehl, K. (2019a). *How to use WeChat for business: A guide for marketers.* Retrieved from https://blog.hootsuite.com/wechat-marketing/

Sehl, K. (2019b). *How to use Pinterest for business: 8 strategies you need to know.* Retrieved from https://blog.hootsuite.com/how-to-use-pinterest-for-business/.

Shareef, M. A., Mukerji, B., Alryalat, M. A. A., Wright, A., & Dwivedi, Y. K. (2018). Ads on Facebook: Identifying the persuasive elements in the development of positive attitudes in consumers. *Journal of Retailing and Consumer Services, 43*, 258–268.

Sharma, L. (2017). *5 ways to encourage user generated content on social media.* Retrieved from https://www.socialmediatoday.com/social-business/5-ways-encourage-user-generated-content-social-media

Simpson, J., Ohri, L., & Lobaugh, K. (2016). *The new digital divide: The future of digital influence in retail*. Retrieved from https://www2.deloitte.com/us/en/insights/industry/retail-distribution/digital-divide-changing-consumer-behavior.html

Skrovan, S. (2017). *Why researching online, shopping offline is the new norm*. Retrieved from https://www.retaildive.com/news/why-researching-online-shopping-offline-is-the-new-norm/442754//

Stewart, T. (2018). *Case study: Estée Lauder looks to Instagram influencers on multi-brand campaign*. Retrieved from https://mobilemarketingmagazine.com/case-study-estee-lauder-companies-visual-amplifiers-vamp-instagram-influencer-marketing

Tafesse, W. (2016). An experiential model of consumer engagement in social media. *Journal of Product and Brand Management, 25*(5), 424–434.

Tafesse, W. (2020). YouTube marketing: How marketers' video optimization practices influence video views. *Internet Research, 30*(6), 1689–1707.

Teng, K. (2019). *Choosing the right social platforms for your business*. Retrieved from https://www.yellow.com.au/business-hub/choosing-the-right-social-platform-for-your-business/

Thomala, L. L. (2020). *Number of active WeChat messenger accounts Q2 2011-Q2 2020*. Retrieved from https://www.statista.com/statistics/255778/number-of-active-wechat-messenger-accounts/

Thomas, L. (2018). *Estée Lauder companies' influencer marketing campaign provides social strategy insights*. Retrieved from https://www.bandt.com.au/estee-lauder-companies-influencer-marketing-campaign-provides-social-strategy-insights/

Twitter. (2019). *Q3 2019 letter to shareholders*. Retrieved from https://s22.q4cdn.com/826641620/files/doc_financials/2019/q3/Q3-2019-Shareholder-Letter.pdf

Vrountas, T. (2019). *4 reasons why you can't ignore Facebook advertising*. Retrieved from https://instapage.com/blog/4-reasons-facebook-advertising-cant-be-ignored

Vrountas, T. (2020). *User-generated content: Why it's effective and how to use it in your marketing campaigns*. Retrieved from https://instapage.com/blog/what-is-user-generated-content

Wojcik, S., & Hughes, A. (2019). *Sizing up Twitter users*. Retrieved from https://www.pewresearch.org/internet/2019/04/24/sizing-up-twitter-users/

Wolfe, J. (2018). *Want faster airline customer service? Try tweeting*. Retrieved from https://www.nytimes.com/2018/11/20/travel/airline-customer-service-twitter.html

Wouters, C. (2016). *The effect of negative user-generated content on consumer-based brand equity: Comparing brand loyal versus non-loyal customers in the luxury wine market*. Master dissertation, University of Cape Town.

Xu, X., & Pratt, S. (2018). Social media influencers as endorsers to promote travel destinations: An application of self-congruence theory to the Chinese generation Y. *Journal of Travel and Tourism Marketing, 35*(7), 958–972.

.

# Optimizing the Use of Four Major Social Media Platforms

8

## 8.1 Facebook

Facebook is an ideal social media platform for achieving significant sales and maximizing business value. First, Facebook can enable a firm to reach one-fifth of the world's population (Vrountas, 2019). Facebook daily active users (DAU) reached a staggering 1.7 billion in the first quarter of 2020 (Facebook, 2020). In terms of monthly active users (MAU), Facebook users outnumber the total users of Twitter, Instagram, Pinterest, and LinkedIn combined (Vrountas, 2019). Second, Facebook can be very precise on reaching target customers. The ad targeting options of Facebook include, among others, demographics, interests, behaviors, and connections (Kim, 2019). For example, Facebook allows firms to target a specific segment of customers (34–44 years old, married, unemployed housewives who live in a specific US city). Third, customers regard Facebook as a key source for purchasing information. On average, Facebook users click one ad every 3 days (Newberry, 2019a, 2019b). This Facebook statistic also implies that users pay attention to Facebook ads, rather than just tuning ads out (Newberry, 2019a, 2019b). Furthermore, Facebook takes the lion's share (80.4%) of US social referral to e-commerce sites in comparison to other platforms: Instagram (10.7%), Pinterest (8.2%), Reddit (0.4%), and Twitter (0.3%) (eMarketer, 2019). In terms of e-commerce business owners, Facebook can be used to advertise their websites to increase website traffic. Finally, Facebook introduces additional features such as "Website Custom Audiences" to increase remarketing effectiveness (Vrountas, 2019). A firm's remarketing effort is providing marketing communication to people who have previously visited its website or platform. Considering that purchase abandonment is commonplace for many e-commerce companies, effective remarketing is crucial for firms to capture value from customers who could have purchased products on their website previously. The Website Custom Audiences feature enables marketers to inject a snippet of HTML code onto their webpages, and then, marketers can display Facebook ads to people who would visit those webpages (Vrountas, 2019). According to a recent report, Facebook had nine million active

F. J. Martínez-López et al., *Social Media Monetization*, Future of Business and Finance, https://doi.org/10.1007/978-3-031-14575-9_8

advertisers (Clement, 2020). In summary, Facebook is a top-performing social media platform for advertising and other business campaigns.

### 8.1.1  Facebook's Algorithm on Promoting and Demoting Posts and How to Increase the Visibility of Posts

Before a firm begins posting commercials on Facebook, they need to understand how the algorithm works, i.e., which and how posts are chosen to be presented to viewers. By publishing interesting content that can always be shown to target customers, the firm's Facebook marketing campaign can be deemed effective and meaningful. In a nutshell, three key factors work hand in hand to push a post to a viewer: (a) information regarding who a viewer usually interacts with; (b) the media format in the post (e.g., video, link, and photograph); and (c) the popularity of a post (Cooper, 2020). Furthermore, Facebook also provides surveys for users to determine which posts are more preferable for them. To leverage the Facebook algorithm, the following actions are recommended:

1. *Creating Engaging Posts Is Key to Increasing the Visibility of Such Posts on Facebook.* All approaches to improve the Facebook algorithm for the firm are centered on increasing user engagement. In order to get a firm's posts ranked in the News Feed, the firm needs to create posts that attract user comments and/or instigate user sharing and conversations (Ennis-O'Connor, 2018). However, firms should be wary of using click bait to get more clicks or views. The Facebook algorithm can identify and demote click baits. The posts that encourage responding with a single word or an emoji will be demoted by Facebook (Ennis-O'Connor, 2018).
2. *Well-Timed Posts Get More Visibility on Facebook.* The most appropriate time to post on Facebook is whenever a firm's audience is most likely to see and engage with its content (Tien & Aynsley, 2019). Facebook promotes newly created posts for audiences. For example, on the basis of Facebook data, the best time to post B2B brand content on Facebook is between 9:00 and 14:00 EST on Tuesday, Wednesday, or Thursday (Tien & Aynsley, 2019).
3. *Video Content Is Currently the Most Prevalent Media Format on Facebook.* About 69% of marketers report that video content performs best on Facebook ad campaigns (Dopson, 2019). In terms of video length, it is recommended that a firm limits branded videos between 15 and 90 s (Regev, 2019). When a video hits 90 s in length, user engagement begins to decrease considerably (Forte, 2019).
4. *Posting Consistency Can Ensure Sustainable Customer Engagement.* A social media marketer needs to keep her posts consistently showing up in the audience's News Feed. This is the key to engaging the audience on Facebook (Cooper & Tien, 2020). Professionals suggest using a social media calendar to ensure the consistency of social media posting. A social media calendar is a well-organized and scheduled social media marketing plan for arranging social media posts distributed across dates. Planning out social media calendar months in advance

and scheduling posts ahead of time will save social media marketers from finding trends and viral events and searching for ideas every day (Aboulhosn, 2020). Using a social media calendar is able to guarantee the consistency of posting on Facebook (Cooper & Tien, 2020).

5. *Facebook Paid Ads Are More Effective in Reaching Customers.* The Facebook algorithm has been oriented toward offering more meaningful social media content for users. Therefore, commercial content less relevant to users is not encouraged to be shown in users' News Feed. However, Facebook advertising features allow firms to reach target customers by employing specific customer profiles. Facebook ads can get a firm's branded content in front of the people who most likely desire such a firm's offerings (Newberry, 2019a, 2019b). Because Facebook advertising is a major approach for many firms to reach customers, its use will discussed in further detail in a later section.

6. *Power of Facebook Social Networks Can Be Leveraged to Increase the Reach of Social Posts.* Information sharing on Facebook offers users the opportunity to maintain relationships and express themselves (French & Read, 2013). Facebook is often used to share information about users' daily activities (Cho et al., 2015). Hence, it is recommended that firms offer information and messages that can benefit viewers' online social life. For example, a firm can express a specific suggestion about a healthy lifestyle, and this opinion may resonate with its Facebook followers. Then, followers may be willing to adopt this suggestion and share the Facebook post with their contacts and groups to share the healthy lifestyle suggestion.

## 8.1.2 Facebook Advertising

Facebook ads are a specific ad form that uses Facebook's advertising solution. Facebook describes its advertising solution as follows:

> With a few clicks, you can run ads across Facebook, Instagram, Audience Network and Messenger. By making a single campaign, you can reach people on all of their favourite apps and websites.[1]

Based on this definition, Facebook's advertising feature not only works for ads running on Facebook, but also includes ads running on other platforms owned by Facebook Inc. As previously mentioned, Facebook paid ads are effective for reaching target customers because organic content that firms generate for commercial purposes is less likely to appear in users' News Feed according to the current Facebook algorithm. Facebook has various ad targeting options. Overall, Facebook's ad targeting options are comprised of demographics, interests, behaviors,

---

[1] see Facebook's official introduction: https://www.facebook.com/business/ads

connections, and remarketing (Lister, 2020).[2] In this section, we discuss how to effectively run advertising campaigns on Facebook.

### 8.1.2.1 Set Campaign Objectives for Facebook Ads

Setting campaign objectives in Facebook can help Facebook optimize a firm's ads for the outcomes the firm desires (Gotter, 2019). There are currently 11 Facebook campaign objectives which can be categorized into three classes: awareness, consideration, and conversion (Gotter, 2019). The following explanations of campaign objectives and specific business goals are adapted from Facebook for Business (n. d.).

(A) Awareness. The awareness objective aims to arouse public interest in a firm's products. This objective can be further broken down into two specific objectives: brand awareness and reach.
   (A1) Brand Awareness: increase customers' awareness of a firm's brand.
   (A2) Reach: expose a firm's ad to as many people as possible in the audience that the firm defined.
(B) Consideration. The consideration objective aims to prompt people to think about a firm's product or service and search for more information.
   (B1) Traffic: lead people from Facebook to any URL the firm chooses, such as a website's landing page, a shopping app, or other appropriate information source.
   (B2) Engagement: reach customers who are more likely to engage with the firm's post. Engagement entails likes, comments, and shares.
   (B3) App Installs: lead people to the app store where they can download the firm's app.
   (B4) Video Views: share videos of a firm's business with Facebook users likely to watch the video.
   (B5) Lead Generation: generate leads for a firm's business. The ads will collect information from customers who are interested in the firm's product such as subscriptions for business solutions.
   (B6) Messages: communicate with prospects to cultivate interests in a firm's business.
(C) Conversion. The conversion objective focuses on how to encourage people who are interested in the firm's business or offering to purchase or use the firm's product or service.
   (C1) Conversions[3]: encourage people to take a specific action on the firm's site, such as adding an item to a shopping cart, downloading a game app, registering for an e-commerce site, or buying an item directly.

---

[2] For more details about Facebook's ad targeting options, please see Lister (2020).

[3] Facebook for Business (n.d.) defines a goal "conversion" (C1) for the campaign objective "conversion" (C). We do not think that a specific goal should be labeled as its upper objective;

(C2) Catalog Sales: present products from a firm's online shopping store's catalog to generate sales.

(C3) Store Traffic: promote store information to people in the vicinity of a physical store.

### 8.1.2.2 Understand Facebook's Ad Targeting Strategy and Define the Target Audience

As previously mentioned, Facebook offers several targeting options to help firms find prospects. Firms can use these options to target specific customers such as 25- to 35-year-old female customers. In particular, we introduce a specific targeting option that is easily overlooked by firms.

In practice, there are many shoppers who visit a firm's e-commerce website and select products on such website, but then leave without making a purchase. In order to minimize these cases, firms can try using Facebook Pixel. Facebook Pixel is a code that a firm can plug into the backend of their website (Lee, 2018). The code tracks users' online behaviors on the website, so the firm can target website visitors based on their online behaviors (Lee, 2018). Pixel allows firms to retarget users who have abandoned a shopping cart, who have viewed the product webpage or who have subscribed to online campaigns (Lee, 2018).

However, this remarketing approach could entail an ethical issue. Is it ethical that Facebook collects user behaviors on other websites and uses such behaviors as a basis to conduct more precise remarketing activities? In other words, is it ethical that Facebook rolls out Facebook Pixel for firms or brands to retarget potential customers? In recent years, Facebook has been criticized because they monetize users' data without their consent, which constitutes a serious threat to their data security and privacy. This breach of privacy could lead to a loss of Facebook users. Therefore, this data-driven business model may need to be refined in the future. In the long term, the Facebook business model has to be amended to focus on fostering user trust, which implies that user privacy and data security are as crucial as monetization (Burt, 2019). In particular, user trust and monetization go hand in hand for Facebook's long-term success (Burt, 2019).

### 8.1.2.3 Set Ad Placements on Facebook

Facebook offers several places for paid ad placement. Research reveals that where a firm places their ads can change the click-through rates (CTRs) by around 400% (Animalz, 2019a, 2019b). As higher CTRs are associated with higher conversions rates, different Facebook ad placements could result in different marketing consequences such as different conversion rates (Animalz, 2019a, 2019b). In this section, we discuss various Facebook ad placements.

---

calling them "actions," for instance, would be more suitable because this specific objective aims to elicit Facebook users' specific actions.

1. Ads in News Feed

   Placing ads in Facebook News Feed is one of the most popular ad placement options. If a firm decides to place their ads in Facebook News Feed, its ad will appear in Facebook users' News Feed. This placement option is effective for advertising because ads appear as regular Facebook posts. However, it can also be a relatively expensive option because Facebook charges per 1000 ad impressions (Lawrance, 2019). The advertising fee is closely tied to how many impressions are achieved.

2. Ads in Facebook right column

   Facebook layout has changed significantly since it began. Facebook now leaves less room for right column ads. It has promoted more native ad places for News Feed ads. But research revealed that right column ads can achieve up to three times more user engagement when used in tandem with News Feed ads (Animalz, 2019a, 2019b). Right column ads, while more expensive than News Feed ads (Animalz, 2019a, 2019b), are recommended when a firm attempts to convert shoppers who have previously visited its website, into buyers (Animalz, 2019a, 2019b). Hence, right column ads are more effective when Facebook Pixel is used to retarget potential customers.

3. Ads in Instant Articles

   Instant Articles are a native format in which publishers publish instant and interactive articles on Facebook. On mobile devices, instant articles load four times faster than regular mobile website links, and instant articles can drive a traffic lift of approximately 44% t.[4] Facebook allows firms to place an ad every 350 words in each Instant Article (Constine, 2017). A firm should therefore create an audience network and customize its ad placements in its Instant Articles so that these ads can be shown to the audience network.

4. In-Stream Video Ads

   Facebook in-stream ads can be placed before, during, or after video content shared on Facebook. This ad placement is quite similar to YouTube ads. The Facebook in-stream videos placement allows a firm to deliver 5–15 s video ads for users watching videos on Facebook (Lawrance, 2019). The biggest issue associated with this ad placement is that it interrupts Facebook users' video-watching experiences (Lawrance, 2019). It is expected that in-stream videos ads may not get much user engagement compared to other ad placements such as News Feed ads (Lawrance, 2019).

5. Messenger Ads

   As said in the bestselling book, *The Cluetrain Manifesto,* "markets are conversations" (Levine et al., 2009). Accordingly, marketing should be framed in a human voice instead of in purposeful promotions (Levine et al., 2009). In other words, today's customers are unlikely to passively receive obsolete and uniform content. They prefer to access digital content that is more interactive and

---

[4]Data are taken from Facebook. Please see Facebook's advertising solutions: https://www. facebook.com/formedia/solutions/instant-articles

communicative. Facebook Messenger is a real-time messaging platform that allows users to have conversations with others. Messenger ads are essentially messages containing commercial information, which are quite different from conventional News Feed ads. Facebook reported that 53% of customers are more likely to purchase items from a firm or a brand if they can message them (Smith, 2019). The first type of Messenger ad is sponsored message ads. This ad placement allows a firm to deliver sponsored message ads directly to users who had conversations with the firm (McHale, 2020; Lawrance, 2019). The second type of Messenger ad is Messenger home ads. Messenger home ads are a banner ad that is presented in the Messenger home menu (McHale, 2020). As Facebook Messenger leaves messages in users' inboxes, message ads can achieve higher customer engagement in contrast to other Facebook ads. Also, as Messenger ads send real-time notifications to users, firms can reach targeted customers faster (Smith, 2019).

### 8.1.2.4 Set Ad Budgets and Schedule on Facebook

Before spending money on Facebook ads, firms should understand Facebook's ad display mechanism. In a traditional advertising model (e.g., a newspaper), advertisers need to purchase an ad position for displaying their ads. As ad positions are limited and there could be several advertisers vying for positions, displaying an advertiser's ad depends on whether such advertiser's ad bid is higher than other competitors. Facebook's ad display mechanism is similar. An ad auction is used to determine which ad is shown to a user at a particular moment. The major nuance between Facebook's ad auction and a traditional ad auction is that the winning ad is not solely determined by the highest bid that an advertiser offers. In order to win an ad auction, the following three factors are considered[5]:

(a) *Bid*. The bid that an advertiser offers for an ad can help determine whether such an ad will win the auction or not. Basically, the more an advertiser is willing to pay for displaying their ad, the more likely it is that the ad will win the auction. The special part of Facebook's ad auction is that the winning ad may not be the highest bid. Facebook also takes user-centered factors into account.

(b) *Estimated Action Rates*. The action rate refers to an estimated rate at which a particular Facebook user will take an action (e.g., purchase and download) when facing the ad. According to Facebook, this rate is the likelihood that displaying an ad to a user generates the expected outcome of the advertiser.

(c) *Ad Quality*. The ad quality is measured by several sources such as feedback from users viewing or hiding the ad and other ad attributes (e.g., withholding information). The higher quality the ad, the more likely the ad will be shown to a user.

---

[5]The factors that determine whether an ad can win the ad auction are adapted from Facebook's Business Help Center. The original webpage is: https://www.facebook.com/business/help/4302911 76997542?id=561906377587030

In contrast to a traditional ad auction, the uniqueness of Facebook's ad auction is that Facebook ads are quite personalized. As Facebook users' digital time and personal energy are limited, Facebook has to decide which ad is most meaningful and relevant for each user. Each time a Facebook user is exposed to a Facebook ad, an ad auction occurs automatically to decide which ad to show to the user next on the basis of three factors mentioned previously. This user-centered ad auction guarantees the success of Facebook's advertising business.

A firm's Facebook advertising budget is divided into daily budgets and lifetime budgets. When a daily budget is set for a Facebook ad, a maximum monetary amount is set for Facebook to run a firm's ad each day (Morgan, 2020). In other words, in the daily budget mode, Facebook will try to spend the limited ad budget every day. In contrast, when a lifetime budget is set for a Facebook ad, the ad budget will be spent for the entire campaign (Morgan, 2020). In the lifetime budget mode, there is no limit on the budget of a particular day. If an ad performs exceptionally during a particular day, Facebook tends to consume more of the budget to win more ad auctions and reach more customers. Hence, the lifetime budget can amplify the impact of the ad on certain days. If the ad did not have many impacts on a certain day, Facebook would become more conservative in consuming the budget. In daily budget mode, advertisers need to schedule their ads and set an end date for the ad campaign (Morgan, 2020). Advertisers need to study their target customer behavior, sales, and market trends to customize the ad scheduling. It is preferable to turn ads on when an advertiser's target audience is online. On the lifetime budget mode, advertisers can select hours and dates for Facebook to deliver their ads to users.

### 8.1.2.5 Define Ad Formats, Insert Ad Content, and Launch Facebook Campaigns

Previously, we have discussed campaign objectives, targeting options, ad placements, ad budgets, and schedules. The final step in creating a Facebook ad is defining ad formats, inserting ad content, and launching the advertising campaigns.

First, advertisers need to define the ad format. Facebook currently offers these ad formats: image, video, slideshow, carousel, and collection.[6] Here, we focus on carousel ads and collection ads. Carousel ads are an ad format that allows up to ten images or videos to be displayed within a single ad (Animalz, 2019a, 2019b; Donnelly, 2020). Facebook users can browse carousel ads with a swipe-through menu (Animalz, 2019a, 2019b). On the surface, collections ads are similar to carousel ads, allowing multiple images or videos to be displayed in a single ad (Animalz, 2019a, 2019b). But collection ads are created for e-commerce and product discovery (Animalz, 2019a, 2019b). Tapping on images in collection ads can lead users instantly to a product webpage, where the purchase can be eventually completed.

---

[6]The discussion on Facebook ad formats is adapted from the website of Facebook for Business: https://www.facebook.com/business/learn/lessons/tips-for-choosing-the-right-ad-format?ref=search_new_0#

Second, firms need to create ad content based on the given ad format. Despite the fact that we have placed a lot of emphasis how firms can extract maximum value from Facebook ads by using Facebook advertising features, the most crucial factor of running a successful advertising campaign is developing quality ad content. Facebook users are similar to all other social media users in that high-quality ad content is more appealing. Furthermore, quality ad content will determine ad viewers' value perceptions about the ad and also increase trust in the ad content (Bakr & Tolba, 2016).

Following these choices, the advertising campaign is ready to launch. Facebook will deliver ads to specific customers at the given placements on the basis of the budget mode. As Facebook's commercial features have been imitated by many other social media platforms, the following sections will not detail similar features that are shared by other social media platforms.

## 8.2  Instagram

### 8.2.1  Instagram's Most Important Updates for Social Commerce

Instagram Shopping[7] is Instagram's most crucial function for enabling firms and brands to achieve monetization through e-commerce. Instagram has reported that 70% of shopping enthusiasts use Instagram to discover products. Instagram found that, when Instagram users were inspired by an item found on Instagram, they would attempt to purchase the item immediately. Instagram Shopping is not a single shopping feature on Instagram. It is a set of features across Instagram that allow users to shop through media content wherever they are in the platform: (a) Shop, a storefront on a business profile page that can be customized and allow viewers to shop directly on the profile page; (b) Shopping Tag, a tag that can be used by firms to highlight products from their catalog in stories and in-feed; (c) Instagram Shop, an e-commerce-style in-app shopping destination where users can discover items and brands they love from across Instagram; (d) Collections, a feature that allows firms to organize products into themes; (e) Product Detail Page, an Instagram page that displays all important information on a product including pricing, descriptions, and media; (f) Shopping Ads, an advertising feature by which firms can reach customers at scale by increasing the online presence of their social posts; (g) Checkout on Instagram, a shopping feature that allows users to purchase items securely and seamlessly using Facebook Pay without leaving social media; (h) Live Shopping, a livestreaming channel for firms to sell items through Instagram Live.

---

[7]This section is adapted from Instagram's shopping solution: https://business.instagram.com/shopping. Firms that are interested in Instagram shopping are welcome to visit this website to access more information about this key function.

## 8.2.2   Instagram Stories

Instagram Stories allow a user to share photos and videos to their "Story" which is accessible to the user's followers. Instagram Stories will disappear 24 h after being released (Bernazzani, 2020). This ephemeral feature has become Instagram users' favorite: 500 million users use Instagram Stories every day (Functionalmedia, 2020). One in four Millennials and Gen Z-ers look for stories of the products and services they want to buy (Functionalmedia, 2020). Instagram Stories are also created on the firms' side: One-third of the most viewed Instagram Stories are from firms (Functionalmedia, 2020).

In this section, we will illustrate how firms can employ Instagram features to boost sales of products displayed in Instagram Stories. First, adding shoppable stickers to Instagram Stories can create a seamless shopping experience for customers and boost online sales. The use of shoppable stickers can helps firms to tag products from their inventory or e-commerce site in the story (Carbone, 2019). The stickers can be a shopping bag icon or a textual sticker that is shown in the story (Carbone, 2019). When customers click the shoppable sticker, they can see the item name, price, and description (Carbone, 2019). Second, Instagram rolls out countdown stickers by which firms elicit the interest of followers and get more traction with their promotion events and sales activities (Chacon, 2018). When a firm shares a story about an upcoming event such as an in-store sale or new product launch, the firm can add a countdown sticker that will count down to a set date and time (Chacon, 2018). In particular, this countdown feature allows the firm's followers to subscribe to the countdown event, which will send them a notification when the countdown ends (Chacon, 2018). Finally, Instagram can display the marketing effectiveness of a firm's Instagram Story. Basically, Instagram displays how many shares, replies, profile visits, and sticker taps each story generates; it also shows how many impressions, follows, and leads each story creates. It is noteworthy that Instagram only saves these metrics for 2 weeks (Warren, 2020). Firms can leverage other social media marketing analytic products to get extensions with regard to the duration of social media metrics (Warren, 2020).

## 8.2.3   Instagram Live Shopping

Live Shopping, an interactive and remote shopping mode, is one of the most important Instagram updates. As people have become accustomed to social distancing and online meeting due to the outbreak of COVID-19, Live Shopping became a new shopping trend. Instagram is a front runner among social media platforms in terms of livestream e-commerce. In contrast to traditional e-commerce, real-time interactions are a crucial characteristic of livestream e-commerce (Ko & Chen, 2020). Livestreamers can use this Instagram feature to immediately interact with viewers and sell items via an "Add to Bag" button at the bottom of the livestream. If viewers are interested in the item and click this button, the item will be added to their "shopping bag" and the purchase can be made via Checkout on Instagram. For example, Beauty influencer Nikita Dragun attracted approximately 43,000 of her 8.3 million followers to a Live Shopping event about a beauty tutorial of her branded product (Flora, 2020). This livestream achieved 33,000 product page impressions, and 5000 products were added to customers' shopping bags (Flora, 2020).

Despite the fact that livestream e-commerce is now surging, this novel e-commerce mode will be a strategic wave of the future for small businesses. Instagram Live Shopping is a strategic enabler for small business owners to offer sophisticated real-time content for their customers. They can simultaneously react to customers' comments and inquiries. As customer needs and doubts are recognized and effectively responded to, small business owners are better able to serve customers and achieve higher sales.

## 8.3   WeChat

### 8.3.1   The Business Value in Chinese Markets

WeChat is a social media and messaging app mainly targeting at consumers in China. WeChat was released as a messaging app around a decade ago by its parent company Tencent (Sehl, 2019a, 2019b). It quickly became "an app for everything," offering users gaming, ridesharing, e-shopping, and e-government services (Sehl, 2019a, 2019b). The WeChat monthly active users (MAU) are currently over 1.2 billion (Thomala, 2020). Allen Zhang, the creator of WeChat, asserted that many Chinese media users spend approximately one-third of their online time on WeChat (see Li, 2019). Firms interested in a country with no access to Facebook, Instagram, and Twitter can leverage this app to reach new users and increase monetization.

### 8.3.2   Using WeChat for Business

Firms first need to create a WeChat business account. In the WeChat ecosystem, there are four types of business accounts: Subscription Account, Service Account, Mini Program, and WeChat Work. The Subscription Account is used to broadcast content to all of a firm's followers. This account is particularly suitable for media companies or brands. Firms can post once a day with one to six articles at the time of each publishing (Chinese Social Media, 2019). The post is framed as a content menu on which followers tap to view one or more articles. According to one study, over 32% of official account operators have sold merchandise, about 40% offered customer services or public services, and approximately 34% cut down communication costs by over 30% (China Academy of Information and Communications Technology Industry and Planning Research Institute, 2018).

The Service Account focuses on offering e-service. It allows firms to access the service functions that Wechat offers: WeChat Pay, WeChat Stores, Instant Customer Service, geo-location services, HTML 5 campaigns, posting four times per month (one to six articles at once) with push notifications, WeChat Mini Programs, Voice recognition, URL shortening, and multiple QR codes per account (Chinese Social Media, 2019). Service Account owners can communicate with followers via WeChat, which is quite similar to Facebook Messenger. For example, customers can ask questions about a product or a service by messaging the Service Account. If Service Account owners insert AI-powered chatbots for customer service, customers who make an inquiry can get automated answers immediately. If customers are not satisfied with automated answers, a human customer service agent will respond to customer inquiries. We can see that WeChat purposefully creates a more socially focused online browsing experience for users by imposing a restriction on the number of posts for Service Accounts and Subscription Accounts. This restriction also forces firms to produce high-quality content to engage customers.

The WeChat Work account is most suitable for corporate users. WeChat Work is an enterprise social media solution. When a firm creates a WeChat Work account, its staff can use WeChat to clock in/out, have video conferences, make payments, and give administrative examinations and approvals, among other options. WeChat Work accounts can not only create a social media enterprise solution for internal organizational affairs, but also connect to external WeChat users. For example, many customers want to use WeChat to conveniently communicate with sales reps, but they do not want sales reps to access their social content shared that is shared on their WeChat. If a firm creates a WeChat Work account, a customer can add a sales rep as a WeChat Work friend which means that WeChat will be limited to a few business functions between the customer and the sales rep. The customer's online social circle is not available for the sales rep.

Creating a Mini Program account enables a firm to run an app in WeChat. For example, an e-commerce firm may want to reach all WeChat users. They can create a Mini Program account and develop a Mini Program for merchandising products via WeChat. Mini Programs is an on-demand app that users can use without installing it. The invention of Mini Programs brings about ease of use for apps that are not frequently used. This feature is particularly appealing for people who do not want their smartphone installed with an excessive number of many apps. In addition, WeChat is equipped with a payment function, so payments in WeChat can be completed without leaving WeChat. WeChat Mini Programs saw transactions of over 800 billion yuan (USD115 billion) in 2019, a considerable growth of 160% year over year (CIW Team, 2020). WeChat Mini Program daily active users (DAU) exceeded 400 million in Q1 2020 (CIW Team, 2020). These statistics show that WeChat Mini Programs can lead to extensive business opportunities.

Second, WeChat integrates online and offline information. This integration allows WeChat users to connect and access online and offline information simultaneously. For example, a fashion store embeds product promotions information into a quick response (QR) code and places this code in its store. When customers use WeChat to scan the code, they will access the webpage of the store's product promotions. The combined use of QR codes and WeChat allows firms to reach and serve customers offline. A firm can wrap their WeChat account in QR codes, so that any customers scanning these codes are able to follow its WeChat account and access customer service via WeChat. In short, WeChat's integral capability enables firms to extend their network, offer customer service, and nurture leads (Ross, 2020).

Third, advertising via WeChat is a good option. WeChat ads can be divided into Moment ads and Official Account ads. Moment ads are similar to Facebook's News Feed ads. Such ads are shown to WeChat users who browse social content shared by their friends. The Official Account ads are banner ads or card ads appearing at the bottom of a WeChat post. Advertisers do not have to place such ads in their posts. WeChat also allows such ads to appear in articles posted by other creators as long as article readers are target customers of such ads. WeChat ads' difference from Facebook ads lies in a restriction on ad placements. In many Chinese cities, only one Moment ad is allowed to be shown in each users' Moment. Each WeChat article basically only has one section to place an ad. This restriction demonstrates that WeChat developers do not want to over-monetize WeChat users, but rather focus on WeChat's social attributes instead of commercial attributes. Indeed, social networking sites are essentially a platform for users to connect to the world and their friends. This networking feature should be available for more people and increase the entire society's welfare by reducing transaction costs in networking, messaging, and making deals.

Finally, WeChat shows a high level of connectivity and compatibility. WeChat can connect to and be compatible with smart artifacts and information systems. For example, WeChat has partnered with Caesars Entertainment and Ayla Networks, creating a "Hotel Room of the Future" experience in Las Vegas (Hwei, 2015). WeChat enables hotel customers to control the room's facilities (Hwei, 2015): WeChat enables users to dim lights, open blinds, adjust room temperature, and lock doors, among other options (Hwei, 2015). Because WeChat users can directly use this app to book hotels and make payments, this WeChat-based smart hotel solution is particularly useful for Chinese tourists in Las Vegas. WeChat plays a key digital assistant role in a hotel visitor's entire journey, creating seamless consumption experiences.

## 8.4  Pinterest

Pinterest is an American image sharing and social media platform designed for the discovery of inspiration and ideas (Gershgorn, 2019). Pinterest is one of the most popular social apps in the USA. According to Pinterest's earnings report, during Q4 2019 Pinterest had 335 million monthly active users (MAUs) (Pinterest, 2020). Among these users, 73.7% are located outside the USA (Pinterest, 2020). Research reveals that 62% of Generation Z and Millennials want visual search capabilities to discover and identify the products quickly (ViSenze, 2018). Pinterest fulfills this customer demand using its image search capability. As a consequence, approximately 84% of weekly active users (WAUs) use Pinterest to help them decide what to buy and 83% of WAUs have made a purchase based on content they see from brands or firms on Pinterest (Sehl, 2019a, 2019b).

### 8.4.1  Key Terms in Pinterest Marketing

The following are key terms used in Pinterest marketing [adapted from Sehl (2019a, 2019b)]:

(a) Pins: The primary type of post published on Pinterest. Pins are a photograph, video, or text, and can link to a website source.
(b) Promoted Pins: Pins that firms pay for to increase their online visibility. Such pins will appear with a "Promoted" label.
(c) Rich Pins: Particular types of Pins that offer more information for the user including price to install buttons. Currently, there are four types of Rich Pins: Product Pins, Recipe Pins, Article Pins, and App Pins.
(d) Shop the Look Pins: A shoppable Pin in which firms can add product tags. Pinterest users can use such pins to shop by tapping on the white dots in the Pin.
(e) Boards: Used to group Pins around a certain theme or topic. For example, an apparel brand can use Boards to present all branded dresses.
(f) Group Boards: Boards that can be edited by more than one person. Group Boards are particularly suitable for consumers to co-create branded content for a firm's marketing purposes.
(g) Audience Insights: Pins analytics that Pinterest business accounts have access to. Firms can use this function to track the key metrics of their advertising campaign.
(h) Pinterest Lens: A visual search feature that allows users to take a picture and access relevant content on Pinterest.
(i) Pincodes: QR codes that can be scanned and that link viewers to a firm's board of profiles.

### 8.4.2  Tips to Improve Pinterest Marketing

First, firms need to understand that Pinterest can provide a unique browsing experience for customers. Pinterest is designed to inspire users and create a collection of visual content. Many firms have noticed the power of social networking sites and have added a "Share it on Facebook" button or a "Tweet it" button on their product webpages. But in most circumstances, other social media platforms do not organize and display social media content in an organized fashion; i.e., a branded post is usually mixed with other irrelevant posts. In contrast, Pinterest is different. The image sharing platform will organize and present images in a coordinated manner. For example, when users are searching for shoes on Pinterest, a firm's shoe images will be presented with other similar shoes images. Machine learning or artificial intelligence technology is behind this function. Hence, customer engagement is enhanced by organized images.

Second, lighter- and warm-colored images are more preferable than dark in most circumstances. Research shows that lighter- and warm-colored images are more re-pinned than darker images (Gotter, 2016). We are not implying that darker- and cold-colored images should never be used. We merely provide evidence that lighter-and warm- colored images seem to be more attractive in the eyes of most Pinterest users. The choice of a product image's color framing should be congruent with its target customers, brand, advertising campaign, and communication platforms.

Third, Pinterest Boards can be used for marketing. Firms could not only pin more images, but also actively use Boards to bundle together relevant product images. For example, beauty brand Glossier creates individual Boards for lip, brow, and other makeup ideas (Sehl, 2019a, 2019b). Glossier creates a Board called "Makeup Ideas: Lips." In the Board, customers can find inspiration for the lip look they desire. The Glossier Board currently has 71,150 followers.

Fourth, search engine optimization (SEO) is necessary for Pinterest marketing. As previously mentioned, Pinterest is a visually focused platform. A tremendous amount of visual content is produced and shared every day. It is difficult to search for images when most searches are text-based. Hence, how do a firm's Pins or other visual contents stand out? SEO is the key to increasing such content's discoverability on Pinterest. In order to optimize the visual search results of a firm's Pin or Board, it is important for the firm to name the Pin or Board creatively and precisely. Precise keywords and creative descriptions are beneficial in creating a SEO-friendly Pin or Board. For example, IKEA USA created an interesting description for its Board "Living Rooms": "Your living room is where you share your life with others. Fill it with comfortable seating and stylish décor for your family and friends to enjoy. Browse for IKEA living room ideas that fit every size space and budget."[8] In this description, IKEA adds keywords that are relevant to the brand and products, such as "living room," "comfortable seating," "stylish décor," and "IKEA living room ideas" to facilitate the discoverability of this Board (Gilbert, 2020). Moreover, optimal ratios should be taken into consideration when creating Pins (Gilbert, 2020). The most popular choice for a picture is 2:3 ratio or $600 \times 900$ pixels (Gilbert, 2020). With the prevalence of mobile phones, more and more people are accustomed to using mobile social apps. Hence, vertical Pins should be more comfortable for mobile phone users. Accordingly, when a Pin is more agreeable to users, it is more likely to be discovered by users.

Last, Audience Insights and other Pinterest analytic tools can be used to assess the performance of a firm's Pinterest marketing. Pinterest offers insights about a firm's Pinterest profile and their audience. The platform also displays the outcomes (Impressions, RePins) of a firm's advertising campaign. By delving into the information, a firm can determine which campaign does or does not reach their expectation and make changes in their marketing plan accordingly.

In summary, we have presented how firms use four social media platforms for business. Despite the fact that there are numerous social media platforms, the

---

[8]The description of IKEA USA's Board "Living Rooms" can be seen at https://www.pinterest.com/IKEAUSA/living-rooms/. This Board is a successful case in Pinterest marketing, getting almost half a million followers. IKEA nicely organizes different Pins in different product segments. It is quite convenient for customers to find relevant furniture and décor on the Board.

selection of the social media platform is not the most important choice for the success of social media monetization. The key is what outcomes a firm expects to see and which customers a firm targets. The most engaging social media content can be simultaneously viewed at multiple social media channels by users. We use this chapter to demonstrate the different characteristics of four social media platforms. Our summary suggests that the best use of social media is to understand and fully leverage the different characteristics and features of these platforms. Based on our observations, Facebook remains the most influential platform for generating leads and earning profits.

## References

Aboulhosn, S. (2020). *How to create a social media calendar that works*. Retrieved from https://sproutsocial.com/insights/social-media-calendar/

Animalz. (2019a). *Facebook carousel ads and Facebook collection ads: The powerhouse combo*. Retrieved from https://adespresso.com/blog/facebook-ad-types-collection-ads-carousel/

Animalz. (2019b). *Everything you need to know about Facebook ad placement to improve conversions*. Retrieved from https://adespresso.com/blog/facebook-ad-placement-improve-conversions/

Bakr, Y., & Tolba, A. (2016). Antecedents to SMS advertising acceptance: A grounded theory approach. *International Journal of Internet Marketing and Advertising, 10*(1–2), 28–53.

Bernazzani, S. (2020). *Instagram stories: What they are and how to make one like a pro*. Retrieved from https://blog.hubspot.com/marketing/instagram-stories

Burt, A. (2019). *Can Facebook ever be fixed?* Retrieved from https://hbr.org/2019/04/can-facebook-ever-be-fixed

Carbone, L. (2019). *How to drive sales with shoppable Instagram stories stickers*. Retrieved from https://later.com/blog/shoppable-instagram-stories-stickers/

Chacon, B. (2018). *How to use the countdown sticker for Instagram stories*. Retrieved from https://later.com/blog/instagram-stories-countdown-sticker/

China Academy of Information and Communications Technology Industry and Planning Research Institute. (2018). *Build an innovative community of shared ecosystem and foster new drivers of economic growth*. Retrieved from https://www.dropbox.com/s/e2mge1oser0jbnk/WeChat%20Economic%20%26%20Social%20Impact%20Report%202017.pdf?dl=0&utm_source=CAICT+Report&utm_campaign=833b04783d-EMAIL_CAMPAIGN_2018_04_11&utm_medium=email&utm_term=0_afc2cd30e2-833b04783d-269754381

Chinese Social Media. (2019). *WeChat for business: Which account is best for me*. Retrieved from https://tenbagroup.com/wechat-for-business-which-account-is-best-for-me/

Cho, I., Park, H., & Kim, J. K. (2015). The relationship between motivation and information sharing about products and services on Facebook. *Behaviour and Information Technology, 34*(9), 858–868.

CIW Team. (2020). *WeChat statistical highlights 2020; mini program DAU >300m*. Retrieved from https://www.chinainternetwatch.com/30201/wechat-stats-2019/

Clement, J. (2020). *Number of active advertisers on Facebook 2016–2020*. Retrieved from https://www.statista.com/statistics/778191/active-facebook-advertisers/

Constine, J. (2017). *At least Facebook's unfair Instant Articles now let sites show more ads*. Retrieved from https://techcrunch.com/2017/03/09/deal-with-the-blue-devil/?_ga=2.163816380.2029006907.1601976803-2043516331.1598023850

Cooper, P. (2020). *How the Facebook algorithm works in 2020 and how to make it work for you*. Retrieved from https://blog.hootsuite.com/facebook-algorithm/

Cooper, P., & Tien, S. (2020). *How to create a social media content calendar: Tips and templates.* Retrieved from https://blog.hootsuite.com/how-to-create-a-social-media-content-calendar/

Donnelly, G. (2020). *How to create awesome Facebook carousel ads that convert.* Retrieved from https://www.wordstream.com/blog/ws/2018/05/21/facebook-carousel-ads

Dopson, E. (2019). *The best Facebook ad content for driving awareness & sales.* Retrieved from https://databox.com/the-best-facebook-ad-content?utm_source=zest.is&utm_medium=referral&utm_term=zst.5c8445af8100a

eMarketer. (2019). *US social referral share to ecommerce sites, by platform, Q1 2019 (% of total).* Retrieved from https://www.emarketer.com/chart/227803/us-social-referral-share-ecommerce-sites-by-platform-q1-2019-of-total

Ennis-O'Connor, M. (2018). *How to increase organic reach and create more engaging content on Facebook.* Retrieved from https://medium.com/@JBBC/how-to-increase-organic-reach-and-create-more-engaging-content-on-facebook-28bcaef016b3

Facebook. (2020). *Facebook Q1 2020 results.* Retrieved from https://s21.q4cdn.com/399680738/files/doc_financials/2020/q1/Q1-2020-FB-Earnings-Presentation.pdf

Facebook for Business. (n.d.). *Help: Choose the right ad objective.* Retrieved from https://www.facebook.com/business/help/1438417719786914

Flora, L. (2020). *Instagram's livestream shopping sees early beauty adopters.* Retrieved from https://www.glossy.co/beauty/instagrams-livestream-shopping-sees-early-beauty-adopters/

Forte, J. (2019). *Beating the algorithm: 11 Essential Facebook video secrets.* Retrieved from https://www.jeffbullas.com/facebook-video-secrets/?utm_source=zest.is&utm_medium=referral&utm_term=zst.5c603cad953b0

French, A. M., & Read, A. (2013). My mom's on Facebook: An evaluation of information sharing depth in social networking. *Behaviour and Information Technology, 32*(10), 1049–1059.

Functionalmedia. (2020). *The 8 types of Instagram stories you need to be using.* Retrieved from https://functional-media.com/the-8-types-of-ig-stories-you-need-to-be-using/

Gershgorn, D. (2019). *Pinterest is distancing itself from social networks as it goes public.* Retrieved from https://qz.com/1579086/pinterest-is-distancing-itself-from-social-networks-as-it-goes-public/

Gilbert, H. (2020). *Pinterest SEO: 12 tips to optimize your pins for search.* Retrieved from https://later.com/blog/pinterest-seo/

Gotter, A. (2016). *26 tips to improve your Pinterest marketing.* Retrieved from https://www.socialmediaexaminer.com/26-tips-to-improve-your-pinterest-marketing/

Gotter, A. (2019). *How to choose the right Facebook objectives for every campaign.* Retrieved from https://www.disruptiveadvertising.com/social-media/facebook-objectives/

Hwei, L. (2015). *Control your hotel room via a WeChat app? It's possible.* Retrieved from https://vulcanpost.com/136211/wechat-ayla-networks-turns-phone-remote-hotel-room-future/

Kim, L. (2019). *How to be smart and precise with Facebook ad targeting.* Retrieved from https://medium.com/marketing-and-entrepreneurship/how-to-be-smart-and-precise-with-facebook-ad-targeting-90db67487f1b

Ko, H. C., & Chen, Z. Y. (2020). Exploring the factors driving live streaming shopping intention: A perspective of parasocial interaction. In *Proceedings of the 2020 International Conference on Management of e-Commerce and e-Government*, pp. 36–40.

Lawrance, C. (2019). *Facebook ad placements for marketers: How to make the right choices.* Retrieved from https://www.socialmediaexaminer.com/facebook-ad-placements-for-marketers-how-to-make-right-choices/

Lee, K. (2018). *How to master Facebook ad targeting & zero-in on your audience.* Retrieved from https://sproutsocial.com/insights/facebook-ad-targeting/

Levine, R., Locke, C., Searls, D., & Weinberger, D. (2009). *The cluetrain manifesto.* Basic Books.

Li, Y. (2019). *Mark Zuckerberg wants Facebook to emulate WeChat. Can it?* Retrieved from https://www.nytimes.com/2019/03/07/technology/facebook-zuckerberg-wechat.html

Lister, M. (2020). *All of Facebook's ad targeting options (in one epic infographic).* Retrieved from https://www.wordstream.com/blog/ws/2016/06/27/facebook-ad-targeting-options-infographic

McHale, B. (2020). *The ultimate guide to Facebook ad placement optimization.* Retrieved from https://www.wordstream.com/blog/ws/2018/01/08/facebook-ad-placement-optimization

Morgan, M. (2020). *Facebook ads daily vs. lifetime budgets: Pros & Cons.* Retrieved from https://www.wordstream.com/blog/ws/2019/02/19/facebook-ads-daily-vs-lifetime-budgets

Newberry, C. (2019a). *How to advertise on Facebook in 2020: The definitive Facebook ads guide.* Retrieved from https://blog.hootsuite.com/how-to-advertise-on-facebook/

Newberry, C. (2019b). *33 Facebook stats that matter to marketers in 2020.* Retrieved from https://blog.hootsuite.com/facebook-statistics/#advertising

Pinterest. (2020). *Pinterest Q419 earnings report.* Retrieved from https://s23.q4cdn.com/958601754/files/doc_financials/2019/q4/2019-Q4-IR-Earnings-Presentation-12320.pdf

Regev, Y. (2019). *10 expert tips to improve your Facebook video marketing.* Retrieved from https://www.socialmediatoday.com/news/10-expert-tips-to-improve-your-facebook-video-marketing/554182/

Ross, L. (2020). *Everything you need to know about WeChat QR codes for businesses.* Retrieved from https://www.chooseoxygen.com/en/blog/everything-you-need-to-know-about-wechat-qr-codes-for-businesses

Sehl, K. (2019a). *How to use Pinterest for business: 8 strategies you need to know.* Retrieved from https://blog.hootsuite.com/how-to-use-pinterest-for-business/

Sehl, K. (2019b). *How to use WeChat for business: A guide for marketers.* Retrieved from https://blog.hootsuite.com/wechat-marketing/

Smith, B. (2019). *4 ways Facebook messenger ads are awesome (& how to set them up).* Retrieved from https://www.wordstream.com/blog/ws/2017/10/31/facebook-messenger-ads

Thomala, L. L. (2020). *Number of active WeChat messenger accounts Q2 2011-Q2 2020.* Retrieved from https://www.statista.com/statistics/255778/number-of-active-wechat-messenger-accounts/

Tien, S., & Aynsley, M. (2019). *The best time to post on Facebook, Instagram, Twitter, and LinkedIn.* Retrieved from https://blog.hootsuite.com/best-time-to-post-on-facebook-twitter-instagram/#facebook

ViSenze. (2018). *New research from ViSenze finds 62 percent of generation Z and millennial consumers want visual search capabilities, more than any other new technology.* Retrieved from https://www.businesswire.com/news/home/20180829005092/en/New-Research-from-ViSenze-Finds-62-Percent-of-Generation-Z-and-Millennial-Consumers-Want-Visual-Search-Capabilities-More-Than-Any-Other-New-Technology

Vrountas, T. (2019). *4 reasons why you can't ignore Facebook advertising.* Retrieved from https://instapage.com/blog/4-reasons-facebook-advertising-cant-be-ignored

Warren, J. (2020). *The ultimate guide to Instagram stories for business.* Retrieved from https://later.com/blog/instagram-stories-for-business/#analytics

# Cases and Analyses of Companies Leveraging Social Media

**9**

This chapter aims to present the newest practices in social media marketing. We provide details of these practices and explain why the analyzed companies are considered winners in the era of social media. Nine cases of companies leveraging social media are introduced. This chapter focuses on how these companies use social media; therefore, their corporate strategy and business policy (matters of secondary interest for our purposes) are only concisely mentioned. We have included traditional retail brands such as Nike and Estée Lauder as well as online retailers such as Amazon and Pinduoduo. These companies have been chosen due to the success of their social media strategies.

## 9.1    Nike

Nike is an American brand that focuses on the design, development, marketing, and sale of sports apparel, equipment, and accessories. Personalization is a key in Nike's product design and marketing strategy. As social media is able to push personalized social ads and recommend content that meets users' personal needs, Nike has been proactively using social media to promote their products and services. Most importantly, Nike generates significant sales and customer equity via social media marketing. Nike, as a sport brand, needs to perform well on social media because sports are a sociable activity and sporting events can create a huge social media buzz in many circumstances (Jovana Banovic, 2011).

Nike is one of the most influential brands on social media. Since Nike first began using social media, the company has accumulated millions of followers. The origins behind such success are that Nike fleshed out a sophisticated social media marketing strategy from the beginning. Nike is a pioneer in this space having recognized that social media would play a determinant role in fashion brand marketing. The company has deployed a multiplatform strategy using Facebook, Twitter, and Instagram, among other platforms. For example, in 2010, Instagram had just rolled out. At that moment, many firms were unfamiliar with how to use the platform to market their

F. J. Martínez-López et al., *Social Media Monetization*, Future of Business and Finance, https://doi.org/10.1007/978-3-031-14575-9_9

products. In contrast, Nike was skilled in creating high-quality visual content. Nike's Instagram posts reached around 300,000 to 400,000 likes from followers, which was impressive with respect to social media practices at this time (Jovana Banovic, 2011). It appears that Nike has an inherently "social gene" in terms of using social media for marketing and branding purposes. Furthermore, Nike was exceedingly versatile in social media. For example, Nike Belgium was using QR codes in a social media campaign to promote its shoes by letting customers "like" different crazy-shaped jogging routes (Schonfeld, 2010). Nike accumulated "likes" for the Facebook campaign by letting customers scan QR codes in posters or on Nike store windows (Schonfeld, 2010). This approach to collecting "likes" was novel because it led in-store customers to online campaigns. Around 2011, Nike was increasingly aware that there was no one-size-fits-all social media marketing strategy. At that time, many brands were still using a single social media account to serve all customers. However, given a brand like Nike, which has numerous product lines from footwear to sports equipment, it was unlikely that all customers of different products could be reached with social media content produced by a single account. Nike has created specific accounts to target specific customers. It has created over 300 social media profiles related to a set of products and geolocations (Ravi, 2018a, 2018b). For example, on Twitter, Nike has its main social media account Nike (@nike) and also has the specific account Nike Basketball (@nikebasketball) to target basketball fans. Nike Basketball posts content directly related to basketball events or megastars, so content produced by Nike Basketball can generate higher engagement rates among basketball fans in contrast to content produced by Nike's major Twitter account. In order to promote its forthcoming new product LeBron 18, Nike Basketball tweeted "strive for greatness" and called out LeBron James (@kingjames) in the tweet. Basketball fans can see what basketball shoes their favorite superstar wears on the court. Nike Basketball also shared a page with inspiring words signed by LeBron James. Product promotion tweets related to this product received numerous likes in just a few days.

During 2013, Nike noticed that social media users were becoming more demanding. Users wanted social media content to be more visual and interactive. Photograph-focused Instagram posts were becoming more and more popular since mobile app versions of such social media platform became prevalent among worldwide smartphone users. Nike, accordingly, rolled out more visual and interactive Instagram content for its followers. One of the most successful Instagram marketing campaigns that Nike launched at this time was their PHOTOiD program. This program gave followers an option to create custom Nike footwear based on colors in their favorite Instagram photographs (Ditty, 2015; Heble, 2015). Basically, users could upload photographs to a Nike PHOTOiD landing page where they could automatically design their own custom shoes based on the colors displayed in the image (Ditty, 2015; Heble, 2015). This campaign was a great success among Nike's Instagram followers (Heble, 2015): More than 100,000 shoes were created by PHOTOiD users in the first week, and an 8% click-through rate was achieved to buy shoes on Nike ID.

A few years later, Nike continued to push forward their social media marketing by spending considerable amounts of money on social media marketing. They hired additional sport stars to promote the Nike brand and communicate its values and beliefs to social media followers. From Roger Federer and Rafa Nadal to LeBron James, Michael Jordan, and Cristiano Ronaldo, among other big names, Nike undoubtedly relies on sports megastars for their marketing purposes (Ravi, 2018a, 2018b). For example, in February 2017, Nike launched the "Equality" campaign during Black History Month and ran a video post featuring Serena Williams and LeBron James (Ravi, 2018a, 2018b). Nike did not solely spend money on such megastars; they also placed their attention on social media influencers. For example, social media influencers were recruited to promote Nike's new Air Vapormax series. Nike partnered with a father–son duo who ran a popular YouTube channel "What's Inside?" and were famous for cutting up objects to showcase what is inside (Influencer Marketing, 2020). In the campaign, the digital celebrities created several videos in which they used the branded messages in the individual themes of their channel, including a video where Nike Air Vapormax was cut to show what was inside the shoes (Influencer Marketing, 2020). This video was viewed more than 3.6 million times, and received 32,000 likes (Influencer Marketing, 2020). This social media campaign effectively created hype for the new product on social media.

Nike continues to further develop their social media marketing strategy. After intense social media marketing activities across several years, Nike has learned what social media content is most appealing for which customers (Relevantly, 2020). For example, if targeted customers are children, Nike's social media content will be entertaining and fun; if targeted customers are teenagers, Nike will design social media content transpiring pop culture and youth culture. Furthermore, the company has learned that monetization is not always direct and straightforward, e.g., creating sales by adding a buy button in a social post allowing customers to directly buy products they discovered in the post. Indirect monetization is more effective in terms of monetization performance. Nike can lead viewers who have viewed one of their social posts to their Facebook main page, wherein viewers can access more social media content created by the company (Relevantly, 2020). It is an interesting research question to further examine what factors determine this social media content referral strategy. In particular, it is interesting to study which viewers of certain social media content should be led to an e-commerce webpage to complete the purchase and which viewers are better directed to a social webpage or a brand information webpage to access more social or brand information.

To summarize, Nike has been very successful in social media marketing. The company has moved beyond social media as a channel. Social media has been framed as a value creation platform generating value with customers. Social media marketing should not be just a tool to catch consumers' attention. Nike has demonstrated that it can also be a source of competitive advantage.

## 9.2    Adidas

Adidas is a German multinational corporation focusing on designing and manufacturing sportswear, clothing, shoes, and sport equipment. Adidas is the second largest sports brand after Nike.

Facebook is a major battlefield between sports brands. In terms of football apparel and shoes, Nike used ex-Real-Madrid's superstar Cristiano Ronaldo in brand promotions, while Adidas brought Barcelona FC's superstar Lionel Messi to the fore of its marketing campaigns on Facebook (Joseph, 2013). Adidas was making Messi the sole star of its online football campaign and viewing Facebook as the primary marketing channel because the company looks to widen its lead over Nike in the burgeoning football apparel market (Joseph, 2013). Unlike other brands which mostly recruit celebrities to front social media campaigns, Adidas placed a major focus on the personal and direct involvement of influencers in the campaign planning process (Gilliland, 2017). In other words, Adidas has a close partnership with influencers. Influencers have their say in defining their social media marketing campaigns. Influencers are able to share social media content containing Adidas information in their own fashion. Social media is a place where a firm works hard to shape a brand but may also run into a brand reputation crisis. Social media has been used by customers to create negative word of mouth (WOM) and online complaint that can damage a brand's reputation (Pfeffer et al., 2014). Adidas was specifically concerned with its negative social media sentiment and received fewer negative comments compared to other name brands (Isaieva, 2019). In more recent years, Adidas tended to use Instagram rather than Twitter most likely because Adidas targets younger customers who make up the majority of Instagram users. Twitter was more frequently used by Nike (Isaieva, 2019).

Adidas's social media advertising strategy is quite interesting. Its social ads seem to be culturally congruent with target consumers. As many of Adidas' consumers are young, Adidas creates youth elements in their social ads and wins over consumers' recognition by focusing on young consumers' street culture and subcultures such as Brit-pop and hip-hop (Gilliland, 2017). In particular, such ads can create hype among young consumers, ultimately generating more social media leads and increasing the virality of social ads. Furthermore, Adidas actively used the newest Instagram feature, Checkout On Instagram. The ease-of-use checkout feature allows for users to order and pay for a product they discovered in an Instagram post with such a feature. In the first 3 months of 2019, Adidas' online sales increased by 40% year over year, which Kasper Rorsted, the Adidas' CEO, has attributed largely to Instagram (Joseph, 2020). "Product launches and Instagram's checkout tool were the two most important things for our online sales business in the first quarter," the CEO said (see Joseph, 2020).

Adidas also focuses on the emerging market. Weibo is China's Twitter. China Insight Report finds that Adidas earned 80% of all Weibo engagement on activewear brand accounts from December 2017 to November 2018 (Flora, 2019). This was mainly because Adidas generated Weibo posts featuring its brand ambassador Jackson Yee, a member of the superstar boy band TFBoys (Flora, 2019). It was rare that a foreign brand knew so well about what Generation Z likes and curated its social media content for Generation Z in China. While Adidas only created around 50% of Weibo brand posts that Nike created, they achieved customer engagement approximate 30 times as much as Nike (Flora, 2019).

To summarize, Adidas has shown how effective social media marketing can be and how a firm can make a difference in today's homogenized social media marketing actions. Basically, different advertisers, different ad content and formats, different endorsers, different customers, and different social media platforms can be employed to achieve a novel social media marketing strategy. On the basis of Adidas's social media marketing, we see that social media marketing can play a strategic role in growing a firm's sales. It is of paramount importance for a brand to create a specific subculture for a customer segment. Social media has been a cultural catalyst in formulating and shaping people's beliefs and values about a brand. Adidas uses social media to influence young customers by collaborating with influencers and creating content specifically designed for such young customers' values and beliefs. By innovating social ad content and social ad endorsement and targeting specific customer segments, Adidas has used social media to create a competitive advantage and drive product sales.

## 9.3    Estée Lauder

Estée Lauder is a leading manufacturer of quality skincare, makeup, fragrance, and hair care products (Estée Lauder, 2019). The company sells its products in approximately 150 countries under a number of name brands including Estée Lauder, Clinique, Origins, Bobbi Brown, La Mer, Jo Malone London, Aveda, and Too Faced (Estée Lauder, 2019). Estée Lauder currently has approximately 2.5 million followers on Facebook and 3.9 million followers on Instagram. The company's number of followers on social media has outperformed many other beauty brands.

Estée Lauder's success on social media relies on creating sophisticated content, similar to professional commercials or television ads. For example, in order to promote its new Paint-On Liquid LipColor collection (a set of matte, vinyl, or metallic lip colors), Estée Lauder recruited four professional models (Parisi, 2017). These models, wearing the Paint-On Liquid LipColor, were depicted in a video where they appeared in various environments, from a swimming pool to a fancy restaurant, accompanied by the song "Our Lips Are Sealed" by the band The Go-Gos (Parisi, 2017).

Estée Lauder has a portfolio of brands including Mac, Mecca, Clinique, La Mer, Estée Lauder, Glossier, and Aesop. In order to promote these brands, it recruited 60 influencers to promote 37 products from across Estée Lauder's brand portfolio (Stewart, 2018). All influencers were given the freedom to choose what products they wanted to post about and to create the content they preferred (Stewart, 2018). On the one hand, the freedom in product choice and content creation enables influencers to endorse products congruent with their established social image on social media platform, making product endorsement posts more authentic and credible (Thomas, 2018). On the other hand, Estée Lauder can also examine how different brands produce differential outcomes in terms of social media reach and user engagement (Thomas, 2018). As a consequence, Estée Lauder gained 120 pieces of content created by the influencers, which reached over 3.3 million users and achieved an overall engagement rate of 3.8% (Stewart, 2018). The findings indicated that the most popular beauty product was skincare (Thomas, 2018). Influencers and their followers are more interested in skincare than other beauty products (Thomas, 2018). The firm spent over $900 million on influencer marketing solely in the USA (Mirreh, 2019). The firm even committed 75% of its advertising budget on social media influencers from macro-influencers to micro-influencers based on this success (Mirreh, 2019).

The case of Estée Lauder shows two key elements of social media marketing. First, social media content is exceedingly important in obtaining optimal social media marketing performance. Estée Lauder deems the creation of social media content to be as crucial as the creation of legacy TV ads. The firm spent a significant amount of money on developing social media content. The quality content in turn builds an appealing social image for the firm. Second, social media influencers are a key part of Estée Lauder's social media strategy. In particular, the company provides influencers with a high level of freedom. This approach enables influencers to create content specific to their followers, which led to a large customer engagement rate. This case implies that influencers are the core of social media marketing. Influencer marketing is quite different from endorser marketing. As social media influencers' personal influence is reliant on their specific content (e.g., food bloggers' food recipe posts, beauty bloggers' makeup tips, and sport bloggers' sporting content), the effectiveness of influencer marketing relies on whether the endorsed product can naturally be advertised in such a particular type of content. In other words, unlike traditional endorsers, social media influencers usually are skilled in creating a particular type of content (e.g., beauty micro-bloggers use their makeup techniques to create makeup-related posts). They need to assure congruence between shared content and endorsed product. Previous endorser marketing literature has noted the importance of an endorser's congruence with brands, products, and customers. However, what social media content contains and how social media content displays the content should also be congruent with the influencer in the case of social media marketing.

## 9.4　L'Oréal

L'Oréal is a French cosmetics company. It is currently the top beauty manufacturer in the world in terms of beauty sales (Collins et al., 2020). It reached around 30 billion euros of sales in 2019 (L'Oréal, 2020). Its goal is "to offer each and every person around the world the best of beauty in terms of quality, efficacy, safety, sincerity and responsibility to satisfy all beauty needs and desires in their infinite diversity" (L'Oréal, 2020).

Beauty products such as cosmetics and hair dyes are very unique in contrast to ordinary consumption goods. The value of a beauty product varies as different consumers (e.g., White, Black, Asian, and Hispanic) use the products in different situations (e.g., offices, schools, and parties). In addition, consumers do not know whether a beauty product matches their appearance before opening the package and using the product. Once open, beauty products are not resalable in most circumstances. In other words, the mismatch risk between a beauty product and a consumer's needs can be high when a consumer has not previously bought or tried the product. In order to alleviate this mismatch risk, several digital solutions have been adopted by L'Oréal. The French brand has been aware that digital technologies are revolutionizing the codes of the beauty experience and has launched more than 20 services such as virtual makeup, hair color try-out, skin diagnosis, and other personalized recommendation mechanisms (L'Oréal, 2020). In order to achieve this digital transformation, since 2012, L'Oréal has taken a set of measures including operating digital technology incubators, rolling out AI-powered products, increasing the agility and responsiveness of its production facility, recruiting and hiring talent, and acquiring AI companies (Marr, 2019). All these measures show that digital marketing is an essential element of L'Oréal's corporate strategy. The French brand has therefore endeavored to digitize its business. In particular, L'Oréal has acquired Modiface, an augmented reality (AR) technology company for beauty brands (Marr, 2019). Modiface provides the ability to precisely perform beauty try-on simulations and live video. The AR technology is not just a business buzz. As technology allows consumers to see themselves modeling different shades of lipstick and other beauty products, L'Oréal has seen online conversion rates as much as tripled after buying Modiface (Gwynn, 2019). Fifteen companies including Amazon, Boots, and AS Watson have included L'Oréal's virtual try-on technology in their platforms and apps (Abboud, 2020). This technology has been a competitive advantage during the pandemic crisis for the cosmetics company (Abboud, 2020).

More recently, L'Oréal has also partnered with social media platforms to create a better shopping experience for social media users. Pinterest, a photograph sharing platform, has rolled out a "Try On" option that allows users to virtually try on beauty products (Faull, 2020). Basically, Pinterest shoppers can use the option to see themselves modeling different products featured in the social media platform (Faull, 2020). Furthermore, L'Oréal's partnership with social media platforms has been important for maintaining their online visibility during the COVID-19 pandemic. US prestige beauty sales dipped by 14% in 2020 Q1 (Collins, 2020). As people are less likely to go to public places for social interactions, it is reasonable that they also have a lower willingness to purchase cosmetics and beauty products. However, with the prevalence of online meetings and conferences, people need to pay attention to their digital appearance when having online interactions with others. Snap Camera users can beautify their social presentation by using L'Oréal's AR looks (e.g., virtual hair color, digital makeup) in Snap Camera (Williams, 2020). By incorporating branded content in Snap Camera, L'Oréal can still sustain a high level of public awareness and promote direct social sales through the app to offset the decline in store sales (Williams, 2020). L'Oréal also took other measures to sustain its brand image during the pandemic. Social media has been a substantial channel in L'Oréal's communication with customers. L'Oréal used social media platforms (including Instagram, Twitter, etc.) to announce that they would speed up the production of hand sanitizers and offer them free of charge and would also donate millions of dollars to nonprofit organizations for people in need (Leelathipkul, 2020). The company reported that this act of social responsibility gained a considerably high customer engagement rate, which was nine times higher than the average customer engagement of social media marketing campaigns (Leelathipkul, 2020). L'Oréal also used social media to indicate that they would not lay off any workers or cut anyone's salaries (Leelathipkul, 2020). These efforts in communicating L'Oréal's corporate social responsibility (CSR) can help create a credible and responsible corporate image. The corporate image is particularly crucial for the sales of beauty products which relies on customers' trust in the beauty company because beauty products mostly consist of chemicals and are put on human skin. Based on the brand's 2020 half-year results, despite the fact that the brand witnessed a decrease in sales ($-11.7\%$) in the first 6 months, the brand still accomplished a staggering $64.6\%$ growth in e-commerce (L'Oréal Finance, 2020).

To summarize, L'Oréal's practices have offered us valuable insights regarding the social media marketing of beauty products. The incorporation of novel technology such as AR and AI enables the company to more precisely offer a beauty solution tailored to each consumer's preferences and facial features. Also, when the business environment changes (e.g., the COVID-19 pandemic), a company needs to agilely respond to the change. In particular, partnering with or acquiring technology companies is one approach for a traditional company to obtain digital capabilities in response to the environmental change.

## 9.5  Zara

Zara is one of the largest and most famous fashion retail brands worldwide. It offers male and female clothing, children's clothing, shoes, and accessories (Roll, 2020). Zara contributes the most sales to the Spanish company Inditex, compared to other Inditex brands (Inditex, 2020).

The success of Zara lies in its strategic focus on the use of social media, particularly Instagram. The Spanish brand heavily relies on Instagram to promote products and generate buzz for its ever-changing product lines (Mediakix, 2019). The social media strategy is cohesive with the brand's fast fashion strategy. Zara is able to develop new designs year-round and puts the designs in production for a short period, thus reducing the worry about large stocks of unsold product (Store Setup, 2019). These limited production runs ensure that customers know their clothing will be relatively unique in contrast to the mass-produced items of seasonal retailers (Store Setup, 2019). As this fast fashion strategy focuses on continually producing new products, it is also difficult for Zara to keep customers updated about new products. The content dissemination nature of social media enables Zara to publish attractive, visual content and keep customers informed about new arrivals.

The brand's Instagram account serves an online catalog into the brand's new arrivals (Mediakix, 2019). If consumers access Zara's Instagram main page, they can find the current fashion trends in the latest posts. This fashion-focused content marketing strategy has attracted 40.2 million followers on Instagram. The brand also knows the popularity of social videos. Approximately 32% of its Instagram posts were videos (Ravi, 2018a, 2018b).

Furthermore, Zara utilizes a different approach with influencer marketing on Instagram. For example, they launched a "Timeless" campaign featuring influencers over the age of 40 (Ravi, 2018a, 2018b). This social media campaign employs fashion industry veterans Malgosia Bela, Yasmin Warsame, and Kristina de Coninck who discuss the effect of aging on their personal style (Ravi, 2018a, 2018b). Such social media marketing does not explicitly advertise products per se, but this approach can implicitly influence consumers' beliefs and values about Zara. In terms of the selection of influencer marketing, Zara tends to use regular models that look more like ordinary Instagram users in their promotional posts (Schlossberg, 2015). Zara does not blindly hire celebrities to endorse their brand because endorsement effectiveness relies on the congruity between endorsers and customers (Gaied & Rached, 2010; Xu & Pratt, 2018). As another example, on their #iamdenim campaign, Zara recruited influencers to advertise their denim products. Zara let influencers create raw content and convey the idea that their real denim was for real, everyday people (Amazonassociates, 2020). The use of reputable influencers and the emphasis of the accessibility of prices ensured the success of the social media marketing campaign (Amazonassociates, 2020). Apart from the use of reputable influencers, Zara has realized that micro-influencers can also play their part in social media marketing. Out of 2421 influencers, Zara collaborated with 522 micro-influencers (Editorial Team, 2019). This strategy has been proven to be a good one because the brand's earned media value (value created from earned media in which the social media exposure was obtained through social word of mouth, blogs, online product reviews, etc.) was considerable at 175 million euros (Editorial Team, 2019).

Zara has demonstrated that micro-influencers should not be ignored in social media marketing. In 2019, Zara opened its online store for South African shoppers (Deyana, 2019a). Sixty micro-influencers were recruited to promote Zara's online store and vouchers used in the campaign (Deyana, 2019a). Thanks to social media conversations and user interactions around Zara's new online stores on social media platforms like Instagram, the branded hashtag #DearSouthAfrica used in the campaign reached an audience of over six million people in 1 day, before the online store was even launched (Meltwater, cited in Deyana, 2019a). As a consequence of these efforts, Zara's Instagram marketing performance was more satisfactory than its main competitors' (e.g., Uniqlo) in terms of social media following and marketing performance.

To summarize, Zara's success consists of three aspects. First, success of social media marketing relies on whether a brand emphasizes the role of social media in their entire marketing activities. Also, the social media marketing strategy should be in line with the other business strategies of the company, such as production strategy.

Second, Zara's success has indicated that value-focused marketing communication (communicating about brand values and perspectives) can outperform its merchandise-focused counterpart (communicating about product attributes and benefits). Last, companies should not blindly select an influencer due to his or her popularity or reputation. Zara's success has shown that suitable influencers can also create satisfying marketing outcomes. Despite the fact that micro-influencers have lower social media following than macro-influencers, this does not mean that micro-influencers are less persuasive in terms of the effectiveness of brand endorsement. Micro-influencers have a smaller audience because the followers are following the influencer due to a specific field such as female beauty, travel, and entertainment. Therefore, micro-influencers can be more influential and credible than macro-influencers because a higher level of shared value is achieved between a micro-influencer and her target audience. This explains why micro-influencers were influential and effective in Zara's social media campaigns.

## 9.6    Coca-Cola

The Coca-Cola company is a beverage corporation. Coca-Cola focuses on developing, manufacturing, and selling beverage products. It was the third biggest beverage companies worldwide based on $37 billion in sales in 2019 (Bedford, 2020). Coca-Cola's competitive advantage comes from its strong brand image and awareness (Adamkasi, 2018). A key to sustaining this brand image and awareness is its capacity to create captivating advertisements (Adamkasi, 2018).

Marketing plays its part when a product cannot outperform its competitors. Despite the fact that Coca-Cola tastes slightly different than Pepsi, most people cannot tell the difference (Lubin, 2012). In the era of social media, social media marketing has been Coca-Cola's key approach to increasing brand awareness and achieving strategic goals. Coca-Cola uses a multiplatform strategy to build its brand image and awareness:

1. YouTube. Coca-Cola joined YouTube in January 2006. Currently, its YouTube channel has 3.4 million subscribers and had almost 2.7 billion views in 2020. For example, its most viewed video, titled "Vai no Gás (English translation: Go on Gas)," received around 127 million views. This number of views is high considering the video was released in 2019. The Vai no Gás ad targets young consumers and conveys an energetic lifestyle implying that young people should drink Cokes with gas. It aims at arousing viewers' intrinsic motivation to have a cold Coke with gas during summer time. The YouTube ad did not use celebrities. The characters in this video are young Coca-Cola consumers. Furthermore, in the video, viral music and video games are highlighted, which can create high affinity among 13- to 24-year-old consumers (see Robin, 2019). The high congruity between the YouTube ad and the target consumers made young consumers more engaged in viewing the ad, leading to the virality of the social ad on YouTube.

2. Facebook. The company's Facebook page has reached around 106 million followers and has received around 106 million likes. The Facebook page is used by the brand to advocate fan interaction. Social ads, celebrity endorsements, and games apps are shared by the brand to increase fan engagement. Coca-Cola also has fan pages for other products like Coca-Cola Zero and Diet Coke (Dravid, 2016). Coca-Cola endeavors to use Facebook (including a Logout Experience, Target and Reach Blocks, and Page Post ads in the News Feed) to promote its brands and products (Facebook for Business, 2014). The outcome of Facebook marketing has shown that Facebook is a strong complement to Coca-Cola's TV campaign and has generated optimal outcomes (the information and the following data were adapted from the full case study in Facebook for Business, 2014):

(a) 27% of Coca-Cola's incremental sales were created by Facebook. However, only 2% of the gross media budget was consumed.
(b) For every 1 euro spent on Facebook, a ROI of 2.74 euros was created.
(c) 35% of total buying behavior was caused by the synergistic effect of Facebook ads and TV ads.

3. Twitter. Coca-Cola's Twitter account currently has 3.3 million followers. Different from other social media accounts, Coca-Cola actively uses the hashtag feature in Twitter to build brand awareness. For example, on May 17, 2020, Coca-Cola tweeted, "Restaurants make more than food. They make our birthdays special, our date nights romantic, our big moments feel like a celebration. Give your favorite spot some love using the hashtag #WeLoveThisPlace." Coca-Cola encourages followers to create tweets using the hashtag #WeLoveThisPlace to let more consumers know about the WeLoveThisPlace campaign.
As another example, Coca-Cola Turkey (@CocaCola_TR) used Twitter to build brand awareness by sponsoring the Turkish national football team around Euro 2016 (Twitter, n.d.). Coca-Cola Turkey first used the First View feature (when users log on to Twitter, the video using this feature will appear at the top of users' timelines) in Twitter to create huge awareness for its #HaydiMilliTakım (#ComeOnNationalTeam) campaign (Twitter, n.d.). Furthermore, in order to boost the social sharing of the video used in the campaign, a customized button, Tweet #HaydiMilliTakım, was introduced to make it easier for viewers to participate in the campaign. As a result, the campaign generated key outcomes (the information and the following data were adapted from the full case study in Twitter, n.d.):

(a) Six million impressions and 25,000 tweets were generated.
(b) An average engagement rate of 2.2% was achieved.
(c) The association between the Coca-Cola brand and the Turkish national team was reinforced.

4. Instagram. Coca-Cola's Instagram currently has 2.8 million followers and 190 posts. While Coca-Cola did not post content on Instagram as frequently as on other social media platforms, the views of its posts on Instagram were not trivial. For example, on World Kindness Day in 2019, Coca-Cola's Instagram posted a photograph with "Kindness starts with _____." The company

encouraged its Instagram followers to share things with which kindness starts. This post got approximately 14,100 likes.

Another example from Instagram is when Coca-Cola kicked off a social media campaign #ThisOnesFor in 2017 to promote Coca-Cola's original Coke beverage throughout Western Europe (Deyana, 2019b). Fourteen Instagram influencers in fields ranging from fashion to sport and travel were recruited to promote product consumption and customer engagement (Deyana, 2019b). The influencers endorsed the Coca-Cola brand by creating Instagram content related to sharing a Coke with their relatives or friends and included @cocacolaeu and #ThisOnesFor in their endorsed content (Deyana, 2019b). The campaign received respectable outcomes [the information and the following data were adapted from Deyana (2019b)]:

(a) Over 173,000 likes, 1600 comments, and an average engagement rate of 7.8% were generated in the campaign.
(b) Coca-Cola increased their brand awareness and successfully attracted the attention of younger demographics in the region of Western European.

Most recently, as racism issues arose in the USA, the Coca-Cola company paused all social media activities for at least a month, effective July 1st (Coca-Cola Company, 2020). The company asserted that they will take the time to reassess their advertising policies to avoid offensive social media content (Coca-Cola Company, 2020). To summarize, Coca-Cola uses a multiplatform strategy, and it specifically adapts its content marketing strategy to the social media platform used.

## 9.7   Hyatt

Previously, we have listed six brands encompassing cosmetics, fashion, and beverages. In recent years, social media marketing and monetization have gone beyond these product categories. The industries of tourism and hospitality have also used social media for marketing and monetization purposes. Due to this wave of social media marketing use in the tourism and hospitality sectors, we include this case from the hospitality sector.

Hyatt Hotels Corporation is a global hospitality company with a world-class brand. Hyatt mostly offers hotel and resort services for both business and pleasure. As of the end of 2019, Hyatt achieved a total revenue of $5 billion (Hyatt Hotels Corporation, 2020). Hotel service quality cannot be assessed beforehand, so a firm like Hyatt relies on its strong brand image and marketing capabilities to outperform similar hotel services offered by firms like Hilton, Marriott, Holiday Inn, Hampton Inn, and Shangri-La. Hyatt places their "world-class brands" as the first competitive advantage among its other advantages (please see its 2019 financial report: Hyatt Hotels Corporation, 2020). To sustain this brand image worldwide, Hyatt has embraced social media marketing and has been a pioneer in applying this marketing approach in the hospitality sector.

Hyatt has used social listening to monitor marketing campaigns and predict key trends or topics that could generate higher customer engagement (Gigante, 2013). On the basis of social listening, Hyatt amends its content marketing strategy to avoid its content being offensive to viewers (Kaye, 2013). Hyatt relied on social data (e.g., negative comments or conversations) to determine whether an ad campaign should be continued, suspended, or replaced by alternative content (Gigante, 2013). Hyatt also used predictive analytics and proprietary metrics to assess a social buzz or trend's potential trajectory and prospective impact on customers (Gigante, 2013).

Social marketers should not just focus their attention on products or services. Corporate social responsibility (CSR) can also be a key vehicle to build brand awareness in social media marketing. Existing literature recommends that social media should be used as a tool to communicate a firm's CSR efforts (Kesavan et al., 2013). YouTube has been used to showcase many inspiring videos of Hyatt colleagues volunteering in local community service programs (Lwarburt, 2015). These efforts can demonstrate Hyatt's corporate social responsibility and add value to its world-class brand. A distinguishing approach of Hyatt's social media marketing is that Hyatt employees were used as a central element of the entire social media campaign. Hyatt employees were encouraged to share photographs, stories, and insights related to Hyatt on social media platforms such as Facebook, Twitter, and Instagram (Lwarburt, 2015).

Hyatt has also masterminded several social media campaigns using influencers. In April 2018, in order to increase awareness in a local community and highlight specific areas (e.g., Corn Maiden restaurant, the spa services, the resort grounds, and the horse stables) of a Hyatt hotel in New Mexico, 50 Instagram micro-influencers were recruited to participate in an exclusive VIP influencer event (Jenkins, 2018). These influencers were told to share Instagram content based on their tour and experience of the resort. The outcomes of the influencer marketing campaign were successful (Jenkins, 2018): 576 Instagram posts were generated containing 743 photographs and 15 videos. The #HyattTamaya hashtag used in the campaign reached 68,178 people and made around 602,142 impressions from April 21 to April 29, 2018, and the customer engagement in such a short period consisted of 23,068 likes and 989 comments.

In summary, we find that social media can be used in multiple sectors including hospitality. Hyatt has demonstrated the effective use of social media can generate business value and build its world-class brand.

## 9.8  Amazon

Amazon is an American multinational technology firm. The company's major businesses include, but are not limited to, e-commerce, cloud computing, digital streaming, and grocery retailing.

Amazon's foray into social media sites is quite interesting. The company actively leverages several social media platforms for marketing and e-commerce sales. It also created its own social media platform, Spark, in 2017. It once called Spark an

"Instagram meets e-commerce" initiative (Lincoln, 2017). Akin to Instagram, Spark is a social media platform producing user-generated images and photographs. Ideally, Spark is used to keep Amazon's consumers engaged with products within its own social media channel instead of using other social media channels (Lincoln, 2017). Amazon has noticed that consumers' product discovery journey is becoming diverse. The traditional product discovery journey of searching for products in Amazon's website is becoming obsolete. As social media increasingly dominates consumers' digital time, social media can also be a key source for people to discover items online. The introduction of Spark is intended to help convert social media content viewers into buyers at the point of discovering a product on the social platform. However, Amazon has since shut down Spark. An article published on Forbes indicated that there could be two reasons why such a platform failed (see Masters, 2018). During the period 2017–2018, English speaking markets were not ready to accept such commercialized social platforms (Masters, 2018). Another reason is that the Spark application neglected a key partner, consumer brands who sell on Amazon (Masters, 2018). Spark did not offer incentives for consumer brands to produce high-quality content. In essence, Spark failed to create synergies between consumers, brands, and Amazon's e-commerce platform. Spark did not meet customers' social needs and did not consider the role of marketer-generated content in building a commercialized social media platform.

Amazon also applies a multiplatform social media strategy to merchandise items and build an attractive brand image. Facebook, Instagram, Twitter, Snapchat, and others have been included in Amazon's marketing mix. Given that each platform has its own attributes and different target demographics, Amazon's approach to each social media platform varies. For example, Amazon created its Instagram account and included a link (amazon.com/alexaaccessibility) to its main page. Users who click this link would go to an Amazon product webpage to get more information about the AI-powered speaker, Alexa Echo. Linkages that lead social media users to Amazon.com are easy to use. But this approach is limited to a singular shopping mode: Consumers discover a product in a social post, get interested in purchasing the product, click the purchase link, and complete the purchase on the Amazon webpage. In order to innovate the way consumers find interesting products, Amazon has collaborated with Snapchat and allows users to scan a product or its barcode using Snapchat to search for the product within Amazon's product offerings (Dean, 2018). Once used, this visual search feature can pop up a webpage that displays product information (e.g., product price and reviews) and a purchase button for purchasing the product or similar products (Boland, 2018). This strategic partnership between Amazon and Snapchat can create monetization potential for both parties. Amazon can leverage social traffic to create more e-commerce sales. Snapchat can monetize this visual search feature by optimizing search results and displaying paid ads in those results. Although Snapchat did not reveal whether it was receiving affiliate revenue from Amazon for each sale made through the visual search feature (Boland, 2018), the social media platform may also take a cut from Amazon's e-commerce sales.

In order to fully leverage the power of online social networks, Amazon also rolled out the Amazon Influencer Program.[1] Influencers of social media platforms such as Facebook, YouTube, Twitter, and Instagram can join this program, recommend products, and take a commission for sales. The commission rates vary from 10% for Amazon's private-label fashion line to 1% for digital items such as video games (Johnson, 2019). Given these rates, the program can create a considerable stream of income for influencers (Gailis, 2020). The program can help in current influencer marketing on social media platforms. In the previous marketing mode, followers would have to ask for the influencer to send them a link to the particular product showcased in the video. If multiple items' links are requested, it is tedious for influencers to respond to all requests in a timely manner. In contrast, the Amazon influencer program allows the influencer to create their own store, with a URL, on Amazon, including concrete product categories such as decor items, baby items, beauty items, and accessories. Influencers can include the link in their social post. When clicked by viewers, the link can direct their followers to the influencer's store. For example, Laura Fuentes shared a video related to clean eating recipes on YouTube in January 2020. She included a link to her Amazon store underneath the YouTube video. Viewers can then click this link to browse products recommended by her and complete the purchase on Amazon.

To summarize, Amazon has been exploring and exploiting the power of online social networks. In particular, Amazon leverages its online presence as one of the largest online retailers in the world and tries to break down the silos between its mature e-commerce platforms and social media platforms, encompassing the use of visual search technology and the creation of Amazon Influencer Program.

## 9.9 Pinduoduo

Pinduoduo is one of the largest e-commerce platforms in the world. Pinduoduo is currently the second largest e-commerce player in China. The core value proposition of Pinduoduo is to create and promote a relatively novel e-commerce concept and shopping experience of "team purchase" (Huang, 2018). The team purchase concept is defined by consumers posting in social media platforms and advocating others to purchase items together, i.e., as a team (Wang et al., 2011). Consumers can launch a team purchase in order to bargain with sellers for lower prices, better deals, or more services (Wang et al., 2011).

The proliferation of Pinduoduo's social commerce business relies on a collaboration with the dominant Chinese social media platform, WeChat. Helped by the popularity of WeChat in China, Pinduoduo has acquired numerous users by attracting WeChat's social traffic. Tencent, WeChat's parent company, holds an 18.5% stake in Pinduoduo (Boyd, 2020). The collaboration with WeChat allows WeChat users to access Pinduoduo's e-commerce site without exiting WeChat.

---

[1]More information can be seen at affiliate-program.amazon.com/influencers

WeChat users do not need to download and install the Pinduoduo app. They can find a mini-version of the Pinduoduo app by searching for it in WeChat and using it for shopping-related activities. Furthermore, WeChat offers an integral payment method, WeChat Pay, for all in-app transactions; consumers just click "pay," enter their password, and the payment is done. This gives Pinduoduo buyers great ease of shopping when using the mini-version app of Pinduoduo in WeChat. Pinduoduo uses the large social clout of WeChat to assign consumers to team purchases (Hill, 2019). The desire for a good deal (more price bargaining power), the enjoyment of sharing interesting product information (more fun when shopping together), and the ease of sharing a purchase link (just one click to share) drive consumers to share Pinduoduo links with their WeChat groups or WeChat Moments (akin to the News Feed in Facebook) to launch a team purchase (Hill, 2019). It is a savvy move by Pinduoduo to integrate itself into WeChat's digital business ecosystem (technical infrastructure, payment features, third-party software compatibility, etc.) to grow e-commerce sales (Boyd, 2020). Fueled by the popularity of WeChat, Pinduoduo's approximate consumer acquisition cost was merely $2 per consumer, significantly lower than the $39 and $41 for major competitors JD.com and Taobao, respectively (Natanson, 2019). The low consumer acquisition cost is a competitive advantage for Pinduoduo and has helped the firm accomplish its "viral growth" strategy. As WeChat is very "sticky" for users, Pinduoduo has achieved a very high 7-day retention rate (77%) compared to other e-commerce platforms in China (Natanson, 2019). These figures show that social media can be a key source of competitive advantage for an e-commerce platform. Pinduoduo also cemented its social commerce by offering socially focused features such as Price Chop. Price Chop is an interesting feature that allows consumers to get items free by sharing a link with their friends (Hariharan & Dardenne, 2020). Basically, a consumer needs to share the link with as many friends as possible and ensure that every friend has clicked the link (no purchase required) to chop the price of an item down to zero (Hariharan & Dardenne, 2020).

To summarize, Pinduoduo is a good case in point to show how social media can be a source of competitive advantage. Social media can be integrated in the design of a firm's business model to create value for customers.

## 9.10  Managerial Implications

Several interesting managerial implications can be drawn from the above cases.

1. The emphasis of social media marketing by a firm is a cornerstone of social media marketing excellence. If a firm aims to achieve marketing excellence by using social media channels, it should stress the role of social media channels in their marketing strategy. All cases included in this chapter support this point. If a firm's emphasis on social media marketing is absent or lacking, it is unlikely that social media users' engagement and participation in the firm's social media campaigns are valued by the firm. When a firm stresses the importance of social media

marketing, social marketers take greater care of their social media users' needs and motives. It is then possible for the firm's social media channel to generate high customer engagement and, most importantly, social sales.

2. Social media influencers have been widely used in social media marketing. It can be found that almost all of our sample firms used influencer marketing tactics. We define influencers as individuals having a significant and meaningful social media following. Usually, an influencer is renowned in a particular field such as sport, female health, fashion, and cosmetics. In the above cases, we have seen that even world-famous brands such as Coca-Cola recruit influencers to promote their products. Influencer marketing can indeed produce optimal outcomes for firms. Furthermore, firms should not blindly recruit macro-influencers (those influencers having over one million followers) to perform marketing campaigns. We show that micro-influencers (those influencers with anywhere between one thousand to one million followers) are also influential in creating customer excitement and engagement.

3. Social media can be a source of competitive advantage and value creation. L'Oréal, Zara, Coca-Cola, and Amazon are pioneers in social media marketing and have offered valuable insights into what methods and tools brands may use in the era of social media. Pinduoduo is an inspiring example for future firms. It shows how social value is incorporated in its business model. The social shopping concept "team purchase" approaches a gap in current e-commerce practices: Most existing e-commerce platforms mainly offer a solitary shopping experience. The enjoyment and happiness of shopping together are absent in the traditional e-commerce model. Pinduoduo's close alignment with social media platforms makes it possible to shop with others and meet people's desire to buy products at lower prices.

## References

Abboud, L. (2020). *L'Oréal glimpses its digital future amid pandemic.* Retrieved from https://www.ft.com/content/ab917d5d-e601-44ba-9a2c-53dbb2146dc7

Adamkasi. (2018). *Competitive advantage of Coca Cola.* Retrieved from https://www.competitiveadvantageanalysis.com/competitive-advantage-of-coca-cola/

Amazonassociates. (2020). *9 examples of great influencer fashion marketing campaigns.* Retrieved from https://amazon-affiliate.eu/en/9-examples-influencer-fashion-marketing-campaigns/

Bedford, E. (2020). *Global beverage market: Leading companies 2019, based on sales.* Retrieved from https://www.statista.com/statistics/307963/leading-beverage-companies-worldwide-based-on-net-sales/

Boland, M. (2018). *Will snapchat excel in visual search?* Retrieved from https://arinsider.co/2018/09/26/can-snapchat-excel-in-visual-search/

Boyd, C. (2020). *Pinduoduo: Everything you need to know about PDD, China's third-biggest ecommerce site.* Retrieved from https://medium.com/@clarkboyd/pinduoduo-everything-you-need-to-know-about-pdd-chinas-third-biggest-ecommerce-site-38ac42086e47

Coca-Cola Company. (2020). *Coca-Cola to pause all social media activity in July.* Retrieved from https://www.coca-colacompany.com/news/coca-cola-to-pause-all-social-media-activity-in-july

Collins, A., Fine, J. B., & Wynne, A. (2020). *Top 10 largest beauty manufacturers.* Retrieved from https://wwd.com/beauty-industry-news/beauty-features/top-10-largest-beauty-manufacturers-1203620799/

Collins, A. (2020). *U.S. prestige beauty sales dip 14 percent in Q1.* Retrieved from https://wwd.com/beauty-industry-news/body-care/coronavirus-prestige-beauty-sales-dip-14-in-q1-1203623656/

Dean, S. (2018). *Snapchat is partnering with Amazon to let users shop through their smartphone cameras.* Retrieved August 23, 2022, from https://www.latimes.com/business/technology/la-fi-tn-snap-amazon-20180924-story.html

Deyana. (2019a). *Why Zara's #DearSouthAfrica micro-influencer campaign made waves across social media?* Retrieved from https://www.webcelebs.com/news/why-zaras-dearsouthafrica-micro-influencer-campaign-made-waves-across-social-media/

Deyana. (2019b). *#ThisOnesFor the success of Coca-Cola's Instagram campaign.* Retrieved from https://www.webcelebs.com/case-studies/thisonesfor-the-success-of-coca-colas-instagram-campaign/

Ditty, A. (2015). *Inside Nike's Instagram strategy.* Retrieved from https://www.business2community.com/instagram/inside-nikes-instagram-strategy-01247413#:~:text=Focus%20on%20your%20audience&text=They%20do%20a%20great%20job,of%20the%20community%20to%20share

Dravid, R. (2016). *Coca-Cola's global reach using the social media platform.* Retrieved from https://www.digitalvidya.com/blog/coca-colas-global-reach-using-the-social-media-platform/

Editorial Team. (2019). *The best-performing brands in influencer marketing 2018 and their secrets to success.* Retrieved from https://influencerdb.com/blog/best-performing-brands-influencer-marketing-2018/

Estée Lauder. (2019). *2019 annual report.* Retrieved from https://media.elcompanies.com/files/e/estee-lauder-companies/universal/news-and-media/media-resources/resources-and-reports/reports/2019-elc-10k.pdf

Facebook for Business. (2014). *Coca-Cola sees success with brand marketing on Facebook.* Retrieved from https://www.facebook.com/business/news/coca-cola-sees-success-with-brand-marketing-on-facebook

Faull, J. (2020). *L'Oreal signs up for Pinterest's roll out of AR tech.* Retrieved from https://www.thedrum.com/news/2020/01/28/l-oreal-signs-up-pinterest-s-roll-out-ar-tech

Flora, L. (2019). *Adidas gets fashion-forward in China.* Retrieved from https://www.gartner.com/en/marketing/insights/daily-insights/adidas-gets-fashion-forward-in-china

Gaied, A. M., & Rached, K. S. B. (2010). The persuasive effectiveness of famous and non famous endorsers in advertising. *IBIMA Business Review, 2010,* 474771.

Gailis, G. (2020). *Amazon influencer guide.* Retrieved from https://klintmarketing.com/amazon-influencer/

Gigante, M. D. (2013). *How Hyatt used social media data to determine its ad campaign agenda.* Retrieved from https://www.mdgadvertising.com/marketing-insights/how-hyatt-used-social-media-data-to-determine-its-ad-campaign-agenda/

Gilliland, N. (2017). *How Adidas Originals uses social media to drive sales.* Retrieved from https://econsultancy.com/how-adidas-originals-uses-social-media-to-drive-sales/

Gwynn, S. (2019). *How L'Oreal, Eve Sleep and Dunelm are using media to drive ecommerce.* Retrieved from https://www.campaignlive.co.uk/article/loreal-eve-sleep-dunelm-using-media-drive-ecommerce/1667275

Hariharan, A., & Dardenne, N. (2020). *Pinduoduo and the rise of social E-commerce.* Retrieved from https://www.ycombinator.com/library/2z-pinduoduo-and-the-rise-of-social-e-commerce#footnote2

Heble, A. (2015). *Nike gains new customers through Instagram.* Retrieved from https://www.digitalvidya.com/blog/nike-gains-new-customers-through-instagram/

Hill, N. (2019). *PinDuoDuo: 0 to $24 billion in 3 years with social commerce*. Retrieved from https://www.groupify.de/insights/2019/8/9/pinduoduo-0-to-24-billion-in-3-years-with-social-commerce

Huang, Z. (2018). *2018 letter to shareholders*. Retrieved from https://investor.pinduoduo.com/news-releases/news-release-details/letter-shareholders

Hyatt Hotels Corporation. (2020). *2019 annual report on form 10-K*. Retrieved from https://s2.q4cdn.com/278413729/files/doc_financials/annual_2019/H-10-K-12.31.19-FINAL-FILED-2.20.20.pdf

Inditex. (2020). *Annual report 2019*. Retrieved from https://www.inditex.com/documents/10279/645708/2019+Inditex+Annual+Report.pdf/25aa68e3-d7b2-bc1d-3dab-571c0b4a0151

Influencer Marketing. (2020). *8 influencer marketing case studies with incredible results*. Retrieved from https://influencermarketinghub.com/influencer-marketing-case-studies/

Isaieva, Z. (2019). *Nike vs Adidas: Who's on top with social media*. Retrieved from https://youscan.io/blog/nike-vs-adidas-who-is-on-top-with-social-media/

Jenkins, C. (2018). *2018 #HyattTamaya InstaMeet influencer event at Hyatt Regency Tamaya resort and spa*. Retrieved from https://www.simplysocialmedianm.com/blog/2018-hyatttamaya-instameet-influencer-event-at-hyatt-regency-tamaya-resort-and-spa

Johnson, L. (2019). *Amazon is paying influencers big commissions to sell its products, and it's open to anyone. Here's how to sign up*. Retrieved from https://www.businessinsider.com/amazon-influencer-how-to-make-money-2019-2?IR=T

Joseph, S. (2013). *Adidas brings Messi and Facebook to the fore*. Retrieved from https://www.marketingweek.com/adidas-brings-messi-and-facebook-to-the-fore/

Joseph, S. (2020). *'It's having a positive impact': Instagram is driving Adidas' online sales*. Retrieved from https://digiday.com/marketing/its-having-a-positive-impact-instagram-is-driving-adidas-online-sales/

Jovana Banovic. (2011). *How Nike use social media [case study]*. Retrieved from http://jovanabanovic.com/2011/12/16/nike-use-social-media-case-study/

Kaye, K. (2013). *How social data influenced Hyatt to pull part of campaign days before launch*. Retrieved from https://adage.com/article/datadriven-marketing/social-data-influenced-hyatt-pull-part-a-campaign/243539

Kesavan, R., Bernacchi, M. D., & Mascarenhas, O. A. (2013). Word of mouse: CSR communication and the social media. *International Management Review, 9*(1), 58–66.

L'Oréal Finance. (2020). *2020 half-year results*. Retrieved from https://www.loreal-finance.com/eng/news-release/2020-half-year-results

L'Oréal. (2020). *2019 annual report*. Retrieved from https://www.loreal-finance.com/system/files/2020-03/LOREAL_2019_Annual_Report_3.pdf

Leelathipkul, T. S. (2020). *How L'Oréal Paris makes the best use of social media during COVID-19?* Retrieved from https://medium.com/@tita.suphattiya/how-lor%C3%A9al-paris-makes-the-best-use-of-social-media-during-covid-19-516107c55c33

Lincoln, J. (2017). *Why Amazon's new social media site should not be ignored*. https://www.inc.com/john-lincoln/dont-ignore-amazon-spark-especially-if-you-sell-a-.html

Lubin, G. (2012). *Here's the real difference between Coke and Pepsi*. Retrieved from https://www.businessinsider.com/the-difference-between-coke-and-pepsi-2012-12?IR=T#:~:text=%22Pepsi%20is%20sweeter%20than%20Coke,raisiny%2Dvanilla%20taste%20of%20Coke.&text=Turning%20to%20nutritional%20content%2C%20Pepsi,Coke%20has%20slightly%20more%20sodium

Lwarburt. (2015). *Hyatt gets social media right by making it personal*. Retrieved from http://smbp.uwaterloo.ca/2015/10/hyatt-gets-social-media-right-by-making-personal/

Marr, B. (2019). *The amazing ways how L'Oréal uses artificial intelligence to drive business performance*. Retrieved from https://www.forbes.com/sites/bernardmarr/2019/09/06/the-amazing-ways-how-loral-uses-artificial-intelligence-to-drive-business-performance/#3e4c6e8f4bba

Masters, K. (2018). *Here's everything that's wrong with Amazon spark*. Retrieved from https://www.forbes.com/sites/kirimasters/2018/05/20/heres-everything-thats-wrong-with-amazon-spark/#632e0b4b65eb

Mediakix. (2019). *How Zara became one of the best brands on Instagram*. Retrieved from https://mediakix.com/blog/best-brands-on-instagram-zara-channel-followers/

Mirreh, M. (2019). *Estée Lauder commits 75% of its advertising budget to influencers*. Retrieved from https://talkinginfluence.com/2019/08/27/estee-lauders-commits-75-of-its-advertising-budget-to-influencers/

Natanson, E. (2019). *The miraculous rise of pinduoduo and its lessons*. Retrieved from https://www.forbes.com/sites/eladnatanson/2019/12/04/the-miraculous-rise-of-pinduoduo-and-its-lessons/#2160f9c81f13

Parisi, D. (2017). *Estée Lauder's multipart #LipsToEnvy campaign shows Facebook video confidence*. Retrieved from https://www.luxurydaily.com/estee-lauders-multipart-lipstoenvy-campaign-shows-facebook-video-confidence/

Pfeffer, J., Zorbach, T., & Carley, K. M. (2014). Understanding online firestorms: Negative word-of-mouth dynamics in social media networks. *Journal of Marketing Communications, 20*(1–2), 117–128.

Ravi, K. (2018a). *6 ways Nike built a strong brand on social media*. Retrieved from https://blog.unmetric.com/nike-social-media

Ravi, K. (2018b). *How Zara built an engaging brand on social media*. Retrieved from https://blog.unmetric.com/social-media-strategy-zara

Relevantly. (2020). *Nike case study: How Nike Facebook ads are used to drive sales*. Retrieved from https://relevantlymarketing.com/news/how-nike-facebook-ads-are-used-to-drive-sales

Robin. (2019). *Virals of the year: Coca Cola celebrates bubbles in Brazil to get over 120m views*. Retrieved from http://www.netimperative.com/2019/11/28/virals-of-the-year-coca-cola-celebrates-bubbles-in-brazil-to-get-over-120m-views/

Roll, M. (2020). *The secret of Zara's success: A culture of customer co-creation*. Retrieved from https://martinroll.com/resources/articles/strategy/the-secret-of-zaras-success-a-culture-of-customer-co-creation/

Schlossberg, M. (2015). *Zara has one key advantage over Gap and J. Crew*. Retrieved from https://www.businessinsider.com/how-instagram-is-helping-zara-take-over-the-fashion-world-2015-9?IR=T

Schonfeld, E. (2010). *Slap A QR code on that product so that people can like it*. Retrieved from https://techcrunch.com/2010/10/18/likify-qr-code/

Stewart, T. (2018). *Case study: Estée Lauder looks to Instagram influencers on multi-brand campaign*. Retrieved from https://mobilemarketingmagazine.com/case-study-estee-lauder-companies-visual-amplifiers-vamp-instagram-influencer-marketing

Store Setup. (2019). *Fast fashion strategy: How Zara took over the fashion World*. Retrieved from https://startbusinessjourney.com/zara-fast-fashion-strategy/

Thomas, L. (2018). *Estée Lauder companies' influencer marketing campaign provides social strategy insights*. Retrieved from https://www.bandt.com.au/estee-lauder-companies-influencer-marketing-campaign-provides-social-strategy-insights/

Twitter. (n.d.). *Coca-Cola Turkey reinforces a football sponsorship with First View*. Retrieved from https://marketing.twitter.com/emea/en_gb/success-stories/coca-cola-turkey-reinforces-football-sponsorship-with-first-view

Wang, J. J., Zhao, X., & Li, J. J. (2011). Team purchase: A case of consumer empowerment in China. *Journal of Consumer Affairs, 45*(3), 528–538.

Williams, R. (2020). *L'Oréal rolls out 1st beauty AR lenses on Snap's desktop app*. Retrieved from https://www.mobilemarketer.com/news/loreal-rolls-out-1st-beauty-ar-lenses-on-snaps-desktop-app/577054/

Xu, X., & Pratt, S. (2018). Social media influencers as endorsers to promote travel destinations: An application of self-congruence theory to the Chinese Generation Y. *Journal of Travel and Tourism Marketing, 35*(7), 958–972.

# Part IV

# Knowhow for Social Media Companies to Garner Maximal Revenue

# Monetization Strategy Implementation for Social Media Companies

10

## 10.1 Critical Success Factors of Social Media Monetization

This chapter introduces key aspects of social media monetization. From a network perspective, the value of social media relies on the number of social media users. The more users a social media platform has, the more attractive it is for advertisers, brands, and other business users. This explains why daily active users (DAUs) are so important for defining the popularity of social media. A significant number of users offer a solid base for a social media platform to profit and optimize monetization.

### 10.1.1 User Acquisition

It is more and more difficult to acquire users on social media platforms. According to a recent report published on September 23, 2021, the number of available apps in the Google Play Store reached 2.79 million (Statista Research Department, 2021). Only a few social media platforms, such as TikTok, Pinterest, and Reddit, can dramatically grow their DAUs in the current competitive environment. In this section, we will expand on methods a social media platform can put in place to attain new users.

1. *Increase the Exposure of Social App* via *App Store Optimization.* The app store is among the first priorities for companies to increase the exposure of a social app. According to Google, the app store accounts for 40% of app discovery (see Hammadabid, 2021). App Store Optimization (ASO) is the process of increasing and maximizing an app's visibility in an app store (Hammadabid, 2021). First, the app title needs to be developed to incorporate keywords. According to MobileDevHQ (now renamed Tune), the proper inclusion of keywords in the title can lead to a 10.3% increase in app rankings (see Rampton, 2015). The number of words, characters, and syllables should always be considered in creating an app name. It is recommended that an app name be condensed into one or two words with a maximum of nine or ten characters. Existing popular

© The Author(s), under exclusive license to Springer Nature Switzerland AG 2022
F. J. Martínez-López et al., *Social Media Monetization*, Future of Business and Finance, https://doi.org/10.1007/978-3-031-14575-9_10

social apps such as Facebook, Twitter, and Reddit all follow this principle. Second, the app description is the prime place to depict its key features. The description should be accurate and realistic. Inaccurate or unrealistic descriptions may lure users to download an app, but, in the long run, nonrepresentative descriptions will only damage an app's popularity and will not help to obtain a significant network effect. Unrealistic expectations on app performance could lead to bad user reviews (Klimow, 2016). Credible apps, on the other hand, will attract loyal users (Klimow, 2016). Third, user ratings and reviews are a key factor in determining a user's decisions regarding such app. Considerable positive reviews, including four-star or higher ratings, can signify a social app's high usability and positive features. It is suggested that a social app encourage users to provide a positive app review and a high rating. The social app can offer rewards for users who give reviews in exchange for such features as ad-free content or access to paid content for some period of time. Finally, ASO can be considerably enhanced by increasing the downloads of the app. This requires efforts mentioned below to heighten the influence of app marketing.

2. *Create User Personas for Precision Marketing.* User personas are archetypical users whose goals and attributes can elucidate the needs of a major user group (Faller, 2019). User personas can be created via a template that includes behavior patterns, goals, attitudes, and other demographic information (Faller, 2019). There is no social media platform that dominates various users across different demographics or mental schema. Facebook, for instance, cannot replace YouTube which focuses on video content. Soul, an online social app, provides a good example of a company growing its user base by creating precise user personas. Soul is a social app matching users with similar hobbies or personalities using AI-enabled technology. Users can socially interact with others after being categorized based responses to a quiz (Lahiri, 2021). Soul has acquired over 100 million users since its inception just 4 years ago, with monthly active users (MAUs) jumping to over 30 million (PRNewswire, 2021). The app has hit multiple markets including China, North America, Japan, and Korea (PRNewswire, 2021). Soul was valued at over $1 billion and has privately filed for a US initial public offering (IPO) (Lahiri, 2021). A clear user persona was created to promote the social app. The app mainly targets singles who seek to fulfill their social needs. Most of its users are single university students and other single workers whose ages range from 25 to 35. After clearly delineating its target users, Soul's user acquisition strategy is designed to find users in these demographics. For example, Soul's "Young People's Social Metaverse" ad can be seen at several places, from billboards to other social media platforms. The value that this ad seeks to deliver is clear: decreasing young people's loneliness.

3. *Create Social or Public Value for All Networked Users to Promote the Social Media Together.* When a social media platform offers free access to all users, the socially connected service obtains a feature of social welfare (Dohrmann et al., 2015). This social value creation is the prerequisite of monetization (Dohrmann et al., 2015). Once social value or public value is created, all networked users should benefit and are motivated to promote the social media platform together.

The social or public value becomes greater when more users access the service. Social media is a media platform that enables everyone's use of the public media resource to advertise, promote, and share content. Social media can be used for delivering news, sharing traffic information, increasing marketing exposure, client service, and asking for support (Agrawal, 2016). The value has been injected into daily life. For example, WeChat, a social app combining a mobile payment feature, has been adopted by utility companies (e.g., gas, electricity, water) to remotely collect utility fees. Potential users are encouraged to download this social app and use it to pay utility fees so that they do not have to make a payment at a physical service station.

4. *Snowballing the Social Media User Network by Leveraging Existing Users*. Snowballing is a viral growth process in which a business starts small, but quickly builds momentum. Imagine that a social app has 1000 users, and each user can contact ten people to download the app. If the appeal for downloads is successful, the app can then reach 10,000 people. Again, newly acquired users can contact more people and repeat this process. This viral growth process is termed snowballing. The snowball effect relies on creating a buzz for a social app and encourages existing users to attract more users. For example, Soul creates a buzz among millennials because it is a social app specifically focusing on social activities between young people (e.g., online parties, online games, online dating). Existing Soul users are willing to share this app and encourage friends to join their online social circle.

Social media can acquire more users by using marketing strategies that may also be used for promoting other products or services. The key aspects mentioned above should be closely tailored to the particularities of social media. Conventional advertising channels, such as mass media, email, and website banners, can also be used for acquiring users.

## 10.1.2 User Retention

User retention is an app strategy that focuses on encouraging users to continue coming back to the app (Kazmi, 2021). It can be measured by a retention rate that is the percentage of users who continue using the app divided by all users acquired at the beginning of a period. Retention is measured by dividing the number of users who installed and opened the social app on day 0 by the number of users who used the app on day X (AppLovin, 2021). If this rate is too low, it indicates that most users eventually decide to leave the app. The retention rate can be measured after a period such as 1, 10, or 30 days. A common mistake of new social apps is using clickbait to induce users to download and register, but this unethical marketing strategy can result in low user retention.

User retention is important for social media monetization. Low retention rates could indicate low user satisfaction with the current social app or imply that competitors with better technology, service, or features are in the same domain

(AppLovin, 2021). Current users' dissatisfaction with the current app and resulting shift to a competitor's app leads to weak monetization performance.

1. *Bond Existing Users with Others*. Previously, we discussed the role of a network effect in social media business. The network effect does not only attract new users to join the network, but also keeps existing users at the network. Social media connects users with others, bonding users together. An individual user who leaves the platform will lose all connections with his or her social network friends. This is a major reason why dominant social media platforms such as Facebook or WeChat thrive. The classic motivational theory, Maslow's Hierarchy of Needs, indicates that individuals have a need of belonging. Maslow's Hierarchy refers to a need for interpersonal relationships and being part of a group or community (McLeod, 2020). According to a survey of 594 social network users and 608 microbloggers in China, social media users' sense of belonging is positively related to the strength of their habit of using social media (Liu et al., 2018). Social media platforms should increase their users' sense of belonging, thus increasing user retention. Platforms should intentionally create more connections between users. For example, Facebook will recommend potential friends for a user based on the user's profile information and established connections. Facebook also creates communities for users with shared interests, so that they are able to interact with others in the communities.

2. *Consistently Generating New Social Media Content*. Utilitarian value and hedonic value are predictive of social media users' behavior of posting social media content and their continued use of social media (Chen et al., 2011). Social media users' motives to acquire utilitarian value and hedonic value can be fulfilled by generating and accessing new social media content. Sharing, viewing, and commenting on social media content produced by icons on social media drives fans to continually use the social media platform. Social media platforms, particularly small social media platforms such as brand communities or school forums, can periodically organize campaigns to promote the co-creation of social media content. For example, the cellphone brand OnePlus's BBS (bulletin board system) recently organized a photography contest titled "Silhouette Moment" among BBS users to memorialize the Fall of 2021. All OnePlus users can share three photographs with test descriptions on the brand community and can participate in this campaign. Winners of the contest win rewards like OnePlus 9 or Never Settle T-shirts. This campaign received very favorable responses. Appealing autumn photographs were shared on the BBS and these photographs successfully attracted many views and clicks.

   The richness of social media content creates an immersive experience for users, which may lead to *social media addiction* (Hou et al., 2019). From a business perspective, it is favorable for a social media platform to develop users who are addicted to using and viewing the social media content on the platform. However, from an ethical perspective, a user retention model based on user addiction is unethical and may hurt users, particularly adolescents and children. Misleading, pornographic, and fake contents are spreading on social media. Research has shown that social media addiction is positively related to depression, anxiety, and insomnia (Bányai et al., 2017; Koc & Gulyagci, 2013; Shensa et al., 2017; van Rooij et al., 2017) and negatively related to subjective well-being, vigor, and life satisfaction (Błachnio et al., 2016; Hawi & Samaha, 2017; Uysal et al., 2013). This dark side of social media needs to be considered in the process of social media monetization. Monetization is not an act solely focusing on making money. The goal of monetization should be to help a firm survive and thrive. Consequently, the firm with sustainable revenue can more confidently weather a turbulent environment and fulfill its corporate social responsibility. In the case of social media, a social media platform with sustainable advertising revenue can more confidently play a role in creating more social welfare for all users. For example, a social media platform with higher advertising revenue can more confidently roll out an adolescent version of the platform in which adult-related social media content is strictly controlled.

3. *Develop Dynamic Capability to Compete in a Competitive Environment.* Dynamic capability is a high-order capability to cope with an unstable environment. Dynamic capability can be defined as "the firm's ability to integrate, build, and reconfigure internal and external competencies to address rapidly changing environments (Teece et al., 1997, p. 516)." As we know, there are numerous social media platforms: Facebook, Twitter, Instagram, Snapchat, TikTok, and YouTube, among others. Social media has become a battlefield for Internet companies to compete for online traffic. In China, many new social apps appear in app stores every year. With the advent of machine learning, 5G, cloud computing, and other technologies, disruptive innovations in social media are fundamentally changing the features of social media. How to avoid disruptive innovations from competitors has become a challenge for existing social media platforms. Dynamic capability is a strategic capability for a social media company to weather the rapidly changing environment and competitor innovations. Specifically, based on dynamic capability theory, social media companies need to scan the environment and identify opportunities in the market, develop and select opportunities, and adapt existing business models (Kump et al., 2019; Teece, 2007). For example, Facebook, the leading social media platform in the world, has made 13 attempts to clone Snapchat (The Guardian, 2016). Facebook recognized the opportunities in its competitor's novel features and developed and mobilized resources to incorporate similar features in its own platforms. In retrospect, if Facebook had kept focusing on its original version, it would be difficult for Facebook to catch up with the trends in the competitive environment. Apart from identifying opportunities from competitors, Facebook stresses the role of an innovative culture. At Facebook, over 18,000 employees were seeking innovative ideas and creations (Clifford, 2017). "I think the strategy of Facebook is to learn as quickly as possible what our community wants us to do, and that encourages a culture that encourages people to try things and test things and fail," said CEO Mark Zuckerberg (see Clifford, 2017). This innovative strategy has driven Facebook to evolve from version 1.0 to version 340.0, a persistent product sequencing process (Helfat & Raubitschek, 2000). This product sequencing

process entails the co-evolution of organizational knowledge, capabilities, and products over time, which leads to competitive advantage in a rapidly changing environment (Helfat & Raubitschek, 2000).

4. *Develop App Features to Meet Users' Needs in Presenting Best Selves.* Social media is an online platform where users want to present their best selves while interacting with others online. The symbolic interaction theory indicates that an object or a person's meaning (e.g., social status and impression) is generated by means of human interaction (Aksan et al., 2009). For example, an attractive social presence in social media can be defined by a significant number of likes or positive comments. People rely on feedback from others to define their social meanings, i.e., the *looking-glass self* (Solomon, 2018). Therefore, social media should meet users' need for presenting an attractive self-image online. In practice, many social media platforms have adopted this strategy. They create attractive digital avatars for users to virtually interact with others or enable users to digitally manipulate their digital presence (such as selfie beautification). For example, the social app QQ allows users to create customized digital avatars on the social platform. QQ even creates paid features for users to pay for more attractive digital decorations or images for their digital avatar.

Essentially, user acquisition and user retention are the two pillars of social media monetization. Social media cannot achieve high monetization performance unless a significant number of users are acquired and retained. A large number of users can ensure online traffic, creating possibilities for actors in social media to earn profit. In fact, some strategies could be useful for attracting new users as well as keeping existing users. Kuaishou, a leading video social app in China, invited celebrities to become users of the app and share their daily lives in the social app. For example, Chinese movie megastar Jackie Chan opened his first video social account on Kuaishou on October 27, 2021 (The Information Daily, 2021). Kuaishou has been committed to offering entertainment content for more ordinary users by shortening the distance between stars and users (The Information Daily, 2021). By partnering with megastars like Jackie Chan, Kuaishou is able to attract new users and keep existing users who want to get more information about Mr. Chan.

## 10.2   Strategies for Monetization

Social media platforms are not solely created for commerce. Instead, social media is a means of communication for people to exchange information. Therefore, how an informative vehicle can become a "money maker" requires entrepreneurs' deliberate elaboration. In essence, social media monetization requires that firms find an appropriate *track* to monetize its social traffic or users. A competition track refers to a competitive field in which a firm competes with other firms. Different tracks could provide different characteristics (Geng, 2021). For instance, a firm in one track could rely on investment and natural resources to compete, while in another track its competitiveness could depend on technological innovation (Geng, 2021). Powered

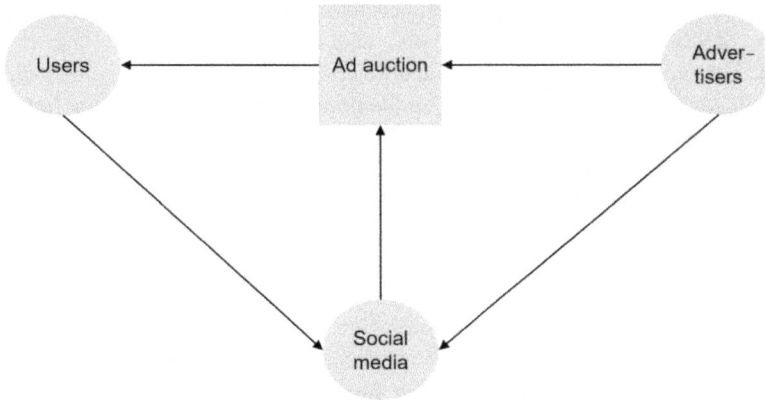

**Fig. 10.1**  Social media's advertising business (source: authors' elaboration)

by advances of new technology such as cloud, machine learning, and mobile technology, new business opportunities emerge and give birth to many business unicorns in tracks such as smart logistics, healthcare, AI, New Entertainment, New Retail, and Internet education.[1] Advertising business has been a common competition track for most social media companies. Social media companies choosing this track need to compete with other advertising channels such as mass media and other social media channels. In this chapter, we present two main tracks that have been proven successful in existing social media cases: advertising and social commerce.

## 10.2.1  Advertising Strategy

Advertising is most social media platforms' main monetization strategy. Social media's advertising model is presented in Fig. 10.1. Social media can collect users' data such as behavioral patterns, location information, and user profiles. At the same time, advertisers pay social media for their commercials to be advertised and customize their advertising demand such as targeting specific consumers, user action rates, user engagement, and conversion rates by defining the content of commercials. Social media collects data from both sides and uses the data to establish and upgrade their ad auction algorithm. This algorithm considers the relevancy and creativity of each commercial as well as the bid of each advertiser. The best advertiser wins the ad auction and is able to present their commercial to the specified audience.

This strategy has proven successful for many popular social media platforms such as Facebook and Snap. According to Facebook's 2020 annual report (Facebook Inc., 2021), advertising generates substantially all the revenue for Facebook Inc. Their

---

[1] On the list, here comes the unicorn!—2019 China Unicorn List release. Market Watch, 2020(08), 7–15.

report revealed that the advertising revenue (in millions) for 2018, 209 and 2020 was $55,013, $69,655, $84,169, respectively, and accounted for over 95% of total revenue. The report also revealed that marketers pay for ad products either directly or through advertising agencies based on the number of impressions or actions such as clicks by users. In another example, according to Snap's 2020 annual report (Snap Inc., 2021), the company derived most of their revenue from advertising. The fiscal report revealed that, for the years 2018, 2019, and 2020, advertising revenue represented around 99%, 98%, and 99% respectively, of total revenue. Interestingly, Snap's report also revealed the potential risk in the advertising business: The advertising business relies heavily on the social media's ability to collect and disclose data and metrics related to users.

Indeed, in recent years, different countries and regions have focused their attention on the protection of user data. The European Union (EU) has enacted the General Data Protection Regulation (GDPR). The GDPR aims to elevate individuals' control of and protect their rights related to personal data. The California State Legislature also rolled out the California Consumer Privacy Act (CCPA) to enhance privacy rights for residents of California, United States. Since September 1, 2021, China's Data Security Law (DSL) has taken effect. This law requires any individual or organization in Chinese territory to effectively protect and legitimately use data and to consistently protect that data. Social media companies that fail to properly collect, use, and store user data could be fined by these regulators. For example, it was reported that Facebook was fined $5 billion by the Federal Trade Commission and must update and adopt new privacy and security measures (Snider & Baig, 2019). The fine was the largest penalty ever imposed on a firm for violating consumers' privacy rights (Snider & Baig, 2019).

## 10.2.2  Social Commerce Strategy

Social commerce strategy is defined as a social media platform's strategic move into e-commerce by incorporating e-commerce features into the platform. As shown in Fig. 10.2, the social commerce business is more complicated than the advertising business. First, the social media platform needs to introduce e-commerce features. The e-commerce features include, but are not limited to, e-commerce stores, product description webpages, user comments, and buyable buttons. The goods purchased through social media platform can be tangible or intangible. For example, social media has embraced forms of online social activities such as online streaming and social gaming, wherein users can purchase virtual items to decorate their digital selves or tip their favorite streamers. Similar social metaverse options (social virtual world) are promoted by many social media platforms. This is also the reason why Facebook Inc. changed its name to Meta (Rodriguez, 2021). Sellers can leverage these features to create their e-commerce stores and merchandise products via the social media platform. Buyers can browse and purchase items directly through the social media platform using these features. E-commerce activities can also occur out of the social media's walled garden. For example, hypertext linkage technology can

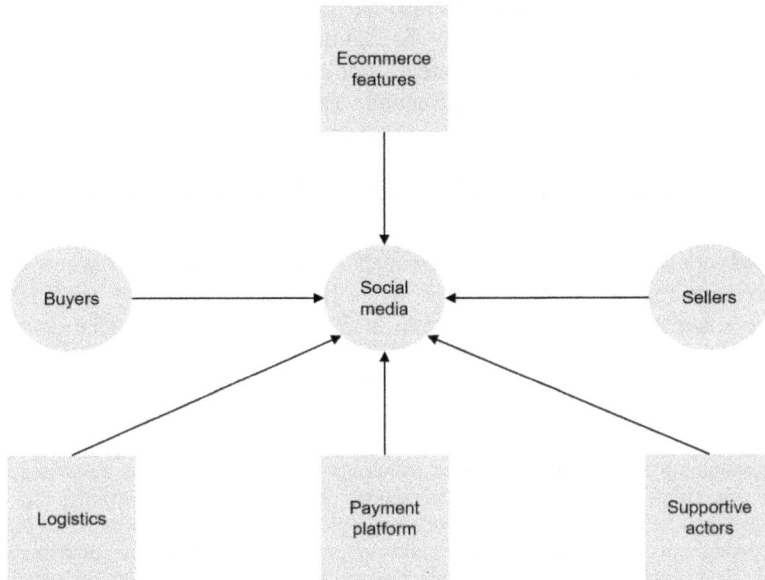

**Fig. 10.2** Social media's social commerce business (source: own elaboration)

be used to lead a buyer from a seller's social media post to an external shopping website. The e-commerce deal is completed on the external website instead of the social media platform. Social media can profit by boosting the seller's social media posts or taking a cut from deals made through a post. Finally, social commerce, like e-commerce, needs logistics, payment platforms, and other supportive aides. Payment platforms embedded in social media enable users to make payments directly through social media. For example, Facebook Pay is available when Facebook users make donations, purchase items on Facebook Shop and Marketplace, and pay for games or event tickets.[2] Logistics are necessary for sellers to fulfill the product delivery process. Although the social media company does not need to own a logistics segment, the social media platform should be able to display shipment information for buyers to confirm this information. Apart from logistics and payment platforms, other supportive aides could play a part in the social commerce business. Insurance for product quality or return shipments could be necessary to protect buyers from being deceived by sellers' fraudulent behavior. It is also possible to incorporate a credit program in social commerce to show buyers and sellers' past transaction credibility. For instance, sellers can be assigned a lower rating if they have received higher return rates, more negative comments, and more consumer complaints.

---

[2] The information related to Facebook Pay is adapted from pay.facebook.com/facebook/ (retrieval date: October 30, 2021).

The social commerce strategy has also been established as successful by some leading social media platforms despite the fact that this strategy is relatively immature compared to the advertising strategy. For example, Kuaishou is a pioneer in creating its own e-commerce infrastructure. This video-based social app allows items to be sold within the app and Kuaishou takes a cut from each deal completed in the app. According to its 2020 Annual Report (Kuaishou Technology, 2021), the total e-commerce Gross Merchandise Value (GMV) was RMB 381,168.5 million, which was staggering considering the e-commerce feature had only recently been introduced into the app. According to the 2020 report, their social media saw growth in the average repeat purchase rate go from 45% in 2019 to 65% in 2020. The company noted the following steps taken in 2020 to enhance its social commerce business:

> In 2020, we continued to support the improvement of our ecosystem, as well as to provide more products and services to address our users' needs, thereby further enhancing the trust and encouraging interactions among users, merchants and our platform. First, we invested in ecommerce infrastructure to facilitate transactions on our platform by providing various tools to help merchants manage their stores on our platform. Second, we incentivized high-quality merchants, as well as supported middle and long-tail merchants by providing training to help them improve their service capabilities and quality. Third, we were dedicated to strengthening platform governance, especially quality control and merchant supervision. We are pleased to see that the overall customer purchasing experience and satisfaction were further optimized. (Kuaishou Technology, 2021, p. 9)

Hua Su, Co-founder of Kuaishou, is one of the leaders incorporating e-commerce into video-based social media. Kuaishou is redefining how e-commerce is exploited in the era of mobile Internet and social media. Previously, the underlying risk in e-commerce was the natural separation between sellers and buyers. Kuaishou uses videos as the main outlet to merchandise items via the social media platform. The platform uses an AI-powered algorithm to find and locate target consumers. Kuaishou enables the use of short social videos that include a shoppable button which users can tap to purchase the item featured and allows livestreamers to merchandise items to viewers in real time. The video format of commercialized social media content enables buyers to see real people promoting items, thus creating higher trust beliefs.

Weibo is another successful example of social commerce. Unlike Kuaishou, this Chinese social media platform focuses on partnering with established e-commerce companies to monetize social commerce. According to Weibo's 2020 Annual Report (Weibo Corporation, 2020), Weibo offers social commerce solutions for their users to administer e-commerce on Weibo. This report revealed that, from April 2013 to January 2016, Weibo had a strategic collaboration with Alibaba and other companies which explored social commerce business. Furthermore, Alibaba merchants can use Weibo to connect to Weibo users. The report demonstrated that revenues generated from the strategic partnership with Alibaba accounted for around 30% of Weibo's total revenues from 2013 to 2015. The success of Weibo relies on the "content ecosystem," a term coined in its annual report (Weibo Corporation,

2020). According to the report, Weibo provides content creators with opportunities to monetize their social assets through e-commerce, subscription, tipping, and other means. In other words, Weibo builds its social commerce business by empowering content creators to profit from commercial activities on Weibo. The more monetary outcomes content creators can achieve from Weibo, the higher monetization performance Weibo will achieve.

This win–win business logic drives Weibo toward a user-centric monetization strategy. Specifically, content creators can merchandise tangible products (e.g., facial masks, Bluetooth speakers, and watches) and intangible goods (e.g., paid articles, copyrighted music, and crafted menus) to their fans. Content creators can also reap monetary benefits by getting virtual gifts from fans. Weibo can take commissions from completed purchases of tangible and intangible products. Fans also need to pay to send some virtual gifts. According to Weibo's 2020 Annual Report, value-added service accounted for $203.8 million in revenue generated from VIP membership, livestreaming, and game-related services (Weibo Corporation, 2020).

In the following chapter, we will discuss in greater detail social media's advertising and social commerce business, i.e., how these monetization strategies are orchestrated as business models for achieving monetization. In particular, we will explore how multiple businesses align for social media companies in order to extract maximum value. Furthermore, we will explain why basic social media services are offered for free, but additional value-added services can be offered for a fee.

# References

Agrawal, A. J. (2016). *It's not all bad: The social good of social media.* Retrieved September 29, 2021, from https://www.forbes.com/sites/ajagrawal/2016/03/18/its-not-all-bad-the-social-good-of-social-media/?sh=d3b4d4c756fb

Aksan, N., Kisac, B., Aydin, M., & Demirbuken, S. (2009). Symbolic interaction theory. *Procedia—Social and Behavioral Sciences, 1*(1), 902–904. https://doi.org/10.1016/j.sbspro.2009.01.160

AppLovin. (2021). *What is a good retention rate and why does it matter?* Retrieved October 16, 2021, from https://www.applovin.com/blog/what-is-retention-rate/

Bányai, F., Zsila, Á., Király, O., Maraz, A., Elekes, Z., Griffiths, M. D., et al. (2017). Problematic social media use: Results from a large-scale nationally representative adolescent sample. *PLoS One, 12*, e0169839. https://doi.org/10.1371/journal.pone.0169839

Błachnio, A., Przepiorka, A., & Pantic, I. (2016). Association between Facebook addiction, self-esteem and life satisfaction: A cross-sectional study. *Computers in Human Behavior, 55*, 701–705. https://doi.org/10.1016/j.chb.2015.10.026

Chen, W. K., Huang, Y. S., & Hsu, P. Y. (2011). Hedonic values and utilitarian values as predictors of social media participation. In *Proceedings of the International Conference on Electronic Business (ICEB)*, pp. 45–51.

Clifford, C. (2017). *How Mark Zuckerberg keeps Facebook's 18,000+ employees innovating: 'Is this going to destroy the company? If not, let them test it.'* Retrieved October 18, 2021, from https://www.cnbc.com/2017/06/05/how-mark-zuckerberg-keeps-facebook-employees-innovating.html

Dohrmann, S., Raith, M., & Siebold, N. (2015). Monetizing social value creation—A business model approach. *Entrepreneurship Research Journal, 5*(2), 127–154.

Facebook Inc. (2021). *Annual report 2020.* Retrieved October 30, 2021, from https://www.annualreports.com/HostedData/AnnualReports/PDF/NASDAQ_FB_2020.pdf

Faller, P. (2019). *Putting personas to work in UX design: What they are and why they're important.* Retrieved September 28, 2021, from https://xd.adobe.com/ideas/process/user-research/putting-personas-to-work-in-ux-design/

Geng, M. (2021). Transforming track to build a new pattern of high-quality development in Henan. *Henan Daily,* 2021-10-14(005).

Hammadabid. (2021). *7 Activities to grow your online business in 2021.* Retrieved September 27, 2021, from https://techgave.com/7-activities-to-grow-your-online-business-in-2021/#:~:text=According%20to%20Google%2C%2040%20percent%20of%20apps%20are,publishers%20are%20not%20investing%20in%20app%20store%20optimization

Hawi, N. S., & Samaha, M. (2017). The relations among social media addiction, self-esteem, and life satisfaction in university students. *Social Science Computer Review, 35,* 576–586. https://doi.org/10.1177/0894439316660340

Helfat, C. E., & Raubitschek, R. S. (2000). Product sequencing: Co-evolution of knowledge, capabilities and products. *Strategic Management Journal, 21*(10–11), 961–979. https://doi.org/10.1002/1097-0266(200010/11)21:10/11<961::aid-smj132>3.0.co;2-e

Hou, Y., Xiong, D., Jiang, T., Song, L., & Wang, Q. (2019). Social media addiction: Its impact, mediation, and intervention. *Cyberpsychology, 13*(1), 4. https://doi.org/10.5817/CP2019-1-4

Kazmi, R. (2021). *User retention: Why Is it so important?* Retrieved October 15, 2021, from https://www.koombea.com/blog/user-retention/

Klimow, A. (2016). *How to create a credible description for the app store.* Retrieved September 28, 2021, from https://vironit.com/how-to-create-a-credible-description-for-the-app-store/

Koc, M., & Gulyagci, S. (2013). Facebook addiction among Turkish college students: The role of psychological health, demographic, and usage characteristics. *Cyberpsychology, Behavior and Social Networking, 16,* 279–284. https://doi.org/10.1089/cyber.2012.0249

Kuaishou Technology. (2021). *Annual report 2020.* Retrieved October 30, 2021, from https://ir.kuaishou.com/static-files/9b436e92-fd39-404c-877e-c3b0d9b92b80

Kump, B., Engelmann, A., Kessler, A., & Schweiger, C. (2019). Toward a dynamic capabilities scale: Measuring organizational sensing, seizing, and transforming capacities. *Industrial and Corporate Change, 28*(5), 1149–1172. https://doi.org/10.1093/icc/dty054

Lahiri, A. (2021). *Chinese AI social app soul secretly files for $300M US IPO: Bloomberg.* Retrieved September 28, 2021, from https://finance.yahoo.com/news/chinese-ai-social-app-soul-125449774.html

Liu, Q., Shao, Z., & Fan, W. (2018). The impact of users' sense of belonging on social media habit formation: Empirical evidence from social networking and microblogging websites in China. *International Journal of Information Management, 43,* 209–223. https://doi.org/10.1016/j.ijinfomgt.2018.08.005

McLeod, S. (2020). *Maslow's hierarchy of needs.* Retrieved October 17, 2021, from https://www.simplypsychology.org/maslow.html

PRNewswire. (2021). *Soul app hits the 30 million MAU milestone in four years, riding a nascent social network trend.* Retrieved September 28, 2021, from https://www.benzinga.com/pressreleases/21/02/n19439480/soul-app-hits-the-30-million-mau-milestone-in-four-years-riding-a-nascent-social-network-trend?utm_campaign=partner_feed&utm_source=yahooFinance&utm_medium=partner_feed&utm_content=site

Rampton, J. (2015). *The beginner's guide to app store optimization.* Retrieved September 28, 2021, from https://www.forbes.com/sites/johnrampton/2015/10/16/the-beginners-guide-to-app-store-optimization/

Rodriguez, S. (2021). *Facebook changes company name to Meta.* Retrieved October 31, 2021, from https://www.cnbc.com/2021/10/28/facebook-changes-company-name-to-meta.html

Shensa, A., Escobar-Viera, C. G., Sidani, J. E., Bowman, N. D., Marshal, M. P., & Primack, B. A. (2017). Problematic social media use and depressive symptoms among US young adults: A nationally-representative study. *Social Science & Medicine, 182*, 150–157. https://doi.org/10.1016/j.socscimed.2017.03.061

Snap Inc. (2021). *Annual report 2020*. Retrieved October 30, 2021, from https://s25.q4cdn.com/442043304/files/doc_presentations/presentation/2021/Snap-Inc.-2020-Annual-Report.pdf

Snider, M., & Baig, E. C. (2019). *Facebook fined $5 billion by FTC, must update and adopt new privacy, security measures*. Retrieved October 30, 2021, from https://www.usatoday.com/story/tech/news/2019/07/24/facebook-pay-record-5-billion-fine-u-s-privacy-violations/1812499001/

Solomon, M. R. (2018). *Consumer behavior: Buying, having, and being* (12th ed., Trans. by Xiaoyan Yang et al.). Renmin University Press.

Statista Research Department. (2021). *Google play: Number of available apps 2009–2021*. Retrieved September 27, 2021, from https://www.statista.com/statistics/266210/number-of-available-applications-in-the-google-play-store/

Teece, D. J. (2007). Explicating dynamic capabilities: The nature and microfoundations of (sustainable) enterprise performance. *Strategic Management Journal, 28*(13), 1319–1350. https://doi.org/10.2307/20141992

Teece, D. J., Pisano, G., & Shuen, A. (1997). Dynamic capabilities and strategic management. *Strategic Management Journal, 18*(7), 509–533. https://doi.org/10.1002/(SICI)1097-0266(199708)18:7<509::AID-SMJ882>3.0.CO;2-Z

The Guardian. (2016). *Facebook makes 13 attempts to clone Snapchat. Lucky for some?* Retrieved October 18, 2021, from https://www.hitc.com/en-gb/2016/11/11/facebook-makes-13-attempts-to-clone-snapchat-lucky-for-some/

The Information Daily. (2021). *Jackie Chan joined Kuaishou, opening the world's first short video social account*. Retrieved October 29, 2021, from https://new.qq.com/omn/20211027/20211027A08UKK00.html

Uysal, R., Satici, S. A., & Akin, A. (2013). Mediating effect of Facebook addiction on the relationship between subjective vitality and subjective happiness. *Psychological Reports, 113*, 948–953. https://doi.org/10.2466/02.09.18.PR0.113x32z3

van Rooij, A. J., Ferguson, C. J., van de Mheen, D., & Schoenmakers, T. M. (2017). Time to abandon internet addiction? Predicting problematic internet, game, and social media use from psychosocial well-being and application use. *Clinical Neuropsychiatry, 14*, 113–121.

Weibo Corporation. (2020). *Annual report 2020*. Retrieved October 31, 2021, from http://ir.weibo.com/static-files/9d492ab8-3e17-47e4-bbf4-ad8d01473ca4

## 11.1 The Social Business: A PESTLE Analysis

The external environment of a social media company encompasses social, legal, and economic aspects that can significantly influence a firm's strategy for monetization. For example, if a social media company breaches a user data protection law, it could incur a large fine or even be banned from offering social media service by user data protection organizations or legal institutions. A legitimate business model is of paramount importance for a social media company to achieve sustainable monetization.

PESTLE analysis, an extension of PEST analysis, is a situational tool used in strategic analysis. PESTLE is the abbreviation for the political, economic, social, technological, legal, and environmental aspects in a firm's environment that could influence the business. Each social media company needs to consider these six aspects when devising its strategy and business model.

1. *Political Analysis.* Social media is a key new media channel in the twenty-first century that cannot be ignored by governments. Social media and social media companies are influencing and being affected by politics. After the 2020 presidential election, right-leaning Facebook pages dominated the discussion around elections and voting, attracting more comments than both left-leaning and ideologically nonaligned pages combined (Gogarty & Martiny, 2021). Right-leaning pages received over 2.7 billion interactions on over 645,000 Facebook posts (Gogarty & Martiny, 2021). Social media is becoming a barometer of American politics. Social media is frequently used for analyzing key political campaigns (Meier et al., 2022) and has also been employed by politicians and election campaigns to promote their political ideology. One result of these actions is that Facebook's previous practice of allowing any type of political ads to be posted to the site has been criticized (Freund, 2020). Even misleading and problematic political statements have been advertised on Facebook without oversight. To combat this situation, Facebook has made efforts to increase the

transparency of political ads. For instance, posters of political ads need to meet certain criteria rolled out by Facebook if their ads are to be displayed (Freund, 2020). These criteria include allowing viewers to see who sponsored the ad and what location and age group the ad is targeting (Freund, 2020). In summary, the social media business is intertwined with today's political environment.

2. *Economic Analysis*. Users' in-app spending has been increasing over time. The statistics reported below by a recent study (Stancheva, 2021) show the potential of future app monetization:

    (a) In 2020, the amount consumers are spending on in-app purchases was USD380 billion globally.

    (b) It is estimated that app revenue will grow to the staggering amount of USD935 billion in revenue in 2023.

    The app economy continues to increase. More online spending is expected in the near future. This trend is a positive factor, implying social media companies may continue to increase profits. As more people are willing to purchase or pay for in-app services or items, additional approaches can be employed by social media companies to monetize their users. For example, Sina Weibo, a microblogging platform, has initialized its content monetization program due to the fact that more and more people are willing to pay for premium content shared on Weibo. A subscription-based monetization mode has been created for Weibo users to access premium content such as healthy recipes, lottery purchases, and investment advice shared by premium content creators.

3. *Social Analysis*. From a global perspective, society has shown great interest in using social media. The statistics offered by Dean (2021) reveal this fact:

    (a) 4.48 billion users currently use social media globally, which is double the 2.07 billion social media users in 2015.

    (b) Over 93% of Internet users are on social media.

    (c) Globally, the average time a person spends on social media per day is 2 h 24 min.

    (d) Facebook was the largest social media company, with 2.9 billion monthly active users (MAUs), followed by YouTube (2.3 billion MAUs), WhatsApp (2 billion MAUs), and WeChat (1.2 billion MAUs).

    Even though social media seems very attractive to society, social media invokes problems that should be highlighted. As discussed in the previous chapter, social media usage may lead to users' depression, anxiety, and insomnia, and eventually decrease one's life satisfaction. This negative influence of social media on users' well-being can be controlled by minimizing usage. According to a study documented by a research team from the University of Pennsylvania, limiting social media use to around half an hour per day could lead to a significant improvement in well-being (Hunt et al., 2018). Nobel (2018) stated, "... not all social media is created equal." Nobel (2018) further noted the negative social influences of social media: Facebook is "highly comparative" and may encourage users to create ostentatious characters that cause us to compare our lives with others; Twitter can be devastating when people are trolled by negative comments;

Dating apps may be helpful for creating a romantic relationship—or they may cause users to become upset about "too many swipe left rejections."

4. *Technological Analysis.* In recent years, new technology has emerged that revolutionizes social media features. Artificial intelligence (AI) is perhaps the most influential of these technologies. AI enables social media companies to increase advertising precision, so that social media advertising becomes more attractive for advertisers. AI is built on social data. The accuracy of AI grows when more social data is used by the algorithms inside the AI technology. AI technology can be used in social media to forecast social media content users' preferences or to build interrelation rules between social media content. The forecast feature can be used for providing social media content relevant to users' interests. The interrelation rules can identify and build interrelations between social media contents that users view; thus, a social media platform can recommend content related to content viewed by users. For example, TikTok uses AI technology to offer more relevant social media content that matches users' interests. Different social media content will be displayed for different users. This differentiated content strategy can significantly increase user satisfaction with relevant social media content. Augmented reality (AR) is another technology that has been adopted by social media. AR filters and lenses enable social media users to add virtual items or decorations to their pictures or videos, making pictures or videos more attractive. Snapchat also launched Shoppable AR by which users can try a certain brand's product using an AR lens. Then, a button appears which leads users to the brand's landing page where they are able to buy the item.

5. *Legal Analysis.* Social media can be a double-edged sword. It raises contentious issues such as copyright infringement and the delivery of misinformation. Therefore, it is necessary to consider the related legal aspects in order to protect social media users. Copyright infringement should be considered to protect creative and original user-generated content shared in social media. Due to the significant amount of user-generated content, it may seem impossible to hold back the wave of copyright infringement in the era of social media. Social media is a platform designed for producing and exchanging content. It is common to see content creators encourage others to distribute content on social media. The sharing of social media content can create impact for content marketing. But not all content creators are willing to see their creative content misused or shared on social media without their authorization. The mix of different content creators' motives can cause difficulties in imposing restrictions on copyright infringement. To combat the copyright infringement issue, countries have undertaken several legal measures. For example, China has refined their Copyright Law. China's laws now include an art category named "video and audio arts," and China increased the fine for copyright infringement of up to CNY five million. Accordingly, major social media platforms, aware of the severity of this issue, have taken steps to crack down on this. Many social media platforms have put stricter regulations and content filters in place regarding content upload to avoid copyright infringement.

Misinformation is another controversial issue in social media. Unlike traditional mass media formats such as television and newspapers, there is a lack of "gatekeepers" controlling information flow for most social media. Research has found that falsehoods spread significantly farther, faster, deeper, and more broadly than truth (Vosoughi et al., 2018). False news reached more people than true news; the top 1% of false news spread to between 1000 and 100,000 people, whereas true news rarely spread to more than 1000 people (Vosoughi et al., 2018). Psychological research also revealed that repeatedly reading misinformation makes it seem less unethical to share misinformation regardless of whether an individual believes it (Effron & Raj, 2020). Repeated misinformation may reduce the moral condemnation that it receives by making it feel intuitively true (Effron & Raj, 2020). For example, U.S. election misinformation is an increasing problem (Deagon, 2020). In 2020, America's political competitors put the nation's electoral process in the crosshairs with fake news stories and doctored videos on social media (Deagon, 2020).

6. *Environmental Analysis*. Social media is used as a news outlet for environmental issues and as a catalyst for environmental activism. Traditional mass media cannot comprehensively report all environmental issues; social media can draw people's attention to environmental issues that may have been overlooked. When a virulent red tide hit Florida's coast in 2021, this event was not reported on any mass media sources (Puentes, 2021). However, over 5.8 million viewers watched a TikTok video made by Paul Cuffaro that reported on the devastating death of fish that resulted from the event (Puentes, 2021). Social media users have used social media to report environmental issues such as deforestation, water conservation, and species extinction. Research has also noted the positive relationship between social media use and pro-environmental behavior. For example, Ai et al. (2021) found that social media use is positively related to voluntary garbage sorting. The mechanism between social media use and pro-environmental behavior can be explained by the social cognitive theory (Bandura, 2001). This theory implies that individuals' learned behavior can be formed by observing the behavior of others and the outcomes of such behaviors, either in real life or on social media (Bandura, 2001). Exposure to pro-environmental issues on social media means people can observe actual pro-environmental behaviors and obtain the experience of performing pro-environmental behavior (Ai et al., 2021). Based on the PESTLE analysis, we find that social media is closely connected to many factors. Running a social business needs to take these factors into consideration. In summary, a modern social business is an ELSE (ethical, legal, social, and economic) business.

## 11.2  Business Model Design

Business model design describes the pattern by which a company makes money. A business model includes three elements: *content*, *structure*, and *governance* (Zott & Amit, 2010). *Content* indicates what activities are to be performed in the business model; *structure* denotes how such activities are linked and sequenced; *governance* defines the persons performing the activities and the places for performing them (Zott & Amit, 2010). The process of business model design follows five steps: identifying product/service elements, business model theming, value-creating mechanism design, value proposition, and business model implementation (Lee et al., 2011). Business model themes can be configured by four elements: novelty, lock-in, complementarities, and efficiency [more detailed information on business model theming can be found in Zott and Amit (2010)].

Existing studies detail the components of business model design and delineate the process of business modeling. Bouwman et al. (2008) offered the STOF framework: service (e.g., value proposition and target group), technology (e.g., value delivery system), organization (e.g., roles, task assignment), and finance (e.g., revenue model). Osterwalder and Pigneur (2010) provided the classic business model canvas: key partners, key activities, key resources, value propositions, customer relationships, channels, customer segments, cost structure, and revenue streams. El Sawy and Pereira (2013) added more components for business model design and developed the VISOR framework: value proposition, interface, service platforms, organizing model, and revenue/cost. Business model researchers have also followed the procedure of design thinking in business modeling. A generic business model design process can follow the process of understanding, observing, defining, ideating, prototyping, and testing (Geissdoerfer et al., 2016). Similarly, He and Ortiz (2021) presented a design framework consisting of portrayal, exploration, prototype, and evaluation.

However, generic business modeling approaches may not perfectly line up with all social media companies' specific business models. Most social media platforms are offered at no charge and are offered by their respective corporations with the intent of monetizing the labor of their users (Srauy, 2015). Social media can be beneficial when users keep using the platform despite social media platforms' ability to monetize users' free labor (Srauy, 2015). Social business models can be characterized by the degree to which social value creation is monetized and the level of revenue generated in excess of costs (Dohrmann et al., 2015). This is a major difference from other types of corporations. Also, due to the heterogeneity of social media platforms, it is difficult for a social media platform to simply imitate another platform. For instance, we all know the Facebook business model is based on advertising. But only Facebook has been so successful with the advertising business model. Furthermore, the ways to monetization are diverse for social media. Different monetization approaches generate different outcomes. The causes and effects of a social business model remain ambiguous. Research has revealed that small changes in a social business model can generate a significant impact on monetization and market performance (Dohrmann et al., 2015). Therefore, modeling a social business is a difficult task. In this chapter, we will categorize existing social business models and discuss how these models are formulated.

## 11.3    Business Modeling for Core Businesses

### 11.3.1 Advertising Business Modeling

Among social media companies, Facebook's advertising-based business model represents the classic social business model. In the model, four actors (Facebook, advertisers, users, and publishers) are participating in the value creation process. Facebook advertisements will not just appear on Facebook News Feed, Facebook right-hand column, Instagram, and Messenger, but also Facebook's external Facebook Audience Network (FAN).[1] FAN allows advertisers to extend their advertising campaigns off Facebook's site and onto other websites, apps, and videos using targeting data. Put simply, users may see the exact same advertisements across the Web. The distinguishing feature of Facebook's business model is that there is a "virtuous circle" where advertisements that match users' preferences produce better outcomes for advertisers, which means more advertising revenue for publishers (Fumagalli et al., 2018). Therefore, internal or external actors can "sell" their advertising resources for advertisers. The Facebook case demonstrates the power of leveraging advertising resources in or off the social media platform.

1. *Building Advertising Architecture.* Programmatic technologies are leading the wave of digital advertising (McGuigan, 2019). Programmatic advertising is a relatively new application of automatic technology that leverages large datasets to disseminate deeply personalized marketing materials to target customers incorporating real-time pricing and bidding (Benady, 2015; White & Samuel, 2019). The most common programmatic advertising on social media is real-time bidding. Real-time bidding is an automatic auction process that enables advertisers to bid on ad space from social media on a cost-per-thousand-impressions basis (Bonacci, 2021). Social media's advertising business model relies on this ad bidding mechanism. In this process, a social media platform will first gather a user's data such as interests, clicks, history, locations, and user profile information. After a period of data collection, this user will be assigned a value by the social media platform. Each time the user swipes up and is about to see an advertisement, real-time bidding is activated. The system will offer an opening price to various advertisers based on this user's assigned value. The highest bid wins and that advertiser can show the user the advertisement. Apart from real-time bidding, social media can also allow programmatic direct. Programmatic direct refers to a form of advertising that allows advertisers to buy advertising space at fixed prices directly from social media platforms, overcoming real-time bidding auctions but with the perk of getting a guaranteed number of impressions on social media (Kovalenko, 2021).

---

[1] Facebook for Developers. Retrieved March 1, 2018, from https://developers.facebook.com/?locale=en_UK

However, programmatic direct advertising is not perfect. Social media platforms are faced with the dilemma of pursuing the acquisition of more detailed information about users to provide more personalized offerings yet doing so increases the possibility of creating a sense of fear among consumers (Samuel et al., 2021). Consumers have displayed concerns over the ethical use of social data (White & Samuel, 2019). Moreover, the automation of advertising does not guarantee the effectiveness of advertising. When just a few advertising platforms use programmatic direct advertising technology, it could be competitive, but if consumers were saturated with programmatic, data-driven advertising, they could become exhausted with such personalized advertisements. Notably, *the right to be forgotten* is stressed in today's digital world. Therefore, programmatic direct advertising technology is a double-edge sword for social media platforms.

2. *Defining the Pricing Model and Bidding Strategies.* The pricing model is the foundation of an advertising business model. A pricing model is comprised of four types: cost per action (CPA), cost per impression (CPI), cost per click (CPC), and cost per view (CPV). CPA refers to the cost of getting a user to both click on an advertisement and perform a desired action (Duncan, 2020). With CPA, the advertising fee is charged when users take actions such as completing an email signup, downloading an app, clicking the "like" button, or directly making a purchase. CPI is the expense a firm incurs every time its social advertisement is displayed to a potential consumer (Clardie, 2021). CPI helps advertisers see if an advertising campaign is reaching a large enough audience to justify the expense (Clardie, 2021). A type of CPI that has been widely adopted by social media platforms is cost per mile (CPM). CPM refers to the price of one thousand advertisement impressions on a social media webpage (Kenton, 2022). CPC is a pricing model used in advertising campaigns, particularly app user acquisition, in which advertisers pay each time a user clicks on their ad (Dogtiev, 2022). As a metric, the CPC rate has a long history and is the metric for many online advertising campaigns (Dogtiev, 2022). CPV denotes the price an advertiser pays for a view on social media (Gollin, 2018). For example, the average industry CPVs on Facebook are between USD0.1 and USD0.15 (Nedelko, 2021).

Based on the pricing model(s), social media can offer advertisers several bidding strategies or options. For example, LinkedIn offers three bidding strategies: manual, target cost, and max delivery.[2] The manual strategy sets an amount to bid on in an auction. Target cost sets target cost per key result and the social media platform automatically adjusts the bid amount to get the highest results while staying within the limit of target cost. Max delivery allows the social media platform to automatically bid to get the max results with the best budget efficiency. Under the different bidding strategies, the advertising fee is charged by different pricing models such as CPC and CPM. Consequently, different bidding strategies lead to different outcomes. For the manual option, advertisers have

---

[2]The discussion on LinkedIn is adapted from https://www.linkedin.com/help/linkedin/answer/a421112?lang=en (retrieval date: March 29, 2022). More information can be seen in this linkage.

more control over their bidding. For the target cost option, advertising cost is more stable. For the max delivery option, no bid management is necessary. The advertising outcome relies on automatic intelligence technology.

3. *Expanding Social Networks and Routinizing Advertising Business.* The success of an advertising business model depends on the scale of social networks. A larger scale of social networks enables advertisers to more easily find target consumers, and social media becomes more attractive for advertisers. The scale-up of social media activates the network effect which means the value of a social media platform is dependent on the number of users who leverage it (Stobierski, 2020). Previously, we have discussed several aspects of the architecture or foundation of building an advertising business model. Due to the heterogeneity of different firms, different firms' advertising business models will be quite different, as will be the financial performance of business models. It is still to be determined what causes the performance difference of advertising business models. For example, Facebook's advertising business model is not unknown to later followers. Facebook's first mover advantage enables this social media platform to accumulate a larger scale of social networks; therefore, later advertising-based social media platforms will find it difficult to catch up to Facebook.

The performance of a social business model relies on multiple internal and external factors. The PESTLE factors previously discussed could affect business model performance. From a resource-based view, organizational resources could shape organizational capability which eventually affects the model performance. Business modeling is a dynamic, evolutionary process that interacts with internal and external factors. Therefore, the perspective of evolutionary economics is more suitable for reviewing the construction and development of business models (Nelson & Winter, 1985). Evolutionary economics is more effective in analyzing the dynamic, competitive business environment than neoclassical economics (Nelson & Winter, 1985). This theory argues that the fate of a firm is determined by its environment and how its environment rewards its heritage of routines (Nelson & Winter, 2002). This point implies that social media monetization is not merely incorporating commercial features into the social media platform. It is more important for a social media platform to create and routinize monetization activities which are approved and can be rewarded by the environment comprised of substantial users. In contrast to previous studies showing that business models can be dissected into different components (see Bouwman et al., 2008; Osterwalder & Pigneur, 2010; El Sawy & Pereira, 2013), we argue that business modeling should not only be aimed at creating a value creation structure, but also define a set of patterns or routines to activate, standardize, and sustain the monetization process. In other words, business models can be characterized as a set of processual patterns (Beynon-Davies, 2018). In order to successfully monetize users, social media companies need to develop a habitual way to turn social value into revenue. This view echoes reality. In fact, successful social media companies will not easily change their monetization approaches. Even though Facebook's versions have been updated many times, their advertising-based monetization routine has not significantly changed. This path dependency mechanism stabilizes a firm's monetization performance.

***Profiting from Advertising*** After creating a routinized advertising system, additional conditions need to be met to successfully profit from this advertising business. Teece (1986) offered an interesting framework of profiting from technological innovation that encompasses three components: regimes of appropriability, the dominant design paradigm, and complementary assets. The regime of appropriability refers to the design of intellectual property rights or the feature of the technology itself that determines a firm's ability to capture the profit generated (Teece, 1986). Social media companies file patents to obtain the regime of appropriability. For example, Meta has been focusing on filing and acquiring patents that support their mission to enable people to build community and bring the world closer together (Chan, 2019). Interestingly, Meta does not just file patents that are relevant to their current plans (Chan, 2019). Many of their patents are not incorporated into their social media platforms, but rather focus on future-looking technology and building future competitive advantage (Chan, 2019).

Dominant design features refer to the technological feature that has become the de facto standard (Horan, 2017). Due to the existence of dominant design, social media platforms are different from each other without being fundamentally different (Markides & Geroski, 2008). Tinder, an online dating and geosocial networking application, established the "swipe right" to like or "swipe left" to dislike other users' profiles. The "swipe right" or "swipe left" feature has been a dominant design feature for many social media platforms. Accordingly, competitors imitate the dominant design. Once a social media feature is popular in the market, competitors can analyze what is special about it and then roll out their imitation which may be even more dominant. It is worth mentioning that the innovator rolling out the dominant design feature may run into an innovator's imitation dilemma (Davis & Aggarwal, 2020). In the competition of digital innovation, imitators often outperform the original creators (Davis & Aggarwal, 2020). For example, TikTok, a short video sharing platform, has had to defend imitators like Meta's Reels (Davis & Aggarwal, 2020).

When constructing a profitable business model, firms need to understand that a social media platform with many daily active users does not necessarily lead to profitability. Complementary assets are supportive assets located downstream of the innovation chain, encompassing assets for innovation such as manufacturing capabilities, distribution channels, service networks, and complementary technologies (Teece, 1986). Therefore, complementary assets need to be considered in the process of building a business model. In terms of social media platforms' advertising business, complementary assets could be social media analysts, third-party applications, and supportive developers. These complementary assets play their part in shaping a social media platform's advertising business.

## 11.3.2  Social Commerce Business Modeling

Social commerce refers to an e-commerce model where consumers place orders for products or services directly through social media platforms (Marticio, 2021). In current social commerce practice, both tangible and intangible products are sold via social media platforms. Recently, major social media platforms have expedited their move into e-commerce. Facebook launched its biggest move into e-commerce with Facebook Shops (Chacon, 2020). This new e-commerce feature allows small businesses to create e-stores on both Facebook and Instagram (Chacon, 2020). Instagram Checkout is available to all eligible firms and content creators in the United States (Warren, 2020). This Checkout feature allows users to make a purchase without leaving the social media platform, creating a frictionless shopping process (Warren, 2020). With the rising demand for direct shopping on Pinterest, this social media platform has provided a Shop tab, a special tab which users can use to search and browse in-stock inventory from online retailers (Canning, 2020). TikTok partnered with Shopify and rolled out Shopping buttons. Video ads that can display a call-to-action button that will lead viewers to a Shopify store (Mayfield, 2021). We can see that even though most social media platforms rely on advertising to monetize, they are also proactive in finding new ways to monetize.

1. *Building E-Commerce Architecture.* E-commerce architecture is the foundation of social commerce business. There are two routes to build it. One is for the company to create its own e-commerce architecture and e-commerce ecosystem. Another is for the company to incorporate third-party e-commerce platforms, creating commercial and financial information exchange between a social media platform and an e-commerce platform. In practice, we see most social media platforms either adopt the latter route or use both approaches. But there are social media platforms offering their own e-commerce features for social users. For example, Kuaishou, a social video sharing app, blocked Taobao's (the dominant e-commerce platform in China) links and has developed its own e-commerce business (Fu, 2022).
   To present a complex example of a social commerce business model, we will discuss the entire e-commerce architecture a social media platform may need to bolster social commerce activities. E-commerce architecture represents a coherent structure of e-commerce systems and can be classified into four subsystems (see Fig. 11.1). The first subsystem is the information exchange subsystem. This subsystem provides for the exchange of item information between sellers and buyers. Sellers can present their items in social media content or incorporate their item information in social media buy buttons. The second subsystem is the finance subsystem. This subsystem offers payment and finance features for buyers and sellers. This subsystem should be highly secure to ensure payment security. The third subsystem is the credit subsystem. This subsystem aims to assess all entities' credibility in social commerce. An entity will be assigned higher credit if he or she performs credibly, for example, never selling counterfeit products or falsely showing low return rates. This credit subsystem is of

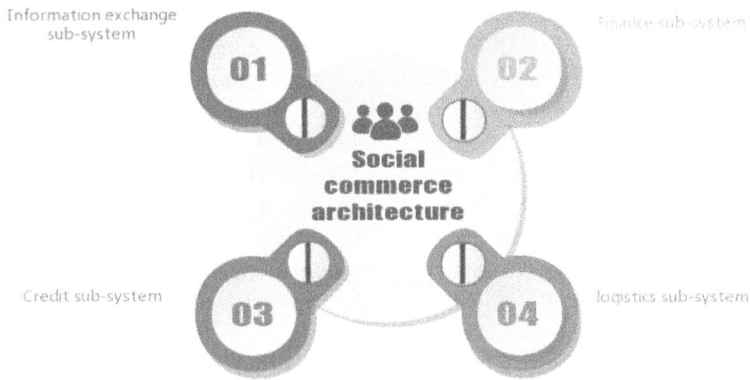

**Fig. 11.1** Subsystems of social commerce (source: own elaboration)

paramount importance for social commerce where trust is difficult to create in comparison to physical retailing. The final subsystem is the logistics or fulfillment subsystem. Once an order is placed, the social media platform should display shipment information for buyers to estimate the arrival date. This logistics subsystem should support forward and backward logistics for buyers to receive and return items.

2. *Empowering Users to Sell on Social Media.* The social commerce business model is a model that depends on a large number of users, and these users' participation in social selling is a key for the flourishing of social commerce. To prompt users' participation in social commerce, it is necessary to understand their needs. Social sellers need to establish a powerful brand image. Social media should enable brands to create a social media page where brands can add a portal for their online stores. It is strongly recommended that a social media platform create its own e-commerce infrastructure so that buyers can browse items without leaving the platform. Sina Weibo, China's answer to Twitter, offers a verification tag for official brands to ensure buyers are purchasing from the official brand stores and that buyers will not be scammed by counterfeit products.

Moreover, social media can offer support for increasing buyers' engagement in brands' marketing campaigns. As coined by the Canadian communication theorist Marshall McLuhan, "the medium is the message." Social media can largely determine consumers' perceptions of a firm. The variety of social media content formats enables a brand to create appealing content for its users. The creating, cloning, and dissemination of social media content can become a fashion or a buzz increasing consumer engagement and brand memory. For example, in 2021, MXBC, a Chinese beverage chain brand, became a powerful brand when its "I love you, you love me" song went viral on social media. The amplification mechanism of social media played a key role in enlarging the influence of this song. Social media should enable brands to create community to foster brand love. Brand community in social media can identify people with shared interests and increase the interactions between a brand and its fans.

However, social media companies need to be careful when using their media power. Social media should be a technology for good. Commercialized media content may or may not be beneficial for human beings' welfare. For example, unhealthy opinions could be advocated by high-calorie food brands, causing people to become obese. Good technology is needed to promote accountable brands and authentic brand information. Social media companies cannot just be paid to promote commercials without discretion. Unfortunately, most social media algorithms are still failing to combat misleading content (Daws, 2021).

3. *Creating and Capturing Social Value.* Business models describe the creation and capture of value. Social commerce business models are centered on the social value shared by users which is a public value shared by the social media platform and users on the platform. The value creation is facilitated by free-to-use social media services and social commerce features. In practice, social commerce features such as social media buy buttons and livestreaming e-commerce are offered free of charge. The creation of an online store on social media is streamlined. A seller needs to create a store name and stock the store with items, and then, a seller is prepared to sell items on social media. Research has found that social media usage can lead to an increase in product awareness, enhanced relationships with consumers, new customers' acquisition, and enhanced ability to reach consumers globally, and promotion of local businesses (Jones et al., 2015).

A social media platform needs to find a way to capture the social value that it created. Even though different types of social media platforms, such as interest communities and social networks, may have different business model structures (Diao et al., 2015), their ways to monetize via social commerce could be similar. In essence, incorporating e-commerce features into a social media platform allows it to become an online marketplace. First, social media can capture the created value by charging a service fee to users. For example, Sina Weibo charges a brand a service fee if they want their social media account to be officially verified. Second, social media can make money from boosting social media content wrapped with shoppable features. Essentially, this is an advertising mode. Apart from charging advertising fees such as cost per clicks or views, social media can also take a percentage from each sale. Last, regarding intangible products such as articles, pictures, and videos, social media can charge a sub-scription fee for users who want to access premium content. This value capture mechanism is built on the freemium model which means the basic service is offered at no charge, but the premium service has a fee. Social media platforms, such as Facebook and Sina Weibo, have adopted this business model.

Based on Teece's (1986) model discussed above, we can discover why social commerce may only constitute a small percentage of a social media platform's total revenue. Social commerce is a new way to promote products and services, but it is not the sole place to shop online. Hence, it is hard for social media platforms to obtain the regime of appropriability.[3] Also, e-commerce technology is quite common and social commerce features are widely adopted by social media platforms. Many social media platforms are merely following traditional e-commerce players' e-commerce design architecture and not creating their own e-commerce design paradigm. In fact, advertising is more suitable for social media companies which are not dependent on fixed assets. Their asset-light model easily succeeds when they need to deploy significant fulfillment networks and highly secure payment systems. When first moving into social commerce, they do not have much bargaining power with logistics companies and finance sectors. These assets impose restrictions on a social media platform's capacity and capability with regard to its e-commerce operation.

### 11.3.3  Hybrid Business Modeling

When we delve into the underlying logic behind the advertising business model and the social commerce business model, we find that they are two different models. The advertising business model converts media resources into advertising revenue. The social commerce business model leverages marketplace power to reach monetization. It can be compared to a car equipped with an internal combustion engine and an electric power system (Furr, 2016). This is a hybrid business model composed of two or more distinct business models (Furr, 2016). We expect that more business models could be incorporated into social media platforms, such as e-tourism, online dating, and manpower recruitment. Therefore, this dynamic process of business model renewal also leaves an issue for social media companies, i.e., how they add a new business model into the existing business model. In another words, the dynamics of social business model evolution remains uncertain.

From a retrospective view, we can examine how a social media platform like Facebook or WeChat hybridized its advertising business model and social commerce business model. Both Facebook and WeChat started with their advertising business and then launched their social commerce business. First and foremost, preliminary efforts in developing social networking services are not mutually exclusive of future social commerce business. For example, Facebook's Profile, Timeline, Verified Page, and Trending features are designed for social interaction; however, these social features also play a role in promoting social commerce. For example, consumers can decide whether a seller is credible or professional by looking at his or her Timeline and Profile. Similarly, WeChat's Moment, Mini Program, and Home Page are useful tools for supporting social commerce activities. Moment can display WeChat users' public posts as well as commercials. Mini Programs can be used for e-commerce activities.

---

[3]Recall that the regime of appropriability refers to the design of intellectual property rights or the feature of the technology itself that determines a firm's ability to capture the profit generated.

Next, key movements toward commercialization may not appear in a commercial way. They could be a consequence of *serendipity*. Advertising has been purposefully considered a way to monetization for WeChat, but not for social commerce. WeChat Pay, a payment interface and infrastructure, is developed and owned by WeChat. This payment feature was initially introduced for WeChat users to send money between users and to make mobile payments. With the advent of the social shopping era, people began to shop on social media. WeChat Pay immediately became a vital e-commerce infrastructure for bolstering social commerce activities. When a user wants to purchase an item shared by an external seller on WeChat, they do not need to leave their credit card information for the seller. At the point of payment, WeChat Pay will automatically appear for users to enter their pin numbers. As this payment feature has been previously used by WeChat users' in their daily lives, users' trust in using the payment feature spilled over into social shopping contexts, which makes WeChat commerce more credible for new entrants.

Last, experimentation or a testing process occurs when different business models are hybridized. Facebook is one of the pioneers in social commerce and started to experiment with its buy button around 2014 (see Krug, 2014). However, following a series of trial and error, Facebook's buy button did not come to fruition. Facebook started social commerce by providing Facebook Marketplace in 2017 and cooperated with PayPal to launch a payment service in 2017. Facebook would finally operate Facebook Shop in 2020 (Chacon, 2020). After years of experimentation, social commerce has become an organic part of Facebook's ecosystem. More recently, Meta, Facebook's parent company, has plans to make its own "Zuck Bucks" (Ridzaimi, 2022). They are "reputation tokens" or "social tokens" which can be used for rewarding "meaningful contributions in Facebook groups" (Ridzaimi, 2022). Although it remains unclear how these tokens will be monetized, it is clear that Meta is attempting to identify additional sources of revenue.

To summarize, it can take years to hybridize different business models on a social media platform. The hybridization process of experimentation prescribes that a social media platform continually innovates and seeks new revenue sources. The hybrid business model is built on the social value and functions brought about on social media platforms. A social feature could be useful for commercial functionality.

## References

Ai, P., Li, W., & Yang, W. (2021). Adolescents' social media use and their voluntary garbage sorting intentions: A sequential mediation model. *International Journal of Environmental Research and Public Health, 18*(15), 8119. https://doi.org/10.3390/ijerph18158119

Bandura, A. (2001). Social cognitive theory of mass communication. *Media Psychology, 3*, 265–299.

Benady, D. (2015). Programmatic: Packed with potential and peril. In *Catalyst* (pp. 13–19). Charted Institute of Marketing.

Beynon-Davies, P. (2018). Characterizing business models for digital business through patterns. *International Journal of Electronic Commerce, 22*(1), 98–124. https://doi.org/10.1080/10864415.2018.1396123

Bonacci, J. (2021). *What is real-time bidding? Real-time bidding in under 5 minutes.* Retrieved March 24, 2022, from https://www.webfx.com/blog/marketing/real-time-bidding/#:~:text=Real-time%20Bidding%20Definition%3A%20Real-time%20bidding%20%28RTB%29%20is%20an,for%20one%20thousand%20people%20to%20see%20your%20ad

Bouwman, H., Faber, E., Haaker, T., Kijl, B., & De Reuver, M. (2008). Conceptualizing the STOF model. In H. Bouwman, H. De Vos, & T. Haaker (Eds.), *Mobile service innovation and business models.* Springer. https://doi.org/10.1007/978-3-540-79238-3_2

Canning, N. (2020). *How the new Pinterest shop tab drives more sales for your business.* Retrieved April 5, 2022, from https://later.com/blog/pinterest-shop-tab/

Chacon, B. (2020). *Facebook & Instagram launch "shops" to help small businesses sell online.* Retrieved April 5, 2022, from https://later.com/blog/facebook-shops/

Chan, J. (2019). *How patents drive innovation at Facebook.* Retrieved April 5, 2022, from https://about.fb.com/news/2019/08/how-patents-drive-innovation/

Clardie, M. (2021). *What is cost per impression?* Retrieved March 29, 2022, from https://www.clearvoice.com/blog/what-is-cost-per-impression/#:~:text=You%20can%20calculate%20the%20cost%20per%20impression%20on,per%20impression%20is%20%240.0125%20%28%2450%20cost%20divided%20by%204%2C000%29

Davis, J., & Aggarwal, V. (2020). *The innovator's imitation dilemma: TikTok and Facebook in context.* Retrieved April 5, 2022, from https://knowledge.insead.edu/entrepreneurship/the-innovators-imitation-dilemma-tiktok-and-facebook-in-context-14961

Daws, R. (2021). *Social media algorithms are still failing to counter misleading content.* Retrieved April 6, 2022, from https://artificialintelligence-news.com/2021/08/17/social-media-algorithms-are-still-failing-to-counter-misleading-content/

Deagon, B. (2020). *Fake news in 2020 election puts social media companies under siege.* Retrieved March 17, 2022, from https://www.investors.com/news/technology/fake-news-2020-election-puts-social-media-companies-under-siege/

Dean, B. (2021). *Social network usage & growth statistics: How many people use social media in 2021?* Retrieved November 29, 2021, from https://backlinko.com/social-media-users

Diao, Y., He, Y., & Yuan, Y. (2015). Framework for understanding the business model of social commerce. *International Journal of Management Science, 2*(6), 112–118.

Dogtiev, A. (2022). *Cost per click (CPC) rates 2022.* Retrieved March 29, 2022, from https://www.businessofapps.com/ads/cpc/research/cpc-rates/

Dohrmann, S., Raith, M., & Siebold, N. (2015). Monetizing social value creation—A business model approach. *Entrepreneurship Research Journal, 5*(2), 127–154. https://doi.org/10.1515/erj-2013-0074

Duncan. (2020). *What is cost per action and how is it calculated?* Retrieved March 29, 2022, from https://zyro.com/learn/cost-per-action/

Effron, D. A., & Raj, M. (2020). Misinformation and morality: Encountering fake-news headlines makes them seem less unethical to publish and share. *Psychological Science, 31*(1), 75–87. https://doi.org/10.1177/0956797619887896

El Sawy, O. A., & Pereira, F. (2013). VISOR: A unified framework for business modeling in the evolving digital space. In *Business Modelling in the dynamic digital space. SpringerBriefs in digital spaces.* Springer. https://doi.org/10.1007/978-3-642-31765-1_3

Freund, J. (2020). *Facebook's political advertisement Regulations in Georgia.* Retrieved November 28, 2021, from https://caspianpolicy.org/research/articles/facebooks-political-advertisement-regulations-in-georgia

Fu, Z. (2022). *Kuaishou to block Taobao and JD links and concentrate on its own e-commerce business amid public trust crisis.* Retrieved April 5, 2022, from https://en.pingwest.com/a/9877

Fumagalli, A., Lucarelli, S., Musolino, E., & Rocchi, G. (2018). Digital labour in the platform economy: The case of Facebook. *Sustainability (Switzerland), 10*(6), 1757. https://doi.org/10. 3390/su10061757

Furr, N. (2016). *Hybrid business models look ugly, but they work.* Retrieved April 7, 2022, from https://hbr.org/2016/03/hybrid-business-models-look-ugly-but-they-work

Geissdoerfer, M., Bocken, N. M. P., & Hultink, E. J. (2016). Design thinking to enhance the sustainable business modelling process—A workshop based on a value mapping process. *Journal of Cleaner Production, 135*, 1218–1232. https://doi.org/10.1016/j.jclepro.2016.07.020

Gogarty, K., & Martiny, C. (2021). *Right-leaning Facebook pages have earned billions of interactions on election-related posts since the presidential election.* Retrieved November 27, 2021, from https://www.mediamatters.org/facebook/right-leaning-facebook-pages-have-earned-billions-interactions-election-related-posts

Gollin, M. (2018). *Facebook ad costs explained: CPM, CPC, CPA and more.* Retrieved March 29, 2022, from https://www.falcon.io/insights-hub/topics/social-media-roi/facebook-ad-costs-explained-cpm-cpc-cpa-and-more/

He, J., & Ortiz, J. (2021). Sustainable business modeling: The need for innovative design thinking. *Journal of Cleaner Production, 298*, 126751. https://doi.org/10.1016/j.jclepro.2021.126751

Horan, C. (2017). *An engineer's take on the theory of dominant design.* Retrieved April 5, 2022, from https://www.intercom.com/blog/dominant-design-engineering/

Hunt, M. G., Marx, R., Lipson, C., & Young, J. (2018). No more FOMO: Limiting social media decreases loneliness and depression. *Journal of Social and Clinical Psychology, 37*(10), 751–768. https://doi.org/10.1521/jscp.2018.37.10.751

Jones, N., Borgman, R., & Ulusoy, E. (2015). Impact of social media on small businesses. *Journal of Small Business and Enterprise Development, 22*(4), 611–632. https://doi.org/10.1108/ JSBED-09-2013-0133

Kenton, W. (2022). *Cost per thousand (CPM).* Retrieved March 29, 2022, from https://www. investopedia.com/terms/c/cpm.asp

Kovalenko, I. (2021). *What is programmatic direct advertising.* Retrieved March 24, 2022, from https://smartyads.com/blog/what-is-programmatic-direct-advertising/

Krug, N. (2014). *Facebook buy button: Game changer or fail.* Retrieved April 7, 2022, from https:// sociallight.net/social-media/facebook-buy-button/

Lee, J. H., Shin, D. I., Hong, Y. S., & Kim, Y. S. (2011). *Business model design methodology for innovative product-service systems: A strategic and structured approach.* In 2011 Annual SRII global conference. IEEE, pp. 663–673.

Markides, C. C., & Geroski, P. A. (2008). *Fast second.* Retrieved April 5, 2022, from https://hbr. org/2008/02/fast-second

Marticio, D. (2021). *What is social commerce?* Retrieved April 5, 2022, from https://www. thebalancesmb.com/what-is-social-commerce-5211572

Mayfield, D. (2021). *TikTok for e–commerce: How to sell your products with social commerce.* Retrieved April 5, 2022, from https://www.blog.shippypro.com/tiktok-for-ecommerce/

McGuigan, L. (2019). Automating the audience commodity: The unacknowledged ancestry of programmatic advertising. *New Media and Society, 21*(11–12), 2366–2385. https://doi.org/10. 1177/1461444819846449

Meier, F., Bazo, A., & Elsweiler, D. (2022). Using social media data to analyse issue engagement during the 2017 German Federal Election. *ACM Transactions on Internet Technology, 22*(1), 3467020. https://doi.org/10.1145/3467020

Nedelko, D. (2021). *How much does Facebook advertising cost? 2020/2021 update.* Retrieved April 8, 2022, from https://marketerknows.com/facebook-advertising-cost/

Nelson, R. R., & Winter, S. G. (1985). *An evolutionary theory of economic change.* Belknap Press.

Nelson, R. R., & Winter, S. G. (2002). Evolutionary theorizing in economics. *Journal of Economic Perspectives, 16*(2), 23–46. https://doi.org/10.1257/0895330027247

Nobel, J. (2018). *Does social media make you lonely?* Retrieved November 29, 2021, from https:// www.health.harvard.edu/blog/is-a-steady-diet-of-social-media-unhealthy-2018122115600

Osterwalder, A., & Pigneur, Y. (2010). *Business model generation: A handbook for visionaries, game changers, and challengers*. Wiley.

Puentes, C. (2021). *Social media and environmental activism: An evolving relationship*. Retrieved March 17, 2022, from https://smea.uw.edu/currents/social-media-and-environmental-activism-an-evolving-relationship/

Ridzaimi, S. (2022). *Zuck Bucks? Meta is reportedly ditching crypto for in-app tokens as its Metaverse currency*. Retrieved April 7, 2022, from https://technave.com/gadget/Zuck-Bucks-Meta-is-reportedly-ditching-crypto-for-in-app-tokens-as-its-Metaverse-currency-29460.html

Samuel, A., White, G. R. T., Thomas, R., & Jones, P. (2021). Programmatic advertising: An exegesis of consumer concerns. *Computers in Human Behavior, 116*, 106657. https://doi.org/10.1016/j.chb.2020.106657

Srauy, S. (2015). The limits of social media: What social media can be, and what we should Hope they never become. *Social Media and Society, 1*(1), 1–3. https://doi.org/10.1177/2056305115578676

Stancheva, T. (2021). *17 app revenue statistics—Mobile is changing the game in 2021*. Retrieved November 28, 2021, from https://techjury.net/blog/app-revenue-statistics/

Stobierski, T. (2020). *What are network effects?* Retrieved March 30, 2022, from https://online.hbs.edu/blog/post/what-are-network-effects

Teece, D. J. (1986). Profiting from technological innovation: Implications for integration, collaboration, licensing and public policy. *Research Policy, 15*(6), 285–305. https://doi.org/10.1016/0048-7333(86)90027-2

Vosoughi, S., Roy, D., & Aral, S. (2018). The spread of true and false news online. *Science, 359*(6380), 1146–1151. https://doi.org/10.1126/science.aap9559

Warren, J. (2020). *Instagram checkout: Everything you need to know*. Retrieved April 5, 2022, from https://later.com/blog/instagram-checkout/

White, G. R. T., & Samuel, A. (2019). Programmatic advertising: Forewarning and avoiding hype-cycle failure. *Technological Forecasting and Social Change, 144*, 157–168. https://doi.org/10.1016/j.techfore.2019.03.020

Zott, C., & Amit, R. (2010). Business model design: An activity system perspective. *Long Range Planning, 43*(2–3), 216–226. https://doi.org/10.1016/j.lrp.2009.07.004

# Information System and Structure Design for Social Media Monetization

**12**

## 12.1 Structure and System Design for Social Advertising

Information system (IS) and structure design establish the foundation for successful social media monetization. Previously, we have focused on discussing the conceptual and theoretical aspects of social media monetization. In this chapter, we will focus our attention on more practical knowledge about how to design an IS and structure design for social media monetization. The design research produces new insights for social media monetization because it applies existing theory and knowledge in a field of practice, and, most importantly, updates, refines, and advances our perceptions and knowledge about social media monetization in the iterative and interactive process between designers and artifacts. IS design research has been relevant to theory and knowledge for action, i.e., a form of how-to-do knowledge (Gregor, 2006).

It is inappropriate to view social media system design as merely a technical issue. This technocentric view has raised severe issues in practice. Cutting-edge technologies such as artificial intelligence (AI), data mining, and social media analytics are viable in practice, but they have not been completely embedded in our social system. The social system considers ethical issues and legal consequences related to new technology, and many of these issues have not yet been properly resolved. For example, when Facebook deceived users about their ability to control the privacy of their personal information, the Federal Trade Commission imposed a historical $5 billion penalty and demanded that Facebook increase accountability and transparency.[1]

The term "socio-technical" is defined as the symbiotic relationship between society and technology, and a socio-technical system is based on this relationship

---

[1] FTC Imposes $5 Billion Penalty and Sweeping New Privacy Restrictions on Facebook. Retrieved May 6, 2022, from https://www.ftc.gov/news-events/news/press-releases/2019/07/ftc-imposes-5-billion-penalty-sweeping-new-privacy-restrictions-facebook

F. J. Martínez-López et al., *Social Media Monetization*, Future of Business and Finance, https://doi.org/10.1007/978-3-031-14575-9_12

(Cox, 2018). The socio-technical system stresses humans' subjectivity. It also considers human factors that determine the performance of a technical system such as knowledge, motivations, values, and perceptions (Cox, 2018). These intrinsic elements may derive from situational, cultural, and contextual factors (Cox, 2018). The socio-technical perspective is tailored to social media system design. Social media is an interactive content exchange platform that relies on a large number of users to create and share content. Active users drive a thriving social media platform which is why major social media platforms care about the number of their daily or monthly active users. Research has also indicated that IS design research should delve into generating knowledge for the design of IS systems and view IS systems as socio-technical systems (Carlsson, 2007, 2010). The socio-technical view has been deemed a key foundation in IS design science research (Baskerville et al., 2007; Carlsson, 2010; McKay & Marshall, 2008).

## 12.2  Design Goals

In this chapter, we will discuss the design framework of social media for monetization. Existing social media has met a set of significant needs. Therefore, a successful strategy would not merely include replicating what exists or deconstructing existing social media platforms such as Facebook. At the same time, the existing framework of social media platforms should be studied. From the socio-technical view, existing social media platforms have been tested and proven in the market. Hence, we should understand existing design and develop new designs in order to address the current problems that existing social media platforms do not.

Privacy breaches, fake news, information overload, overcommercialization, and copyright violation are major problems for existing social media platforms. Because of these problems, many people have abandoned social media. A recent behavior, coined "social media detoxification," refers to "voluntary attempts at reducing or stopping social media use to improve well-being" (El-Khoury et al., 2021). After a detoxification period, people reported a positive change in mood, less anxiety, and better sleep quality (El-Khoury et al., 2021). A recent survey conducted by the Washington Post-Schar School found that the majority of adults did not trust social media platforms such as Facebook (72% distrust rate), Instagram (60% distrust rate), TikTok (63% distrust rate), WhatsApp (53% distrust rate), and YouTube (53% distrust rate) (see Open Thought, 2022); 64% of Americans thought that social media has a negative impact on the USA (see Open Thought, 2022).

If these problems cannot be properly addressed, it is meaningless to discuss monetization. Privacy protection, accurate information, appropriate commercialization, and legitimate operations are "hygiene factors" that determine users' continued use of social media. Monetization is a higher-order goal for social media design. Preventing or resolving these problems is a lower-order goal for design. For example, social media platforms can introduce privacy policies, data encryption, and data collection restrictions that protect user privacy. Therefore, while we do not intend to act in the way of software engineers, we will suggest key design features, principles, policies, and functions for social media to successfully reach monetization. A characteristic of this research is its focus on designing principles or mechanisms for constructing a *responsible* and *profitable* social media platform.

## 12.3  Social Media Content

Social media is a content exchange platform, and content is the most valuable asset of a social media platform. If a social media platform's content is not appealing, fewer and fewer users will continue to use the platform. The first component of a social media platform is social media content generation. Social media allows users to create original content and share exciting life moments. Social media content can be textual, graphic, audio, and video. Recently, social media video apps have become popular. In 2021, TikTok stated that it had one billion active users, denoting exponential growth of the social video app (Bursztynsky, 2021). Short video social media apps can bring more immersive experiences for users.

Social media content can be instant messages between two friends, shared information in social community, or social media posts in news feeds. Social media content can be directly monetized by incorporating commercial features. Sina Weibo has been exploring content monetization since 2014. This microblogging platform incorporated content subscription features in microblogs. Content creators can offer free initial content (e.g., first chapters in a novel) and charge followers for access to the rest of the content. A microblogging platform can take a percentage from creators' earnings. This has been a proven strategy in social media content monetization. Facebook cloned Patreon, a subscription-based content platform, to create similar content monetization modes for luring creators with cash rewards (Constine, 2018).

Social media platforms are facing several important failings with regard to social media content. These flaws are undermining the base of social media monetization. Misinformation is the most severe problem for social media. Recently, the Russia–Ukraine war has been viewed as "the first TikTok war" as war-related information is simultaneously shared in social apps such as TikTok (Brown, 2022). Some accounts are real, but there is concern about misinformation shared on the app (Brown, 2022). As reported by NewsGuard, TikTok was feeding false and misleading content about the Russia–Ukraine war to users within 40 min of their signing up to the app (Cadier et al., 2022). During the COVID-19 pandemic, social media platforms have been spreading accurate and inaccurate information (Gabarron et al., 2021). A large amount of misinformation about the pandemic was shared on social media and led to an increase in social anxiety and damage to our mental health, which led to users' distrust in social media content. To analyze the motivations behind widespread misinformation on social media, we first ask a question: Do social media users really care about the authenticity of social media content? On the one hand, people should care about the authenticity of social media content because social media has become a major source of information for many people. The authenticity of social media content influences our life, society, and economy. The representative case was the

Associated Press's (AP's) fake tweet of "explosions at the White House" (Downing, 2018) due to their account being hacked. Just after the AP's Twitter account was hacked and the fake tweet about explosions at the White House was posted, the Dow Jones Industrial Average dropped 150 points in seconds (National Post Wire Services, 2013). Within 3 min, the AP stated that its account had been hacked and the tweet was fake; however, this 3-min market plunge briefly wiped out over \$100 billion of the S&P 500's value (National Post Wire Services, 2013). On the other hand, some people intentionally create deceptive content and share it on social media. Research has revealed that, due to people's social media sharing, fake news spreads faster than true news (Langin, 2018). Driven by the fear of missing out (FOMO), people follow the pleasure principle and may participate in the spreading of fake news (Beesley, 2018). The more views a piece of fake news receives, the more likely it is to reach a wider audience. Fakes news leverages the content recommendation algorithms of social media. We recommend that algorithm designers step in and figure out how to crack down on the spreading of fake news. In fact, there have been pioneering studies about using machine learning to combat fake news (Aneja & Aneja, 2021). Apart from developing social media algorithms, multiple stakeholders should participate in harnessing social media misinformation. Social media can include a feedback feature for users to report biased, fake, misleading, and other toxic social media content. Government, nonprofit organizations, and policy-makers can also create laws, rules, and regulations for combating misinformation. The involvement of multiple actors and stakeholders should largely enrich the socio-technical system, which should eventually create a shared responsibility structure that minimizes social media misinformation.

Advertising is the most common way for social media platforms to monetize social media content. Advertising and e-commerce features can be incorporated into social media content in several ways. The simplest way is to allow content creators to incorporate a link in their social media feeds. This link can lead viewers to an external website to complete purchases. As social media feeds and external websites are isolated from each other, this brings frictions in the purchase path from a social media platform to an external website. Social media can monetize on this by creating an ad bidding strategy based on cost per clicks or cost per mile.

Another way to incorporate e-commerce into social media content is for a social media platform to create its own e-commerce infrastructure. For example, Facebook created its own Facebook Shop (Cohen, 2020). This shopping feature enables sellers to share their products and offers with consumers and easily tag their products in Facebook posts to boost sales (TeckSolver, 2020). According to Facebook's vice president of ads, Dan Levy, Facebook will still focus on advertising and also take a "small fee" on each transaction (Cohen, 2020). While the creation of its own e-commerce infrastructure sounds interesting, this move creates more workload for e-commerce players because they need to operate their social commerce shops and update stock information, offer real-time consumer service, and fulfill orders placed by social media. Social media platforms should not be designed in a way to increase business users' workload, so it is not always the best solution to create an e-commerce infrastructure. Recently, headless, or customizable, commerce is on the rise. In headless commerce, the e-commerce backend area is independent, yet still connected with the content management end (Ruder, 2021). This new commerce mode enables a single engine to power diverse online storefronts including social media posts (Ruder, 2021). Headless commerce makes it possible for e-commerce players to simply use a core e-commerce system to manage all sales channels including social media channels. This headless mode is convenient for e-commerce players and allows them to focus on operating their own e-commerce business. Accordingly, social media should enable this connection between its platform and headless commerce systems. This loose cooperative structure between social media and external e-commerce systems should be beneficial for both parties. Social media platforms can avoid over-monetizing users by becoming an all-in-one app. At the same time, e-commerce players can focus on their core business systems and create more relevant social media feeds for their social media followers.

## 12.4 Social Media Profile and Social Media Connection

It is unlikely that social media platforms offer us the meaningful connections we really desire. Alexandria (2018) stated, "social media helps keep me connected to my communities, but social media itself is not my community." Social media is often deemed a way to lessen loneliness; however, it commonly makes people feel lonelier.[2] The main problem with the status of current social media is that it is losing its merit as a platform for making friends and having social interactions and is turning into a platform packed only with entertainment content. Entertainment has become the content of all our discourse (see Postman, 1987); consequently, information on social media is becoming less valuable than the entertainment value that it delivers. Therefore, our first priority should be to redefine the concepts of "friends" and "connections" on social media. It is time for social media to go back to its roots and enable people to find true friends and build meaningful connections. True social media friends should reflect real-life or the virtual social ties that a person enjoys. Social media helps us build, maintain, or restore relationships we have in the real world and the virtual world. It fills up holes in our real social networks that are difficult to maintain, such as long-distance relationships. Meaningful connections are built over time, in exchanges of mutual openness, empathy, and other mutual beneficial aspects (Otte, 2019). Many social media networks contain a large number of fake accounts, social bots, and online trolls. However, more mission-driven technology companies are surfacing and creating socially focused platforms such as Talkspace, seven Cups, and Friended (Otte, 2019). These social apps aim to cater to the desire for safe, honest, and meaningful social interactions (Otte, 2019). Soul is

---

[2]Social Media Increases Depression and Loneliness. Retrieved May 12, 2022, from https://healtharchivee.com/social-media-increases-depression-and-loneliness/#:~:text=Social%20Media%20Increases%20Depression%20and%20Loneliness.%20Social%20media%2C,social%20media%20isolates%20people%20and%20leads%20to%20depression

a social app that demonstrates how a pure social app can gain momentum within today's competitive online traffic. It has approximately 34 million monthly active users. Soul creates a secure, comfortable environment for users to efficiently connect and interact with others, enabling users to freely express their ideas and content and receive responses from others. Apart from using artificial intelligence to match people with similar interests, Soul conceals users' real identity and social class in order to create equal relationships between users (CYzone, 2021). This is a major difference from most social media platforms in which key influencers generate more impact and obtain more attention. In other words, there are two design strategies for social media profiles and social connections. The first strategy is allowing users to display their social status and identity. The other is hiding or blurring users' real identity and status to promote more unbiased connections between strangers.

Social media profiles and social media connections can include monetization elements. Social media profiles contain textual and graphic information about a social media user. In order to combat misinformation and fake accounts, social media profile verification is a way to increase the authenticity of social media profiles and verify a social media user's real identity. Social media profile verification ensures a user can find the user he or she intends to interact with. Sina Weibo is an example of successfully monetizing social media profiles. Weibo is a Twitter-like social media platform with a substantial active user base. Celebrities, athletes, brands, politicians, and many other individuals and organizations are using Weibo to interact with their followers. If there was no profile verification, a person could mimic a celebrity's social media profile and use this social media account to deceive the celebrity's followers. Weibo imposes a verification mechanism to avoid impersonation and to guarantee authentic information sharing. A symbol "V" is displayed with verified social media profiles. Weibo charges a fee for verification, but government, media, education, and other social welfare organizations are eligible for a waiver of the fee. Verification can significantly increase user trust in the authenticity of social media profiles. It ensures that it benefits brands wanting to use their social media account for marketing and sales.

Social media connections are the social relationships a social media user has in a particular social network. As mentioned previously, lack of meaningful connections is a rising problem faced by social media platforms. The mission of a social media platform should be to help users find friends, whether these friends are in real life or virtual. It is common that social media platforms allow users to use an identifiable name, code, or graphic for ease in adding social media friends. From a business perspective, this is a key way for physical businesses to connect and keep customers. Physical businesses can include quick response (QR) codes in their physical stores. QR codes are scanned in store allowing visitors to follow the business's social media account. The design of social media should enable local businesses to build a proprietary network of customers. Social media, accordingly, is a tool used by business to serve their customers. For example, a flower store can offer a discount promotion for customers following the store's social media account. The store can periodically feed followers their newest flower arts and promote the sale of flowers. Another way to build social media connections is recommending new friends or persons who a social media user may be familiar with. As mentioned previously, Soul, an anonymous social app, uses machine learning (ML) to recommend new friends with similar interests. However, Soul has not found a way to monetize their ML-based social media connections. LinkedIn, a professional social networking platform, has found a way to monetize social media connections by offering a hiring and recruitment service. LinkedIn Recruiter is a recruitment platform for human resource (HR) managers that helps firms find and connect with talents they may want to hire. The recruitment platform enables HR managers to search for any candidate on LinkedIn using a keyword search, a Boolean search and over 20 other search filters.[3] Social media community is also a way to find and build social media connections. Firms can use social media community, a key place to conduct firm–customer interactions, to forge competitiveness and reach monetization. We discuss the design features and principles of social media community in the next section.

## 12.5  Social Media Community

Social media community involves the use of social media users to participate in a community and feel a sense of belonging to the community (Tarigan et al., 2022). Research has indicated that consumers' participation in a social media brand community can help develop brand trust and loyalty, and that consumer–brand identification plays a key role in shaping consumer–brand relationships (Coelho et al., 2018). Social media communities can be categorized into different types. First, communities of interests are communities where people share similar interests. For instance, a brand community allocates consumers with a similar interest in the brand. Second, communities for information sharing are social groups where people share information with each other. For example, residents join a social media community for sharing and viewing information shared by others. The community for information sharing wipes out the efforts of directing information on an individual basis. The last type of social media communities is task-focused communities. This type of social media community is oriented toward user collaboration in fulfilling tasks. For example, Workplace for Facebook is an enterprise version of Facebook allowing business users to create groups in which colleagues work together to complete tasks.

Due to the anonymity of social media community, hate speech, online trolls, and cyberbullying are jeopardizing and tarnishing the entire community. Therefore, it is necessary to take steps to prevent this type of negative content from being shared in community. Social media design features can be included to combat negative content sharing. Social media community needs to design and create a respectful culture that encourages community members to act in a friendly manner when sharing, viewing, and reacting to social media content. Abusive, harassing, profane, misleading, and bullying speeches should be banned from community. A respectful

---

[3]LinkedIn Recruiter. Retrieved May 14, 2022, from https://business.linkedin.com/talent-solutions/recruiter

culture relies on creating an organizational structure, administrative guidelines, and community management features to support these goals. For example, Baidu Tieba is a social platform where users can join a particular community in a particular domain. This platform was a place that spreads misleading information and hates speech, but it has been evolving its regulation principles and mechanisms to combat these negative community posts. Baidu Tieba has found that users' self-regulation is key to manage community in various domains such as schools, stars, regions, literature, and healthcare. The administrators of these online communities are the key to implementing the self-regulation policy. Therefore, Baidu Tieba has elaborated detailed guidelines and rules for people wanting to be an administrator of an online community. "Mission, inheritance, mutual assistance, and friendship" are the four pillars of a competent Baidu Tieba administrator. Community administrators should monitor posts in the community and reject or wipe out those posts involving hate speech or misleading information. The election of community administrators even goes through a democratic process in which community members need to participate to vote for their desired administrator. The community administrators also ensure the community posts are on topic, keeping shared content relevant for community members.

Social media is substantially different from traditional media. A key in a social media platform's regulation is balancing the support of free speech with the suppression of misinformation, conspiracy theories, and other inappropriate content (Ghosh, 2021). Penalties such as demonetization, suspending, or even banning social media accounts can be adopted to crack down on inappropriate social media content. However, it remains unclear how to decide the appropriateness of social media content. A simple retributive approach could harm a social media platform's reputation as a place to speak freely. YouTube increased their regulatory level and implemented a system of demonetization for videos involving sensitive topics such as pornography, child abuse, and graphic content (Bagwell, 2018). Demonetization for videos means that video creators will receive lower revenue from the sensitive videos or from their channel (AIR, 2021). However, the problem arises when the demonetization rules, which remain extremely unclear, are inadvertently adopted to censor videos related to politics, current events, and other sensitive topics (Bagwell, 2018). It would be implausible to blindly mark all political content as sensitive, even if the content may seem uncomfortable. In order to avoid the risk of demonetization, content creators should reform their social media channel, follow the guidelines and policies imposed by the social media, and alleviate the risk by spreading polished, sanitized, and mainstreaming content in social media platform (AIR, 2021). At the same time, the penalties imposed by social media could drive content creators to other platforms such as Patreon which is less strict in moderating and censoring content distributed in the platform.

The regulation system for social media community should include external regulators. Governments and nonprofit organizations should develop regulations for the social media community. External regulation can force social media platforms to update their privacy contracts with users and promote users' compliance with the principles and rules agreed upon in the social media community. The

Cyberspace Administration of China has specifically rolled out a regulation about the Internet community. It requires the Internet forum community service provider to fulfill their responsibility in information security systems and to not use the forum to publish and disseminate information prohibited by laws and regulations.[4] In the USA, there are several players involved in developing a regulatory system for social media; Federal regulators, state legislators, and Congress are influential regulators for social media (Coldewey, 2020). However, social media allows for the diversity and multiplicity of options and opinions, while governments' one-size-fits-all policy could threaten social media and free speech (Ortner, 2019). Therefore, it is imperative to find a way to regulate social media which is more equitable to relevant stakeholders such as users, content creators, social media platforms, and governments.

In the era of big data and artificial intelligence, the monetization and regulation of social media community and content need new insights into the relationship between humans and technology. Big data analytics and artificial intelligence are a dominant technological force for social media content delivery and identification. The delivery of advertisements and commercial posts relies on a machine-based process to recognize target consumers. Likewise, the identification of misinformation and sensitive social media content involves the use of machine learning, along with visual and textual recognition techniques. Substantial social media content is created and shared in social media community, making it difficult for humans to moderate and manage all content. Machine learning is an inevitable tool in detecting inappropriate content. But machine learning-based algorithms are easily prone to mistakes in content decisions; for instance, YouTube used automated age restrictions to unfairly block some creators' videos and then noticed this mistake and stated that they would amend it (Solsman, 2020).

## 12.6  Social Commerce Features in Social Media

Social commerce injects e-commerce features into social media platforms. Social commerce features can be included in social media content, profiles, connections, and communities. First, we will discuss basic social commerce features.

1. *Buy Buttons*. Buy buttons are navigation features for social media users to access more product information and complete a purchase within social media. There are a vast variety of buy buttons: purchase icons, clickable figures, shopping carts, and product tags, to name a few. Buy buttons connect a social media platform to an e-commerce platform. The buy buttons are at the core of social commerce and have substantially commercialized social media and social interactions. The

---

[4]The Cyberspace Administration of China (CAC) announces the Regulations on the Administration of Internet Forum Community Services (with full text). Retrieved May 16, 2022, from http://www.sic.gov.cn/News/91/8409.htm

inclusion of a buy button in social media content can move a social media user's mindset from a browsing mindset to a commercial or shopping mode. Many social media platforms have adopted and incorporated buy buttons into their platforms.

Dr. Rachel Plotnick (2018), the author of *Power Button: A History of Pleasure, Panic and the Politics of Pushing*, provides a comprehensive discussion of why people like buttons, from pushing a button to turn on the television, to clicking a button to "like" something on social media. She argues that button pushing became a means for digital command, which ensured "effortless, discreet, and fool-proof control." Button pushing fulfills people's desire for power and brings about instant gratification (Plotnick, 2018). Social media buy buttons are easy to use. When a buy button is featured in a promotional post, it removes the effort of users leaving the social media platform and going to a shopping platform to search for and purchase the product promoted in the post. If a default payment option has been set up and linked with a consumer's credit card, with just a simple push of the buy button, the consumer has completed the purchase and only needs to wait for the delivery of the item. Social media buy buttons boost impulse purchases on social media, and largely facilitate consumerism on social media.

2. *Social Media Shops*. Shops can appear on a social media user's profile page or main page. The shops present all items sold by the social media user. Since its interception, social commerce has been criticized as using new media channels to monetize naive consumers. It is the invention of social media shops which has laid the foundation for the social media marketplace. Social media is not merely a channel to merchandise goods; instead, it changes and shapes the substantial aspect of our consumption. Social media shops enable social media to become an actual marketplace where firms can leverage their social media influence to develop a brand. This value-added approach was recently discovered and adopted by many social media companies.

Kuaishou, a social video app, is an example of the evolution of social commerce.[5] Started around 2018, Kuaishou lacked its own e-commerce infrastructure and mostly relied on influencers or streamers using their personal influence to promote items. With the popularity of social commerce, particularly livestreaming e-commerce, Kuaishou's e-commerce market was quickly dominated by a few powerful influencers. Since 2019, Kuaishou has been creating its own supply chain to ensure well-designed supplies for its e-commerce market. It also encouraged influencers to create their personal brand and establish livestreaming infrastructure. TikTok, another pioneer in social video apps, was also exploring what distinguishes social commerce from traditional e-commerce. Both TikTok and Kuaishou have been extensively finding ways to create distinguished social commerce. They were aware that building exclusive social media brands is the

---

[5]The case study about Kuaishou was adapted from Kuaishou e-commerce evolution: From barbarism to prosperity. Retrieved May 17, 2022, from https://www.chinaz.com/2022/0516/1395603.shtml

key for long-term successes. In 2022, Kuaishou initiated a Kuai brand support program, and they plan to spend 23 billion yuan to cultivate 500 Kuai brands encompassing multiple sectors such as beauty, apparel, and food. The feature Kuaishou Shop was officially created for boosting Kuai brands and Kuaishou e-commerce. There are several salient characteristics of Kuai brands. First is the intertwined relationship between the influencer's personal brand and the product brand. Second is the immersive shopping experience brought about by interactions between influencers and fans. Last are the repeated purchases derived from the proprietary social community owned by the influencer. Traditional e-commerce platforms do not possess these characteristics. In essence, successful social commerce builds a strong emotional tie between influencers, brands, and fans.

3. *Social Media Wallets*. A social media wallet provides users with convenience and security when making payments while shopping on social media. Users enter their credit card information in their social media profile and set up a default payment method for social shopping. More sophisticated social media wallets allow users to deposit money and access additional financial products. The inclusion of a social media wallet feature enables users to complete the purchase once they click the buy button because their mailing address and payment information are securely stored in the social media platform and are automatically used for social shopping.

   Milanović (2022) argues that the ultimate digital wallet will come from a social media platform and not a fintech company. The author believes that social media can unify consumer data in one comprehensive profile; as consumers do not compartmentalize when they want to make payments, social media wallets offer consumers the ease of having their information on-hand when they want to make payments. However, the development of social media wallets may be controversial in terms of consumer privacy. Social media has collected so much consumer data about our social lives that if a social media platform also accessed and saved our purchase history, there may be little to no consumer privacy remaining. Joint data mining techniques or other data capture techniques can precisely describe and reveal any consumer's identity.

4. *Group Buying*. Under group buying, consumers enjoy a discounted group price if they are willing and able to coordinate their purchases (Jing & Xie, 2011). Group buying allows sellers to benefit from consumers' social interactions, i.e., using a discount to lure informed consumers to act as "sales agents" to reach other consumers (Jing & Xie, 2011). Social media communities, particularly brand communities, are also used for group buying. Brands can share commercials in community for members to initiate group buying. Social media can also launch group buying by partnering with external e-commerce platforms. Pinduoduo is one such e-commerce platform for group buying. Consumers can also share a product post in WeChat for other WeChat users to participate in the group buying. Group buying is a disruptive force for China's traditional markets. Many consumers participate in coordinating their orders to receive discounts by

purchasing in bulk. During the pandemic, group buying skyrocketed and provided retailers with the opportunity to clear out their inventory (Vadhera, 2021).

5. *Subscription and Ad-Free Premium*. Subscription means that consumers pay monthly, quarterly, or annually for premium social media content. It is a commercial feature widely adopted by online streaming platforms such as Netflix. In general, social media has been offered free of charge, but premium content and features will only be accessible to subscribed users. YouTube Premium is a subscription feature for individuals, families, and students. It allows users to have an ad-free experience, bundle YouTube music, and have offline or background listening. Sina Weibo's paid subscription feature allows microbloggers to charge their fans a subscription fee to access premium content created or shared by the microbloggers.

Subscription-based social media has a promising future. However, the way existing social media handles users may be problematic. User-generated data are used to develop and enhance the recommended content and advertising in social media. Meanwhile, users are targeted by social media advertisements for commercial purposes, regardless of their interests in those commercials. With the advent of the attention economy, scarce attention resources drive some content creators to exaggerate and spread unproven stories and deceitful content. The exploitation of social media users seems unstoppable and betrays the original purpose of introducing social media: to connect people and build community. In other words, social media should increase its usage value instead of the reverse and find a way to boost its commercial value in the service of advertisers. People are rethinking the role of social media in our society, our social circle, and our life. Practitioners and researchers are actively exploring what the future of social media should be (see Appel et al., 2020; FameLIV, 2022). How social media will be presented and what it is going to offer could be completely different in the future. However, the way social media views its users may change. Subscription-based social media is a way to disrupt the current social business model. Subscription-based social media does not need to exploit users for increasing the precision of content recommendation or to push advertisements and saturate social media channels. It enables a completely different social business model. Social media may once again become an ideal place for sharing exciting or memorable moments in our lives. The premium features supplied by social media can include bigger storage space, unlimited viewable posts, advanced search filters, and the ability to undo left swipes, among others (Open Thought, 2022). Nonsubscribed users are also free to access social media; therefore, free access to social media is guaranteed (Open Thought, 2022).

## 12.7   Structure and System Design for Gamification

Gamification refers to the incorporation of game elements into nongame contexts (Butler & Spoelstra, 2021). The history of gamification helps us to understand what gamification is and how it benefits us. Key features arose from the Boy Scouts around 1908.[6] The Boy Scouts awarded members badges to recognize their achievements.[6] In fact, four of their gamification elements, *rewards*, *badges*, *recognition*, and *achievements*, have been adopted by today's social media platforms. Research has shown that badges lead to more active user responses (Hamari, 2017). Recently, Facebook rolled out Facebook Group Badges which include New Member, Rising Star, Conversation Starter, Conversation Booster, Visual Storyteller, Greeter, Founding Member, and others (Vizor, 2020). These badges are used for increasing users' engagement in Facebook groups. Facebook has also rolled out the Top Fan Badge which is awarded for the most active fans on a page to make them stand out (Vizor, 2020). Douyu, an online streaming platform, also introduced Fan Badges. Douyu's Fan Badges represents a fan's closeness with his or her favorite streamer. Fans can increase this closeness measure by sending virtual gifts to the streamer. The Fan Badge is associated with higher recognition. The higher level (from level 1 to level 30) of Fan Badge enables a fan to get virtual gifts such as virtual glow sticks and send these gifts to the streamer. The higher level of Fan Badge also enables a fan to use colorful comments in the livestreaming room. When a fan forgets to send gifts to a streamer for over 7 days, he or she loses this closeness score.

Rewards are a prominent feature used by Chinese social media platforms. The lite version of Kuaishou uses Kuai coins to reward users browsing videos shared on the platform. Kuai coins can be exchanged for Chinese dollars. Watching social videos shared on Kuaishou allows users to accumulate Kuai coins and earn real money. Kuaishou has also rolled out other in-app games for users to play and get rewards from. Rewards for users help to ensure the number of daily active users. Livestreamers on Kuaishou can receive virtual gifts from their audience. Virtual gifts can also be exchanged for real money. Livestreamers present their talent such as singing, dancing, and gaming techniques to get rewards from audiences. Meta has also considered making "Zuck Bucks" and is exploring "social tokens" or "reputation tokens," which could be used as rewards for meaningful contributions in Facebook groups (Peters, 2022).

Research has found that the inclusion of gamification elements is generally associated with greater brand engagement (Summers & Young, 2016). Consumer engagement is often activated by presenting social achievements on social media. NikeFuel, a part of the Nike+ campaign, encourages consumers to work out and share their results by unlocking special trophies after achieving a certain level of outcome (Wells, 2014). Every time consumers receive a reward, they can share the

---

[6]The History of Gamification (From the Very Beginning to Now). Retrieved May 20, 2022, from https://www.growthengineering.co.uk/history-of-gamification/

achievement on social media channels and increase brand visibility (Wells, 2014). What drives the success of badges, achievements, and other gamification on social media? First, achievements set up consumer expectation. The achievements require consumers to complete specific tasks or requirements. For a trophy or badge in health marketing, consumers need to work out for a specific amount of time. The requirements contained in the achievement create an expectation for consumers. Second, the attainment of achievements exhibits individuals' personal capability and satisfies the human need for self-actualization as in Maslow's Hierarchy of Needs. Third, the accomplishment of an achievement signals a future challenge. The growth in challenging goals is a key for the success of gamification. If a person felt no challenge in a campaign or social media game, he or she would probably switch to an alternative with more challenging missions. In the case of Douyu, there are users arguing that higher levels (higher than 30) should be provided for high-level users to distinguish themselves from others. Fourth, psychological flow is a state of mind characterized by a user's participation in an activity that is in the sweet spot between effort and ability (Madigan, 2016). Achievements and feedback in gamification design promote users' psychological flow and motivate users to engage in online activities (Madigan, 2016). Last, achievements are a way to make higher achieving users stand out from lower achieving users. The inclusion of achievements and badges in social media design is a way to boost star users' recognition.

Despite the fact that some social media platforms have attempted to add gamification elements into their social media platforms, it remains unclear how social media platforms monetize these gamification elements. In most cases, gamification is used to retain users and increase daily active users.

## References

AIR. (2021). *YouTube demonetization: How to continue making money from your channel.* Retrieved May 16, 2022, from https://air.io/en/youtube/youtube-demonetization-how-to-continue-making-money-from-your-channel

Alexandria, C. (2018). *Does social media really give us the meaningful connections we want?* Retrieved May 12, 2022, from https://whyy.org/articles/does-social-media-really-give-us-the-meaningful-connections-we-want/

Aneja, N., & Aneja, S. (2021). Detecting fake news with machine learning. In M. Tripathi & S. Upadhyaya (Eds.), *Conference proceedings of ICDLAIR2019. ICDLAIR 2019. Lecture notes in networks and systems* (Vol. 175). Springer. https://doi.org/10.1007/978-3-030-67187-7

Appel, G., Grewal, L., Hadi, R., & Stephen, A. T. (2020). The future of social media in marketing. *Journal of the Academy of Marketing Science, 48*(1), 79–95. https://doi.org/10.1007/s11747-019-00695-1

Bagwell, L. (2018). *Is demonetization censorship?* Retrieved May 16, 2022, from https://www.theodysseyonline.com/demonetization-censorship

Baskerville, R. L., Pries-Heje, J., & Venable, J. (2007). Soft design science research: Extending the boundaries of evaluation in design science research. In: *Proceedings of the 2nd international conference on design science research in information systems and technology*, Pasadena, CA.

Beesley, K. (2018). *Why does fake news spread faster than real news?* Retrieved May 11, 2022, from https://www.psychologytoday.com/us/blog/psychoanalysis-unplugged/201804/why-does-fake-news-spread-faster-real-news?msclkid=5a20c0ebd13111ec9ba60017619db8dd

Brown, S. (2022). *In Russia-Ukraine war, social media stokes ingenuity, disinformation.* Retrieved May 9, 2022, from https://mitsloan.mit.edu/ideas-made-to-matter/russia-ukraine-war-social-media-stokes-ingenuity-disinformation?msclkid=78f8f25fcf9e11ec9e8611c0bd2dba69

Bursztynsky, J. (2021). *TikTok says 1 billion people use the app each month.* Retrieved May 9, 2022, from https://www.cnbc.com/2021/09/27/tiktok-reaches-1-billion-monthly-users.html?msclkid=f01838cccf4a11ec91178e420747728c

Butler, N., & Spoelstra, S. (2021). The theology of gamification. In *Academy of Management Proceedings.* https://doi.org/10.5465/AMBPP.2021.13007abstract

Cadier, A., Labbé, C., Padovese, V., et al. (2022). *WarTok: TikTok is feeding war disinformation to new users within minutes—Even if they don't search for Ukraine-related content.* Retrieved May 9, 2022, from https://www.newsguardtech.com/misinformation-monitor/march-2022/

Carlsson, S. A. (2007). Developing knowledge through IS design science research: For whom, what type of knowledge, and how. *Scandinavian Journal of Information Systems, 19*(2), 75–85.

Carlsson, S. A. (2010). Design science research in information systems: A critical realist approach. In A. Hevner & S. Chatterjee (Eds.), *Design research in information systems: Theory and practice* (pp. 209–233). Springer.

Coelho, P. S., Rita, P., & Santos, Z. R. (2018). On the relationship between consumer-brand identification, brand community, and brand loyalty. *Journal of Retailing and Consumer Services, 43*, 101–110. https://doi.org/10.1016/j.jretconser.2018.03.011

Cohen, L. (2020). *What is Facebook shops? Here's what you need to know.* Retrieved May 9, 2022, from https://www.dailydot.com/debug/facebook-shops/?msclkid=ca901684cf9711eca1df21de7ad7d606

Coldewey, D. (2020). *Who regulates social media?* Retrieved May 16, 2022, from https://techcrunch.com/2020/10/19/who-regulates-social-media/

Constine, J. (2018). *Facebook builds Patreon, Niche clones to lure creators with cash.* Retrieved April 1, 2021, from https://techcrunch.com/2018/03/19/facebook-creator-monetization/

Cox, S. A. (2018). *Socio-technical systems model.* Retrieved May 6, 2022, from http://www.managinginformation.org/socio-technical-systems-model/

CYzone. (2021). *Soul's secret to success: Tackle social pain points and make friends with Gen Z.* Retrieved May 12, 2022, from https://www.cyzone.cn/article/646831.html

Downing, H. (2018). *Opinion: The importance of credibility in the social media era.* Retrieved May 11, 2022, from https://irmagazine.com/technology-social-media/opinion-importance-credibility-social-media-era?msclkid=a3629ae9d12c11ec8204863509f73438

El-Khoury, J., Haidar, R., Kanj, R. R., Bou Ali, L., & Majari, G. (2021). Characteristics of social media 'detoxification' in university students. *The Libyan Journal of Medicine, 16*(1), 1846861. https://doi.org/10.1080/19932820.2020.1846861

FameLIV. (2022). *What is the future of social media?* Retrieved May 18, 2022, from https://fameliv.com/2022/05/02/what-is-the-future-of-social-media/

Gabarron, E., Oyeyemi, S. O., & Wynn, R. (2021). COVID-19-related misinformation on social media: A systematic review. *Bulletin of the World Health Organization, 99*(6), 455–463A. https://doi.org/10.2471/BLT.20.276782

Ghosh, D. (2021). *Are we entering a new era of social media regulation?* Retrieved May 16, 2022, from https://hbr.org/2021/01/are-we-entering-a-new-era-of-social-media-regulation

Gregor, S. (2006). The nature of theory in information systems. *MIS Quarterly: Management Information Systems, 30*(3), 611–642. https://doi.org/10.2307/25148742

Hamari, J. (2017). Do badges increase user activity? A field experiment on the effects of gamification. *Computers in Human Behavior, 71*, 469–478. https://doi.org/10.1016/j.chb.2015.03.036

Jing, X., & Xie, J. (2011). Group buying: A new mechanism for selling through social interactions. *Management Science, 57*(8), 1354–1372. https://doi.org/10.1287/mnsc.1110.1366

Langin, K. (2018). *Fake news spreads faster than true news on Twitter—Thanks to people, not bots.* Retrieved May 11, 2022, from https://www.science.org/content/article/fake-news-spreads-faster-true-news-twitter-thanks-people-not-bots?msclkid=5a20a297d13111ecbe832e139afb01bb

Madigan, J. (2016). *Why do achievements, trophies, and badges work?* Retrieved May 21, 2022, from https://www.psychologyofgames.com/2016/07/why-do-achievements-trophies-and-badges-work/#foot_text_3447_2

McKay, J., & Marshall, P. (2008). *Foundation of design science in information systems.* Sparks working paper, RISO (research into information Systems in Organisations), Faculty of information and communication technologies, Swinburne University of Technology, Melbourne.

Milanović, N. (2022). *Why a social media platform will win the digital wallet war.* Retrieved May 17, 2022, from https://content.11fs.com/article/why-a-social-media-platform-will-win-the-digital-wallet-war

National Post Wire Services. (2013). *Dow Jones plummets, then recovers after fake AP tweet of explosions at the White House.* Retrieved May 11, 2022, from https://financialpost.com/investing/dow-jones-plummets-then-recovers-after-fake-ap-tweet-of-explosions-at-the-white-house?msclkid=56602f49d12f11ecac53dbca34dd7fbc

Open Thought. (2022). *Shifting social media incentives with the subscription model.* Retrieved May 17, 2022, from https://www.openthoughtblog.com/shifting-social-media-incentives-with-the-subscription-model/

Ortner, D. (2019). *Government regulation of social media would kill the internet—And free speech.* Retrieved May 16, 2022, from https://thehill.com/opinion/technology/456900-government-regulation-of-social-media-would-kill-the-internet-and-free/

Otte, L. (2019). *Making real connections in the age of social media.* Retrieved May 12, 2022, from https://www.psychologytoday.com/us/blog/the-human-connection/201912/making-real-connections-in-the-age-social-media

Peters, J. (2022). *Meta is reportedly making 'Zuck Bucks'.* Retrieved May 21, 2022, from https://www.theverge.com/2022/4/6/23013896/meta-facebook-zuck-bucks-finance-financial-services-products

Plotnick, R. (2018). *Power button: A history of pleasure, panic and the politics of pushing.* The MIT Press.

Postman, N. (1987). *Amusing ourselves to death.* Methuen.

Ruder, T. (2021). *Why headless e-commerce is vital for any social media monetization strategy.* Retrieved May 9, 2022, from https://innotechtoday.com/why-headless-e-commerce-is-vital-for-any-social-media-monetization-strategy/#:~:text=With%20headless%20commerce%2C%20the%20e-commerce%20backend%20is%20separate%2C,monetization%2C%20your%20storefronts%20are%20your%20social%20media%20feeds

Solsman, J. E. (2020). *YouTube AI to automatically block videos that violate age restrictions.* Retrieved May 16, 2022, from https://www.cnet.com/tech/services-and-software/youtube-machine-learning-to-put-automated-age-restrictions-blocks-on-videos/

Summers, J. D., & Young, A. G. (2016). *Gamification and brand engagement on Facebook: An exploratory case study.* In Twenty-second Americas Conference on Information Systems, San Diego.

Tarigan, Z., Jonathan, M., Siagian, H., & Basana, S. (2022). The effect of e-WOM through intention to use technology and social media community for mobile payments during the COVID-19. *International Journal of Data and Network Science, 6*(2), 563–572.

TeckSolver. (2020). *What is Facebook shop? And how to create FB shops?* Retrieved May 9, 2022, from https://www.tecksolving.com/facebook-shop/

Vadhera, K. (2021). *What is China's community group buying trend & how does it work?* Retrieved May 17, 2022, from https://jungleworks.com/what-is-chinas-community-group-buying-trend-how-does-it-work/

Vizor, D. (2020). *Top fan badge—Facebook group & page badges explained.* Retrieved May 20, 2022, from https://www.group.app/blog/facebook-badges/

Wells, M. (2014). *Gamification, social media and success: 4 prime examples.* Retrieved May 21, 2022, from https://www.mainstreethost.com/blog/gamification-content-marketing-tactic-social-media/

## 13.1 Risks in Social Media Monetization

When a user swipes left, swipes right, browses, likes, and shares a piece of a post or video on a social media platform, the monetization system of the platform notes these actions and processes the user's social media usage behavior. Noncommercial content, which seems to have no relation to social media monetization, could be preferred by the user. However, the user's preference has been collected and utilized by the system to depict the user persona and detect user preferences. This information can be "monetized" at an appropriate moment by pushing a social media advertisement or a social media post containing a shopping link. This describes the basic workings of social media monetization which is quite different from our view of conventional business. Social media monetization is a novel economic schema that hybridizes commercial elements (e.g., advertisements, shopping information) and social elements (e.g., friends, community) in the service of optimal economic benefits. In the era of big data, artificial intelligence, headless e-commerce, and other frontier computing and commerce technologies, the monetization process is becoming more algorithmic, automatic, and cost-effective. The advertisement auction process in a social media platform can be automatically conducted in a way advertisers' desire. The product(s) contained in a social media post can be precisely recommended to target users with a specific persona. It is expected that, in the future, the automation and precision of social media monetization will be further elevated and elaborated. Given this, we cannot help asking where we should locate humans in the algorithm-based economic system and what we should do when the system goes wrong?

Risk is a term that describes the uncertainty and severity of the consequences of an activity that is related to something humans' value (Aven & Renn, 2009). Social media monetization could lead to several consequences related to these values. Social media essentially is an online platform for social interactions. However, when monetization is highlighted by a social media platform, the platform will inevitably be oriented toward commercialization. For example, in 2019, Kuaishou released the "Photosynthesis Plan" and declared a hefty budget of 10 billion yuan within a year to support 100,000 quality content creators.[1] "Open traffic, Grows at the speed of light" was the theme for this plan.[1]

Social media imposes certain restrictions on creators for monetizing their content. For example, content creators need to fulfill specific requirements in order to monetize on YouTube. They need to have over 4000 watch hours in the previous 12 months and 1000 subscribers to start making money (Linetsky, 2022). If they have met these standards, they can click the "$" sign next to a video to start monetizing with advertising (Linetsky, 2022). Likewise, Kuaishou has initiated a Kuaixiang program which requires creators to have over 10,000 followers. When creators have reached this level, the social media platform can incorporate advertisements or advertising features (e.g., a shopping button or a download button) in or next to videos generated by the creators. We see that social media platforms are actively leveraging the network of content creators and imposing requirements related to the number or the action of followers for identifying commercially valuable creators. Therefore, creators wanting to reach monetization have to comply with these requirements and attract more followers and more attention. The compliance with these requirements makes it difficult for certain content creators to monetize. For instance, classic art and high culture seem to be absent from social media.

Furthermore, it is hard for content creators to attract eyeballs using social media content without the content being retouched or beautified. Plain, genuine, and original narratives or videos are scarce; more frequently seen are exaggerated, digitally edited, polarizing, and extreme media content. When nonstop mediocre content is dominant on a media platform, content creators may leave or disconnect from the platform (Postman, 1987). As such, we are no longer inspired to action by the social media content we receive; we are only driven to develop opinions and form perceptions of it (Postman, 1987). This is an obvious pitfall for long-term success of a social media platform. Attention-based monetization strategies place less focus on the regularities in life and places higher priority on what is considered irregular.

From Twitter's tweets, Facebook's news feed, to YouTube's video recommendations, how people obtain and consume information today is filtered through the lens of social media algorithms. Social media algorithms decide what content people see every day. Machine learning or script-based algorithms shape the experience of browsing content on social media. Social media platforms have been criticized due to their algorithm-based business model. Discussion around whether this particular business model and the dominant market power of social media giants spawn unsound goals that ultimately harm people and society is common (Kaye, 2021). The inherent risks in existing social media monetization practices are its

---

[1] Kuaishou released the "Photosynthesis Plan," supporting 100,000 high-quality creators with a flow of 10 billion yuan within a year. Retrieved May 31, 2022, from https://www.36kr.com/p/1724063465473

algorithmic-based content recommendation mechanisms. Social media algorithms are the mechanisms that a social media platform utilizes to prioritize and push content based upon what it determines will be most relevant or interesting to a viewer (Liberg, 2021). However, a consequence of this is the creation of a techno-cratic governance regime where social media users' experiences or feelings are shaped and determined by the expertise and judgment of algorithm developers and product teams (Burrell et al., 2019) This regime would entail automatic mechanisms using machine intelligence to replace human intelligence in deciding which social media content should be pushed toward which users. The appropriateness of content would be fully decided by machine. This media content recommendation mecha-nism is particularly salient in comparison to traditional mass media which relies on humans to act as gatekeepers of media content. Social media platforms like Facebook reach monetization with these algorithms. The content recommendation and advertisement bidding algorithms play a key role in social media monetization. For example, Facebook's content recommender and advertising auction are highly mature and have helped Meta earn billions of dollars in 2021 alone (see Meta, 2022).

The individual and social benefits that an algorithmic system brings should not come at the price of either equity or fairness (Blacklaws, 2018). It was reported that Facebook's ad-serving algorithm discriminates by gender and race (Hao, 2019). For instance, if there exists a bias against a certain race of women which causes fewer viewers to view, like, or comment on their social media posts, the content recom-mender of the platform will amplify the bias against these women in order to optimize their advertising effectiveness (Brown, 2021). Unfairness and discrimina-tion against a particular race or gender make it more difficult for content creators to monetize from social media, creating a risk for the existing algorithmic-based monetization model. Facebook (renamed Meta) has been sued by the Department of Housing and Urban Development for housing discrimination, in direct conflict with the firm's long-lasting effort to combat discrimination in its ad-serving system (Brandom, 2019). Facebook was discriminating against people based on who they are and where they live (see Brandom, 2019). Meta even clearly indicated the potential risk incurred by class action lawsuits based on claims related to advertising, algorithms, and consumer protection in their most recent annual report (Meta, 2022).

## 13.2  Risks in Social Media Demonetization

Demonetization, often referred as "Adpocalypse," is a process in which content creators are denied paid ads or other commercial features for their self-generated content (Zappin et al., 2021). As a consequence, the revenue for these content creators is decreased, and their content is less likely to be promoted by the platform or is even banned (Zappin et al., 2021). YouTube's demonetization of content comes in two forms: demonetization of an entire channel and demonetization on a video-by-video basis (see Zappin et al., 2021).

Demonetization is achieved by content moderation, which is a strategy widely adopted by social media platforms to crack down on misinformation and abusive and inappropriate content. Content moderation refers to "the screening, evaluation, categorization, approval or removal/hiding of online content according to relevant communications and publishing policies" (Flew et al., 2019, p. 40). In the case of the Chinese social app Kuaishou, moderated content can be demoted, restricted in terms of its social media influence, and even removed. A content creator's content will be moderated when one of the following requirements is met: First, when an account posts too many commercials, it will be moderated by the platform. Posting too many commercials leaves viewers with a negative impression of the platform. Second, social media content infringing on other copyrights will be moderated. This policy aims to reduce unoriginal content and protect others' copyrights. Third, social media posts containing malicious, misleading, and illegal content will also be moderated. Lastly, it has been reported that low-quality content, based on some parameters such as the number of views and the number of referrals, will also be restricted in terms of social media influence.[2] However, the specific parameters the platform follows to demote social media content or restrict its influence remain opaque.

In another example, YouTube employs machine learning-based algorithms in content moderation and follows a retributive approach to penalize "convicted" YouTubers via demonetization (Ma & Kou, 2021). YouTube's content censorship algorithm is also opaque and remains a black box to the world (Outay et al., 2021). YouTubers have been confused about "flip-flopping" monetization icons on their videos and feel it is hard to discern what is and is not acceptable by YouTube's guidelines and standards (Alexander, 2018). Some content creators are sprinting to other social media platforms with fewer monetization restrictions. What *is* known is that the monetizable YouTube videos need to follow "advertiser-friendly" guidelines (Alexander, 2018). Different videos are aligned with different monetization icons. A green "$" icon means that the video is earning revenue from the broadest set of advertisers and YouTube Red (see Sans, 2017). A yellow "$" icon means that the video is eligible to earn revenue in YouTube Red, but is running limited advertisements or even running without advertisements because it has been marked as either not suitable for all advertisers or has been fully demonetized because it does not fulfill YouTube's guidelines (see Sans, 2017). A dark "$" with a backslash means that the video is not earning any revenue from advertisements nor YouTube Red due to copyright or community guideline infringements (see Sans, 2017).

The algorithm-based moderation shapes YouTubers' labor conditions and pushes them to apply the practical knowledge they have learned about the moderation algorithms (Outay et al., 2021). A recent study reported how YouTube publicly celebrates and respects LGBTQ+ people's diversity with respect to race, nationality, gender, and other characteristics (Rodriguez, 2022). Meanwhile, the social media platform privately discriminates against LGBTQ+ users who publish videos about queer sex education, lesbian sexuality, and other topics which are in conflict with the platform's advertising and community guidelines (Rodriguez, 2022). Caplan and

---

[2]How to restore restricted traffic in Kuaishou? Why is it restricted? Retrieved May 25, 2022, from https://hongshen.net/hong/21520/

Gillespie (2020) exposed YouTube's tiered governance approach in which different actors (e.g., amateurs, organization, and YouTube's contracted creators of original content) are held to different standards in different ways. The authors argue that YouTube prioritizes the interests of advertisers over the needs of creators: Established media personalities were deemed more "advertiser-friendly," and user-created content was policed separately, more restrictively, and through different mechanisms causing an over-dependence on biased algorithms (Caplan & Gillespie, 2020). Kumar (2019) reported the chilling effect brought about by the public fear of demonetization. The resulting loss of viewership had consequences far beyond YouTubers' dissatisfaction with YouTube's demonetization policy. The policy denoted a substantial change in YouTube's incentive structure and is likely to discourage YouTubers from generating content in "sensitive" content categories, potentially leading to a shift from a multiple, free, and heterogeneous content platform to a more polished, advertiser-friendly, and homogeneous platform (Kumar, 2019).

YouTube has been amending its demonetization policy due to the incurred controversy. However, the rumblings among the creator community have not diminished (Kumar, 2019). Despite the fact that YouTube has been working on this agenda for over 5 years, it remains questionable how effective demonetization really is and how best to send a signal to creators bumping up against the boundaries of what is acceptable behavior on YouTube (see Sato, 2022). A recent study shows that, on YouTube, the adoption of external monetization platforms (e.g., Patreon, Amazon, and Etsy) is expanding and increasingly prevalent (Hua et al., 2022). YouTubers can include a link along with their demonetized videos for viewers to donate money or purchase the item featured in the video. YouTube wants to be a gatekeeper using content demonetization to wipe out problematic content. However, the wide adoption of alternative monetization strategies by YouTubers complicates YouTube's role as a gatekeeper: The problematic content remains and spreads on the platform, and creators continue to make money off the platform (Hua et al., 2022). The demonetization policy becomes ineffective when alternative monetization approaches are available for content creators.

We find that Western social media and Eastern social media are different from each other and their demonetization policies follow the mainstream values derived from their culture. However, despite the fact that many social media platforms espouse and emphasize diversity on their sites, mainstream values and discourse limit diversity by imposing an implicit censorship mechanism—demonetization. The influence of "dissent" is minimized, and the "dissenting creators" are deprived of the ability to earn revenue. When a social media platform's monetization system merely follows "advertiser-friendly" guidelines, the promotion or demotion of social media content depends on its compatibility with advertisements. These guidelines will shape and force content creators to generate more monetizable content in order to avoid their generated content being demonetized. The demonetization policy will dampen creators' enthusiasm and excitement about creating unconventional and diverse content. Furthermore, as the diversity of a social media platform's content decays, it likely increases the probability of the platform's failure. Hence, the consequences of an inappropriate demonetization policy could be a risk factor related to a social media platform's survival.

## 13.3  Challenges in Social Media Monetization and Demonetization

### 13.3.1  Free Speech and Content Moderation

Content moderation seems to put free speech at risk. Content moderation affects free speech because social media platforms can determine which social media content deserves to be promoted/demoted and kept/removed according to existing standards or regulations (De Gregorio, 2019). Social media companies enjoy discretion in deciding how to moderate content by interpreting social media users' right to free speech according to the companies' own legal, economic, and ethical guidelines (De Gregorio, 2019). Digital celebrities in social media are persons attracting high levels of attention from a significant number of users. These influential users lead to more commercial value not only for social media platforms but also for brands and advertisers. Austin Li and Viya, two top Chinese livestreamers, raked in billions of dollars in less than 13 h by monetizing their social media followers via live e-commerce (Cheng, 2021). If a social media platform prioritizes influential users, it becomes doubtful whether the platform will take down content generated by these users or mark as incitement or abusive information (Panday, 2020). Real cases are increasingly occurring in the regulatory context, and platforms are being accused of showing bias in their decision making (Panday, 2020). The dilemma between free speech and content moderation arises from the user-centric attribute of social media. Social media is a user-centric content production and exchange platform. Users are the producers and consumers of social media content. This user-centric attribute makes it hard for social media platforms to guarantee that numerous users have freedom of speech, and all user-generated contents are socially desirable.

### 13.3.2  Goals in Conflict

Social media has become a powerful platform and has attracted numerous individuals, families, and businesses. Social media content creation, livestreaming, and social e-commerce have allowed many people to work and earn a living from these domains. For example, livestreaming has been adopted by many Chinese regional governments to promote local products and increase local employment rates. In China, social media platforms play a key role in a regional governments' toolkit for diminishing poverty and creating societal wealth. The essential economic form of social media monetization is a gig economy. In essence, social media platforms are not much different from sharing platforms such as Uber. In the Uber business model, drivers offer transportation services and charge passengers a fee for the service. Uber takes a percentage from the fee. Uber drivers are therefore gig workers, not Uber employees. Social media platforms are doing the same. In a social commerce mode, social sellers use a social media platform to sell goods, and the platform takes a percentage from sellers' sales. In a social media advertising mode, content creators create original and creative content to attract audiences wherein social media advertisements are explicitly or implicitly included. Advertisers pay a fee for their social media advertisements. The social media platform shares a part of the advertising revenue with the content creators.

The goal of a social media platform is not always coordinated with the goals of the many content creators and may even be in conflict. A recent study shows that Twitter users complain that Twitter sometimes works against what the platform wants (increasing user engagement, preserving advertising revenue) (Burrell et al., 2019). The research indicated the consequences of a reliance on profit-seeking social media platforms to make decisions for the larger common good (Kumar, 2019). Social media's goal is higher advertising revenue or more profits from social media transactions, while social media workers desire higher revenue from their content. The latter requires the social media platform to take more social responsibilities and develop the ability to cultivate and monetize social value. Obviously, a higher percentage of revenue sharing with social media labor will benefit these creators, but the question is how the social media platform also retains a fair share.

We also analyze the two major economic forms of social media monetization: promoting/demoting content and social advertising. People should be aware that social commerce is quite different from traditional e-commerce. The major difference is the product search mode. In traditional e-commerce, search engines are actively used by shoppers to browse specific products. The results of a product search can be "manipulated" by the e-commerce platform to prioritize paid sellers (sellers who pay for their product search results to be optimized), but small business players can still stand out from others because there are consumers using other search rules such as ascending prices or descending sales. In contrast, the search engine-based approach is basically nonexistent in social commerce since social media users do not shop in the same way as they do in a traditional e-commerce platform. Social shopping is more similar to window shopping. The social media posts or content is the storefront of social sellers. The key is which seller's posts should be promoted for more views and which seller's posts should be demoted. The sales of social sellers are largely reliant on whether their social media content is promoted by the platform or not. The social advertising model is even more problematic. Social media workers publish original and creative content, while the platform can demonetize or even deprive them of the ability to earn a living. Most algorithmic demonetization mechanisms remain unclear and opaque. As formal contractual protection is absent between social media workers and the social media platform, it seems that the platform is not liable for the legal consequences expressed in existing labor regulation and laws. The loose cooperative structure between the platform and the workers facilitates the expansion of scale of the gig economy, but at the same time spawns a new form of labor exploitation. For example, Facebook was criticized for manipulating users' social instinct to make them addicted to the site (Perez-Breva, 2018).

Recently, people have taken some initial steps to harness this imbalance in the platform–worker relationship. Research has also indicated that post-punishment support is necessary for social media content creators to improve and optimize their labor (Ma & Kou, 2021). YouTube's YouTube Partner Program (YPP) and similar revenue sharing mechanisms in social media are the next step to ensure creative workers are earning proper payback and compensation (see Caplan & Gillespie, 2020). The YPP is a new form of labor contract, governing the varieties of creative production on YouTube (Caplan & Gillespie, 2020). The Chinese Ministry of Human Resources and Social Security, National Development and Reform Commission, and other departments have rolled out guidelines to safeguard the rights and interests of workers in a new form of employment (Ministry of Human Resources and Social Security et al., 2021). The guidelines explicitly indicate the necessity of safeguarding the labor security rights and interests of workers in new forms of employment and aim to promote the standardized and sustainable growth of the platform economy (Ministry of Human Resources and Social Security et al., 2021).

### 13.3.3  The De Facto Algorithm and the Algorithm Imaginary

As mentioned previously, social media platforms' monetization and demonetization policies and backend algorithms are unclear and stratified (Caplan & Gillespie, 2020). Social media users form "conservative bias" which obscures how a social media platform monetizes or demonetizes social media content and update their revenue sharing arrangements (Caplan & Gillespie, 2020). The opacity of social media algorithms' content promotion/demotion introduces the notion of the algorithmic imaginary:social media users' ways of thinking about what algorithms are, what they should be, and how they should function (Bucher, 2017). The notion of the algorithmic imaginary implies the "social power" of social media algorithms (Bucher, 2017).

A recent study conducted by Zhang et al. (2020) shows that content creators tend to "play with" or "please" social media algorithms using individual or collective tactics. For example, it is common to see video creators on Kuaishou encourage followers to hit the like button on the video created by them. In this case, creators assume that more likes lead to more views and wider reach, which eventually creates a bigger impact. Social media creators and audiences' algorithmic imaginary significantly influence how people treat social media and content shared on it. This imaginary is not always beneficial. When content creators assume that exaggerated content is more likely to be promoted by the content recommender algorithm, redundant content is often found on the platform.

Social media users' imagination of a social media algorithm forms "folk theories" about the algorithm. Folk theory is a common lay belief about an object, based on known facts, hearsay, or individual experiences (Hansen, 2012). Folk theories significantly influence human behavior because they are collective wisdom and reinforced by personal or others' experiences. Research reveals that folk theories of algorithmic recommendations provide a constructive way to broaden our understanding of users' agency in their interaction with algorithms (Siles et al., 2020). Platform users' admiration of folk theories about algorithms offers them actionable directions and resources to take actions or enact resistance with respect to algorithms (Siles et al., 2020). In the process, social media users' sense-making strategies about algorithms are context-specific, triggered by specific cues such as expectancy violations (Swart, 2021).

Research reveals that content creators have mixed feelings about social media algorithms (Zhang et al., 2020). They are pleased about the algorithm-based traffic distribution amplifying their social media impact and popularity and are upset about the algorithm demoting them and their content when they have been inactive for a period (Zhang et al., 2020). Content creators are also concerned about the changes in the algorithm's orientations. Many social media platforms are run by self-serving social media companies pursuing profits. Social media companies need to consider their strategic planning and the dynamic environment. For example, a social media startup quickly tries to obtain a large number of daily active users (DAUs) so that it is preferred by the capital market and has more opportunities for investors. The social media algorithm during this period is oriented toward obtaining more DAUs. The social media platform is more likely to monetarily incentivize content creators to encourage them to produce creative and attractive content. However, when the social media platform wants to create more profits via social media advertisements, e-commerce, and e-gaming, the social media algorithm will comply with business policy and put a higher priority on the more commercialized social media content.

## 13.4  Building Accountability for Social Media Monetization and Demonetization

In order to face the risks and challenges of a social media company, accountability is of paramount importance. However, research on accountability in social media monetization and demonetization is scarce. In 2018, Facebook made the following statement about their privacy policy:

> We are accountable. In addition to comprehensive privacy reviews, we put products through rigorous data security testing. We also meet with regulators, legislators and privacy experts around the world to get input on our data practices and policies.[3]

This shows that Facebook is serious about "being accountable." They have endeavored to offer data-secured services and engaged multiple entities such as regulators, lawmakers, and experts in the process. On the basis of this case, we discuss the accountability issues of social media monetization and demonetization, structuring the discursive opinions derived from accountability studies, and

---

[3] Giving You More Control of Your Privacy on Facebook. Retrieved June 7, 2022, from https://about.fb.com/news/2018/01/control-privacy-principles/

uncovering the actors, modes, and strategies for a social media company to monetize their users in socially desirable ways.

## 13.4.1 Overview of the Accountability Framework for Social Media Monetization and Demonetization

The definition of accountability can help us identify the subjects and objects in the accountability framework. Bovens (2007) defined accountability as "a relationship between an actor and a forum, in which the actor has an obligation to explain and to justify his or her conduct, the forum can pose questions and pass judgement, and the actor may face consequences" (p. 447). Bovens (2007) views accountability as a social *relationship* between an *actor* and a *forum*. The actor is obliged to explain and justify their innocence or offer an *account*, while the forum can judge what he said, concur or oppose the justification, and let the actor incur *consequences* (Bovens, 2007). The five lenses (actor, forum, relationship, account, and consequences) were also adopted by previous research to study accountability (see Wieringa, 2020). We adopt this definition and apply this accountability theory in our study.

### 13.4.1.1 Actor

Who should be reporting the account or be responsible for the risk and failure in social media monetization and demonetization? Who should be responsible when social media monetization is achieved at the cost of making people addicted to social media? And who should be responsible when an innocent content creator's social media content is demoted or even banned for a mistaken decision made by the algorithmic content moderation system? On the one hand, the operator of a social media platform does not need to develop all algorithms by themself but may delegate external developers to develop algorithms for them. On the other hand, data generated in social media platforms is not only used for the platform, but also shared and used by third parties. Facebook application programming interface (API) is an example. A Facebook API enables third-party developers to add, retrieve, and delete data on the Facebook social media platform.[4] Given this, who are considered the responsible actors when something with the platform goes wrong? Should the social media company, the external developer, or both of them be blamed? In the Cambridge Analytica scandal, the political consulting firm Cambridge Analytica was at the center of an ongoing controversy over the alleged harvesting and use of Facebook (now named Meta) users' data, which was reportedly utilized to direct messages for political campaigns including Donald Trump's presidential election and the Brexit vote (Meredith, 2018). When first revealed, both companies denied "any wrongdoing" (Meredith, 2018). However, it seemed that their denial was ineffective. By the end of 2020, Cambridge Analytica and its parent company had shuttered their doors (Otlowski, 2020). Meta has incurred investigations, litigation,

---

[4]Facebook APIs. Retrieved June 3, 2022, from https://rapidapi.com/collection/facebook-apis

and also issued endless apologies both from the company and the chief executive Mark Zuckerberg (Otlowski, 2020). Four years after the scandal, the District of Columbia sued Zuckerberg over Cambridge Analytica privacy breaches and seeks to hold him personally liable for the scandal (Gordon, 2022).

Three actor roles have been distinguished: decision makers, developers, and users (Wieringa, 2020). Decision makers are those who have the right to decide the overall design of the system and specific technical features (Wieringa, 2020). Developers are often seen as the responsible party in developing the algorithm system with the value-laden biases and are held responsible for the algorithm's decisions (Martin, 2019). The last actor is the user of the system, and their engagement with it (Wieringa, 2020). The users of a social media platform are using the platform and consenting to the "terms of use." The peculiarity of a social media platform is that its users are "productive." Social media users generate data for training and developing algorithm biases. Users also can spread misinformation across the platform using social networking and messaging features offered by the platform. There are also professional users of social media using social media data to generate analytic insights for marketing, consulting, and other purposes. Cambridge Analytica is an example of the latter.

The multiplicity of actors implies that building accountability for a social media platform is not solely determined by the social media company. Accountability is a collective outcome of multiple actors' behaviors. The social media platform is the focal actor who establishes accountability for media content, monetization, demonetization, algorithm fairness, and transparency. Third-party developers are obliged to ethically and legally collect, share, and utilize social media data, and interact with users without taking advantage of them. Furthermore, content creators and most social media audiences do not use social media to spread misinformation, hate speech, extremist, and other harmful content. The collective attribute of accountability in social media settings also denotes that, when the social media platform goes wrong and someone needs to pay for it, each actor tends to escape their responsibility and even deny any wrongdoing because it is usually difficult to distinguish one actor's fault from another. For example, if the content recommender algorithm is biased to recommend hate speech to users, it is difficult to figure out which actor is responsible for this. The recommender algorithm is developed by algorithm developers and gets trained by social media data generated by users.

### 13.4.1.2 Forum

Social media has become an online platform for people to interpret, judge, and discuss public affairs. What if the platform has a self-serving purpose to make more profits? Considering the danger of an unmonitored media platform, there should be judicial places to mitigate risks in the process of social media monetization and demonetization. Conventional forums are divided into five roles on the basis of accountability relationships: political accountability (e.g., political representatives); legal accountability (e.g., judges); administrative accountability (e.g., auditors examining a system); professional accountability (e.g., peers or fellows); and social accountability (e.g., citizens) (Bovens, 2007).

First, political accountability is the responsibility of an entity for the political system. Regarding to social media's political accountability, Ceron (2017) wrote a book titled *Social Media and Political Accountability*. In this book, Ceron (2017) discussed how social media platforms enhanced politicians' accountability and the responsiveness of the political system and how the offline behavior of politicians was affected by the platforms. Social media platforms have been a "political propaganda machine," having fundamentally transformed today's political system. Research has found that social media does improve accountability by informing the public and facilitating the organization of protests (Zhuravskaya et al., 2020). However, it is important to point out that social media can lead to polarized political views and even have a significant influence on democratic elections.

Second, legal accountability concerns the liability of an entity with respect to current laws or regulations. In recent years, many countries have enacted laws and regulations to govern algorithmic systems, including the Algorithmic Fairness Act and the Platform Accountability and Consumer Transparency Act in USA and the General Data Protection Regulation (GDPR) in Europe. The existing laws and regulations are mostly used to govern digital platforms; therefore, in practice, the generic regulatory weapons need to be further refined and amended.

Third, administrative accountability is related to the obligation of an administrator to protect people who are vulnerable to the abuse of power of the administrator and the responsibility of the administrator to deliver satisfactory value. We cannot merely use a single legal/illegal dimension to measure and regulate all affairs in social media. Administrative agencies are another forum for evaluation, including internal and external administrators. In order to combat criticism over how Facebook handles hate speech, violent extremism, and other issues; the company created a court-like Oversight Board which is intended to provide a new way for users to appeal content decisions on both Facebook and Instagram (Yurieff, 2021). This board can reverse content decisions made by the two platforms. For example, the board withdrew the previous removal of an Instagram post from a Brazilian user that aimed to raise people's awareness about breast cancer (Yurieff, 2021). The previous content was removed because it contained five photographs containing women's nipples, which the board declared permissible in light of Facebook's own policy exception for "breast cancer awareness" (Yurieff, 2021).

Fourth, professional accountability deals with an accountability relationship between a professional and her peer group (Bovens, 2007). There are many social media platforms owned by different companies, but they follow some common rules and routines. In some industries, similar companies can initiate an industrial association or even a cartel. The industrial conventions and routines offer guidelines and instructions for companies in the industry, including explicit or implicit restrictions on product price, competition rules, and business ethics. However, in practice, the forums for professional accountability in the social media industry are lacking. We recommended companies launch and organize peer-review committees to scrutinize social media platforms, particularly their monetization activities. In fact, due to the "black box" nature of social media algorithms, professionals and experts on the peer-review committees are more capable of analyzing and detecting problems in a social media platform than an industry association.

Last, social accountability is an accountability relationship dealing with a wider stakeholder: society as a whole. Research notes that wider society would need scientific communication to explain an algorithm system and how it works (Bryson & Winfield, 2017). NGOs, citizen organizations, and individual citizens are the judge of a company's misconduct. With respect to algorithmic systems, research argues that algorithms should be made inspectable by a wider range of people (Fink, 2018). Social media platforms can be categorized into types of firms that create revenue by utilizing the social mission of a free social network (Dohrmann et al., 2015). As Mark Zuckerberg said in congressional testimony, "Yes, there will always be a version of Facebook that is free" (see Castillo, 2018). Free-to-use online social networking is a key social mission of social media like Facebook. The problem is social media platforms are creating value *with* the social mission, not *for* the social mission (Dohrmann et al., 2015). The social forum steps in when social media platforms pursue monetization goals at the cost of damaging public interests. In reality, it can be seen that a forum has more than one type of accountability relationships with actors. For example, a forum could step into the legal and the administrative accountability relationships with other actors and impose legal and administrative restrictions.

First, the involvement of too many forums can create chaos for social media companies. Only among the USA, Congress, state legislators, Federal Communications Commission (FCC), and the Federal Trade Commission (FTC) can forums currently regulate U.S. social media companies. The involvement of too many forums or regulators leads to a coordination problem between forums. Second, excessive regulation is another barrier for social media companies' survival and may eventually discourage the future of the vibrant gig economy brought about by social media platforms and companies. Finally, the workings of social media platforms and social media algorithms remain a black box for external regulators. It is not judicial for a regulator to impose sanctions on a social media company without a comprehensive understanding about the exact nature of the wrongdoing, who was responsible, how it was done, and why. This "detective work" requires an external regulator to open the black box and override the boundary between public power and private entities. For example, as a consequence of FTC's investigation on Facebook's Cambridge Analytica scandal, the FTC will legitimately have more access to Facebook's internal privacy decisions (see Fair, 2019).

### 13.4.1.3 Accountability Relationships

Previously, we discussed possible actors and forums in social media monetization. In different types of accountability relationships, actors are interacting with different types of forums. We now delve into the accountability relationship and study what the relationship brings about for each party. Accountability relationships should not be deemed a burden by social media companies. In fact, it is a form of authorization. The establishment of an accountability relationship authorizes social media companies to do business within the restrictions which have been agreed upon. A significant risk for a business is the ambiguity of restrictions, regulations, or laws. In an ambiguous regulatory environment, an entrepreneur will never know when his or her business may be forcibly shut down by regulators. A proper accountability relationship will clearly indicate the extent to which an actor should explain their conduct to the public and the forum. The actors accordingly know what is permitted by the forum. Furthermore, the restrictions entailed in the accountability relationship prevent a company from abusing its power. When restrictions or regulations are intentionally betrayed by the company, the company will face consequences or sanctions imposed by the forum. Most importantly, building accountability, particularly for social media and its "black box" algorithms, is an iterative, recurrent, and recursive process between actors and forums. We have a long way to go before people find a set of measures and mechanisms to perfectly govern social media monetization and demonetization. The accountability relationship follows a learning process and evolves over time.

The authorization, restriction, and iteration process in accountability relationships has substantial effects on social media governance. These attributes of accountability relationships complicate the governance practice and techniques. Social media platforms are authorized to collect, utilize, and share user data. The question is how far and to what extent a social media platform is authorized to handle user data, and where is the boundary between legitimate use and illegitimate use? Discrimination (e.g., discrimination in race, gender, class, or other characteristics) is a common negative consequence of algorithmic systems. However, current practice lacks established rules to penalize discrimination brought about by algorithmic systems. For example, when race or gender discrimination issues surface in a social media platform, what restrictions or penalties should be imposed and on whom? The complication of social media governance drives today's social media platforms and social media regulators to jointly elaborate and dedicate themselves to accountability relationships.

#### 13.4.1.4 The Account of Social Media Monetization and Demonetization Activities

An account refers to a detailed statement of mutual demands or needs arising out of a relationship between two parties. Brandsma and Schillemans (2013) formulated a conceptual model of the accountability cube (p. 961). The cube encompasses three dimensions of accountability: providing information, discussion, and informal or formal consequences (Brandsma & Schillemans, 2013). Based on this accountability cube, we see that information provision is a key dimension in assessing accountability. The account of an actor's activity can be demarcated into two stages: ex-ante and ex-post accounts. In theory, a sound accountability-building process involves a social media company's ex-ante and ex-post accounts or statements on how it develops, curates, and achieves monetization. However, it is not wise for all types of social media platforms and companies to follow the same bureaucratic procedure. Some social media platforms are small niche platforms tailored to a small group of users. Some social media platforms frequently update their apps. A thorough information provision may be necessary for social media giants like Facebook, Twitter, and YouTube because their effects on society are considerable.

There are not many rules on ex-ante accounts of social media activities, particularly monetization activities, but more general ex-ante rules or regulations are under discussion. In Europe, in order to make sure that certain large online platforms are fair and competitive, and to control their market power, ex-ante rules are being considered to complement the EU competition framework (Geradin, 2020). However, these rules are not specifically designed for social media companies. China is very restrictive in content published on Internet websites or platforms. The certifications of Internet Content Provider (ICP) are a main ex-ante measure to qualify a website or platform to provide Internet content in China without being restricted or banned by the *Great Firewall*—a sophisticated Internet censorship system in China (Anderson, 2012). Depending on the business a company wants to offer, there are two types of ICP certifications, ICP filing, and ICP license (Chu, 2021). The former is required for content providers whose platforms merely offer information (Chu, 2021). The latter is required for platforms or websites with online payment features (Chu, 2021). In order to get this certification, companies need to show that owners have enough expertise and skills to offer Internet content service and comply with Chinese laws.

The ex-post accounts of monetization and demonetization activities are more commonly seen in practice. The forum asks the actor to report what is done, scrutinizes the accounts, identifies risks and problems, and requires the actor to modify their behavior or practice when necessary. As mentioned previously, there are several risks and challenges in the process of social media monetization and demonetization. A decent ex-post account of monetization and demonetization activities will benefit the social media company as well as other stakeholders. The ex-post account reports what is done and modifies behaviors and practices as seen fit, preventing the company from starting down a slippery slope. Existing research recommends that platforms check whether the system still conforms to its initial specifications (Kroll et al., 2017), and the values previously expressed (Pauleen et al., 2017; Cath et al., 2018). Furthermore, it is beneficial to require companies to report how their algorithmic system's decision is made for the forums to review (Diakopoulos, 2015, 2016; Vedder & Naudts, 2017; Cath et al., 2018; Dameski, 2018). We believe it is important for social media giants to disclose and explain how social media algorithms work, what are the privacy policies, how they balance content moderation and free speech, and whether social media laborers are fairly paid. The accounts of these affairs should be sent to different forums or stakeholders. For example, the workings of social media algorithms can be reported to experts for them to review and detect potential biases, lack of transparency, and information asymmetry. Privacy policies can be reported to the appropriate regulators to examine any potential violation of privacy laws. The status quo of content moderation and freedom of speech can be sent to political organizations. Revenue sharing mechanism can be shared with representatives from social media labor.

### 13.4.1.5 Consequences

The forums can impose penalties, restrictions, and sanctions on actors' wrongdoings. Behavioral consequences are the last component in the accountability framework. The deterrence theory of punishment implies that the existence of punishment (e.g., fine, prohibition, and incapacitation) is morally justified because it can deter wrongdoings (Lee, 2017). The presence of deterrence invokes actors' fear of the potential penalties, which is an important incentive in prevention of unethical and illegal behaviors (Lee, 2017). For example, after the FTC's years-long investigation into the Cambridge Analytica scandal and other privacy breaches, the FTC argued that Facebook violated the law by failing to protect data from third parties, using telephone numbers to serve advertisements, and deceiving users that its facial recognition feature was turned off by default (see Kelly, 2019). Apart from the recording-breaking $5 billion fine on Facebook, the FTC has also rolled out new privacy requirements: (a) An independent privacy committee will oversee privacy issues at Facebook; (b) expert compliance officers, who are approved by the independent privacy committee, will conduct the social media platform's daily privacy checks; (c) a third-party assessor, who is appointed with FTC approval, will periodically offer an evaluation of Facebook's privacy practices; (d) the role of CEO Mark Zuckerberg in making final privacy decisions for Facebook will be substantially weakened; and (e) the FTC will legitimately have more access to Facebook's privacy decisions (see Fair, 2019). The lessons from this settlement are beneficial and instructive for other social media companies and social media regulators. This case refined the accountability relationship between a social media company and an external regulator, e.g., how to involve third-party assessors and independent privacy committees, and where the role of a firm leader is located. These restrictions can be adapted for governing other social media companies' wrongdoings.

## 13.4.2 Strategies

### 13.4.2.1 Building a Fair and Ethical Algorithm

Social media monetization and demonetization play a key role in deciding what content a user has the ability to find and consume on a media platform (Zappin et al., 2021). The promotion and demotion of social media users and/or social media content are behind the underlying logic of monetization and demonetization. In other words, in the schema of attention-based monetization strategy, monetization, and demonetization are achieved via promoting or demoting specific users or posts. If a social media post is more likely to see higher impressions or user engagement, it will be promoted by a social media algorithm with possibilities for incorporating commercial features or for displaying follow-up advertisements. By contrast, if a post is unlikely to generate many views, it will be demoted by the algorithm. This mechanism invokes a concern about algorithm fairness. For example, research has revealed that Twitter users expressed fairness concerns when they felt that Twitter was deploying its key resource—attention—in a way that benefited certain users over others (Burrell et al., 2019).

Following this logic, an intuitive way to harness misinformation or harmful content is to inhibit such content before it goes viral on social media. The algorithm is a major approach to identifying harmful content and stopping its spread on social media. Recently, researchers have been actively studying how machine learning and big data analytics are employed to crack down on misinformation. Complex networks, machine learning, data- and text-mining methods, sentiment analysis, and other methods are specifically highlighted by recent research for the prevention, interdiction, and mitigation of threats caused by misinformation (Gradoń et al., 2021). Li (2015) employed machine learning techniques to predict large-scale content censorship. Tanash et al. (2016) focused on finding influential users and communities in censored tweets by using data flow graphics. For example, Twitter has become a useful platform for the dissemination of information and misinformation (Al-Rakhami & Al-Amri, 2020). Al-Rakhami and Al-Amri (2020) analyzed the credibility of information shared on Twitter and proposed an ensemble learning-based framework for verifying the credibility of a vast number of tweets.

Increasing algorithm fairness and transparency have been made an imperative by lawmakers in recent years. Algorithmic systems should comply with the regulatory rule of law (Blacklaws, 2018). For example, in the USA, the Algorithmic Fairness Act was introduced in 2020 and enables the Federal Trade Commission the authority to assess an algorithm's fairness in deciding online advertisement targeting and search results (Kaye, 2021). The Platform Accountability and Consumer Transparency Act was introduced in 2021 and requires online platforms to offer specific information about content they do or do not allow as well as how they decide the enforcement of these content policies (Kaye, 2021). This act would require online platforms to provide transparency reports describing actions they took related to their content moderation policies (Kaye, 2021). In China, the Personal Information Protection Law (draft version) promulgated by the Standing Committee of the National People's Congress in 2020 stipulates the transparency requirements for automated decision making and the fairness and rationality of the results (Wang, 2020). This law confirms the algorithm transparency principle in China's legislation and should play a normative role in the formation of algorithmic order and the achievement of digital justice (Wang, 2020). In Europe, the EU General Data Protection Regulation (GDPR) has provisions that aim to ensure there are no unjustified influence of advanced technology and the capabilities of big data analytics, artificial intelligence, and machine learning on individuals' rights (Blacklaws, 2018). The provisions include articles that require specific transparency and fairness and greater accountability (Blacklaws, 2018).

Designing and creating an ethical and fair algorithmic mechanism for content recommendation and content moderation are a way to prevent discrimination and information asymmetry, and, more importantly, clarify the algorithmic "black box." Social media platforms are open access to society and have significant effects in shaping our cognition about how we look at the world. Therefore, it is necessary to involve a multidisciplinary team of researchers, practitioners, policy-makers, and others to jointly create, set up, and assess the algorithms in the service of building fair and transparent algorithms (Lepri et al., 2018). Given the nature of public goods in social media, the Open Algorithms (OPAL) project, a multipartner socio-technological platform, should be adopted for realizing the vision of a world where data and algorithms are shared and used as levers in support of democracy and development (Lepri et al., 2018).

There is, however, a technical barrier in public understanding (Olhede & Rodrigues, 2017). Machine learning, neural networks, and other algorithms are cutting-edge creations; even data scientists can have a difficult time describing their mechanics in detail. It is even more challenging to do so in a way that enables algorithm fairness to be evaluated and understood (Olhede & Rodrigues, 2017). The complexity of algorithms may hinder platforms from increasing algorithm transparency. For ordinary social media users, they may not be able to nor need to understand the dynamics of a content recommender. But for advertisers, as the advertisement auction algorithm in social media platform is a key to their advertising budget, they should be more motivated to understand how their money is spent on their advertising campaigns. A recent laboratory-based experiment study shows that it does not take much for users to be concerned about the disclosure of the details of algorithms that are perceived to be complex to decision makers, even if people do not fully comprehend them (Lehmann et al., 2022). The algorithm's transparency hinders users' adoption of algorithm-based advice in a particular situation in which the transparent algorithm is perceived to be simpler rather than appropriate (Lehmann et al., 2022). At any rate, it does not matter much whether advertisement auction algorithms are too complex or too elusive. The transparency of the algorithm will increase advertisers' confidence in the algorithm and their adoption of the advice suggested by the system. In the case of Facebook, the transparency of advertisement auction algorithms can help advertisers more confidently choose their bidding strategies such as lowest cost, cost cap, or bid cap.

Due to the opacity of algorithms, algorithm fairness, transparency, and accountability need to be developed in a well-communicated process. A rational communication process enables platforms to conduct a continuous and provisionary assessment of the development, workings, and consequences of algorithms (Buhmann et al., 2020). Following this discursive perspective, Buhmann et al. (2020) constructed a framework for managing algorithm accountability including discourse principles, reputational concerns, and engagement strategies. These authors argued that the discourse of algorithm ethics should follow four principles: participation, comprehension, multivocality, and responsiveness (Buhmann et al., 2020). Furthermore, research points out that effective algorithm accountability needs to engage the broader platforms and agencies where algorithmic systems exist (Reddy et al., 2019). Reddy et al. (2019) introduced the metaphor of detective fiction and argued that "tracing clues to uncover the workings of an algorithm" (p. 6) and "finding out who did it, where, and with what instrument matters" (p. 6) can help effect algorithm accountability, but the resolution is not perfect and "does not bring the culprit to justice on its own" (p. 6). In other words, we may have taken efforts to find out the source, motivation, and workings of a "problematic" algorithm which may have caused a negative consequence such as gender discrimination, for example. These answers are not enough for us to reach the ultimate goal of justice in the digital era. For example, Facebook's ad-serving algorithm has gender and race discrimination issues (Hao, 2019). Algorithm engineers may be able to figure out how and why a certain race of woman is associated with fewer viewers to view, like, or comment on and successfully fix this bias. The accountability issue remains because it is not merely a technical issue related to this bias. This bias derives from culture, social norms, subconsciousness, or even unknown heuristics in some social media users' minds. Algorithms are interacting with humans, using human-generated data to train and elaborate themselves, but humans are the most obscure factor in the socio-technical system. Moreover, the consequences of algorithm responsibility are shaped and determined in relation to existing established legal and ethical principles (Reddy et al., 2019). If using, editing, or sharing copyrighted content in a "socially accepted" way (e.g., cropping a long video into a few seconds) is commonplace in social media, will the victims claim copyright infringement and file litigation? Sloan and Warner (2018) proposed three approaches to achieving algorithm transparency: disclosing source code, transparency without disclosing source code, and informational norms. The two authors sustain that, if acceptable information norms (behavioral regularity in collecting, using, and distributing information) governed the use of predictive analytics, users could more confidently use the algorithm-based results (Sloan & Warner, 2018).

### 13.4.2.2  The Combination of Human Intelligence and Machine Intelligence

Machine intelligence, such as machine learning and big data analytics, is widely adopted to prevent, interdict, and mitigate the dangers caused by misleading, abusive, and other inappropriate content on social media. Graphic recognition and other techniques are used in detecting and automatically filtering out malicious, misleading, or inappropriate content. Social video apps or livestreaming platforms allow streamers and/or content creators to monetize by incorporating clickable advertisements in their livestreaming or shared videos. Graphic recognition can detect and demote inappropriate content such as nudity or guns, so that the system lowers the possibility that the content will be monetized. However, the ambiguous, implicit, and context-dependent nature of human communication makes it difficult for a machine to decide the promotion or demotion of some social media content. Machines are not able to distinguish the meaning of human language in different contexts.

It is possible, however, that social media users may bypass algorithmic surveillance. Even if an anti-piracy system was available, many users know how to circumvent the regulatory system. Digital editing of copyrighted pictures or videos, such as graphic blurring or amending pixels, is a way to circumvent the system. Malicious, harmful speeches can avoid being blocked using language that cannot be understood by machines, but can be understood by human viewers. For example, Douyin and Kuaishou, two social video apps, will demote commercialized videos and therefore many video creators have tacitly adopted a language replacement to stun the content moderation system, using mi (rice in English) to replace yuan (a currency unit of Chinese dollars).

In 2016, AlphaGo, an AI-powered Go game developed by Google's DeepMind, beat the Go game world champion Lee Sedol (Trenholm, 2017). Interestingly, Go experts were puzzled by AlphaGo's moves until they realized that "where a human might play to win by a wide margin, the AI didn't care if it won by a single point. So, it pursued only the slimmest advantage necessary to carry the game" (Trenholm, 2017). The case of AlphaGo has shown that, in the era of machine intelligence, the quality of decisions made by machines can be significantly higher than their human counterparts. As machines have much greater computing and information storage capability, humans, with limited memory resources and cognition, are not able to outperform machines in terms of those advantages. Due to the significant differences in a human decision mode versus a machine decision mode, a "bad" move in the Go game in the eyes of a human is deemed "good" by a machine. Machines can be superior to humans because they are able to identify valuable choices or items that humans cannot. Does the superior performance of machines denote the "shift" in the value or "good/bad" epistemology? We should be aware that machines bring about fundamental changes in the means to how humans find and assess value; more reliance on computing and reasoning, but the underlying logic in value search and assessment has not changed significantly. AlphaGo used two neural networks to find the next move in the board game, a policy network that was developed from millions of master games with a goal of imitating their moves, and a value network that attempted to anticipate the likelihood of winning from each position on the game board (Ross, 2016). Then, a tree-searching network examined consequences several moves ahead (Ross, 2016). The underlying logic in the decision process is not new at all. Humans also make decisions on the basis of prior players' choices and would want to make a choice that has the highest winning probability. This illustrates that the algorithms behind machine intelligence are designed and elaborated by humans and injected with humans' value perceptions and epistemology. Machines are an extension of human knowledge. This view implies that machines and humans are inherently related.

Therefore, it is necessary to combine human intelligence and machine intelligence in establishing technical infrastructure, social media promotion/demotion, and platform development. In other words, in social media settings, machines still rely on humans to develop, refine, and manage the social network and media content platform. Notably, the combination of human intelligence and machine intelligence is not mechanically aligned, but merged in an organic way. In the development process of machine intelligence, humans inject their values and perceptions into machines. Machine intelligence is "value-laden," rather than neutral (Martin, 2019). Human agents ought to be responsible not only for the value weights in machine intelligence, but also for designing who–does–what in the machine-based decision mode (Martin, 2019). Even the automated content moderation system relies on humans to create an index of banned items or categories, and then, the system is able to match social media content to the index (Vincent, 2019). Social media content first needs to be identified by humans and "hashed," meaning it is converted into a unique string of numbers for the machine to process (Vincent, 2019). The algorithm-based content moderation system relies on humans to first define what is "good" and "bad." The developers of the algorithmic system cannot void their accountability. Their values and definitions about misinformation, extremist voices, hate speech, and sensitive content will eventually decide what social media content will be demoted or removed from the social media platform. The ethical performance of a social media platform in front of the paradox between content moderation and free speech is therefore dependent on the humans behind the algorithmic system.

### 13.4.2.3 Self-governance, External Governance, and Co-governance

1. *Self-Governance.* Self-governance relies on a social media platform's self-regulatory efforts. Self-governance is a crucial way to avoid the deviation from an algorithmic process which sometimes produces problematic outcomes. The self-regulatory approach follows the logic of economic liberalism that emphasizes the subjectivity of an economic entity and acts against external regulations or interventions such as governments' regulatory policies. Facebook rolled out its Oversight Board for social media content decisions. The Oversight Board and Facebook's other content regulation systems present the advantages of self-governance: responsiveness, flexibility, greater compliance, and informed and targeted interventions (Arun, 2020). For example, Facebook was able to react nimbly to disinformation about the COVID-19 pandemic, showing the viability and flexibility of the social media's self-regulatory system that which can be difficult for a government regulator (Arun, 2020). Research reveals that online content platforms have the freedom to design content moderation systems, but the established moderation rules need to follow the procedural boundaries defined by the efficacy of fundamental rights between private entities (Hartmann, 2022). The key to self-governance is not merely reviewing social media content shared online, but rather in course correction of the procedures that guarantee that self-governance does not disproportionally damage user rights such as free speech, honor and privacy (Hartmann, 2022). Self-governance easily slips into a performative situation and instrumentalizes moral efforts in building accountability when monetization is the ultimate goal. Self-governance actions without the intrinsic motive to "being an accountable company" have recently been viewed as "ethics washing." Ethics washing is often a part of a company's communication strategy, such as creating an ethics committee and hiring in-house moral ethicists who are not able to shape corporate policies (Bietti, 2019). It has been argued that ethics is being utilized among technology companies as a "performative façade," which leads to ethics being void of intrinsic value and fails to motivate people to conduct themselves ethically (Bietti, 2019). However, we should not dismiss or misunderstand tech companies' ethical efforts, such as Meta's creation of their Oversight Board for withdrawing or revising content decisions made by the Facebook platform. Ethics washing denotes that at the very least, companies that ethics wash are aware of the importance of ethical behavior and accountability. The point is not diminishing ethics washing; instead, we should focus on converting companies' mindsets about instrumentalized forms

of accountability into a new form of accountability driven by intrinsically ethical motives. We also do not think profitability is antithetic to accountability with regard to social media companies and social media business. In fact, future research can explore this area and see under what conditions accountability strategies or ethical measures enable social media companies to earn profits. For instance, in light of current critiques of social media algorithms, under what conditions is a social media platform receiving better user responses when an accountability strategy (e.g., an algorithm transparency statement, a fairness guarantee, or a data security safeguard) is introduced?

2. *External Governance*. The public perception of social media as a public infra-structure intertwined with our everyday lives makes it necessary to include social media platforms in the scope of democratic deliberation and accountability (Kumar, 2019). External governance is a serious public concern. Governance enacted by government entities is the most common form of governance and can be summarized by three aspects: privacy and data protection, the repudiation of intermediary liability protections, and the application of competition and monop-oly laws (Gorwa, 2019). External governance requires that regulation of our lives be justifiable or acceptable to people over whom the rules purport to have authority (Quong, 2018). This governance (termed public reason) acts as a constraint in the accountability of an algorithmic system (Binns, 2018). In other words, the external governance does not merely represent the will of an authorized regulator. The external governance of social media monetization and demonetization is desired and encouraged by people holding commonly shared views. For example, despite the controversy about the algorithm-based ad-serving model, social media users hope that social media monetization is achieved without illegally using their personal data and breaching their privacy. The demonetization system based on algorithmic content moderation should be accurate, precise, and consistent in detecting and demonetizing harmful social media content. The failure of this system in detecting inappropriate spoken content or misjudging good content as bad should not be tolerated. These concerns form the powerful force of public reason and mobilize political resources in society to devise, enact, and implement external regulations. Cusumano et al. (2022) proposed three possible options for governing social media platforms. The first is breaking up big social media companies such as Meta. This move aims to reduce social media giants' enormous market powers. The second option is letting governments directly regulate social media platforms and algorithms. The last option is removing Section 230. This 1996 law protects online platforms from civil liabilities for content they circulate. Section 230 distinguishes social media platforms from publishers who are held more respon-sible for the content they disseminate. Likewise, Zilles (2020) argues that it should not matter if it is humans or machines making the content decision; if a social media platform is banning or censoring some content that does not agree with the platform's values and viewpoints, then it should be considered a publisher. For example, Twitter values the protection of free speech and diversity

and diversity of thoughts, but adopted a different tack when it came to censoring or blocking some social media content (see Zilles, 2020).

3. *Co-Governance.* How social media platforms handle the risk and dilemma of monetization and demonetization should be examined. What a social media platform values is not always congruent with what the public desires. For example, a social media platform sets up an advertiser-friendly policy for its monetization and demonetization system, while social media users desire access to more content regardless of its advertiser friendliness. It is risky to simply rely on social media platforms' self-regulation. More actors need to be involved in social media governance to scrutinize the monetization logic at work with the understanding that these platforms are not monolithic or detrimental in their operations or effects (Lobato, 2016). Co-governance is a mechanism whereby authorities set out objectives to be achieved, but their completion is entrusted to parties that are recognized in the field (e.g., social partners, nongovernmental organizations, or academic organizations) (Finck, 2017). The engagement of corporations, media industries, and civil society in artificial intelligence regulation and governance should be highlighted (Buhmann & Fieseler, 2021). One study concluded that external command-and-control regulation and self-governance incur significant problems in practice and the regime of co-governance emerges as the most appropriate option only under certain conditions (Finck, 2017). By contrast, earlier research found that the developing concept of co-regulation or co-governance is likely to be more constructive, but it is important to assess the bundle of regulatory mechanisms via the application of normative principles (Prosser, 2008). Regulatory regimes of online platforms could be "a cocktail" of different regulatory mechanisms (Prosser, 2008). The monetization and demonetization of social media platforms need to be conducted in a compound regulatory regime involving self-governance, external governance, and co-governance. Previously, we introduced the concept of public reason and its role in external governance. In fact, we believe public reason also explains the workings of societal co-governance. Public reason helps clarify the epistemic standards of a justifiable algorithmic system (Binns, 2018). Relevancy is a key rule to the ad-serving and content recommendation algorithm of social media. The relevancy of a piece of content to a viewer is factored into the process of an advertisement auction. The more relevant the content is to a viewer, the more likely it will be displayed to the viewer. The capabilities of big data analytics could enable the algorithmic system to detect the relevancy between two objects, even if this relevancy relationship is not justifiable for the public. For example, if a man likes educational videos, the system could offer him advertisements related to part-time education degrees. In fact, the relationship between watching educational videos and interest in a part-time degree may be only statistically relevant. It could be that the man has obtained a degree and become more interested in acquiring knowledge. This algorithm-based relevancy creation can become dangerous when the algorithm disregards public reason and pushes harmful content to vulnerable audiences, e.g., pushing pornographic videos to children. The role of public reason here is in opposition and may

deny the relevancy between the harmful content and the vulnerable audience. When a social media platform discloses the algorithm, the relevancy between the harmful content and the vulnerable audience is revealed and therefore can be disconnected.

### 13.4.2.4 Capturing Social Value for Sustainable Monetization

Social mission may seem to be ignored by some social media platforms. Advertising is not Meta's mission. It is "to give people the power to build community and bring the world closer together."[5] The term "mission" seemingly has been abused for commercial purposes and has become a part of a corporate communication strategy. In fact, social mission entails social value that benefits social media companies. By incorporating social mission in a social media company's business strategy and policy, social media companies can identify, create, and capture social value from pursuing the stated social mission. As previously discussed, the goals between a social media platform and social media users are often in conflict. However, we do not think they are irreconcilable. The social responsibilities of a social media company include the advocacy of pro-environmental values, the empowerment of grassroots organizations and small businesses, the creation of societal wealth, the offering of social services, and many other goals that increase social welfare. Monetization is merely a visible outcome for a social media company. More invisible outcomes such as social media brand image and firm reputation can be attained when social media companies pursue the social mission and cultivate social value. The myth is how social media reframes its monetization model by adding social value and social missions in it. Future research can delve into this issue and study how social value is related to a social media company's financial performance.

TikTok, a Chinese social video app, has achieved remarkable success in the Chinese market, but has encountered many barriers and hurdles when the app was offered overseas. U.S. President Donald Trump signed an executive order requiring the app's Chinese owner, ByteDance, to either sell TikTok to an U.S. company or see it forcibly removed from app stores and banned in the USA (Knight, 2021). In order to exist in foreign markets, TikTok was not eager to monetize foreign markets at first and began actively finding ways to present its social value and demonstrate its social responsibility. For example, TikTok launched a social media campaign #LenguaDeSeñasDance in Mexico that aimed to benefit approximately one million people in Mexico and make TikTok the largest Mexican sign language school in the world.[6] During the pandemic, TikTok also launched a $50 million Creative Learning Fund, part of a larger $250 million initiative to benefit communities and help creators with the production of learning content and introduce teachers to the TikTok platform (see Zemach, 2021). At the same time, TikTok is making microlearning

---

[5]Culture at Meta. Retrieved June 10, 2022, from www.metacareers.com/facebook-life/

[6]TikTok bets on teaching Sign Language to one million people in Mexico. Retrieved May 26, 2022, from https://responsabilidadsocial.net/en/tiktok-apuesta-por-ensenar-lengua-de-senas-a-1-millon-de-personas-en-mexico/

(a form of Internet learning which occurs during a users' spare time) a big business (see Zemach, 2021). Many teachers are using TikTok to interact with learners and use the app to keep learners engaged. TikTok can incorporate learning-related commercials in the videos shared by these teachers and share advertising revenue with them.

## 13.5  Concluding Remarks

This chapter has discussed the risks and challenges in social media monetization and demonetization and points out the key role of accountability for a social media company's sustainable monetization. We summarize our main findings as follows. First, today's users' social media usage experience is shaped by machine-based or script-based algorithms. Second, despite the fact that social media companies have been improving their demonetization policy and dynamics, as alternative monetization approaches remain available in social media platforms, the actual effectiveness of these policies is questionable (see Sato, 2022). Third, when a social media platform merely follows "advertiser-friendly" guidelines, these guidelines will shape and force content creators to generate more monetizable content in order to avoid their generated content being demonetized. Fourth, the multiactor character of social media governance implies that building accountability for a social media platform is not solely determined by the social media company; rather, it is a collective outcome of multiple actors' behaviors. The social media company is the focal actor in the accountability system, and we recommend that they disclose their algorithms. We should not diminish social media companies' ethics washing behaviors, but aim to convert companies' mindsets about instrumentalized forms of accountability into a new form of accountability driven by intrinsically ethical motives. Fifth, biases, discrimination, and unfairness caused by social media algorithms are not merely a technical issue. They also result from culture, societal norms, subconsciousness, or even unknown heuristics in social media users' minds. A compound governance regime is recommended for the governance of social media monetization and demonetization. Finally, the social mission of social media platforms cannot be ignored and should not just act as a part of corporate communication strategy. Social media companies need to find a way to cultivate social value from their social mission.

## References

Alexander, J. (2018). *YouTube CEO addresses demonetization anger: 'We know the last year has not been easy'*. Retrieved May 26, 2022, from https://www.polygon.com/2018/4/17/17248464/youtube-demonetization-susan-wojcicki-philip-defranco

Al-Rakhami, M. S., & Al-Amri, A. M. (2020). Lies kill, facts save: Detecting COVID-19 misinformation in Twitter. *IEEE Access, 8*, 155961–155970. https://doi.org/10.1109/ACCESS.2020.3019600

Anderson, D. (2012). Splinternet behind the great firewall of China: Once China opened its door to the world, it could not close it again. *Queue, 10*(11), 40–49. https://doi.org/10.1145/2390756. 2405036

Arun, C. (2020). *The Facebook oversight board: An experiment in self-regulation.* Retrieved May 30, 2022, from https://www.justsecurity.org/70021/the-facebook-oversight-board-an-experi ment-in-self-regulation/#:~:text=Facebook%E2%80%99s%20overall%20content-regulation% 20system%2C%20including%20the%20Oversight%20Board%2C,flexibility%2C%20greater %20compliance%2C%20and%20informed%20and%20targeted%20intervention

Aven, T., & Renn, O. (2009). On risk defined as an event where the outcome is uncertain. *Journal of Risk Research, 12*(1), 1–11. https://doi.org/10.1080/13669870802488883

Bietti, E. (2019). *From ethics washing to ethics bashing: A view on tech ethics from within moral philosophy* (SSRN Scholarly Paper No. 3513182). Social Science Research Network. Retrieved June 9, 2022, from https://papers.ssrn.com/abstract=3513182

Binns, R. (2018). Algorithmic accountability and public reason. *Philosophy and Technology, 31*(4), 543–556. https://doi.org/10.1007/s13347-017-0263-5

Blacklaws, C. (2018). Algorithms: Transparency and accountability. *Philosophical Transactions of the Royal Society A: Mathematical, Physical and Engineering Sciences, 376*(2128), 20170351. https://doi.org/10.1098/rsta.2017.0351

Bovens, M. (2007). Analysing and assessing accountability: A conceptual framework. *European Law Journal, 13*(4), 447–468. https://doi.org/10.1111/j.1468-0386.2007.00378.x

Brandom, R. (2019). *Facebook has been charged with housing discrimination by the US government.* Retrieved May 24, 2022, from https://www.theverge.com/2019/3/28/18285178/ facebook-hud-lawsuit-fair-housing-discrimination

Brandsma, G. J., & Schillemans, T. (2013). The accountability cube: Measuring accountability. *Journal of Public Administration Research and Theory, 23*(4), 953–975. https://doi.org/10. 1093/jopart/mus034

Brown, A. (2021). *How social media monetization is evolving in the face of algorithmic bias: A discussion with Nick McCandless.* Retrieved May 24, 2022, from https://www.forbes.com/sites/ anniebrown/2021/11/14/how-social-media-monetization-is-evolving-in-the-face-of-algorith mic-bias-a-discussion-with-nick-mccandless/?sh=2b0b91d5739e

Bryson, J., & Winfield, A. (2017). Standardizing ethical design for artificial intelligence and autonomous systems. *Computer, 50*(5), 116–119. https://doi.org/10.1109/MC.2017.154

Bucher, T. (2017). The algorithmic imaginary: Exploring the ordinary effects of Facebook algorithms. *Information, Communication and Society, 20*(1), 30–44. https://doi.org/10.1080/ 1369118X.2016.1154086

Buhmann, A., & Fieseler, C. (2021). Towards a deliberative framework for responsible innovation in artificial intelligence. *Technology in Society, 64*, 101475. https://doi.org/10.1016/j.techsoc. 2020.101475

Buhmann, A., Paßmann, J., & Fieseler, C. (2020). Managing algorithmic accountability: Balancing reputational concerns, engagement strategies, and the potential of rational discourse. *Journal of Business Ethics, 163*(2), 265–280. https://doi.org/10.1007/s10551-019-04226-4

Burrell, J., Kahn, Z., Jonas, A., & Griffin, D. (2019). When users control the algorithms. *Proceedings of the ACM on Human-Computer Interaction, 3*, 1–20. https://doi.org/10.1145/ 3359240

Caplan, R., & Gillespie, T. (2020). *Tiered governance and demonetization: The shifting terms of labor and compensation in the platform economy.* https://doi.org/10.1177/2056305120936636

Castillo, M. (2018). *Mark Zuckerberg hints that Facebook has considered a paid version.* Retrieved June 7, 2022, from https://www.cnbc.com/2018/04/10/mark-zuckerberg-there-will-always-be-a-version-of-facebook-that-is-free.html

Cath, C., Wachter, S., Mittelstadt, B., Taddeo, M., & Floridi, L. (2018). Artificial intelligence and the 'good society': The US, EU, and UK approach. *Science and Engineering Ethics, 24*, 505–528. https://doi.org/10.1007/s11948-017-9901-7

Ceron, A. (2017). Social media and political accountability. *Springer International.* https://doi.org/10.1007/978-3-319-52627-0

Cheng, E. (2021). *Chinese livestreamers can rake in billions of dollars in hours. How long will it last?* Retrieved May 25, 2022, from https://www.cnbc.com/2021/11/16/chinese-livestreamers-can-rake-in-billions-of-dollars-in-hours-how-long-will-it-last.html

Chu, N. (2021). *ICP China license: Understanding the essentials and an alternative.* Retrieved June 8, 2022, from https://blog.sinorbis.com/chinese-icp-license

Cusumano, M. A., Yoffie, D. B., & Gawer, A. (2022). *Pushing social media platforms to self-regulate.* Retrieved May 30, 2022, from https://www.theregreview.org/2022/01/03/cusumano-yoffie-gawer-pushing-social-media-self-regulate/

Dameski, A. (2018). A comprehensive ethical framework for AI entities: Foundations. In M. Iklé, A. Franz, R. Rzepka, & B. Goertzel (Eds.), *Artificial general intelligence* (Vol. 10999, pp. 42–51). Springer International. https://doi.org/10.1007/978-3-319-97676-1_5

De Gregorio, G. (2019). Free speech in the age of online content moderation. *Völkerrechtsblog.* https://doi.org/10.17176/20191126-121907-0

Diakopoulos, N. (2015). Algorithmic accountability: Journalistic investigation of computational power structures. *Digital Journalism, 3*(3), 398–415. https://doi.org/10.1080/21670811.2014.976411

Diakopoulos, N. (2016). Accountability in algorithmic decision making. *Communications of the ACM, 59*(2), 56–62. https://doi.org/10.1145/2844110

Dohrmann, S., Raith, M., & Siebold, N. (2015). Monetizing social value creation—A business model approach. *Entrepreneurship Research Journal, 5*(2), 127–154. https://doi.org/10.1515/erj-2013-0074

Fair, L. (2019). *FTC's $5 billion Facebook settlement: Record-breaking and history-making.* Retrieved June 7, 2022, from https://www.ftc.gov/business-guidance/blog/2019/07/ftcs-5-billion-facebook-settlement-record-breaking-history-making

Finck, M. (2017). Digital regulation: Designing a supranational legal framework for the platform economy. *SSRN Electronic Journal.* https://doi.org/10.2139/ssrn.2990043

Fink, K. (2018). Opening the government's black boxes: Freedom of information and algorithmic accountability. *Information, Communication and Society, 21*(10), 1453–1471. https://doi.org/10.1080/1369118X.2017.1330418

Flew, T., Martin, F., & Suzor, N. (2019). Internet regulation as media policy: Rethinking the question of digital communication platform governance. *Journal of Digital Media and Policy, 10*(1), 33–50. https://doi.org/10.1386/jdmp.10.1.33_1

Geradin, D. (2020). *Why is ex ante regulation of systemic online platforms needed on top of competition law?* Retrieved June 8, 2022, from https://theplatformlaw.blog/2020/05/07/why-is-ex-ante-regulation-of-systemic-online-platforms-needed-on-top-of-competition-law/

Gordon, M. (2022). *DC sues Zuckerberg over Cambridge Analytica privacy breach.* Retrieved June 6, 2022, from https://www.cbs42.com/news/business/dc-sues-zuckerberg-over-cambridge-analytica-privacy-breach/

Gorwa, R. (2019). What is platform governance? Information. *Communications Society, 22*(6), 854–871. https://doi.org/10.1080/1369118X.2019.1573914

Gradoń, K. T., Hołyst, J. A., Moy, W. R., Sienkiewicz, J., & Suchecki, K. (2021). Countering misinformation: A multidisciplinary approach. *Big Data and Society.* https://doi.org/10.1177/20539517211013848

Hansen, T. (2012). Parenthood and happiness: A review of folk theories versus empirical evidence. *Social Indicators Research, 108*(1), 29–64. https://doi.org/10.1007/s11205-011-9865-y

Hao, K. (2019). *Facebook's ad-serving algorithm discriminates by gender and race.* Retrieved May 24, 2022, from https://www.technologyreview.com/2019/04/05/1175/facebook-algorithm-discriminates-ai-bias/

Hartmann, I. A. (2022). Self-regulation in online content platforms and the protection of personality rights. In M. Albers & I. W. Sarlet (Eds.), *Personality and data protection rights on the internet:*

*Brazilian and German approaches* (pp. 267–287). Springer International. https://doi.org/10.
    1007/978-3-030-90331-2_11
Hua, Y., Ribeiro, M. H., West, R., Ristenpart, T., & Naaman, M. (2022). Characterizing alternative
    monetization strategies on YouTube. *arXiv*. Retrieved May 31, 2022, from https://arxiv.org/
    abs/2203.10143
Kaye, K. (2021). *Cheat sheet: Senators want more transparency into "addictive" Facebook,
    Twitter and YouTube algorithms.* Retrieved May 31, 2022, from https://digiday.com/media/
    cheat-sheet-senators-want-more-transparency-into-addictive-facebook-twitter-and-youtube-
    algorithms/
Kelly, M. (2019). *FTC hits Facebook with $5 billion fine and new privacy checks.* Retrieved June
    7, 2022, from https://www.theverge.com/2019/7/24/20707013/ftc-facebook-settlement-data-
    cambridge-analytica-penalty-privacy-punishment-5-billion
Knight, W. (2021). *TikTok a year after Trump's Ban: No change, but new threats.* Retrieved May
    26, 2022, from https://www.wired.com/story/tiktok-year-trump-ban-no-change-new-threats/#:
    ~:text=A%20week%20later%2C%20Trump%20signed%20an%20executive%20order,TikTok
    %20in%20a%20deal%20that%20was%20later%20shelved
Kroll, J. A., Barocas, S., Felten, E. W., Reidenberg, J. R., Robinson, D. G., & Yu, H. (2017).
    Accountable algorithms. *University of Pennsylvania Law Review, 165,* 633–705. Retrieved June
    8, 2022, from https://scholarship.law.upenn.edu/cgi/viewcontent.cgi?article=9570&
    context=penn_law_review
Kumar, S. (2019). The algorithmic dance: YouTube's Adpocalypse and the gatekeeping of cultural
    content on digital platforms. *Internet Policy Review, 8*(2). https://doi.org/10.14763/2019.2.1417
Lee, H.-W. (2017). Taking deterrence seriously: The wide-scope deterrence theory of punishment.
    *Criminal Justice Ethics, 36*(1), 2–24. https://doi.org/10.1080/0731129X.2017.1298879
Lehmann, C. A., Haubitz, C. B., Fügener, A., & Thonemann, U. W. (2022). The risk of algorithm
    transparency: How algorithm complexity drives the effects on use of advice. *Production and
    Operations Management.* https://doi.org/10.1111/poms.13770
Lepri, B., Oliver, N., Letouzé, E., Pentland, A., & Vinck, P. (2018). Fair, transparent, and
    accountable algorithmic decision-making processes. *Philosophy and Technology, 31*(4),
    611–627. https://doi.org/10.1007/s13347-017-0279-x
Li, J. (2015). *Predicting large-scale internet censorship—A machine learning approach.* Master
    thesis, University of Virginia.
Liberg, B. F. (2021). *Risk perception of influence operations on social media.* Master thesis,
    Norwegian University of Science and Technology.
Linetsky, T. (2022). *How to earn money on YouTube.* Retrieved May 23, 2022, from https://www.
    wikihow.com/Earn-Money-on-YouTube#:~:text=1%20Set%20up%20and%20build%20your
    %20YouTube%20channel.,months%20and%201000%20subscribers%20to%20start...%20See
    %20More
Lobato, R. (2016). The cultural logic of digital intermediaries: YouTube multichannel networks.
    *Convergence: The International Journal of Research into New Media Technologies, 22*(4),
    348–360. https://doi.org/10.1177/1354856516641628
Ma, R., & Kou, Y. (2021). "How advertiser-friendly is my video?": YouTuber's socioeconomic
    interactions with algorithmic content moderation. *Proceedings of the ACM on Human-
    Computer Interaction, 5*(CSCW2), 429. https://doi.org/10.1145/3479573
Martin, K. (2019). Ethical implications and accountability of algorithms. *Journal of Business
    Ethics, 160*(4), 835–850. https://doi.org/10.1007/s10551-018-3921-3
Meredith, S. (2018). *Here's everything you need to know about the Cambridge Analytica scandal.*
    Retrieved June 3, 2022, from https://www.cnbc.com/2018/03/21/facebook-cambridge-
    analytica-scandal-everything-you-need-to-know.html
Meta. (2022). *Annual report.* Retrieved May 24, 2022, from https://d18rn0p25nwr6d.cloudfront.
    net/CIK-0001326801/14039b47-2e2f-4054-9dc5-71bcc7cf01ce.pdf
Ministry of Human Resources and Social Security, National Development and Reform Commis-
    sion, Ministry of Transport, Emergency Response Department, State Administration of Market

Regulation, State Administration of Medical Insurance, Supreme People's Court, National Federation of Trade Unions. (2021). *Guidelines on safeguarding the rights and interests of workers in new forms of employment.* Retrieved May 27, 2022, from http://www.gov.cn/zhengce/zhengceku/2021-07/23/content_5626761.htm

Olhede, S., & Rodrigues, R. (2017). Fairness and transparency in the age of the algorithm. *Significance, 14*(2), 8–9. https://doi.org/10.1111/j.1740-9713.2017.01012.x

Otlowski, A. (2020). *Two years later: Cambridge analytica and its impact on data privacy.* Retrieved June 6, 2022, from https://www.hipb2b.com/blog/two-years-later-cambridge-analytica-and-its-impact-on-data-privacy

Outay, F., Malik, H., Zappin, A., & Kalaichelvan, K. (2021). Towards understanding the monetization and censorship aspect of streaming media. In *Proceedings—2021 IEEE International Conference on Dependable, Autonomic and Secure Computing, International Conference on Pervasive Intelligence and Computing, International Conference on Cloud and Big Data Computing and International Conference on Cyber Science and Technology Congress, DASC/PiCom/CBDCom/CyberSciTech 2021,* pp. 798–801. https://doi.org/10.1109/DASC-PICom-CBDCom-CyberSciTech52372.2021.00132

Panday, J. (2020). *Exploring the problems of content moderation on social media.* Retrieved May 25, 2022, from https://www.internetgovernance.org/2020/12/23/exploring-the-problems-of-content-moderation-on-social-media/

Pauleen, D. J., Rooney, D., & Intezari, A. (2017). Big data, little wisdom: Trouble brewing? Ethical implications for the information systems discipline. *Social Epistemology, 31*(4), 400–416. https://doi.org/10.1080/02691728.2016.1249436

Perez-Breva, L. (2018). *Opinion: Facebook has to change its business model because it's using us as unpaid laborers.* Retrieved June 8, 2022, from https://www.marketwatch.com/story/facebook-has-to-change-its-business-model-because-its-using-us-as-unpaid-laborers-2018-04-12

Postman, N. (1987). *Amusing ourselves to death.* Methuen.

Prosser, T. (2008). Self-regulation, co-regulation and the audio-visual media services directive. *Journal of Consumer Policy, 31*(1), 99–113. https://doi.org/10.1007/s10603-007-9055-0

Quong, J. (2018). *Public reason. Stanford encyclopedia of philosophy archive.* Retrieved June 2, 2022, from https://plato.stanford.edu/archives/spr2018/entries/public-reason/#WhyPubRea

Reddy, E., Cakici, B., & Ballestero, A. (2019). Beyond mystery: Putting algorithmic accountability in context. *Big Data and Society, 6*(1), 2053951719826856. https://doi.org/10.1177/2053951719826856

Rodriguez, J. A. (2022). LGBTQ incorporated: YouTube and the management of diversity. *Journal of Homosexuality.* https://doi.org/10.1080/00918369.2022.2042664

Ross, P. E. (2016). *AlphaGo wins final game in match against champion go player.* Retrieved June 10, 2022, from https://spectrum.ieee.org/alphago-wins-match-against-top-go-player#toggle-gdpr

Sans, M. (2017). *Get familiar with YouTube's new monetization icons.* Retrieved May 26, 2022, from https://www.dailyrindblog.com/familiar-youtubes-monetization-icons/

Sato, M. (2022). *Alt-right and anti-feminist creators plug their Patreons, custom merch, and solicit outside donations on YouTube, new study finds.* Retrieved May 31, 2022, from https://www.theverge.com/2022/3/22/22991073/youtube-demonetization-alt-right-cornell-study

Siles, I., Segura-Castillo, A., Solís, R., & Sancho, M. (2020). Folk theories of algorithmic recommendations on Spotify: Enacting data assemblages in the global South. *Big Data and Society, 7*(1), 205395172092337. https://doi.org/10.1177/2053951720923377

Sloan, R. H., & Warner, R. (2018). When is an algorithm transparent? Predictive analytics, privacy, and public policy. *IEEE Security Privacy, 16*(3), 18–25. https://doi.org/10.1109/MSP.2018.2701166

Swart, J. (2021). Experiencing algorithms: How young people understand, feel about, and engage with algorithmic news selection on social media. *Social Media + Society, 7.* https://doi.org/10.1177/20563051211008828

Tanash, R. S., Aydogan, A., et al. (2016). *Detecting influential users and communities in censored tweets using data-flow graphs.*

Trenholm, R. (2017). *'AlphaGo': Go ringside for the time AI beat the world's best.* Retrieved June 10, 2022, from https://www.cnet.com/culture/entertainment/alphago-ringside-ai-greg-kohs-interview-deepmind-lee-sedol/

Vedder, A., & Naudts, L. (2017). Accountability for the use of algorithms in a big data environment. *International Review of Law, Computers and Technology, 31*(2), 206–224. https://doi.org/10.1080/13600869.2017.1298547

Vincent, J. (2019). *AI won't relieve the misery of Facebook's human moderators.* Retrieved May 25, 2022, from https://www.theverge.com/2019/2/27/18242724/facebook-moderation-ai-artificial-intelligence-platforms

Wang, Q. (2020). The multiple dimensions of algorithmic transparency and algorithmic accountability. *Journal of Comparative Law, 06*, 163–173.

Wieringa, M. (2020). *What to account for when accounting for algorithms: A systematic literature review on algorithmic accountability. FAT\*.* https://doi.org/10.1145/3351095.3372833

Yurieff, K. (2021). *Facebook's 'supreme court' just ruled against Facebook.* Retrieved June 7, 2022, from https://edition.cnn.com/2021/01/28/tech/facebook-oversight-board-first-decisions/index.html

Zappin, A., Malik, H., Shakshuki, E. M., & Dampier, D. A. (2021). YouTube monetization and censorship by proxy: A machine learning prospective. *Procedia Computer Science, 198*, 23–32. https://doi.org/10.1016/j.procs.2021.12.207

Zemach, D. (2021). *Teaching English with TikTok? How social media is making microlearning big business.* Retrieved May 26, 2022, from https://bridge.edu/tefl/blog/teaching-english-with-tiktok-social-media-making-microlearning-big-business/

Zhang, W., Chen, Z., & Xi, Y. (2020). Traffic media: How algorithmic imaginations and practices change content production. *Chinese Journal of Communication, 14*(1), 58–74. https://doi.org/10.1080/17544750.2020.1830422

Zhuravskaya, E., Petrova, M., & Enikolopov, R. (2020). Political effects of the internet and social media. In P. Aghion & H. Rey (Eds.), *Annual review of economics* (Annual reviews) (Vol. 12, pp. 415–438). https://doi.org/10.1146/annurev-economics-081919-050239

Zilles, C. (2020). *If social media companies are publishers and not platforms, that changes everything.* Retrieved May 30, 2022, from https://socialmediahq.com/if-social-media-companies-are-publishers-and-not-platforms-that-changes-everything/

# Cases and Analyses of Social Media Companies

14

## 14.1 Facebook

In this chapter, we will present cases of two reputable social media giants, Facebook and WeChat, in order to discern how social media companies monetize their social business. We will explain how monetization strategy and monetization actions are used and geared toward generating revenue and conclude with what we can learn from the two cases.

Facebook, founded in 2004, is a California-based online social networking service provider, which is deemed as one of the Big Five tech giants (Google, Amazon, Facebook, Apple, and Microsoft). Facebook, which is widely viewed as one of the most valuable companies in the world, had a market value of over $550 billion and its brand value was ranked 14th in the world in 2019 (Niu, 2019). Mark Zuckerberg co-founded the company with his university fellows and roommates. Its mission statement is "to give people the power to build community and bring the world closer together. People use Facebook to stay connected with friends and family, to discover what's going on in the world, and to share and express what matters to them" (Frier & Chafkin, 2017). Facebook employs a multiscreen strategy. Facebook users can access Facebook's social networking service via PCs, mobile phones, tablets, and smartwatches. Users can use Facebook to browse friends' posts and comments and create a profile page to publicly disclose personal information and data. It was widely reported that Facebook had 2.50 billion monthly active users (MAUs) as of December 2019 (Facebook, 2020). Nevertheless, Facebook ran into several burning issues: user privacy disclosure, manipulation of political elections, a wide spread of fake news and misleading information, and social media addiction.

### 14.1.1 Facebook's Monetization Strategy

According to Facebook's 2020 fiscal report, total revenue was $70.70 billion and of that, advertising revenue was $69.66 billion (Facebook, 2020). Advertising revenue accounted for 98.5% of total revenue. This indicates that Facebook's monetization strategy in essence is an advertising-based strategy (Chaffey, 2013). Facebook can charge individuals or organizations advertising fees by running Facebook ads and sponsored posts.

Despite the fact that many other online advertising platforms have similar services, Facebook's monetization strategy has its own uniqueness. A firm's uniqueness is a component of such firm's competitive advantage (Ulrich & Lake, 1991). The specific uniqueness offers a firm "capabilities that are idiosyncratic and non-imitable" (Ulrich & Lake, 1991, p. 82). Compared to their social media competitors, Facebook's uniqueness lies in a focus on user experience and user growth instead of jumping directly into monetization (Dudovskiy, 2017). This silver bullet helped Facebook win a large percentage of market shares and build its competitive advantage (Dudovskiy, 2017). The uniqueness of Facebook can be summarized by four facets[1]:

1. *Focus on User Experience.* Facebook is a late mover in terms of social media business. Before it was founded, social media pioneers Friendster and MySpace had launched and accumulated millions of users. Compared to these first movers, Facebook used a continual approach on refining user experience. Its platform can meet user needs in accessing standard social networking services as well as displaying a personalized digital presence. By leveraging the network effect, its user experience focus strategy made Facebook popular from its infancy.

2. *Grow and Buy.* With the development of information technology, wireless Internet, and other emerging technologies, Facebook encountered many competitors. For instance, Facebook's initial Web version accumulated a large number of PC-based users. However, the development of wireless Internet made mobile apps popular and disruptive. For example, Instagram is a mobile-first app and focuses on sharing photographs and short videos. This niche position helped Instagram achieve viral growth and accumulate over 50 million users in just a few weeks of introduction (Malik, 2012). By acquiring Instagram, Facebook had the ability to broaden their product lines and shift from PCs to mobile.

3. *Continual Product Innovation.* Facebook has stressed the role of product innovation. This innovation injects vigor into retaining the current user group as well as acquiring new users. Facebook has introduced information service News Feed, instant messaging service Messenger, online streaming service Facebook Live, and many others. In terms of external innovation such as new features rolled out by competitors, Facebook often cloned these and offered similar features to catch up with their competitors. For example, it was reported that Facebook tried to duplicate Snap's features over 10 times (Hern, 2016).

---

[1] The four facets are adapted from Dudovskiy, J. (2017). Facebook Business Strategy and Competitive Advantage. Retrieved from https://research-methodology.net/facebook-business-strategy-and-competitive-advantage/

4. *Seeking New Monetization Opportunities*. If investment in user experience and user growth cannot turn into actual revenue, Facebook's efforts would be in vain. Apart from consolidating its advertising business, Facebook also is continually exploring new monetization opportunities. Facebook rolled out "Facebook Buy Buttons" to move into social commerce around 2014. Despite the fact that this move did not meet users' prior expectations, Facebook provided brands with "Shop Now" buttons to lead followers to these brands' shopping sites. Recently, Facebook also experimented with new paid content features to sell certain videos generated in the community.

To summarize, the success of Facebook's monetization strategy not only relies on creating an online social ads service, but also on the uniqueness that competitors cannot imitate.

## 14.1.2 Facebook's Business Model

Business models can indicate who a firm's customers are, the value a firm creates for customers, how a firm monetizes that value, and the economic explanation of how the firm delivers value to customers and achieves profits as well (Magretta, 2002). In terms of the success of monetization, a business model is a crucial nexus between monetization strategy and monetization actions. It fulfills a gap between a firm's strategic goals and specific actions in detail. Therefore, Facebook's success also relies on a solid business model design to gear up monetization strategy and monetization actions. The business model can therefore be used to discern the sources of a firm's value creation and delineate how a firm's business model links to its strategy (Trimi & Berbegal-Mirabent, 2012). The components of the business model can also indicate what specific actions a firm should take. For example, business models reveal which key partners a firm should build a good relationship with and what key activities a firm should rigorously manage and control.

- *Customers*. In a conventional view, Facebook users are Facebook's major customers. It is their use and content production that is of paramount importance to sustain Facebook's advantage with a huge number of MAUs. However, considering that Facebook allows users to use Facebook for no charge, from a monetization perspective, brands and advertisers are Facebook's de facto customers. It is brands and advertisers who bring about actual monetary value for Facebook. This suggests that Facebook should regard advertisers and brands as its first priority; however, Facebook does not do so. Instead, Facebook views the enormous amount of regular end users as their prized asset and continually works to improve user experience.
- *Value Proposition*. According to Facebook's organizational mission, Facebook aims to empower users to build community and increase the connectivity of the world. It aspires to offer an information-sharing platform where everyone can express themselves and comment and interact with others. In addition to this

value proposition, Facebook also created Marketplace to develop their social commerce business. Users can purchase items from their fellow users by using this commercial feature. Meanwhile, this social media platform offers in-app business with payment solutions by which users can pay third-party agents or companies by using Facebook's payment services.

- *Channels.* Facebook employs a multiscreen strategy. Users can access the social media platform by PCs, smartphones, tablets, and many other mobile devices.
- *Customer Relationships.* Facebook builds good relationships with end users and advertisers. Basically, Facebook needs to extract maximum value from massive users and advertisers. The increase in the number of end users can produce positive outcomes. More users pouring onto the platform can facilitate the content production for the platform and the connectivity between users, therefore making the platform more attractive for users. However, the increase in the number of advertisers can jeopardize Facebook's advertising attractiveness. More advertisers on board will intensify competition and affect the effectiveness of social advertising, making Facebook less attractive for advertisers and other ad service customers. More users will attract more advertisers; however, more advertisers will lead to further commercialization of Facebook and may result in user turnover. Facebook's current customer relationship strategy recognizes and addresses these issues Facebook focuses on acquiring new users and increasing user experience and strictly controls the social ads (displaying an ad among every ten posts) to avoid user aversion.
- *Key Partners.* Creators of content such as short videos, music, and mobile games are crucial partners of Facebook. As there are many third-party applications on Facebook, the company also partners with a significant number of external app developers. As Facebook also rolled out payment solutions, its payment infrastructure needs to partner with credit card companies such as Visa, MasterCard, and PayPal.
- *Key Activities.* In the previous section, we discussed four facets of Facebook's uniqueness. In fact, Facebook's key activities are maintaining its uniqueness and thereby other competitors cannot overtake it. Apart from the four facets, it is necessary to mention that, even though Facebook's core business is social networking services, the company also emphasizes the role of developing financial capabilities. Facebook understood that it is of paramount importance for startups to access sufficient financial resources. Thanks to such efforts in fundraising such as private share sales, Facebook was able to spend $1 billion acquiring Instagram, which is very rare for new ventures.
- *Key Resources.* The brand "Facebook" is Facebook's most priceless resource. However, Facebook was losing its good brand reputation by offering misinformation, fake news, and being involved in political election manipulation. The massive network of users is a key resource of Facebook, which makes the social media platform irreplaceable. As Facebook is a technology company, highly skilled talent is crucial for the company's long-term success. For example, artificial intelligence experts can optimize content recommendation by leveraging machine learning technology.

- *Cost Structure.* The cost structure of Facebook can be divided into two classes. The first class is operating costs, data handling, traffic cost, content acquisition cost, and others. The second class is manpower costs, office spending, and management expenditure.
- *Revenue Stream.* As mentioned previously, ad revenue accounted for over 98% of Facebook's total revenue. A small percentage of the total revenue is payment revenue: Facebook takes a cut from business transactions on the platform. Apart from this, Facebook also proactively looks for new monetization opportunities. For example, its subordinate platform, Instagram, was pushing hard in leading users to complete online purchases without leaving the platform.

In general, Facebook business model explicitly reflects the monetization strategy and delineates how Facebook reaps revenue and realizes profitability. From a managerial view, the business model indicated that monetization actions are not only focusing on how to make money but also managing on key resources, key activities, key partners, and other aspects. For instance, when Facebook cannot sustain a healthy cost structure and not realize profitability, its monetization would not be deemed as successful.

### 14.1.3 Managerial Implications from Facebook's Success

Considering Facebook is not the first mover in social media business, it is necessary to indicate how the company can outpace competitors and what know-how today's social media companies can learn from Facebook's success.

- *Seize the Opportunity to Grow When Regulations are Far from Mature.* Myspace, founded a couple of months before Facebook, was the largest social media platform in the world before 2008. After that, Facebook took the lead. It was considered highly unlikely that Facebook, a student-based startup, could outperform the big company Myspace which had many talented employees including business professionals, MBAs, and Internet engineers. Myspace was acquired by News Corporation for $580 million in 2005. It was expected that Myspace would have exploited the abundant resources offered by the media behemoth and acquired more users and grown its social media business. But the result showed that being acquired by a big company was not always helpful for digital startups. Sean Percival, ex-Vice-President of online marketing of Myspace, once said "the reality was that as time went on, the corporate policies creeped in. The lawyers came in, the accountants. Everything came in. As opposed to being this nimble, fast-moving sports car, they started to become slow" (Dredge, 2015). For example, once Myspace was run by its behemoth parent company, some basic changes or innovations of the platform needed to be processed and evaluated by the parent company's legal and financial departments. By contrast, Facebook was much less restricted by these aspects and therefore could more flexibly move and grow fast. In fact, when social media was new and novel to the public, relevant regulation measures and public policies were far from mature, which actually provides much leeway for nimble, small businesses to move fast and take over the market. However, it does not imply that legal and financial audits are not important for digital companies. In recent years, Facebook has been fined by the UK due to the lack of protection of user data (Waterson, 2018). It was also reported that Facebook was expecting to be fined several billion dollars by the US Federal Trade Commission and the EU due to General Data Protection Regulation (GDPR). To summarize, when regulations are absent or in their adolescent stage, firms should seize the opportunity, move fast, and focus on the growth of business.

- *Evaluate Traditional Business from a Developmental View.* Ad business is a major source of social media companies' revenue. When social media was still novel to people, it was an unsettled issue as to how social media companies could profit from ad business. Click-through rates of Myspace and many other social media platforms were dramatically low (0.04%), which was rather disappointing compared to the rate of banner ads on general websites (Kelleher, 2010). Myspace, as one of the pioneer social media platforms, imitated the advertising approach of general websites and used multiple, large, and animated banner ads on its platform (Kelleher, 2010). This approach was a total mess from the view of today's social media users. "It was one of the most annoying things you could do with an ad, but they (Myspace) just did not care: they had no respect for the users. It was all about monetization. Making money, squeezing every dollar out of it. . ." (Dredge, 2015). By contrast, Facebook focuses on monetization as well as user experience. Facebook does more native and inline advertising which seems more natural and less offensive (Dredge, 2015). Facebook also allows users to block ads they are not interested in, which can make users better targeted for other ads (Kelleher, 2010). The legend of how Facebook can successfully monetize is that the company re-evaluated how ad business should be presented on social media platforms and gradually improved how users interact with commercial content. Social media provides a platform for users to conduct online social interactions with fellow users. In such a *social atmosphere*, it can be very annoying when advertisers jump in and merchandise their goods toward users who are chatting with friends. This does not imply that advertising is inappropriate for social media platforms. Social life cannot shy away from consumerism. Users will use social media platforms to share what they bought and consumed which can be an implicit and organic form of product endorsements and looks less commercial (Boerman et al., 2017). Facebook transformed the traditional advertising approach and fostered a better approach to presenting social ads by considering the social attributes of social media platforms. Brands and advertisers can use influencers to provide social, native ads; Facebook collects user data and offers precise, native ads for each user based on their behavioral pattern and interests.

## 14.2   WeChat

WeChat, released in 2011, is a multifunction social media and mobile payment app with over one billion MAUs. Tencent, a Shenzhen-based Internet technology company, developed WeChat. In 2019, the company was ranked eighth among the world's ten most valuable brands (Shi, 2019). Tencent's mission statement is "improve the quality of life through Internet value-added services" (Liao, 2019a, 2019b). WeChat is a principle product of Tencent's product catalog. WeChat aims to connect people with Internet services and create new business opportunities. It was reported that WeChat created over 22 million jobs in 2018, approximately one-quarter of which earned most of their income through the app (Hu, 2019). WeChat-based information technology solutions are widely used to transform traditional sectors by reducing operating costs, maximizing revenue, and enhancing business efficiency. For example, Shangri-La, a leading firm in the hotel industry, adopted WeChat's e-business solution, and involves WeChat into consumer journey from check-in to checkout (Hospitality Technology, 2019). WeChat's e-business solution sales represented 5% (240 billion yuan) of all companies' spending on information-related investment in the same year (Hu, 2019). In a word, WeChat is a social media platform though its application can be used for individual and business purposes.

### 14.2.1   WeChat's Monetization Strategy

WeChat is free to use, same as Facebook, but its monetization is not as advanced as Facebook. WeChat's monetization strategy can be summarized with four features: advertising, e-service, digital payment, and e-business solutions. It was estimated that WeChat ad business created 380 billion yuan in 2018 (Jufu Finance, 2019). WeChat has a photograph sharing Moment page similar to Facebook's News Feed. Brands and advertisers can push commercials to a target audience in their Moment. Another major revenue source is e-service. It was reported that over 60% of WeChat users use WeChat to shop, order a ride, make reservation, and buy movie tickets, among other services. WeChat is a super app integrating almost all commercial functions related to everyday life. These functions are provided by third-party providers. For example, users can use WeChat to do shopping. This function is provided by Pinduoduo. WeChat can lead massive traffic into Pinduoduo by just creating an interface connecting WeChat and Pinduoduo. In Pinduoduo's IPO report, the company valued the 5-year use of the interface as a $2.85 billion potential asset (Ifanr, 2018) by which Tencent can reap handsome investment revenue from providing this data interface to Pinduoduo. Revenue generated from a digital payment business cannot be ignored. The wide application of WeChat Pay may lead to a cashless society. WeChat users can complete payment by using WeChat Pay. Most recently, WeChat users do not even need to launch the WeChat app. Merchants can use a WeChat-based tablet to gather payment. A single snap of their face can pay all items in their shopping cart (People's Daily Online, 2019). WeChat takes commission fees from each transaction, collects interest from deposits, and offers value service to clients based on data gathered from massive users' use pattern.

In addition, WeChat's Mini Program (mobile applications which can be accessed anytime and anywhere without being installed on a device), digital payment technology, facial recognition, and IoT (Internet of things) technology enable the WeChat product team to offer e-business solutions for the digital transformation of traditional industries. The e-business solution can be used to restructure business processes, improve business operations, and enhance consumer satisfaction. This implies that WeChat can compete with many e-business solution providers and make money from this business. This is mainly due to WeChat's one billion users base (also, most users are in China, which is very powerful for companies concentrating on this market) and the social app's ability to integrate cloud computing, digital payment, artificial intelligence, and many other technologies.

Though advertising is the main revenue source for both WeChat and Facebook, WeChat's ad business is different from Facebook's. Since WeChat launched its social ad business in 2015, WeChat only allowed a social ad to be displayed in users' Moment per day. In March 2018, WeChat permitted adding one more ad into users' Moment per day. This minor adjustment is limited to users who are from large cities such as Beijing and Shanghai; users from medium or small cities still can only find a social ad per day. From this move, we can see that Tencent's WeChat product team is very cautious about commercialization of users' online social lives. By contrast, on Facebook or Facebook's subordinate app—Instagram, more ads will be pushed to users per day. Firm leader personality can influence corporate strategy and alter the outcomes of strategy (Resick et al., 2009). WeChat's monetization strategy is largely affected by its inventor—Allen Zhang. Zhang is Senior Executive Vice President of Tencent and the president of WeChat business. Many top executives from Tencent told Zhang to roll out more commercial features for WeChat to better monetize it. However, Zhang denied their request and asserted that these leaders can add this or that feature after he left Tencent. He infuses a user-centric spirit into the development process of WeChat and untiringly updates WeChat to increase its usability and operating efficiency to meet users' social needs instead of commercial needs. Hence, WeChat, until now, is still considered a social media platform far from being fully monetized (Cantale, 2018). But the reality is that, in such a low commercial orientation mode, WeChat's revenue contribution to Tencent's total revenue has increased by more than 50% year over year since 2013 and is approaching Tencent's core gaming business (Cantale, 2018).

The distinction between WeChat and Facebook does not only lie in the number of ads and leader personality. Affected by a Chinese mindset, the business philosophy behind the product of WeChat is altruism. Pony Ma, the founder of Tencent, once stated that Tencent aspires to be a decentralized empowerment platform (Cao, 2017). WeChat enables small businesses to use the platform to conduct business, and most importantly does not charge any fees for their platform use. It is like renting out counters in a mall without charging monthly rent. Any individuals or organizations can create their Official Accounts—an official home page by which viewers can transact with the owner—on WeChat without any charges. This Official Accounts service has been widely adopted by various sectors such as retail, healthcare, tourism, and government. WeChat's integration with third-party apps leads to the birth of WeChat commerce (W-commerce). Small vendors from JD.com, Pinduoduo, and Vip.com can leverage their personal power in their social circle to merchandise products via Moment and Official Accounts. Viewers encountering such promotional posts or content can click on it and complete the purchase in the WeChat platform or off the platform. WeChat reported that the total sales of W-commerce exceeded 522 billion yuan and the number of W-commerce merchants surpassed 20 million (Chyxx, 2018), while WeChat barely took a fee from sales or merchants. The business logic of altruism is that the success of WeChat relies on the success of massive small-and-medium-size businesses. The more profitable small businesses are, the more users and potential monetization opportunities WeChat will have. This business logic is particularly suitable for a social media business which wants to offer social welfare and create social value for society (Dohrmann et al., 2015).

## 14.2.2  WeChat Business Model

- *Customers*. Users, brands, and advertisers in China are WeChat's major customers. WeChat is now expanding to the global market. The global expansion can help Tencent find foreign brands which are interested in using WeChat's advertising platform to increase brand awareness in China.
- *Value Proposition*. The core value that WeChat created is instant messaging and social networking. Apart from these, WeChat also aims to offer an all-in-one app integrating almost all Internet features, so that various users' needs (e.g., online shopping, e-ticketing, paying for utility, delivery service, and ordering a cab) can be met within the WeChat ecosystem. WeChat even wants to act as an operating system in which users can access apps via WeChat. Given the fact that installation of too many apps can result in the overall decline of smartphone performance, it is quite valuable for users to access such apps on demand without installing them. In addition, because WeChat has such attractive ease-of-use technical features and a huge user base, the company can also act as a crucial vehicle to advance organizations from various industries to digitalize their traditional business.
- *Channels*. WeChat is unlike Facebook in providing a multiscreen service. Its PC version and Web version are comparatively simple and only have a few key features such as instant messaging and social networking. In other words, WeChat employs a mobile-first strategy and focuses on reaching users via mobile channels.
- *Customer Relationships*. WeChat also needs to extract maximum value from users and advertisers. Meanwhile, WeChat is also a crucial platform for providing e-business solutions; therefore, Tencent also needs to maintain a harmonious relationship with industrial customers.

- *Key Partners*. The versatility of WeChat cannot be achieved without partnering with various key actors across many sectors such as e-commerce (JD.com, Pinduoduo), transportation (DiDi Chuxing, Chinese Southern Airline), local business (Dazhongdianping, Meituan), commercial banks (China Everbright Bank, Bank of Beijing), and several others. Many of the partners are leaders in their respective sectors.
- *Key Activities*. The improvement of user experience, product innovation, mergers and acquisition (M&A), and user growth are Tencent's key activities in sustaining WeChat's competitive advantage among other social media platforms. The distinction in key activities between WeChat and Facebook is that WeChat is much more limited to its domestic markets, while the markets Facebook can reach are more worldwide. WeChat is a popular app but its international dominance only covers three countries, leaving a lot of international business money on the table (Culpan, 2018). Tencent is eagerly advancing the global expansion of WeChat through being Snap's largest shareholder and investing $150 million in the US online social community Reddit (Liao, 2019a, 2019b). They have also invited reputable football player Lionel Messi as its global endorser (ESC Editorial Team, 2018). These attempts are seen as Tencent's globalization strategy to export its experience and technology advantage in China to overseas countries such as Malaysia.
- *Key Resources*. The brand "WeChat" is the most crucial resource for WeChat's sustainable success. As a knowledge-intensive tech company, Tencent needs to recruit and develop IT talents for WeChat.
- *Cost Structure*. WeChat is just one product of Tencent's product lines, so it is inappropriate to separate costs related to maintaining the operation of WeChat from Tencent's cost structure. In fact, in order to reduce avoidable taxation and garner benefits from taking Tencent's vast number of businesses and departments as a whole, corporate leaders need to design the cost structure at a corporate-wide level.
- *Revenue Stream*. The majority of revenue comes from advertising, value-added services, and digital payment. Apart from these, WeChat is proactively exploring new revenue sources such as offering e-business solutions and customizable enterprise-versions.

In summary, WeChat's business model can nicely reflect its monetization strategy.

### 14.2.3  Managerial Implications from WeChat's Success

- *Learn to Disrupt the Established Product with a New One*. When Tencent invented WeChat, it was difficult for people to understand why Tencent did so. At that time it appeared that QQ, the product that once helped Tencent survive and thrive in the China's competitive IT market, could have undoubtedly continued to dominate the China market. With the wide adoption of mobile technology and the increasing velocity of mobile Internet, Tencent accordingly rolled out a mobile version of QQ, though the app was weighted down by its desktop version's complicated features (Hariharan, 2017). Users had been used to using QQ with their computers. Therefore, Pony Ma decided to make a bold decision and develop a new, simple mobile app to compete with QQ. Mr. Ma asked several product teams to compete on developing this app. Through this process, WeChat was born. At that time, even many employees of the product team did not believe that WeChat would succeed because the current killer app QQ could fulfill all users' needs. They thought that it was unnecessary to develop what seemed to be a duplicate social app. Meanwhile, there were many similar products such as MiTalk and Youni offered by other reputable tech companies. MiTalk, developed by China's leading smartphone manufacturer Xiaomi, accumulated millions of users quickly and got much public awareness in the China market. But the product manager Allen Zhang firmly believes that WeChat could succeed eventually by offering differentiated value. Three crucial features, voice messages, Shake (an approach to find unknown people) and Moment, differentiated WeChat from their contemporary competitors QQ, MiTalk, and others. Now, despite the fact that WeChat has over one billion users, Tencent has developed new social apps to compete with WeChat and QQ—Weishi—to dig into the gold mine of the social short video business.

- *Do not Just Bet on Advertising.* For online platforms, advertising comes first when leaders brainstorm possible monetization approaches. Facebook's advertising model got much criticism. It has to collect a large amount of user data to offer personalized and native ads for each user, but this approach breaches users' privacy rights (Burt, 2019). The success of WeChat is very inspiring because the app proved that it is possible to find a roadmap to profitability without relying on advertising. In fact, WeChat is very cautious about monetizing via advertising and limits the number of ads to avoid user aversion toward social ads. WeChat tries to explore new approaches of monetization by innovating technologies and catching up with new trends in the digital business. In order to break down the silos between WeChat and external apps or websites, WeChat rolled out WeChat Pay (a payment feature), Mini Programs (in-app programs), and data interface for third-party firms connecting their information system to WeChat. These efforts transformed WeChat into a super app which can profit from enormous businesses. On the one hand, the transformation cannot shy away from the WeChat product team's technological innovation. The product team infused emerging technologies (payment technology, cloud computing, artificial intelligence, etc.) into WeChat. Technological innovation enables WeChat to outperform competitors and offer inspiring new features such as Mini Program and WeChat Pay. On the other hand, this success also relies on Tencent's forward-looking leaders. These Chinese leaders are very crisis-conscious and clearly know that they are always in combat with the turbulent, uncertain environment. For example, when Talkbox rolled out voice messaging, Tencent's leaders quickly noticed that this feature could be a key to the success of an instant messaging app in the China market because Chinese characters are difficult to enter via smartphone keyboard. Therefore, the WeChat product team quickly developed its own voice messaging function and caught up with this trend.

To summarize, Facebook and WeChat are two dominant social media platforms. Each of them has its particular uniqueness and monetization approaches. They provide useful and beneficial insights on how future social media platforms can realize monetization success and find a route to profitability.

## References

Boerman, S. C., Willemsen, L. M., & Van Der Aa, E. P. (2017). "This post is sponsored": Effects of sponsorship disclosure on persuasion knowledge and electronic word of mouth in the context of Facebook. *Journal of Interactive Marketing, 38*, 82–92.

Burt, A. (2019). *Can Facebook ever be fixed?* Retrieved from https://hbr.org/2019/04/can-facebook-ever-be-fixed

Cantale, S. (2018). *What's stopping Tencent from monetizing WeChat in the most obvious way?* Retrieved from https://www.imd.org/research-knowledge/articles/whats-stopping-tencent-from-monetizing-wechat-in-the-most-obvious-way/

Cao, S. (2017). *Tencent CEO Pony Ma's goal is the opposite of a monopoly.* Retrieved from https://observer.com/2017/12/tencent-ceo-pony-ma-speaks-at-fortune-global-forum-in-china/

Chaffey, D. (2013). *Facebook case study.* Retrieved from https://www.smartinsights.com/social-media-marketing/facebook-marketing/facebook-case-study/

Chyxx. (2018). *In 2018, the growth rate of WeChat business market began to slow down, and the industry gradually developed towards standardization and institutionalization [figure].* Retrieved from https://www.chyxx.com/industry/201812/699890.html

Culpan, T. (2018). *The world's most powerful app is squandering its lead.* Retrieved from https://www.bloomberg.com/opinion/articles/2018-07-22/world-s-most-powerful-app-is-squandering-its-lead

Dohrmann, S., Raith, M., & Siebold, N. (2015). Monetizing social value creation–a business model approach. *Entrepreneurship Research Journal, 5*(2), 127–154.

Dredge, S. (2015). *MySpace—What went wrong: 'The site was a massive spaghetti-ball mess'.* Retrieved from https://www.theguardian.com/technology/2015/mar/06/myspace-what-went-wrong-sean-percival-spotify

Dudovskiy, J. (2017). *Facebook business strategy and competitive advantage.* Retrieved from https://research-methodology.net/facebook-business-strategy-and-competitive-advantage/

ESC Editorial Team. (2018). *What is Tencent's strategy to expand in overseas markets?* Retrieved from https://www.ecommercestrategychina.com/column/what-is-tencents-strategy-to-expand-in-overseas-markets

Facebook. (2020). *Annual report.* Retrieved from http://d18rn0p25nwr6d.cloudfront.net/CIK-0001326801/45290cc0-656d-4a88-a2f3-147c8de86506.pdf

Frier, S., & Chafkin, M. (2017). *Zuckerberg's new mission for Facebook: Bringing the world closer.* Retrieved from https://www.bloomberg.com/news/articles/2017-06-22/zuckerberg-s-new-mission-for-facebook-bringing-the-world-closer

Hariharan, A. (2017). *On growing: 7 lessons from the story of WeChat.* Retrieved from https://blog.ycombinator.com/lessons-from-wechat/

Hern, A. (2016). *Facebook tries to clone Snapchat for 8th, 9th and 10th times.* Retrieved from https://www.theguardian.com/technology/2016/oct/31/facebook-tries-to-clone-snapchat

Hospitality Technology. (2019). *Shangri-La group to launch e-services within WeChat ecosystem.* Retrieved from https://hospitalitytech.com/shangri-la-group-launch-e-services-within-wechat-ecosystem

Hu, B. (2019). *Tencent's WeChat created 22 million job opportunities in 2018—Report*. Retrieved from https://technode.com/2019/03/05/wechat-22-million-jobs/

Ifanr. (2018). *The value of a JD WeChat: Not open traffic, billions of first-class*. Retrieved from https://baijiahao.baidu.com/s?id=1619517980294039925&wfr=spider&for=pc

Jufu Finance. (2019). *WeChat can't sit still? Gradually open the business of advertising traffic realization*. Retrieved from https://baijiahao.baidu.com/s?id=1626807874548446139&wfr=spider&for=pc

Kelleher, K. (2010). *How Facebook learned from MySpace's mistakes*. Retrieved from https://fortune.com/2010/11/19/how-facebook-learned-from-myspaces-mistakes/

Liao, R. (2019a). *Tencent promises its technology will 'do good'*. Retrieved from https://techcrunch.com/2019/05/07/tencent-motto-tech-for-good/

Liao, S. (2019b). *Reddit gets a $150 million investment from Tencent and users are posting memes to mock the deal*. Retrieved from https://www.theverge.com/2019/2/11/18216134/reddit-tencent-investment-deal-memes-amount-winnie-the-pooh-tank-man-china

Magretta, J. (2002). Why business models matter. *Harvard Business Review, 80*(5), 86–92.

Malik, O. (2012). *Here is why Facebook bought Instagram*. Retrieved from https://gigaom.com/2012/04/09/here-is-why-did-facebook-bought-instagram/

Niu, E. (2019). *Facebook is no longer a top 10 global brand*. Retrieved from https://www.fool.com/investing/2019/10/18/facebook-is-no-longer-a-top-10-global-brand.aspx

People's Daily Online. (2019). *Is facial recognition the future of smart payment in China?* Retrieved from https://www.telegraph.co.uk/peoples-daily-online/science/facial-recognition/

Resick, C. J., Whitman, D. S., Weingarden, S. M., & Hiles, N. J. (2009). The bright-side and the dark-side of CEO personality: Examining core self-evaluations, narcissism, transformational leadership, and strategic influence. *The Journal of Applied Psychology, 94*(6), 1365–1381.

Shi, Y. (2019). *China's Alibaba, Tencent among 10 most valuable global brands: Report*. Retrieved from http://www.xinhuanet.com/english/2019-06/12/c_138134931.htm

Trimi, S., & Berbegal-Mirabent, J. (2012). Business model innovation in entrepreneurship. *International Entrepreneurship and Management Journal, 8*(4), 449–465.

Ulrich, D., & Lake, D. (1991). Organizational capability: Creating competitive advantage. *Academy of Management Perspectives, 5*(1), 77–92.

Waterson, J. (2018). *UK fines Facebook £500,000 for failing to protect user data*. Retrieved from https://www.theguardian.com/technology/2018/oct/25/facebook-fined-uk-privacy-access-user-data-cambridge-analytica

# Part V

# Buried Treasure in the Roadmap Towards Monetization

# New Technologies to Enhance Money-Making Potential

**15**

## 15.1 Social Media and Artificial Intelligence (AI)

### 15.1.1 Social Media Analytics Enabled by AI

With the advent of data analytics technology, social media sentiment analysis has drawn attention from government, industry, and academia (Chen et al., 2020). Social media sentiment analysis technique is offered as a service by several companies. For example, Wisers, a Hong Kong-based social media analytic company, leverages sentiment analytic technique to offer market opinion monitoring, branding, social word of mouth, public crisis management, and other services. Social media content analytics can help firms understand user emotion and sentiment, recognize patterns and trending topics, and categorize topics and customers by specific brands (Kumar, 2020). Sentiment analysis can help firms understand consumers brand perception and conduct contextual performance analysis of brands and products to obtain competitive insights (Kumar, 2020). There are three basic approaches to conducting sentiment analysis. The rule-based approach relies on specific rules in a scripted language involving natural language processing techniques to produce preset outputs (Malhotra, 2020). The automatic response approach is built on machine learning techniques which simulate human intelligence to perform tasks (Malhotra, 2020). The last approach is a combination of the two approaches, which can produce higher sentiment accuracy. These analytic techniques are useful for ascertaining the cause of a sudden change in the number of fans and user engagement (Kumar, 2020).

The proliferation of social data, such as daily user activities and user background details, has yielded an enormous volume of social data, known familiarly as "big data" (Ghani et al., 2019). Big data generated from social media is expanding at an exponential rate and is the key means to generating insight into human behavior (Matilda, 2016). On the basis of machine learning theory, social data can be divided into different subsamples which can be used for modeling social media user behavior and increasing machine intelligence. The combination of big data and social media

© The Author(s), under exclusive license to Springer Nature Switzerland AG 2022
F. J. Martínez-López et al., *Social Media Monetization*, Future of Business and Finance, https://doi.org/10.1007/978-3-031-14575-9_15

analytics offers a new pathway to push management practice to a higher level (Matilda, 2016).

AI-powered analytic techniques can be monetized in multiple ways. Social data can be categorized in terms of ownership: Some data are exclusively owned by a social media platform, while other data are available and accessible to external individuals or organizations. For example, scientists can use open-source social data and artificial intelligence technology to analyze user sentiment and predict user behavior and cognition. Open-source social data can be leveraged by firms to provide market insights, competitor information, and public crisis information for social media brands. Firms can also achieve monetization by offering to sell such information. Moreover, social media data exclusively owned by a social media platform can be leveraged by the platform to provide more comprehensive service for social media users. Publicly available social media data can be used for training machine intelligence to increase the precision of personalized content recommendations, creating a better user experience. For premium users, exclusive social media data can be used to offer specific services. For instance, using social data, social media can optimize automatic advertisement bidding systems so that premium users' advertising expenditures are more precisely spent in advertising campaigns.

## 15.1.2  Social Media Bots

Social media bots are AI-powered programs specially designed to automatically conduct conversations with social media users. Facebook Messenger and Twitter are among the most popular platforms that support social media bots (Simova, 2019). There are two forms of social media bots. One type is bots which use machine learning to understand the context and intent of a conversation and make more sophisticated and personalized responses. The second type is rule-based bots which follow predefined service scripts to react to consumers' inquiries (Demeku, 2021).

Social media bots can offer 24-h customer service, take orders, and entertain users and more (Simova, 2019). However, bots, even those powered by machine learning, may fail to understand a consumer's questions and provide inappropriate answers to consumers' inquiries. In most cases though, bots outperform humans in terms of their unlimited working time and number of languages mastered. Bots can achieve real-time translation of hundreds of languages. For example, Laiye, a Beijing-based network technology company, developed a smart chatbot system for brands to handle consumers. The system established a knowledge database that includes over 1500 pieces of information, over 20,000 questions, and is able to use natural language processing to analyze consumer inquiries. When interacting with consumers, bots will constantly gather consumer data and profile consumer personalities (for more detail, see Zhao, 2019).

Social media bots are all artifacts derived from human behavior. The problem is that AI-powered bots could act in a way that deviates from human expectations. It has been reported that AI can generate biases related to gender, color, and race.

Social media bots are becoming more realistic (E&T Editorial Staff, 2019). The recent cutting-edge social media bots can imitate a real person. However, anthropomorphic bots could also generate malicious output, such as terrorism content that may radicalize vulnerable audiences, online harassment and hate speech, conspiracy theories and fake news, and misleading information about a company or industry.[1] It is likely because these advanced bots are trained using social media data. Social media bots are a reflection of real humans, even though the reflection may be distorted. Xiaobing, a bot developed by Microsoft China, sparked audience outrage when the bot published harassing and rude statements on Chinese social media platform Weibo (Wang, 2014). In sum, social media bots have a long way to go before they are considered reliable.

### 15.1.3  Social Media and Smart Devices

Wearables have become a common smart device and appear to have a bright future. Wearables such as Google Glass and Apple Watch can support social media apps such as Facebook and Twitter. The adoption of wearables will increase the ubiquity of social media in everyday life (Hammar, 2014). The display screen of a wearable device is normally smaller than a smartphone or computer. Therefore, social media applications designed for wearables should have a wearable device version which has been adapted to the smaller display screen interface. Moreover, social media apps for wearable devices should take into consideration that there is not space for a keyboard on a wearable device. Voice searches are the main search method in a wearable device. Voice searches are more conversational, refined, and specific than keyword searches (Shapiro, 2016). Social apps such as QQ and WeChat are also instant messaging apps in China. These apps become more conversational on wearables such as smartwatches. Wearable device users can send voice messages to communicate with users using various hardware platforms.

With GPS technology embedded in most wearables, it is becoming easier to gather consumer location information.[2] The combination of social media and wearables makes social media marketing more context-specific. Social media advertising can more accurately target consumers in specific areas. On the basis of relevant information and historical data, social apps can push notifications for users to inform them of nearby product information. Considering all these benefits provided by wearables, several social media companies have moved into this new battleground. Facebook partnered with Ray-Ban to launch wearable sunglasses that can record video from the user's perspective (Bhatia, 2021). In 2021, Snap announced a new

---

[1]What Are Social Media Bots? And How Do They Impact National Security? Retrieved April 13, 2022, from https://www.echosec.net/blog/what-are-social-media-bots

[2]3 Ways to Boost Your Marketing with Smartwatches and Wearable Technology. Retrieved April 14, 2022, from https://insights.discoverglobalnetwork.com/digital-commerce/wearable-technology-for-enhanced-marketing

version of it smart glasses, Spectacles that enable Snap users to see virtual images overlaid on their field of vision (Rodriguez, 2021a).

Additional smart devices are also drawing social media companies' attention. The USA introduced smart speakers around 2014, and since that time, over 74.2 million people were using smart speakers in their homes (McNair, 2019). Smart speakers are a new channel to reach consumers. An increasing number of brands and organizations are developing and releasing speaker apps to reach their target audiences (Matthews, 2020). For example, Show my Facebook Photos is an app that runs on Amazon's smart speaker, Alexa. The app links to Facebook users' accounts so that they may view their photographs and albums stored on Facebook on their Alexa device.[3] These apps provide brands more chances to connect with their consumers (Matthews, 2020). Meta, Facebook's parent company, has been a disruptive innovator in smart devices. This company rolled out its smart speakers, Portal and Portal+, in order to place their own smart device in consumers' homes (Bell, 2018). Portal has a smart camera which has a 140° field of view and is able to detect faces and identify people in a room (Bell, 2018). This feature can make social interactions more interesting and immersive by automatically following individuals' movements and gestures.

## 15.2  Social Media and AR/VR

Augment reality (AR) and virtual reality (VR) are other trends in social media platforms. Meta's CEO Mark Zuckerberg has promised to spend $10 billion per year on creating an immersive digital world comprised of avatars (Editorial Staff, 2022). Meta filed several patents related to eye and face monitoring that is incorporated in headsets by means of a small digicam or sensor (Editorial Staff, 2022). For instance, users are able to see a vivid graphic in their line of sight (Editorial Staff, 2022).

VR is "an advanced, human-computer interface that simulates a realistic environment. The participants can move around in the virtual world. They can see it from different angles, reach into it, grab it and reshape it" (Zheng et al., 1998, p. 20). Social VR brings about immersive experiences for users and creates a virtual world where users can interact online. Users can create avatars to act in the virtual world. For example, Rec Room is a VR-based social game that allows millions of users to chat, hang out, explore user-generated rooms, or create new items.[4] It allows users to customize and dress up their Rec Room avatars and find challenging and fun games developed by other users.[4] A recent buzzword is metaverse, meaning a virtual world.

---

[3] Show my Facebook Photos. Retrieved April 15, 2022, from https://www.amazon.com/Amazon-Show-my-Facebook-Photos/dp/B08C6GXLKG/ref=sr_1_1?crid=9JPFLRTYZ9HX&keywords=facebook+skill&qid=1650015833&sprefix=facebook+skill%2Caps%2C319&sr=8-1

[4] Source: Rec Room. Retrieved April 25, 2022, from https://recroom.com/

VR technology can significantly enhance users' virtual experience in the metaverse. In the future, social VR could be a basic technology for the metaverse.

AR is different from VR and can be defined as a technology that is interactive in real time and conjoins the virtual with reality (Turner, 2022). AR cements the presence of physical reality and creates a magical effect for viewers. One popular AR game is Pokémon GO. The Pokémon GO app has generated approximately 600 million downloads worldwide (Rudolf, 2020). Moreover, the app's revenue reached $1 billion in 2020 (Rudolf, 2020). This app enables users to catch virtual Pokémon pets hidden in the physical world. It is also a social game where users can battle others in a virtual gym. While Pokémon GO and other social apps like Snapchat require the use of smartphones, some of the versions of the technology are also supported by wearables like smart glasses (Turner, 2022).

There are three ways to monetize via AR and VR: in-app purchases, increased traffic, and advertising. The adoption of AR or VR represents the trend of *gamification*. Gamification refers to the incorporation of game elements in nongame contexts (Butler & Spoelstra, 2021). A gamified system creates hedonic value for users; e.g., premium digital items can be purchased in-app by users to obtain greater hedonic value. Users can purchase digital items for their digital avatars backed by VR or AR technology. For example, Pokémon GO players can purchase extra Poké balls for catching more Pokémon pets. In-app purchases constitute a major revenue source for many apps.

Increasing traffic is another approach to reach monetization. This approach indirectly increases sales or monetary opportunities. One example of VR technology (which has been widely adopted particularly in hospitality sectors) comes from The Houghton Hotel group (HHG). HHG offers the Houghton skyline penthouse accommodation VR tours on their website.[5] Tourists can click the VR tour link and navigate the video with mouse clicks. VR tours enable tourists to virtually experience the accommodation environment and facilities of the hotels, which may increase the likelihood of tourist reservations. Conversely, AR technology focuses on increasing in-store traffic. In Pokémon GO, physical stores can act as Pokéstops for players to get Poké balls or as gyms for players to have virtual battles with each other. According to the New York Post, New York pizzeria L'inizio Pizza Bar saw sales increase 75% after the store's manager spent $10 to have a dozen Pokémon lured to the location (Whitten, 2016). Simas (2016) recommends physical stores offer promotions for players, such as 15% off for players with in-game achievements. Stores can also encourage players to join the store's mailing list, so they can find out if Pokémon's were caught in the store and also find updates on player promotions.

Advertisements can be planted in virtual worlds created by VR and AR technology. Monetizing via VR ads became an option of social media monetization in the wake of Facebook's experimental ads in Blaston VR (Boland, 2021). (As noted by

---

[5] Source: The Houghton Hotel. Retrieved April 25, 2022, from https://thehoughtonhotel.com/about-us/

Boland (2021), it may take some time for VR usage to reach a high level of advertising monetization.) VR advertisements can be 360° videos or pictures. Similar to regular advertisements, VR advertisements can also be charged based on their cost per click or cost per impression. The pro of VR advertisements lies in creating potentially high advertisement engagement due to higher user engagement (Boland, 2021). However, when users are wandering in a virtual world, it can be annoying to run into advertisements. As more and more VR apps are offered free of charge, advertising is their major revenue source. These apps even require that users view in-app advertisements for a few seconds, which may cause viewers' advertisement aversion instead of interest in them.

## 15.3  Social Media and Blockchain

Today, people are surrounded by centralized financial, media, and communication platforms. These "big black boxes" largely conceal the methods for collecting, handling, and commercializing user data. Many tech giants are so large and complex that their leaders may not be able to fully explain their data management practice in detail. Data and privacy breaches sometimes occur due to the inherent weakness of centralized social media platforms. Blockchain is a decentralized technology that can securely store data. It is a potential solution for creating a more secure and accountable digital system.

Blockchain refers to "a fully distributed system for cryptographically capturing and storing a consistent, immutable, linear event log of transactions between networked actors" (Risius & Spohrer, 2017, p. 386). There are several examples of blockchain-based social media platforms: Sapien, Steemit, Indorse, Sola, and Vevue. Sapien users need a non-fungible token (NFT) passport to become enrolled in the network. This NFT passport is "a new class of digital asset that represents a holder's citizenship within a Sovereign Tribe."[6] In Sapien, user-generated content is vetted by credible individuals who have their own unique NFT passport.

Unlike regular social media, no central authority holds data in a blockchain-based platform (Zakharenkov, 2021). Blockchain social media platforms can generate a collection of interconnected servers used for creating and sharing social media content (Zakharenkov, 2021). Accordingly, the users of blockchain social media have freedom of speech and expression. Traditional social media is a monolithic system where the social media platform monetizes users. Users are basically feeding these monolithic systems a large amount of free information and data without any return (Medium, 2021). In contrast, blockchain social media has a reward system that encourages users to generate social media content. For example, Steemit rewards users with its own cryptocurrency STEEM for publishing and engaging

---

[6]Source: Choose Your Avatar and Blaze a Path Forward. Retrieved April 26, 2022, from https://www.sapien.network/passport

with media content; users are also rewarded for their upvotes and generated content (Medium, 2021).

Blockchain social media platforms are very different from traditional social media platforms. The Blockchain innovation does not indicate a clear way to monetization. It remains unclear how social media data in a decentralized system is monetized and who can reap the benefits. Blockchain-based social platform Uhive is an ideal example. Uhive asserted that the platform was not created for "making money."[7] It rewards users with Uhive Tokens for their active app usage. The tokens can be used as a medium of exchange between users wishing to purchase items on Uhive.[8] Currently, Uhive allows users to purchase tokens which cost approximately $142 for 97,788 tokens.[9] Sapien charges users a fee for purchasing their NFT passport which illustrates an alternative method of monetization.

## 15.4  Social Media and Finance

The combination of social media and finance emerged recently. Social banking is a term that refers to banking activities conducted through social networking channels or social lending services (Enskog, 2016). With the advent of social media technology, today's clients want to use social media to interact with other clients and banking experts (Enskog, 2016). However, when traditional lenders are not able to offer certain financial products (e.g., after a financial crisis), it is more difficult for smaller firms to acquire loans (Enskog, 2016). Social lending or a peer-to-peer (P2P) lending service is a suitable substitute.

WeChat is a pioneer in merging social media and payment services. In 2016, WeChat initiated WeChat Pay which allows users to transfer payments between users. This financial service has been evolving over time; it currently offers four business solutions: cash management, Mini Program pay, "security doctor," and "cash red envelope."[10] Cash management offers secure, convenient, and changeable cash management features. Mini Program pay enables WeChat users to use WeChat Pay for payments in Mini Programs. "Security doctor" is a premium service offered for businesses. It can diagnose the payment security of websites using WeChat Pay and offer suggestions for recovery. "Cash red envelope" is a promotion feature also offered for businesses. Businesses can use this feature to offer specific monetary incentives for their consumers who perform specific actions. For example, businesses can specify that a consumer will receive a 1-yuan red envelope if he or

---

[7] Source: Uhive. Retrieved April 26, 2022, from https://www.uhive.com/

[8] Source: What are the Usages of the Uhive Token? Retrieved April 26, 2022, from https://wiki.uhive.com/kb/what-are-the-usages-of-uhive-tokens/

[9] Source: How to Buy Uhive Tokens? Retrieved April 26, 2022, from https://wiki.uhive.com/kb/how-to-buy-uhive-tokens/

[10] The four business solutions of WeChat Pay are adapted from WeChat Pay's official webpage (retrieval date: April 29, 2022): https://pay.weixin.qq.com/static/product/product_index.shtml

she joins their email list. WeChat Wallet is a banking feature associated with WeChat Pay. WeChat users can deposit money in their WeChat Wallet, and a small amount of interest will be earned.

Recently, Tencent, the parent company of WeChat, has offered a wealth management service, Licaitong and incorporated this service into WeChat.[11] WeChat users can use WeChat Pay to purchase financial products such as banking, insurance, and corporate loans. Moreover, Licaitong can provide users with higher returns on investment. Accordingly, the risk is higher compared to simply depositing money in WeChat Wallet. This financial feature has accelerated the retailing of financial products.

Meta has been investing in the finance sector for several years. They secured an e-money license from the Central Bank of Ireland in October 2016, paving the way for the payment features in Facebook Messenger Europe (O'Hear, 2016). In 2019, Meta pushed hard to replicate WeChat's successful payment feature, WeChat Pay (Kharpal, 2019). The majority of WeChat Pay's revenue comes from commission dollars from online shopping within WeChat and from wealth management services. The online shopping sector and wealth management sector are not as mature in the USA (see Kharpal, 2019). This difference could make it difficult for Facebook to achieve similar success (Kharpal, 2019). Recently, Meta has been unbowed by the rush of companies into the digital banking service area and has a plan for a banking super app (Adams, 2021). We continue to see major social media companies push hard to leverage their social networks to combine social media and financial services, and they continue to explore ways to monetize from financial features. As social media platforms are linking financial service providers and social network users, they are building a brokerage model to profit from this business. For example, WeChat is reportedly charging a fee to Tencent's Licaitong wealth management system users who want to move cash from their WeChat Wallet to deposit in their financial account.

## 15.5   Enterprise Social Media

Most social media platforms focus on daily social interactions such as chatting and dating. But as more and more people use social media platforms as instant messaging platforms and online collaboration platforms, social media platforms have taken note of the potential corporate opportunities of social media platforms. Workplace by Facebook is a business version of Facebook that establishes an online collaboration platform with an appearance similar to regular Facebook (Vigliarolo, 2020). It is an enterprise software that firms can use as their internal enterprise social media platform to interact with their staff (Rodriguez, 2021b). Workplace includes social features such as news feed, groups, live video, events, search, auto-translate, and

---

[11] The discussion on Licaitong is adapted from this site. Retrieved April 29, 2022, from https://www.tencentwm.com/web/v3/about.shtml

trending posts and also supports employee collaboration with internal and external users (Betters, 2016).

Freemium is the monetization model of Workplace. The basic service is offered free of charge, but the premium service charges a fee. The premium version offers more services for organizations willing to pay the fee. For example, the premium version of Workplace allows administrators to conduct administrative actions such as the provision or deletion of accounts and managing corporate community (Animalz, 2018). The premium version is based on a subscription fee for monthly access. The financial performance of Workplace enterprise communication platform has been phenomenal. In 2021, it reached seven million paid users (Rodriguez, 2021b).

WeChat has also initiated their enterprise version of WeChat, Enterprise WeChat, a business-focused communication platform. Enterprise WeChat offers communication experiences similar to WeChat and includes Official Automatic applications such as documents, meetings, emails, schedules, dislikes, and other office tools. Enterprise WeChat also offers different features for different sectors such as retail, education, government, manufacturing, catering, and finance. For example, Enterprise WeChat can be used in a university setting for browsing books from the school library, reserving a seat on the school bus, and topping up their university cards for consumption on campus. China Communications Construction (CCC),[12] a state-owned corporation, is a large construction engineering group ranked 61st in the Fortune 500 (2021). In 2021, its annual earnings were reportedly over 100 billion yuan. They use Enterprise WeChat to merge 48 corporate information systems and integrate over 500 applications, empowering 160,000 employees from 160 countries to work efficiently and synergistically. The daily number of messages in CCC's Enterprise WeChat was over three million. The enterprise version is able to quickly convey and integrate messages and information and saves approximately 30 min per day per employee.

The monetization of Enterprise WeChat differs from Facebook Workplace. It charges a verification fee for firms to verify their identity. Moreover, as each firm is different, Enterprise WeChat reaches monetization by developing a unique version of Enterprise WeChat for each firm. The monetization model is based on specific business solutions that cater to business users' needs. The applications and features of the unique Enterprise WeChat depend on the business solution associated with business users' specific needs. For example, a firm wants to go mobile and use the mobile version of Enterprise WeChat as their internal workflow. The Enterprise WeChat development team can develop a mobile-based workflow specific to this firm's Enterprise WeChat. Therefore, we find that Enterprise WeChat uses a solution-based B2B business model.

---

[12] The China Communications Construction case was adopted from Enterprise WeChat's enterprise cases. Retrieved April 29, 2022, from https://work.weixin.qq.com/nl/index/caselist?id=zgjj

## 15.6  Social Media Monetization in the Future

It is difficult to predict the future of social media monetization. Multiple actors, individuals, organizations, and platforms can use social media to earn profits. Their paths to monetization are diverse and follow different routes. However, we can find some clues about the attributes of future monetization strategies and models based on current social media.

Most firms believe in the neoliberal dogma that argues firms should focus on profitability, governments should minimize their intervention, and people should trust market forces (Harari, 2017). Previously, we have discussed cutting-edge technologies, such as big data, wearables, smart devices, and fintech, in the domain of social media, but technology is merely a factor in shaping future social business. More importantly, socialized humans and society will play a big role in future monetization models. Social media monetization has followed technology-driven logic to boost profits for many years. However, this paradigm has recently been criticized. Historian Yuval Noah Harari (2017) termed Facebook a "social media leviathan" and argued that Facebook is turning Big Data into Big Brother.

Recently, the negative influence of social media technology has surfaced. As Mark Zuckerberg said about his company before Congress in 2018, "We didn't take a broad enough view of our responsibility, and that was a big mistake, and it was my mistake, and I'm sorry" (see Bey et al., 2018). In 2019, people spent approximately 2 h and 22 min per day on social networks (Georgiev, 2022). It is estimated that social media usage will consume 6 years and 8 months of each person's life (Georgiev, 2022). Social media has penetrated every aspect of our society. It weaves an invisible net involving many of us and permeates our economy, politics, culture, and society. By reviewing major social media platforms' who are attempting to combat misinformation and manipulation, Rogers and Niederer (2020) imply that social media platforms are a fertile ground for junk news, troll activities, and the polarization of the political space. The case of the 2016 presidential election in the USA has shown that social media platforms can be used to discredit the basis of a country's election system (Stuart, 2019). Recent research has reviewed the 2020 U.-S. presidential election and found that social media bots not only led to more election-related social media posts, but also fostered social media posts following their own political lines (Chang et al., 2021). In the era of social media, journalism faces a situation where people demand immediate information and want to be informed about events in hours or even minutes. The competitive nature of journalism makes reporters feel forced to spread social media information stories quickly without sufficient effort to verify their authenticity (Fitzpatrick, 2018).

During the COVID-19 pandemic, due to the high levels of alignment between politics and health misinformation, the polarization and subsequent distortions caused by social media have had considerable negative effects on the democratic process as well as public health (Chang et al., 2021). Jiang and Fu (2018) argue that Chinese social media and big data are driven by technological nationalism where a few monopolistic "national champions" dominate the market. They believe the adoption of big data in social media and other Internet platforms is largely technocentric and less reconciled to the humancentric approach that is demanded by people today (Jiang & Fu, 2018). Social media technology is, in some sense, manipulating the meaning of online content. For social media platforms like Facebook and TikTok, their content recommendation algorithm is relevant to likes, views, and comments that content has received. Social media users start to care more about the reactions (e.g., likes or comments) they receive when they share a social media post instead of purely enjoying sharing an exciting moment. Social media technology steps in and can take away our freedom of choice and determine what social media content goes viral or perishes. User actions are then no longer determined or driven by free will. This is a sign of *dehumanization* and *technological panopticon*. We are witnessing how *big data* is converted into *big profits*, but we should think more seriously about how to regulate *big brother as* social media becomes dominant in our lives.

With the advent of cutting-edge technologies such as big data, artificial intelligence, and VR/AR, it is believed that the roadmap of social media monetization will continue to evolve. The monetization approaches of future social media platforms will become much more diverse and undefinable. What is definite is that agents of future social media will expand their monetization models and take technology's double-edge sword effect into consideration. The public will also require future social media to find an unbiased, responsible, and reflective way to reasonably monetize social media data and users. Internal pressure and external pressure push the agents of social media as well as the public to constantly innovate the patterns, practices, and paths of social media monetization. Future social media monetization should not be merely technocentric. It should be developed in a responsible form that demonstrates concern about the dehumanization phenomenon caused by the scale-up of more advanced social computing technology.

## References

Adams, J. (2021). *Inside Facebook's plans for a banking super app*. Retrieved April 29, 2022, from https://www.americanbanker.com/news/inside-facebooks-plans-for-a-banking-super-app

Animalz. (2018). *How to use workplace by Facebook to your advantage*. Retrieved April 29, 2022, from https://adespresso.com/blog/workplace-by-facebook-guide/

Bell, K. (2018). *Portal and Portal+ speakers give Facebook a permanent place in your home*. Retrieved April 16, 2022, from https://mashable.com/article/facebook-portal-portal-plus-speakers-smart-cameras

Betters, E. (2016). *Facebook Workplace: How does it work, what does it cost, and when can you use it?* Retrieved April 29, 2022, from https://www.pocket-lint.com/apps/news/facebook/13912 6-facebook-workplace-how-does-it-work-what-does-it-cost-and-when-can-you-use-it

Bey, J., Tillett, E., & Craver, T. (2018). *Mark Zuckerberg testimony: Facebook CEO open to regulation*. Retrieved May 3, 2022, from https://www.cbsnews.com/live-news/watch-mark-zuckerberg-testimony-senate-judiciary-commerce-committee-facebook-data-breach-today-live/

Bhatia, A. (2021). *Facebook's wearable glasses can succeed where Google Glass flopped*. Retrieved April 14, 2022, from https://tcrn.ch/3i8nX7o

Boland, M. (2021). *Can advertising scale in VR?* Retrieved April 25, 2022, from https://techcrunch.com/2021/07/08/can-advertising-scale-in-vr/#:~:text=One%20of%20VR%E2%80%99s%20 prospective%20revenue%20streams%20is%20ad,billboards%20in%20a%20virtual%20street-scape%20or%20sporting%20venue

Butler, N., & Spoelstra, S. (2021). The theology of gamification. *Academy of Management Proceedings*. https://doi.org/10.5465/AMBPP.2021.13007abstract

Chang, H. H., Chen, E., Zhang, M., Muric, G., & Ferrara, E. (2021). Social bots and social media manipulation in 2020: The year in review. *arXiv*.

Chen, L. C., Lee, C. M., & Chen, M. Y. (2020). Exploration of social media for sentiment analysis using deep learning. *Soft Computing, 24*, 8187–8197. https://doi.org/10.1007/s00500-019-04402-8

Demeku, A. (2021). *How to use chatbots for marketing on social media*. Retrieved April 13, 2022, from https://later.com/blog/chatbots-for-marketing/

E&T Editorial Staff. (2019). *Social media bots becoming more human and difficult to detect, study shows*. Retrieved April 13, 2022, from https://eandt.theiet.org/content/articles/2019/09/social-media-bots-are-becoming-more-human-and-difficult-to-detect-study-shows/

Editorial Staff. (2022). *Facebook patents reveal how it intends to cash in on metaverse*. Retrieved April 16, 2022, from https://www.universalpersonality.com/facebook-patents-reveal-how-it-intends-to-cash-in-on-metaverse/

Enskog, D. (2016). *Social banking—A future business model?* Retrieved April 27, 2022, from https://www.credit-suisse.com/about-us-news/en/articles/news-and-expertise/social-banking-a-future-business-model-201601.html

Fitzpatrick, N. (2018). Media manipulation 2.0: The impact of social media on news, competition, and accuracy. *Athens Journal of Mass Media and Communications., 4*(1), 45–62. https://doi.org/10.30958/ajmmc.4.1.3

Georgiev, D. (2022). *How much time do people spend on social media? [63+ facts to like, share and comment]*. Retrieved May 2, 2022, from https://www.broadbandsearch.net/blog/average-daily-time-on-social-media#:~:text=On%20average%2C%20we%20spend%20144%20minutes%2C%20or%20two,media%2C%20and%20in%20others%2C%20they%20spend%20far%20less.

Ghani, N. A., Hamid, S., Targio Hashem, I. A., & Ahmed, E. (2019). Social media big data analytics: A survey. *Computers in Human Behavior, 101*, 417–428. https://doi.org/10.1016/j.chb.2018.08.039

Hammar, G. (2014). *Is wearable tech the future of social media?* Retrieved April 14, 2022, from https://www.sendible.com/insights/is-wearable-tech-the-future-of-social-media

Harari, Y. N. (2017). *Yuval Noah Harari challenges the future according to Facebook*. Retrieved April 30, 2022, from https://www.ft.com/content/ac0e3b20-0d71-11e7-a88c-50ba212dce4d?platform=hootsuite

Jiang, M., & Fu, K. W. (2018). Chinese social media and big data: Big data, big brother, big profit? *Policy and Internet, 10*(4), 372–392. https://doi.org/10.1002/poi3.187

Kharpal, A. (2019). *Facebook may be looking to replicate a major feature from one of China's top apps. That'll be tough*. Retrieved April 27, 2022, from https://www.cnbc.com/2019/03/13/facebook-wants-to-copy-wechat-pay-with-facebook-coin-payments.html

Kumar, S. (2020). *Text analytics of social media comments using sentiment analysis*. Retrieved April 12, 2022, from https://www.tex-ai.com/text-analytics-of-social-media-comments-using-sentiment-analysis/

Malhotra, S. (2020). *AI explained: Rule-based AI Vs machine learning for enterprises*. Retrieved April 12, 2022, from https://artificialintelligence.oodles.io/blogs/rule-based-ai-vs-machine-learning/

Matilda, S. (2016). Big data in social media environment: A business perspective. In *Social Media Listening and Monitoring for Business Applications* (pp. 70–93). IGI Global. https://doi.org/10.4018/978-1-5225-0846-5.ch004

Matthews, K. (2020). *The state of the smart speaker market in 2020*. Retrieved April 15, 2022, from https://bdtechtalks.com/2020/03/27/the-state-of-the-smart-speaker-market-in-2020/

McNair, C. (2019). *Global smart speaker users 2019*. Retrieved April 15, 2022, from https://www.emarketer.com/content/global-smart-speaker-users-2019

Medium. (2021). *Decentralized social media: Why and How?* Retrieved April 26, 2022, from https://www.ledger.com/academy/blockchain/decentralized-social-media-why-and-how

O'Hear, S. (2016). *Facebook just secured an e-money license in Ireland, paving the way for Messenger payments in Europe*. Retrieved April 27, 2022, from https://techcrunch.com/201 6/12/07/facebook-just-secured-an-e-money-license-in-ireland-paving-way-for-messenger-payments-in-europe/?guccounter=1&guce_referrer_us=aHR0cHM6Ly93d3cuZ29vZ2 xlLmNvbvS8&guce_referrer_cs=vRm7tcsxDqZuQ_ruNct27Q

Risius, M., & Spohrer, K. (2017). A Blockchain research framework. *Business and Information Systems Engineering, 59*, 385–409. https://doi.org/10.1007/s12599-017-0506-0

Rodriguez, S. (2021a). *Snap announces new Spectacles AR glasses, which let you overlay digital objects on the real world*. Retrieved April 15, 2022, from https://www.cnbc.com/2021/05/20/snap-announces-augmented-reality-spectacles-glasses.html

Rodriguez, S. (2021b). *Facebook workplace reaches 7 million paid subscribers*. Retrieved April 29, 2022, from https://www.cnbc.com/2021/05/04/facebook-workplace-reaches-7-million-paid-subscribers.html

Rogers, R., & Niederer, S. (2020). *The politics of social media manipulation*. Amsterdam University Press. https://doi.org/10.5117/9789463724838_ch08

Rudolf. (2020). *Pokémon GO hits $1 billion in 2020, surpassing $4 billion in lifetime revenue*. Retrieved April 25, 2022, from https://pokemongohub.net/post/news/pokemon-go-hits-1-billion-in-2020-surpassing-4-billion-in-lifetime-revenue/

Shapiro, I. (2016). *Wearable technology is the new marketing battleground*. Retrieved April 14, 2022, from https://www.chiefmarketer.com/wearable-technology-is-the-new-marketing-battleground/

Simas, J. (2016). *How to "Lure" Pokémon GO players into your storefront*. Retrieved April 25, 2022, from https://www.shopify.com/retail/how-to-lure-pokemon-go-players-to-your-storefront

Simova, A. (2019). *Social media chatbots: How companies are using them in 2019*. Retrieved April 13, 2022, from https://socialtoolkits.com/social-media-chatbots/

Stuart, A. H. (2019). Social media, manipulation, and violence. *South Carolina Journal of International Law and Business, 15*(2), 100–132.

Turner, C. (2022). Augmented reality, augmented epistemology, and the real-world web. *Philosophy and Technology, 35*, 19. https://doi.org/10.1007/s13347-022-00496-5

Vigliarolo, B. (2020). *Workplace by Facebook: A cheat sheet*. Retrieved April 29, 2022, from https://www.techrepublic.com/article/workplace-by-facebook-the-smart-persons-guide/

Wang, R. (2014). *Microsoft's Xiaoice microblog resurrects foul-mouthed microblog, causing outrage*. Retrieved April 13, 2022, from https://www.qianzhan.com/indynews/detail/283/140 627-c94c19b0.html

Whitten, S. (2016). *Gotta catch 'em all: Pokemon Go is boosting business for restaurants*. Retrieved April 25, 2022, from https://www.cnbc.com/2016/07/12/gotta-catch-em-all-pokemon-go-is-boosting-business-for-restaurants.html

Zakharenkov, A. (2021). *Blockchain social media eliminates centralized control and brings benefits*. Retrieved April 26, 2022, from https://pixelplex.io/blog/blockchain-powered-social-media/

Zhao, H. (2019). *How far is c-end payment away from "gifting" smart healthcare AI to consumers?* Retrieved April 13, 2022, from https://med.sina.com/article_detail_103_2_66369.html

Zheng, J. M., Chan, K. W., & Gibson, I. (1998). Virtual reality. *IEEE Potentials, 17*(2), 20–23. https://doi.org/10.1109/45.666641

Milton Keynes UK
Ingram Content Group UK Ltd.
UKHW020939280923
429557UK00005B/274

9 783031 145773